The Political Economy of the Drug Industry

Florida A&M University, Tallahassee
Florida Atlantic University, Boca Raton
Florida Gulf Coast University, Ft. Myers
Florida International University, Miami
Florida State University, Tallahassee
University of Central Florida, Orlando
University of Florida, Gainesville
University of North Florida, Jacksonville
University of South Florida, Tampa
University of West Florida, Pensacola

The Political Economy of the Drug Industry

Latin America and the International System

Edited by Menno Vellinga

University Press of Florida

Gainesville / Tallahassee / Tampa / Boca Raton

Pensacola / Orlando / Miami / Jacksonville / Ft. Myers

9297353

Copyright 2004 by Menno Vellinga
Printed in the United States of America on recycled, acid-free paper
All rights reserved

09 08 07 06 05 04 6 5 4 3 2 1

A record of cataloging-in-publication data is available from the
Library of Congress.

Title page image: Erythroxylum coca, detail of illustration
by Sir William Hooker.

The University Press of Florida is the scholarly publishing agency
for the State University System of Florida, comprising Florida A&M
University, Florida Atlantic University, Florida Gulf Coast University,
Florida International University, Florida State University, University
of Central Florida, University of Florida, University of North Florida,
University of South Florida, and University of West Florida.

University Press of Florida
15 Northwest 15th Street
Gainesville, FL 32611-2079
http://www.upf.com

In memory of my beloved parents

Klaas Vellinga and Geertje van Foeken

Contents

Figures and Tables

Figures

Tables

Preface

Drug production in source countries has proven to be difficult to control, let alone to eradicate. Drug exporters show a flexibility and inventiveness that beats any controlling agency. The potential supply is virtually unlimited; the trafficking routes to the markets in Europe and the United States are multitudinous. The equipment and inputs used in production and trade, and even the drug shipment itself, can all be easily replaced. The integration of the drug trade into organized crime networks has complicated matters even further.

While debating the pros and cons of the various drug control programs that in the course of the last decades have been defined and put into action, we have to agree that the Andean counter-narcotics effort has not been successful. This applies to all phases: eradication control of precursor chemicals, destruction of production facilities, interception of shipments, control of money laundering, and also to the projects of alternative development. Bolivia has completed an eradication program. However, the social costs have been great and the backlash it has created has led to a resumption of coca cultivation. The lack of adequate information on the functioning of the drug industry has hampered the definition of adequate policies. On the supply side, little is known about the diversity of motivations and circumstances determining coca cultivation as part of peasant household strategies. There is also a lack of precise information on the economic structure of the drug industry, its interaction with the formal economy, its macroeconomic impact, and its infiltration of the political sphere.

In the absence of much information, governments—and in particular the U.S. government—have opted for the "quick fix." Drug control programs were forced onto the respective governments, who—in turn—forced them onto the drug-producing peasantry. International pressures dictated unrealistically short time-spans for these programs and failed to organize adequate contextual support. These programs need to be phased out. In demand countries also, the counter-narcotics policies need to be reconsidered as the strongly repressive approach has hardly had any result. In the United States, the prisons are filling up with drug offenders. The deterring effects, however, seem to be very small. Consumption has not decreased significantly. In various European countries alternative drug policies—including some forms of decriminalization—are experimented with on a relatively large scale, with promising results.

A radical change of strategy is not going to be easy because present policies include support for a wide range of institutions, such as police agencies, security forces, judiciaries, academia, the media, NGOs, and consultancy agencies, all of whom are committed to the continuation of the failed policies of the past. Also, supply suppression will not solve the problems with demand. These policies have accomplished little in the consumer countries and have caused grave problems in the source countries.

The situation of underdevelopment and a continuing lack of economic opportunities in source countries, combined with a persisting demand for drugs in the United States and European markets will continue to reduce the effectiveness of any anti-drug action. The drug industry concerns an economic activity that is well adapted to the conditions of an underdeveloped rural economy. Trafficking could well be seen as a useful way to cope with depressed exports in the formal economy in source countries.

The development of linkages between the drug trade and transnational organized crime has presented new challenges to law enforcement agencies. Only recently has the depth and intensity of such ties in the areas of trafficking and money laundering and their role in financing terrorism and guerrilla activities begun to unravel.

This book will be dedicated to the analysis of the issues mentioned above. It will discuss the alternatives of intervention and control, taking the workings of the industry into account and considering the dynamics of supply and demand. The focus will be on the interaction between economic, political, social, cultural, and legal factors that form part of the political economy of the drug industry.

For each of the producer countries (Bolivia, Peru, and Colombia) and those involved in the export to markets in the United States and western Europe (Mexico, the Caribbean Islands), the functioning of the drug industry, the various efforts to control its development, and the effects on the socioeconomic and political fabric of society should be viewed against the background of: (a) the structure and functioning of the legal economy and the ways of conducting business (the economic culture); (b) the structure of society, its exclusionary nature, and the access to social mobility promoting mechanisms; (c) the structure of power and politics, political culture, and the issue of the legitimacy of official rule. In combination, these elements shed light on the why and how of the rise of the drug industry, its persistent presence in producer countries, and the (non)effectiveness of the various methods of control.

In the areas of production and trade, the drug industry has developed interesting parallels with the dynamics of legal international trade under the influence of increasing globalization and economic integration. In legal as well as in illegal trade, one tries to develop markets at home and overseas, to create market advantage and downstream control, to modernize logistics, to practice technological and product innovation (heroin, crack), and to intervene in the political process in producer and trafficking countries on the basis of accumulated economic power.

At the same time, the drug trade has been producing criminal organizations that behave as enterprise capitalists, operating outside of the law, unhindered by the general cultural standards of civilized society. The Italian and the Russian mafia provide examples of such development and their increasing influence in the drug trade is documented in the book.

At times, these crime syndicates will be operating in coordination with the economic and geopolitical interests of governments. These changes in structure and functioning of the drug industry have affected greatly the possibilities to intervene by law enforcement and counter-narcotic agencies. Various methods of control and their effectiveness in combating the negative impact from drug production and trafficking in producer and consumer countries are being reviewed in the book. It is obvious that the present drug control policies in source countries have dialectical effects, having the tendency to produce results to the contrary.

On the consumer side, substantial differences in demand and in structure of demand prevail between the United States and Europe. They also show substantial differences in drug control strategies. Many European countries are experimenting with alternatives to the "sledgehammer" approach that is being supported by the War on Drugs warriors and advocate the liberalization and decriminalization of drug use. This alternative approach concerns in particular the use of soft drugs, although at a local level experiments are being conducted that include the controlled liberalization of hard drugs for registered hardcore users. The country that has most advanced on this road has been the Netherlands. The Dutch approach has been analyzed in a European context, taking the approaches practiced by other member countries of the European Union into account. The attitude by the European Union toward multilateral initiatives that, as in the case of the Plan Colombia, include a strong element of militarization and the risk of human rights abuses has been very critical and the European position has differed sharply from U.S. policies in this area.

The book concludes with an overview of the general developments within the drug industry, the economic, social, and political effects at the various phases of the commodity chain, and the options of intervention and control. It offers a critical review of the present counter-narcotics policies and discusses alternative ways of intervention. At the same time, it presents a rigidly scientific analysis of an underground economy that has grown to great proportions, undermining the economy and society of the countries where it has been developing its activities.

All chapters are original contributions and have been written by leading Latin American, European, and North American economists, political scientists, anthropologists, sociologists, and criminologists, specialists in the field. The book contains a wealth of information on the drug industry, analyzing all phases of the cocaine commodity chain: from coca-leaf production to the organization of cocaine sales in the consumer countries.

As editor I wish to express my great appreciation to my colleagues who responded enthusiastically to my invitation to participate in the workshop at Utrecht University in June 2001, which led to publication of this book. I gratefully acknowledge the help of Paula Duivenvoorde in preparing the manuscript. The Faculty of Geographical Sciences and the Institute of Development Studies, part of the Urban and Regional Research Center, both at Utrecht University, and the Center of Research of the Netherlands Ministry of Justice have been very supportive of my research interest, and I owe them a debt of gratitude.

Abbreviations

ADN	Party of Democratic Nationalist Action, Bolivia
AECI	Spanish International Cooperation Agency
AUC	United Self-Defense Force of Colombia
CIA	Central Intelligence Agency
CIDAD	Inter-American Drug Abuse Control Commission
CND	United Nations Commission on Narcotic Drugs
DEA	Drug Enforcement Administration
ELN	National Liberation Army
EMCDDA	European Monitoring Center for Drugs and Drugs Addiction
EPL	Army of Popular Liberation
FARC	Revolutionary Armed Forces of Colombia
FELCN	Special Force to Combat Drug Trafficking
GDP	Gross Domestic Product
GNP	Gross National Product
HCL	Cocaine Hydrochloride
INA	National Anti-Corruption Initiative, Peru
INCB	International Narcotics Control Board
INCSR	International Counter-Narcotics Strategy Report
INL	International Narcotics and Law Enforcement Matters
IRA	Irish Republic Army
MIR	Revolutionary Movement of the Left, Bolivia
NDIC	U.S. National Drug Intelligence Center
NGO	Non-Government Organization
ODA	Official Development Assistance
ODCCP	Office of Drug Control and Crime Prevention
OGD	Observatoire Géopolitique des Drogues
OIOS	Office of Internal Oversight Services
ONDCP	United States Office of National Drug Control Policy
PEAR	Special Project on Long-Term Alternative Development, Peru
PRI	Institutional Revolutionary Party, Mexico
SCOPE	Strategy for Coca and Opium Poppy Elimination

UMOPAR   Rural Mobil Patrol Unit
UNDCP   United Nations Drug Control Program
UNGASS   United Nations General Assembly Special Session
USAID   Agency of International Development
WHO   World Health Organization

I

Introduction

The Political Economy of the Drug Industry

Its Structure and Functioning

Menno Vellinga

Coca cultivation, cocaine manufacturing, and the socioeconomic and socio-political contexts in which these processes are taking place have been receiving increasing attention from social science research. Since the mid-1990s an avalanche of publications on drug problems has been published.[1] Within the debate on the production, trade, and consumption of drugs in source countries, concern has been shifting from policy analyses on the macrolevel to the study of the supply side processes on the regional and subregional levels, to the impact on economy and politics in the respective regions, to the linkages with transnationally operating organized crime, and to the effects of the various strategies designed to contain supply.

The small-scale production of coca in the Andean countries did not develop into the "cocaine business" until the mid-1970s. The industry began to boom by the early 1980s, showing spectacular growth in a context of increasing economic crisis and plummeting growth rates. In the coca-producing Andean countries, the state has been on the defense with its inability to fulfill many of its core responsibilities, such as providing justice and personal security to its subjects. The situation has generated a process by which the state and the system it represents have been losing legitimacy. The growing gap between legality and socially acceptable behavior has opened the door to widespread corruption and an explosive growth of criminal and noncriminal underground economies.[2]

The rise of cocaine production and trafficking forms part of this development. Its illegality is greatly affecting the market structure and the strategies of the market parties involved—producers, sellers, and consumers—and has turned violence into a resource whose real or potential use has become an almost "normal" element of market competition. The enormous money interests at the various phases of production and trade have led the entrepreneurs involved to defend market positions at all costs.

Within two decades, coca growing has expanded from the relatively small areas where it was cultivated for traditional consumption to regions covering large parts of Bolivia, Peru, and Colombia. Expansion in the near future into Ecuador, Venezuela, Brazil, and Guyana is not unthinkable. In addition, a growing number of countries have become involved in trafficking and money laundering.

The Cocaine Commodity Chain

Coca is an "easy" crop, and coca growing does not require intensive preparation.[3] The simple tasks of clearing the field by the "slash and burn" method, preparing the seedbeds, transplanting the seedlings, maintaining the field, and harvesting the leaves can easily be performed—and often are—by poor migrants with no agricultural background. In most regions coca is cultivated on small family plots seldom exceeding the size of 2 hectares. It is mostly grown in combination with other market crops and with food crops as part of a diversification strategy.

Coca "plantations" covering extensive areas are very rare. Only in recent years has this phenomenon emerged in Colombia. Most coca cultivation takes place in areas of recent colonization and expansion of the agricultural frontier. The peasant households in these areas have little access to resources such as capital and technology, but account for a relatively large amount of unskilled labor. They adopt coca cultivation as an almost logical choice within their crop diversification strategy. Coca guarantees a continuous flow of income and this continuity is almost as important as the amount of income. Consequently, peasants will respond to a drop in the price of coca leaf by expanding the coca-cultivated area instead of shifting to other crops. Within the diversified agriculture in the frontier areas, coca has been less subject to radical price fluctuations than other crops. It has a secure market that guarantees a steady flow of income to the individual peasant households. This is coca's basic advantage.

At the same time, this advantage gives an idea of the magnitude of the problems that accompany crop substitution. A peasant household can expect to have some income within twelve to fifteen months after having planted coca. The shrub is fully grown after two to three years and will continue to produce for fifteen years or more with three to four crops a year. Coca requires less investment and attention than other crops once it has been planted and will only require manual labor and no special skills. Most peasant families in Bolivia and Peru are familiar with coca. The product is easy to harvest, pack, and transport and in most cases will have an assured market nearby. Under "normal" circumstances, coca would be the ideal income-generating crop to alleviate poverty and rural underdevelopment. Also, the production of cocaine is not a very elaborate or difficult process. The industry is, in fact, perfectly adapted to the conditions of an underdeveloped rural economy: the manufacturing process is not capital intensive, does not have large economies of scale, does not require large amounts of skilled labor, and uses production processes that are relatively easy to organize. These characteristics explain the flexibility with which the industry has been able to respond to the fluctuations in demand in consumer countries, to changes in anti-drug policies, and to repressive operations by the military and law-enforcement personnel. This adaptation also explains why it has been so difficult to find an alternative to the industry.[4]

Coca Production

Who is involved in this production and trafficking of cocaine, and why and how has this involvement come about?[5] Among the coca-producing countries major differences have developed as to the organization of the sector and the market strategies of the entrepreneurs concerned. Before Bolivia embarked on its "option zero" strategy, a certain division of labor had emerged among three countries: Colombia, Brazil, and Mexico. Colombia had become more involved in cocaine production based on coca paste produced elsewhere, and in trafficking, although Brazil and Mexico have been rapidly gaining terrain in this sector. Suppression of coca production in Bolivia and Peru has led to an explosive growth of coca cultivation in Colombia. In Bolivia and Peru the clandestine drug economy had become more interwoven with the formal economy. Many of those involved in drug production and trafficking have been moving back and forth between the two sectors. A small mafia-type drug elite still exists, but it is hardly as prominent as the powerful, well-organized Colombian drug lords of the 1990s. The intensification of repressive policies has strengthened the tendency of these informal and formal sectors to interpenetrate. Generally, repression of the drug industry's activities has resulted in a dispersal of production facilities and a decomposition of the production process into small, technically simple units that do not require a major investment. This way, drug production has become accessible to a wider sector of micro- and small entrepreneurs, who at the same time may be coca-cultivating peasants and managers of small coca-paste-producing facilities. Especially in Peru this activity to produce coca paste or even cocaine base by peasants, who in the past were just selling coca leaf, has become widespread. This way they pocket a greater share of the value added and sell directly to representatives of wholesalers who connect with exporters who, in turn, have a direct link to internationally operating organizations with a heavy presence of Colombian traffickers.

The basic motive for engaging in coca activities and paste production is simple and flows from the countries' long-term structural poverty and under-development and the absence of economic alternatives. In the coca-producing regions, the economic rewards have helped to cushion the worst extremes of poverty, but they have not brought sustained development in terms of improved housing, education, or health. In this way, Bolivia in particular has been repeating its historical role of supplying world markets with a raw material without reaping major benefits.[6] In the late 1980s Bolivia had become heavily dependent on income generated and employment secured by the drug industry. Its legal economy had been undermined by overvalued exchange rates resulting from the massive influx of narco-dollars, by the weakening of local industry, by the collapse of nontraditional exports, and by the boom in financial speculation. Since then, the legal economy has recuperated slightly. However, given the small size of the formal economy in Bolivia a vulnerability to a possible "economic narco-addiction" remains. An important "positive" difference with the Peruvian and Colombian experience, where socially and politically drug-linked violence has been rampant, has been the lack of such widespread violence between druglords and between them and the state. The major Bolivian traffickers' close family and business links may have contributed to this phenomenon.

The Bolivian government, assisted by international organizations, has made the most ambitious effort to control supply. Internationally, alternative development was considered the best strategy to control the supply side of the drug industry in source countries. In Bolivia this effort to combine crop substitution, rural development projects, and law enforcement has not been able to create levels of living that will eliminate the need for coca cultivation.[7] The government campaign to eradicate coca as part of Plan Dignidad has led to widespread resistance by the coca growers, who have organized in a political movement that has become a major player on the Bolivian political scene.

Reducing—let alone eliminating—aggregate coca growing by the world's primary producers of coca leaf in the 1990s has proven to be very complicated.[8] Substitution programs, through which coca growers received funds to induce them to replace coca with other crops, eventually led to the displacement of coca cultivation from project control areas to other areas. The policies of pressuring the Peruvian government, spraying with herbicides, controlling the imports and internal transports of precursor chemicals used in cocaine production, applying military pressure toward the coca growers, and shooting down cocaine transporting planes have booked little progress toward aggregate crop suppression. With alternative development, the difficulties in organizing a proper contextual support system (credit, technical assistance, access to inputs) for a transition to alternative crops in regions located at a great distance from potential markets has frustrated results. In addition, production mobility, as in the case of these supply-control programs, has remained a major concern. Program success does not guarantee that production will not migrate elsewhere. Moreover, in the case of Peru, the alliance between coca growers and the guerilla movement, Sendero Luminoso, hampered supply control up to the mid-1990s. Since then, however, government repression, added to the effects of a destructive fungus attacking Peruvian coca, has led to a decline in production. Nevertheless, there are strong indications that this decline is temporary. Growers have moved from the traditional coca-growing areas in the Upper Huallaga Valley to other locations, and their new crops have only recently entered into full production. In Colombia, the linkages between cocaine production and trafficking and the guerrilla and the paramilitary movements, resulting in an explosive growth in acreage of coca cultivated, have been widely documented and have become an issue of international concern.

The Cocaine Commodity Chain

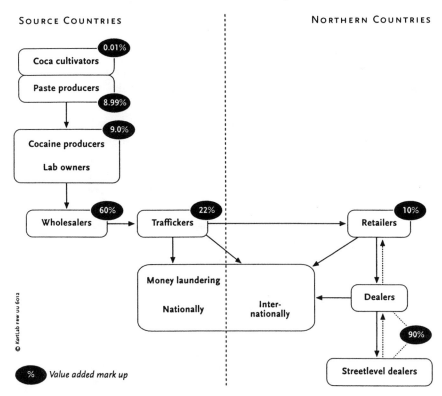

SOURCE COUNTRIES

NORTHERN COUNTRIES

Coca cultivators — 0.01%

Paste producers — 8.99%

Cocaine producers / Lab owners — 9.0%

Wholesalers — 60%

Traffickers — 22%

Retailers — 10%

Money laundering — Nationally / Internationally

Dealers

90%

Streetlevel dealers

% Value added mark up

© KartLab FRW uu 6012

The Industry and Its Entrepreneurs

Most studies on the dynamics of the drug industry that were published in the last few decades are rather descriptive and factual and leave important areas concerning the structure and functioning of the industry untouched. Part of the reason undoubtedly has to do with the difficulties and dangers of doing research, part, also, with an excessive focus on policy options. However, a more profound analysis of the issues is indicated, first, on the microlevel, where the strategies of peasant households should be taken into consideration in the light of the specific economic, social, cultural, and environmental circumstances that influence coca cultivation in their respective regions or subregions. The tradition of coca cultivation and consumption in the Andean region is well-known, and this long-standing familiarity with the crop is obviously an important consideration. However, coca cultivation in the colonization areas in Bolivia, Peru, and Colombia has become part of an extraordinary complex situation that goes far beyond the dictates of tradition.

A good example of the need to take the microlevel factors into account is presented by the history of coca growing in the Chapare in Bolivia and the efforts to control it. The Chapare region in the Department of Cochabamba was populated in the 1950s by waves of migrants directed toward the eastern part of the country following the policy of national integration initiated by the Bolivian government in the 1950s. The 1963 National Colonization Plan designated the Chapare as a preferred destination. As people were encouraged to migrate to the region, especially those living in the desperately poor areas on the Andean Altiplano, the Chapare experienced rapid population growth. In the course of the process, many migrants remained part of a "floating population"; that is, they "floated" between living in the Chapare region and areas of expulsion in the Cochabamba uplands. In 1987 at the time of the coca boom, the Chapare population had grown to a total estimated between 196,000 and 234,000, the difference having to do with the difficulty of calculating this floating population.[9]

The colonization process in Chapare had three different modalities, each resulting in different settlement patterns, interests, and production strategies: permanent migration, semipermanent migration, and agricultural-worker migration. There are differing attitudes toward coca and alternative development among the people who constitute these categories. For the semipermanent migrants, a reduction in the importance of coca would limit their possibilities of combining agricultural activities in their communities of origin with those in the Chapare. For agricultural workers, less coca would mean less employment and more need to look for other destinations of migration. Also among the permanent and semipermanent migrants are a significant number of ex-miners who are escaping from a marginal existence in their *comunidades* on the Altiplano or from narrow valleys in western Bolivia.

These migrants have brought their own backgrounds of fixed organizations of *comunidades* and peasant and miners' *sindicatos* with them to the Chapare.[10] Here, the *sindicatos*—often named after the former miner camps—have come to represent and defend communal interests. Through the years, the *sindicatos* have been the core institutions in Chapare society. Often, and in the absence of state institutions, the *sindicatos* have filled the institutional void, organizing access to land, taking care of essential infrastructure such as constructing rural roads, schools, and health centers, maintaining order in the community, and, above all, providing a link to the political system and official institutions at regional and national levels. In the 1980s the federations of coca growers became one of the most important pressure groups in the country, filling the gap left by the decline of the regular miners' unions.

Coca growers have not always presented a united front on the question of coca eradication and alternative development. The major federations have maintained an ironclad resistance to eradication unless totally compensated by the successful introduction of other marketable crops and/or other economically realistic alternatives, and they lead the present resistance against the policy of complete eradication that is forcefully being pursued by the present national government. Minor federations have generally been more conciliatory.

In the Chapare, various categories of *colonos* have developed their own survival strategies in which coca plays a crucial role. When eradicating coca and organizing alternative development programs, it is indispensable to have a greater understanding of the role and function coca has as a subsistence guarantee. Knowledge of the various household strategies is the key to understanding crop diversification and the importance of coca cultivation. It is clear that peasants give up coca only when they have an alternative source of income that can liberate them from the continuous harassment of security forces and permit them to survive, even though they may have to work harder and earn even less from alternative crops. Instead of such an analysis, government programs have approached coca growers as a homogeneous group, ignoring the diversity among them and the multifunctional role coca cultivation has had for the individual household. The socioeconomic differences among the peasant population, the variety in migration background, and the degree of permanence in settlement, all factors effecting crop decisions, have been ignored. Rather, alternative development programs have adopted a uniform approach, emphasizing a high economic return per hectare as the one and only motivating force in crop decisions. However, the motivations of individual households are varied and often will go beyond simple economic rationality. This situation also helps to explain the variations in coca cultivation at the level of the household, as well as at the regional and subregional levels. In practice, compensation and crop substitution may primarily favor those households that are already better off and that produce coca solely as a source of extra income. In their case, social and legal pressures may work better. In the case of those totally dependent on their income from coca for survival, more attention should be given to the cultivation of food crops and off-farm employment.

Very insightful and provocative analyses of the political economy of the drug industry have been written by Francisco Thoumi in reference to the case of Colombia.[11] He explains how an increasing delegitimation of the regime and the weakening of the state processes accompanied by extremely high levels of violence have led to a growing gap between the legal system (legality) and socially accepted behavior (morality). These developments have created an environment that is experiencing a mushroom-like growth of a high profit and high risk underground business sector in which conflict cannot be resolved through the normal legal channels. Understanding why the drug industry has flourished in the country in the way it has, and the extent to which its growth has affected economy and society, will require knowledge of Colombia's history and political economy. Also, the drug industry has become an integral part of societal dynamics, and any profound analysis will need to include the relationship to the state, the legal private sector, the non-drug underground economy, the political parties, and other social and political organizations. Thoumi maintains that, given the characteristics of Colombia's political economy, the country became an attractive location for the illegal drug industry from early on. Colombia offered conditions that minimized the risks for the cocaine-refining industry, allowed the control of coca-leaf marketing in Bolivia and Peru, and assured a dominating role in the U.S. cocaine market.

For Thoumi, the basic factor behind the country's comparative advantage in the establishment and growth of the illegal drug industry has been the process of delegitimation of the regime. This process has been going on for more than half a century. During this period, the Colombian state has grown increasingly inefficient, unaccountable, and unresponsive to citizen's demands, more and more corrupt, and unable to exert effective control over large areas of the country.[12] At certain points in time, Colombia has shared the characteristics of an increasing delegitimation of the regime and a disintegrating state apparatus losing control over parts of its own territory with other countries in Latin America, and certainly with those in the Andean region. However, the Colombian case is very different from those of the other countries.[13] In Colombia, the delegitimation process began several decades earlier than elsewhere and, moreover, it has continuously been accompanied by extremely high levels of violence. The institutionalization of violence as a "normal" option in the settlement of disputes of any kind has served sectors such as the drug industry. The illegitimate nature of its business precludes resolving conflict through legal channels, which, when added to the high profit and high risk characteristics of the industry, almost automatically will lead to the use of violent means. The regime's delegitimation has been furthered by other factors, such as the long tradition of contraband, black marketeering, and laundering of foreign exchange, experiences that resulted from long-term official exchange controls and restrictive import policies and were transferred to the drug industry. In addition, in Colombia's brand of capitalism, which operates on the basis of a "production-speculation" mentality with little investment in long-term capital equipment, a focus on commerce and quick turnover and high short-term profits has generated an economic "climate" propitious to the growth of a sector like the drug industry. This brand of capitalism is shared with many other countries in Latin America, where it has equally discouraged the development of more stable economic activities and encouraged speculation. In combination, however, with the characteristics of the state-society relationship mentioned above, this brand of capitalism may have had a special impact in the case of Colombia.

Some additional factors should be mentioned that may explain why the drug industry has flourished in Colombia. One major factor concerns the country's complex geography, which has kept many regions isolated and fairly self-sufficient. Large areas of the country have remained outside the government's control, providing safe havens for the production and logistics centers of the cocaine industry. Overseas, the presence of large Colombian migrant communities in the United States has completed Colombia's international competitive advantage in cocaine manufacturing and distribution. The presence of these communities has facilitated downstream penetration of the U.S. market and has permitted the Colombians to organize their own logistics and sales network, bypassing the American wholesalers.

Thoumi's argument that institutional and ethical legacies of the past are important factors that condition the behavior of present economic actors in the drug industry is convincing. However, who are these actors, and what are their operational strategies? How do they define their behavior toward the rest of society, and how do they attempt to incorporate themselves and their capital into the mainstream of Colombian society? Information about these issues is sketchy and sometimes contradictory, and the studies based on empirical research involving actual interviews with industry actors are few in number. There is an urgent need for more information on the way these entrepreneurs operate and run the industry. However, research in such a violent underground sector is extremely difficult and dangerous.

Until the mid-1990s, the industry had been dominated by a small elite of entrepreneurs. This group, at the time estimated at five hundred, supervised every aspect of the business, including the movement of cocaine from source countries to consumer markets, overseas distribution, and the recycling of the proceeds. Trafficking from the same town or region allowed these entrepreneurs to pool their interests through the formation of "cartels" with the intent to maximize export volumes while minimizing risk. Since then, the industry has been transformed. The old cartels have disappeared, and the industry has become fragmented owing to scores of new actors with heterogeneous origins and the lack of consolidation of a new organizational structure.

One of the main objectives of the drug entrepreneurs has concerned their assimilation into mainstream society in order to protect and legitimize their property, legalize at least part of their wealth, obtain an economic status and social recognition comparable to other rich people in the legal circuit, participate in the political process, and access public office. In short, they wished to become respectable citizens. This movement has been strongest in Colombia, obviously because of the strength of its drug elite.[14] However, we have observed similar phenomena in the other countries. Consider the spectacular case of Bolivian drug lord Roberto Suarez Gomez, who as the story goes, in 1984 offered to pay off two-thirds of Bolivia's foreign debt—which at the time stood at 3 billion U.S. dollars—in exchange for government tolerance as a legitimate entrepreneur.

The integration of the drug traffickers into the Colombian economy has been subtle, but pervasive. Thoumi mentions the differences in strategies that have been followed in pursuing assimilation, conditioned as the traffickers are by the diversity in social origins, connections with the national power structure, objectives, and ways of operation. Some of the strategies are confrontational. Interests are being protected through the association with guerrilla movements or through the organization of paramilitary groups in the cocaine-producing regions or in those where extensive investments in real estate have been made. However, most entrepreneurs presently follow a more low-key approach, using their wealth to gain the favor of politicians, clerics, military leaders, and other relevant members of the establishment. The experience in running an illegal industry, based on personal trust and dependency relationships, permits an easy connection with the clientelistic and paternalistic dimensions of the Colombian political system.[15]

The exact degree of economic integration of these entrepreneurs is difficult to ascertain. Drug-related income and capital is notoriously difficult to identify, and the new modern narcos maintain a low profile and use sophisticated methods to hide their identities.[16] The size of the resources produced by the drug industry, added to the widespread illegality of many economic activities and the large underground economy, offers numerous possibilities for laundering capital. Given the widespread lack of respect for laws that apply to economic transactions, and the fact that most firms operate simultaneously in the formal and informal economies, there is no way of establishing where returned drug capital has been invested. The procedure to estimate general socioeconomic impact is most complex and establishing the effects on the political economy of the countries concerned will involve a long list of tradeoffs and social costs. Traditional cost-benefit analysis does not serve in the analysis of these issues.

Business Practices in the Drug Industry

Drug trafficking is the most spectacular sector of the drug industry and the one generating the most added value. Through the years, the drug trade has been increasingly conforming to more general ground rules of legal international trade in such areas as increasing the efficiency of production, the improvement of logistics and transport (containerization), the downstream penetration of markets, and the diversification of product-market combinations. The transformation of the industry in recent years has led to a more flexible cooperation between smaller independently operating entrepreneurs.

An increasing number of countries are getting involved in trafficking, transport, and laundering. Mexico, in particular, has become a transit point in trafficking directed toward the U.S. market, and the Colombians have been losing terrain to the Mexicans.[17] Between 50 and 70 percent of total U.S. cocaine imports are estimated to pass through Mexico. Mexican cartels have come to play an increasingly important role.[18] Traditionally, marijuana and heroin have dominated Mexico's drug trade, and the bulk of the drug money came from the export of these two products, but the cooperation between Colombian and Mexican traffickers has changed this picture. An increase in drug-related corruption and violence has accompanied this development. The liberalization of trade as part of the NAFTA treaty has not only facilitated legal business between the United States and Mexico, but has also opened a wide range of possibilities for illicit activities, including the drug trade. At the same time, liberalization has made it increasingly difficult for the Mexican government to maintain autonomy from U.S. enforcement programs, and the effects of the U.S.-organized War on Drugs have posed challenges to Mexican sovereignty in this matter. The Mexican government has been dragged into a spiral of increasingly punitive programs with the paradoxical effect of making drug trafficking even more appealing. As in Colombia, many people "got an idea." The danger has grown of the formation of powerful organizations in this illegal market that will pose a challenge to the authority of the state. Much research about the organization of drug production and trafficking in Mexico, the entrepreneurs involved, the interaction between the informal and formal economies in this sector of activity, and its macroeconomic impact remains to be done.

The other transit point between the Andean producer countries and the U.S. market is the Caribbean. Its geography and location make the region conducive to drug trafficking; it serves as an almost natural "bridge" between suppliers and consumer markets.[19] The structural weakness of the island economies makes them vulnerable to the enticement of alternative economic opportunities as offered by the drug trade. For the individual Caribbean states, weak and defenseless as they often are to the mighty drug cartels, the consequences are far reaching. The illegal drug traffic threatens their very existence. Drug trade operations and money laundering in the region are accompanied by the all too familiar effects of increased crime, systemic and institutional corruption, arms trafficking, and total distortion of individual economies. The drug business in the Caribbean has become a matter of international concern and has led to coordinated interventions by the United States, Canada, Britain, France, and the Netherlands. These actions reconfirmed the experience from other areas: there is no simple solution to the drug threat. Participation in trafficking feeds on the same manifestations of underdevelopment that preclude the eradication of coca production in the Andean countries. In this situation of massive unemployment and a continuing lack of economic opportunities, a persisting demand for drugs from the U.S. and European markets will reduce the effectiveness of any antidrug action. Trafficking, in addition to increased marijuana production and exports, could then well be seen as a useful way to cope with depressed exports in the formal economy.

Business practices in trafficking have changed over the years. The old generation of cocaine entrepreneurs that dominated the trade in the 1980s and early 1990s and headed the so-called cartels are not in business anymore. They are either dead, in prison (in the United States or in the source country), or retired and their assets have been seized, invested, or deposited in foreign bank accounts.[20] In the course of the 1990s, general changes in international trade were also affecting the way the cocaine market was being organized. Flexibility, the development of a capacity of immediate response to changes in demand, transportation, distribution, and law enforcement activity, became the basic criteria in organizing the trade. The liberalization of international trade has facilitated the penetration of new markets while reducing risk, achieving economies of scale, and modernizing the logistics of supply. It has also permitted an easier coordination with the underground economy in countries overseas. The new entrepreneurs are more low-profile, live a more restrained life-style, and have no criminal records. They operate in total anonymity, refrain from using bank accounts that run the risk of being traced and investigated,[21] do not use telephones or cell phones for business, and prefer personnel messengers to modern means of communication. Their new organizations are small and cell-like. Personnel is often recruited ad hoc as part of complex contracting and subcontracting schemes. Coordination with other organizations takes place on the basis of special knowledge about logistics, communications, security, money laundering, investments, and so on that each may possess. Large-scale stable organizations are avoided in order to reduce vulnerability in the face of repression and active law enforcement.

This does not preclude the possibility of organization among traffickers in order to co-insure shipments, exchange loads, or share intelligence.[22] The breaking up of the cartels put an end to a small number of businesses whose economic power could give them access to the highest level of government organizations (which is still the case in Mexico) and whose capacity to use violence on a massive scale could undermine the state (as in Colombia). At the same time, however, this policy has created in Colombia an estimated number of three hundred small refining and trafficking organizations whose activities are much more difficult to trace. Among them, some fifty organizations stand out. They control the export of cocaine toward northern markets and function in practice as an oligopolistic sector with often savage internal competition.[23] Under this new conjuncture, with the new flexible ways of conducting business and under the conditions imposed by illegality, which would call for a loose organization minimizing risk of detection, many different types of these small enterprises may be interconnected while trying to conclude a deal. Some of these enterprises will be short-lived, single operations, while others will endure for a longer period of time. In many cases, perfectly legal services (for example in transport, money laundering and investment, legal assistance, and so on), will be contracted. At the same time, the business may be extended into society by offering people outside—often friends, politicians, or civil servants—an export organization the opportunity to participate in an export venture as a favor. These new cocaine enterprises are heterogeneous in their structure and operation and, in fact, consist of constantly changing networks tied together through precarious and variable transactions and functioning on the basis of trust *(confianza)*. There is little that makes the notion of cartel, with its suggestion of large, stable, bureaucratic structures, a plausible way of conceptualizing these business operations.[24] This new model of business applies to the cocaine trade directed toward the United States as well as to the trafficking directed toward western Europe, as Damián Zaitch's research on the Colombian drug industry has shown.

Conclusion

So, where do we go from here? Drug production in source countries has proven to be difficult to control, let alone to eradicate. Drug exporters show a flexibility and inventiveness that beats any controlling agency. The potential supply is virtually unlimited: the trafficking routes to the markets in Europe and the United States are multitudinous. The equipment and inputs used in production and trade, and even the drug shipment itself, can all be easily replaced. The linkages with guerrilla and paramilitary movements have created a shield against counter-narcotics action in source countries, while the development of close contacts with transnational organized crime is facilitating operations in the international arena. While considering the pros and cons of the various counter-narcotics programs that, in the course of the past decades, have been defined and put into action, it is easy to see that the Andean counter-narcotics effort has not been successful. This applies to all phases: eradication, precursor chemicals control, destruction of production facilities, interception of shipments, control of money laundering, and projects of alternative development.

The lack of adequate information on the functioning of the drug industry, its effects on economy and society, and the absence of an adequate evaluation of counter-narcotics action has hampered the definition of adequate policies. The following chapters present an effort to fill in a number of blank areas on the map that are of strategic importance with regard to these policy issues. For each of the producer countries (Bolivia, Peru, and Colombia) and those involved in export to markets in the United States and western Europe (Mexico, the Caribbean Islands), the various efforts to control the drug industry and the effects of its operations on the socioeconomic and political fabric of society have been investigated. Basic questions concern the exclusionary nature of society and the limitations it poses to social mobility through legal means, the structure of power and politics, and the legitimacy of official rule, next to the impact of the drug industry on the structure and functioning of the legal economy. These are strategic questions when explaining the why and how of the rise of the drug industry, its persistent presence in source countries, and the lack of effectiveness of the various methods of control, at least in the long-term, as the case of Bolivia has shown.

Eduardo Gamarra explains in his chapter how growing pressure from the United States produced a policy of forceful eradication of coca in Bolivia. The implementation of the plan has brought to light the deep schisms in society between an elite preoccupied with the country's international image, wishing to present Bolivia as a shining example of democracy and economic reform, and the excluded majorities who bear the brunt of a policy that is costing the country 600 million U.S. dollars a year. As an unintended consequence, this U.S.-inspired War on Drugs has pushed Bolivia to the brink of a popular uprising. The resumption of coca cultivation in more distant parts of the Bolivian Amazon is very possible in case the issue of alternative employment for those whose coca has been eradicated is not resolved.

In Peru, as Mariano Valderrama and Hugo Cabieses explain, the United States supported a similar forced coca-eradication strategy. Here also, this strategy had important unintended consequences. Production has been moving to new areas. At the same time, the production of cocaine, which before was left to Colombian traffickers, has increased in Peru. Also, the corrupting influence of the drug trade in the sphere of government and politics has reached new highs, in particular during the reign of ex-president Alberto Fujimori and his advisor Vladimiro Montesinos. However, this illicit industry has not been capable of reaching the level necessary to undermine the state and the licit economy as was the case in Colombia.

Francisco Thoumi describes in his chapter how, over the last two decades, the drug industry has become the major factor influencing the dynamics of the political system in Colombia and how counter-narcotics action has been affected by the lack of a capacity by the state to implement pertinent policies, next to the structural limitations of these policies themselves. The country has been falling apart, subject to an extreme process of social decomposition whose end is unknown.

Rensselaer Lee explains in his contribution how the various counter-narcotics policies that have been implemented in the Andean countries have resulted in a large number of unanticipated problems that not only negated the policy objectives, but have produced results to the contrary. This underlines the "Catch 22" situation in which supply side often finds itself, a phenomenon also noted by Martin Jelsma in his chapter on the Plan Colombia. Mexico has become the major gateway for drug smuggling into the United States. As Luis Astorga indicates, the country is under pressure by the United States to follow a militarized counter-narcotics strategy. This purely punitive approach has not been able to realize its objectives and has generated high levels of corruption that undermine the moral fabric of the Mexican state. As in the Colombian case, the end game is not clear. The Mexican government is waging a war that it can neither win nor lose. The options are few. The strengthening of Mexican official institutions so as to increase their resistance against the enticements of drug-fed corruption would be a long-term objective. On the short-term, and given the pressure from the United States, present counter-narcotics policies will probably continue with the same lack of result as in the past, resulting in a perpetual war.

The Caribbean, another gateway of drugs to the U.S. market, with an economic and political structure that is very different from the other producer and trafficking countries, shows effects that are very similar, although in a more extreme way. Ivelaw Griffith rings the alarm bell for the many small countries that see the power of their states being undermined and their ability to define and execute macroeconomic policy annulled. The multidimensional nature of the drug- trafficking phenomenon also results in multidimensional effects that penetrate all spheres of economic, political, and social life.

The operation of the industry, as shown in the chapters by Reuter and Zaitch, has changed considerably in the course of the 1990s. In the areas of production and trade, the drug industry has developed interesting parallels with the dynamics of legal international trade under the influence of increasing globalization and economic integration. In legal as well as in illegal trade, one tries to develop markets at home and overseas, to create market advantage and downstream control, to modernize logistics, to practice technological and product innovation (heroin, crack), and to intervene in the political process in producer and trafficking countries on the basis of accumulated economic power.[25] New commodity chains are emerging that include sophisticated ways of organizing the business downstream, innovative manners of laundering the proceeds of the trade, and—difficult to trace as Ernesto Savona explains in his chapter—means to coordinate with transnationally operating organized crime in other sectors.

Both Reuter and Zaitch note that in the course of the 1990s, the large organizational structure of the industry came to an end. Flexibility has become the key concept by which drug transactions are governed. Trafficking is operating through networks that function by way of flexible relations among the participants and include symbiotic relations between legal and illegal economic actors. Smuggling and packing methods have become advanced. New communication technology has revolutionized international trade and with it the cocaine trade. Organizations often do not go beyond one or two transactions. They are small and employees are hired ad hoc. Vertical integration is achieved through subcontracting the various specialized tasks with persons that form part of the trust network. This way of organizing operations helps them to escape detection by law enforcement.

The loose organization of the trade may also be one of the reasons why the traffickers did not expand their activities to other illegal activities. At least in the United States, this expansion of operations to other criminal markets has not occurred. Colombian and Mexican traffickers simply have lacked— given the characteristics of their trade—the resources and means to enter other sectors within the United States. In western Europe, however, there is evidence that in recent years an increasing coordination has emerged between Colombian traffickers and internationally operating crime groups of eastern European, Italian, and Middle Eastern background, groups that are engaged in activities through which the drug trade is being integrated into a wider array of criminal activities. There is an increasing evidence—as Bruce Bagley shows—that Russian crime groups are rapidly extending their operations to Central and South America. There may be a certain logic to this involvement of ethnic minorities in trade within the drug industry, given the need to control the greater part of the commodity chain when accumulating the added value at each stage. The illegality of the trade forces traffickers to operate in an atmosphere of trust and the presence of ethnic communities in those places that play a central role in global trade (port cities, major airports, and so forth) supports this need.

What can be done, given these new modes of operation and the dangers of a coordination of activities with transnationally operating organized crime? The War on Drugs—as Rensselaer Lee shows in his chapter—has become an embarrassing failure, even generating an entire chain of counterproductive effects. In the presence of a growing impact of globalizing processes and the increasing ease with which the drug supply is being internationalized, Sandeep Chawla calls for an expansion of multilateral action in order to avoid the bilateral narco-diplomacy that—as Alain Labrousse shows —so often continues to be subordinated to foreign policy considerations. The certification policy of the United States is a good example of the highly political motives that are behind law enforcement and counter-narcotics actions in source countries. Ybo Buruma's criticism of the growing tendency to intervene unilaterally in countries of supply, disregarding questions of national sovereignty, also would point toward the need for coordinated multilateral action. However, the history of multilateral involvement in counter-narcotics action does not leave much room for optimism, as Jelsma notes in his chapter. There is one option of intervention and control that is directed toward demand, but would also indirectly affect supply, and that involves the liberalization of anti-drug regimes and the decriminalization of drug use in the consumer countries. Tim Boekhout van Solinge describes various interesting initiatives that have been developed in several European countries in recent years. Within the European context, the Netherlands has advanced most in this area and—so far—with positive results. The policies are directed mostly toward the use of soft drugs. The cocaine trade and cocaine use, however, have not been object of their initiatives until now.

In the absence of effective action, the drug industry, fed by super profits, has not stopped growing. It has been spreading influence in the economy and politics of the countries concerned. An all-encompassing approach is needed to confront the industry head-on. The inability of the international community to arrive at a consensus on what such an approach in essence should look like will in practice continue to serve the further expansion of the industry.

Notes

1. We would like to mention: Peter H. Smith, ed., *Drug Policy in the Americas* (Boulder, Colo.: Westview Press, 1992); Bruce M. Bagley and William O. Walker III, eds., *Drug Trafficking in the Americas* (Boulder, Colo.: Lynne Rienner, 1994); James Painter, *Bolivia and Coca: A Study in Dependency* (Boulder, Colo.: Lynne Rienner, 1994); La Mond Tullis, *Unintended Consequences: Illegal Drugs and Drug Policies in Nine Countries* (Boulder, Colo.: Lynne Rienner, 1995), Maria Celia del Toro, *Mexico's War on Drugs: Causes and Consequences* (Boulder, Colo.: Lynne Rienner, 1995); Francisco E. Thoumi, *Political Economy and Illegal Drugs in Colombia* (Boulder, Colo.: Lynne Rienner, 1995); Patrick L. Clawson and Rensselaer Lee III, *The Andean Cocaine Industry* (New York: St. Martin's Press, 1996); Elizabeth Joyce and Carlos Malamud, eds., *Latin America and the Multinational Drug Trade* (London: MacMillan, 1998); Madeline Barbara Leons and Harry Sanabría, eds., *Coca, Cocaine, and the Bolivian Reality* (Albany: State University of New York Press, 1997); Ivelaw Lloyd Griffith, *Drugs and Security in the Caribbean: Sovereignty under Siege* (University Park: Pennsylvania State University Press, 1997); Ivelaw Lloyd Griffith, ed., *The Political Economy of Drugs in the Caribbean* (London: MacMillan, 2000); Sewell H. Menzel, *Cocaine Quagmire* (Lanham, Md.: University Press of America, 1997) and *Fire in the Andes* (Lanham, Md.: University Press of America, 1996); Alain Labrousse, *Drogues: Un Marché de Dupes* (Paris: Editions Alternatives, 2000).

2. See Thoumi, *Political Economy and Illegal Drugs,* 2 ff., 133.

3. For the concept commodity chain, see Gary Gereffi, Miguel Korzeniewicz, and Roberto P. Korzeniewicz, "Introduction: Global Commodity Chains," in Gary Gereffi and Miguel Korzeniewicz, eds., *Commodity Chains and Global Capitalism* (Westport, Conn.: Praeger, 1994), 1–14. For an application to the cocaine trade, see Suzanne Wilson and Marta Zambrano, "Cocaine, Commodity Chains, and Drug Politics: A Transnational Approach," in Ibid., 297–316.

4. Ibid., 131; Clawson and Lee, *The Andean Cocaine Industry,* 131 ff.

5. See for the Bolivian case Painter, *Bolivia and Coca;* Leons and Sanabría, *Coca, Cocaine, and the Bolivia Reality.* See for the Peruvian case Julio Cotler, *Drogas y Política en el Perú* (Lima: Instituto de Estudios Peruanos, 1999); also, Julio Morales, *Cocaine: White Gold Rush in Peru* (Tucson: University of Arizona Press, 1989). See for the Colombian case Thoumi, *Political Economy and Illegal Drugs;* and Clawson and Lee, *The Andean Cocaine Industry.*

6. Cf. Roberto Laserna, "La Economía de la Coca en Bolivia: Cinco Preguntas y Una Duda," in Martin Hopenhayn, ed., *La Grieta de las Drogas: Desintegración*

Social y Políticas Públicas en América Latina (Santiago: Comisión Económica para América Latina y el Caribe, 1997), 65–71.

7. For an extensive discussion of this strategy see Menno Vellinga, "Alternative Development and Supply Side Control in the Drug Industry: The Bolivia Experience," *European Review of Latin America and Caribbean Studies,* no. 64 (1998), 7–26.

8. Tullis, *Unintended Consequences,* 95–99; Roberto Lerner, "The Drug Trade in Peru," in Joyce and Malamud, *Latin America and the Multinational Drug Trade,* 117–32.

9. Painter, *Bolivia and Coca,* 3–9. An excellent study of the colonization process can be found in Jim Well and Connie Weil, *Verde Es la Esperanza: Colonización, Comunidad, y Coca en la Amazonia* (La Paz: Editorial Los Amigos del Libro, 1993).

10. On migration to the Chapare, see Michael Painter, *Upland-Lowland Production Linkages and Land Degradation in Bolivia* (Binghamton, N.Y.: Institute for Development Anthropology, 1991), 11 ff.

11. Thoumi, *Political Economy and Illegal Drugs,* passim.

12. These attitudes have grown to supreme levels of irresponsibility among those who govern: see, for example, Andres Oppenheimer, "Elite Colombiana Ve la Guerra Desde la Distancia," *El Nuevo Herald,* July 9, 2001.

13. Thoumi, *Political Economy and Illegal Drugs,* passim. Zaitch offers a good discussion of the impact of the various factors: Damián Zaitch, "Traquetos: Colombians Involved in the Cocaine Business in the Netherlands" (Ph.D. diss., University of Amsterdam, 2000), 29–32.

14. Zaitch, "Traquetos"; Painter, *Bolivia and Coca,* 27.

15. Francisco Leal and Andres Dávila, *Clientelismo, el Sistema Político, y Su Expresión Regional* (Bogotá: Tercer Mundo Editores, 1991), passim.

16. Cf. "La Nueva Generación de la Mafia," *El Tiempo* (Bogotá), September 9, 2001.

17. See Toro, *Mexico's War on Drugs,* passim; Luis Astorga, "Drug Trafficking in Mexico: A First General Assessment," paper presented at the Second Annual Conference of the {sc}most/undep{sc} Project of Economic and Social Transformation Connected with the International Drug Problem, Rio de Janeiro, April 12–14, 1998. The processes of globalization and economic internationalization facilitate a flexibility of international trade of which U.S.-Mexico relations are an example. The drug trade in conjunction with transnational organized crime has been in an excellent position to take advantage of such developments; see Pierre Chavasse, "Globalización: Terreno para la Delincuencia Transnacional," *La Jornada* (Mexico), September 6, 2001.

18. Cf. Gustavo Castillo Garcia, "Expanden Su Radio de Operación los Carteles de la Droga," *La Jornada* (Mexico), July 30, 2001; Will Weissert, "Drug Cartels in Stealth Makeover," *Arizona Daily Star,* August 5, 2002.

19. Cf. Griffith, *Drugs and Security in the Caribbean,* passim.

20. Zaitch, "Traquetos," 45–47.

21. In August 2001, Colombian police discovered 35 million U.S. dollars in cash stashed in the walls of two Bogotá apartments waiting to be laundered and invested; *El Tiempo,* August 25, 2001. Increasingly the proceeds of the drug trade are kept in cash and transported in suitcases or strapped to the body of the traveler. In April

2002, officials at the airport of Cali detained a passenger who was transporting 1.3 million U.S. dollars strapped to his body; *El Tiempo,* April 11, 2002.

22. Zaitch offers a convincing account of these new business practices based on field research in Colombia and the Netherlands. The Netherlands and Spain are the most important gateways to the European cocaine market.

23. "La Nueva Generación de la Mafia," *El Tiempo* (Bogotá), September 9, 2001.

24. An excellent discussion on the use of the term "cartel" can be found in Thoumi, *Political Economy and Illegal Drugs,* 143; also Zaitch, "Traquetos," 49–50.

25. Tullis, *Unintended Consequences,* passim.

II

The Drug Industry

Its Impact on Economy, Politics, and Society
and the Drug Control Effort in Source Countries

2

Has Bolivia Won the War?

Lessons from Plan Dignidad

Eduardo A. Gamarra

For years the target of widespread criticism, Bolivia in the last four years has received more extensive international praise than any other drug-producing country. Beginning in 1998, this country's Plan Dignidad (Dignity Plan) led to the almost complete eradication of coca production in the Chapare Valley, once known as the world's second largest coca-producing region. The premise that underlies Plan Dignidad is rather simple and works mainly as a result of three factors. First, a fundamental conceptual shift occurred in Bolivia's anti-narcotics strategy. Bolivia began to eradicate leaf forcefully; it targeted precursor chemicals, suspended compensated eradication, and militarized the Chapare.[1] Second, the shooting down of airplanes carrying coca paste from Bolivia and Peru into Colombia effectively ended the division of production that once spanned the entire Andean region. Third, production of cocaine came to be concentrated in Colombia in part because of the establishment of a large *zona de despeje* (clear zone) for the Fuerzas Armadas Revolucionarias de Colombia (FARC).[2] This third factor may no longer apply owing to the peace process in Colombia and the suspension of the shootdown policy following the tragic incident in which a small plane flown by a missionary family was mistakenly targeted, resulting in the death of an American citizen and her infant daughter.

Nevertheless, Bolivia's Plan Dignidad enjoyed an enormously supportive round of international attention that lasted until the early part of 2002. The most ecstatic response came from a variety of U.S. government circles ranging from the Office of National Drug Control Policy, to the Drug Enforcement Administration (DEA), and the U.S. embassy in Bolivia.[3] International agencies such as the United Nations Drug Control Program (UNDCP), the Interamerican Drug Abuse Control Commission (CICAD/OAS), and others bestowed praise on the Bolivian effort, and all claimed some share of the responsibility for the success.[4]

The results were indeed impressive. In three years, one less than the plan anticipated, Bolivia eradicated more than 30,000 hectares of coca and all but eliminated the Chapare's role in the drug industry. In June 2001 the Bolivian government claimed it had achieved the elusive goal of "coca cero by 2002."[5] Given the success in the Chapare, the government temporarily shifted its attention to the 14,000 hectares left in the Yungas region of La Paz.[6] This accomplishment was indeed noteworthy in a country that until very recently was the world's second largest producer of cocaine hydrochloride (after Colombia) and which appeared headed toward fulfilling a larger role in the entire illicit narcotics industry.

Bolivia's success, however, must be tempered by a dose of reality. As has been the case in every instance where policy success is claimed, the unintended consequences are large and the concerns over the long-term impact are significant. Clearly policy design and political will were important factors in the achievements of Plan Dignidad. After dramatic confrontations between coca growers and the government it is clear that any eradication campaign must be conducted by taking into account the unions, its leaders, and their political significance in Bolivia. At the same time, however, it is also clear that developments elsewhere were significant to the Bolivian success story.

This chapter attempts both to analyze the impact of Plan Dignidad on Bolivia's narcotics industry and to examine the unintended consequences that have been neglected by those who enthusiastically embraced the results of the eradication program. Human rights concerns are the most cited concerns by critics of Plan Dignidad. Others have manifested worries over the long-term sustainability of the program; in particular, concern has been expressed over the alternative development prospects in the Chapare. Finally, the population of the Chapare, which has long been mobilized around the coca issue, now faces the prospect of unemployment and a political leadership that refuses to admit that all coca produced in the Chapare is for the illicit drugs market.

Moreover, the Bolivian success story needs to be placed within the general Andean context of the Drug War. While Bolivia eliminated coca production in the Chapare, Colombian production surpassed the all-time cultivation high mark of leaf production for the entire region. Bolivia's success is probably linked to the displacement of production toward Colombia, where in 2000 approximately 163,000 hectares of coca were under cultivation. Plan Dignidad was also somewhat related to the overall impact of the Peruvian and Colombian policy to shoot down planes considered to be transporting drugs to Colombian drug labs. The lines of causality are difficult to draw;

these situations appear to have simply occurred at the same time and were not causally related. Nevertheless, Rensselaer Lee's notion that small successes in one region can lead to huge failures elsewhere provides great explanatory power.

El Plan Dignidad

The Bolivian government long argued that the Plan Dignidad was the result of a national dialogue convened in October 1997 to seek consensus on a four point national action plan that included the following categories: opportunity (employment and income); equity (poverty alleviation); institutionality (judicial reform and the fight against corruption); and dignity (drug control). The national dialogue became an important tool to legitimate the government's strategy. Presided over by then Vice President Jorge "Tuto" Quiroga, political party representatives, labor unions, the private sector, academics, and the church participated in the dialogue.[7] In the government's view, an agreement was reached on the basic elements of what was to become the National Action Plan 1997–2002, also known as "For Better Living Conditions."

Claiming that consensus was the basis of the National Action Plan, in December 1997 the Banzer government unveiled the "Strategy for the Fight against Drug Trafficking 1998–2002" (Plan Dignidad), which called for the complete and total eradication of 38,000 hectares of coca by the year 2002, to provide an alternative to the 35,000 families dependent on the coca-cocaine cycle, to carry out a strong interdiction effort, and to implement an aggressive prevention and rehabilitation strategy within a five-year period. The strategy's introductory paragraph states: "The narco-trafficking phenomenon in Bolivia has reached a crucial point: either it is destroyed immediately and definitively or Bolivian society must forever live with it side by side and face all the internal and external consequences that situation implies."[8]

The strategy's total cost in five years was projected to be 952 million U.S. dollars: 108 million for eradication; 700 million for alternative development; 129 million for interdiction; and, 15 million for prevention and rehabilitation. The Bolivian government pledged to finance at least 15 percent of the cost. To finance the rest, the government embarked on an international strategy to obtain support from the United States and multilateral agencies.[9]

Conceptually, Plan Dignidad targeted the interaction among alternative development, eradication, and law enforcement measures. One of the more significant dimensions of the plan was to target the diversion of precursor chemicals. Equally significant was the phasing-out of the coca-compensation policy that paid up to 2,500 U.S. dollars per hectare of coca eradicated voluntarily. Finally, showing the influence of then Vice President Quiroga, the plan established links to a national anti-corruption plan that also received extensive international praise. Quiroga likes to tell a story that he claims prompted him and a group of advisers to design Plan Dignidad.[10] Quiroga relates the embarrassment he felt in Texas during his college days, and later as an employee of IBM, when Americans inevitably linked Bolivia with cocaine.[11] He pledged to eradicate coca to restore dignity to Bolivia so that his daughters would never have to experience his embarrassment. Quiroga also tells of being harassed at airports in Europe because of his Bolivian passport. This story says a lot about the name of the plan and the motivations of the president. It states a lot about the political will required to carry out a controversial plan. While no reason exists to doubt Quiroga's sincerity, these explanations also cloud a fundamental political reality that gave rise to Plan Dignidad.

The Role of Bolivia's International Politics

To understand the origins of the policy, it is perhaps necessary to examine the circumstances surrounding the coming to office of former general Hugo Banzer Suarez in 1997. Key to the emergence of the plan was the severe U.S. embassy scrutiny of Banzer's party, Acción Democrática Nacionalista (ADN), and its relationship with the Movimiento de Izquierda Revolucionaria (MIR). In 1994 accusations surfaced that between 1985 and 1993, the MIR and its leader and former president Jaime Paz Zamora, in particular, had developed a significant relationship with Isaac "Oso" Chavarría, one of Bolivia's most important drug traffickers. Chavarría provided in-kind and cash payments as a contribution to the MIR's quest for the presidency. These linkages allegedly strengthened while Paz Zamora governed Bolivia between 1989 and 1993.[12] The accusations were given so much credibility by the U.S. embassy that in 1996 Paz Zamora's visa to the United States was cancelled in a very public manner. Along with Colombia's president Ernesto Samper, Paz Zamora became an international and national pariah. More importantly, it appeared that his political career had come to an abrupt end. When former general Banzer announced that ADN would not break its coalition with the MIR to contest the 1997 elections, Ambassador Curtis Kamman reportedly told him that he "had chosen the most difficult route." Kamman repeatedly stated that the issue was not the MIR, but individuals questioned by the U.S. government. In many ways then, Banzer faced the difficult task of proving that, despite the reputation of his governmental allies, his new government would be able to carry out a credible counter-narcotics campaign.[13]

Following the inauguration of General Banzer in August 1997 and more expressly after the implementation of Plan Dignidad, the MIR embarked on an expensive, extensive, and successful strategy to secure the restoration of the visa to Jaime Paz Zamora and other prominent members of the party. The details of the operation are still one of Bolivia's most highly guarded secrets. Interviews with U.S. ambassador Manuel Rocha in Bolivia proved insufficient to explain why the United States in 2001 did an about-face on this issue and restored Paz Zamora's visa. Former ambassador Robert Gelhard, who is now retired and in the private sector, claims that he disagreed with the decision to restore the visa.[14] Other former INL officials told the author that the return of the visa was the product of the efforts of a Washington-based law firm and the propitious arrival of the Bush administration. The details will become public one day. For the moment, this incongruous shift in U.S. policy is difficult to explain considering that it had become the cornerstone of Washington's Andean counter-narcotics strategy.

A second factor forcing former general Banzer to demonstrate his government's commitment to fighting drugs was his own previous dictatorial past and allegations about his family's linkages to the narcotics industry and to a series of other networks of corruption. Ambassadors of the United States who have been interviewed over the past decade have repeatedly denied these ties or even that the DEA possessed information about these alleged linkages.[15] On the contrary, ambassadors have generally lavished praise on Banzer for his role in the Drug War. The statements of law enforcement officials interviewed during the same time period provide a notable contrast. In the view of the DEA and other agencies, credible evidence linked Banzer and members of his family and of ADN to the narcotics industry, not only in the 1970s, but also during the post-1985 democratic period.[16] These agents also note that no political party in Bolivia was free of some degree of penetration by the drug industry.

A third factor involved the move on the part of the incoming Banzer administration to turn over the conduct of the Drug War to Vice President Jorge Quiroga, the only person in government who did not have a questionable past.[17] Quiroga quickly became a type of de facto prime minister charged not only with the conduct of Bolivia-U.S. policy, but with conducting the national dialogue and directing the government's economic policy. The vice president also became the government's international poster boy. World Bank president James D. Wolfensohn embraced Quiroga's anti-corruption initiatives, while General Barry McCaffrey took up quoting Quiroga, as did many journalists. Members of the United States Congress were also swayed by Quiroga's style and his ease at communicating Bolivia's message.

It is not hard to be swayed by Quiroga, who speaks perfect U.S. English, commands one-liners in the best U.S. tradition, and delivers impressive power point speeches. "Tuto," as he is known, is as comfortable addressing members of the U.S. House of Representatives as he is speaking to reporters. As effective as he was internationally, Quiroga's effectiveness at home was reduced. During his term as vice president, Quiroga maintained his international reputation but was accused of everything from attempting to topple former general Banzer in a so-called constitutional coup to failing to conduct the government's economic strategy. More important for the purposes of this paper, Quiroga was correctly perceived as the author of Plan Dignidad and was often the target of angry Chapare *cocaleros*.[18]

In his first few months as president, Quiroga was forced to make some critical decisions regarding the continuity of Plan Dignidad. First, he was forced to recognize publicly that in fact *coca cero* had not been attained in June and that a satellite error was responsible for the premature declaration of victory. Second, and most important, facing an inevitable mobilization of the coca-growers federations in the Chapare, Quiroga secretly ordered the entry of four thousand military and police troops into the Chapare. The militarization of the Chapare may have averted massive roadblocks and the like that were scheduled to occur beginning November 6, 2001. The latter decision is the most significant in the sense that it will now be difficult for the government to relinquish control of the Chapare. This also means that the long-term success of Plan Dignidad is related specifically to the long-term presence of security forces in the Chapare.

The Political System and the Narcotics Industry

Unlike other democracies in the Andes, Bolivia has always been a long way from becoming a "narco-democracy." But while the degree of influence on the political system may not be as prevalent, it is also accurate to note that for at least two decades, the Bolivian political system has been severely affected by the proliferation of national and international trafficking organizations. Fewer than two decades ago, one of the most significant worries was the extent to which Bolivian and Colombian narcotics-trafficking organizations had penetrated the political system and its institutions. During the Garcia Meza period (1980–1982), under the most extreme set of circumstances, these organizations were said to have bought themselves a government. Under democracy, trafficking organizations in Bolivia have been able to corrupt judges, policemen, senators, and ministers of state.

Since 1982, every civilian democratically elected government has faced at least one major "narco-scandal" that tainted otherwise laudable efforts in other areas, such as economic and social reform or the continuation of the democratization process. In Table 2.1, a list of the most significant narco-scandals is provided. As can be seen from the list, every democratic government has faced major accusations of involvement with the most prominent drug-trafficking organizations.

As is the case in Colombia, trafficking organizations in Bolivia have sought

Table 2.1. Democracy and Drug-Related Corruption

Administration	Narcotics-Related Scandal
Hernan Siles Ziazo (1982–1985)	Negotiations with the Roberto Suárez organization; accusations against minister of interior of involvement with trafficking organizations
Victor Paz Estenssoro (1985–1989)	Huanchaca Affair, murder of scientist Noel Kempf Mercado; accusations against Minister of Interior and other civilian enforcement officials; Narco-video scandal; accusations against commander of police
Jaime Paz Zamora (1989–1993)	Narcovínculos Scandal involving accusations against President Paz Zamora and the MIR of illicit involvement with the Isaac "Oso" Chavarria trafficking organization; accusations against two of the administrations' ministers of interior of involvement in trafficking or laundering organizations; accusations against other cabinet, subcabinet, and law enforcement officials of involvement with trafficking organizations
Gonzalo Sanchez de Lozada (1993–1997)	Accusations against minister of interior of involvement with the Amado Pacheco trafficking organization*; accusations against the Fuerza Especial de Lucha Contra el Narcotráfico of involvement with the Amado Pacheco organization; accusations of illicit involvement against prominent members of the MNR
Hugo Banzer Suárez (1997–present)	Accusations of links to the Marino Diodato crime family by prominent members of the government, including family ties to Banzer's family

*In the mid-1990s a few organizations existed in Bolivia capable of moving large amounts of refined cocaine directly into Mexico and the United States. The most noteworthy case was that of Amado "Barbas Chocas" Pacheco, who, for at least one decade, smuggled cocaine into Mexico. Pacheco was arrested in September 1995 when his DC-6 loaded with 4.1 tons of cocaine was stopped at the Jorge Chávez airport in Lima, Peru. In contrast to the early days of the Roberto Suarez organization, which boasted that it could deliver 1,000 kilograms per month, the contemporary shipments are massive. For an interesting account of the Pacheco organization see Gerardo Irusta Medrano, *De Huanchaca al Narcoavión* (La Paz: Editorial Gráfica Latina, 1995).

to influence the course of broader policy by providing funds for electoral campaigns. All major parties have been suspected of receiving illicit funding from drug-trafficking organizations. The aforementioned case against the MIR and former president Paz Zamora is the most notorious, although accusations were not made until after he left office in 1994. While the MIR took the rap, including a four-year jail term for party leader Oscar Eid, other parties have gone unpunished. In 1988, for example, ADN was accused of receiving funding from the Roberto Suárez organization for its 1985 campaign. If the charges against these parties are true, the flexibility of trafficking organizations is also noteworthy. In their efforts to finance several presidential campaigns in 1985, 1987, and 1989, these organizations did not bet on a single candidate; instead they made sure that all likely winners got some contribution. This pattern is not unlike the behavior of prominent lobby groups in the United States.

A second major strategy of trafficking organizations was to circumvent ongoing law enforcement and military campaigns aimed at dismantling their illicit business. While numerous examples of this type of activity exist, two are noteworthy. In 1986, the MNR minister of interior, Fernando Barthelemy, was accused of delaying law enforcement activities against trafficking organizations in the Huanchaca area even after a prominent scientist was murdered when he and his team mistakenly ran into a drug lab.[19] In 1991, the United States temporarily halted economic assistance when the MIR minister of interior, Guillermo Capobianco, named a suspected trafficker as the head of the Fuerza Especial de Lucha Contra el Narcotráfico (Special Counter-Narcotics Force-FELCN) in an alleged scheme to provide cover for trafficking organizations.[20] These schemes generally also involved suborning law enforcement and military officials. As a result of the prevalence of these corrupt ties, many activities funded by the United States were carried out without prior knowledge of Bolivian government officials.[21]

The very process of democratization had the paradoxical effect of democratizing the structure of organized crime, thus making democratic governments more vulnerable. As the military and police connections of the important organizations, such as that of Roberto Suárez, suffered important setbacks in the early 1980s, smaller and bolder competitors proliferated. In some measure, this proliferation increased the challenges for law enforcement and military institutions to combat drug trafficking. Democratization allowed trafficking organizations to restructure, retool, and accommodate changing circumstances dictated by the changing nature of the marketplace, more effective law enforcement efforts, or transformations in the domestic political scene. In contrast to the authoritarian period when corrupt military governments were intertwined with a single large trafficking organization, democratic governments have had to face multiple organizations with significant transnational connections.[22] In the final analysis, in 1997 Plan Dignidad had the difficult task of dealing with this entirely revamped structure of organized crime in Bolivia where Colombians were not as important and where at least fifteen Bolivian organizations dominated the industry.[23]

Bolivia's Poor Performance in Drug War Indicators

A fifth factor that led to the launching of Plan Dignidad was the poor performance of Bolivia in terms of eradication and seizures between 1993 and 1997. (See Table 2.2.) Former president Gonzalo Sánchez de Lozada gave the Drug War little attention while focusing most of his efforts on the implementation of an ambitious state reform agenda. As a result, in March 1995, for the first time, Bolivia was decertified but was granted a national interest waiver because of its poor showing on eradication. Furthermore, Ambassador Kamman issued a confidential ultimatum—threatening to decertify the country by June 30, 1995 if coca-eradication targets were not met—that moved the Bolivian government in two significant directions that would pave the road for Plan Dignidad.

In fact, Sánchez de Lozada presided over the escalation of military involvement in the Drug War owing primarily to threats by the United States to decertify Bolivia. Faced with this inevitable fate, the Bolivian government

Table 2.2. Eradication and Seizures Under the Sánchez de Lozada Administration

	1997	1996	1995	1994	1993
Net Cultivation (ha)*	45,800	48,100	48,600	48,100	47,200
Eradication (ha)	7,026	7,512	5,493	1,058	2,397
Cultivation (ha)	52,826	55,612	54,093	49,158	49,597
Seizures					
Coca Leaf (mt)	50.60	76.40	110.090	202.13	201.25
Coca Paste (mt)	0.008	—	0.05	0.02	0.01
Cocaine Base (mt)	6.57	6.78	4.60	6.44	5.30
Cocaine HCL (mt)	3.82	3.17	3.59	1.02	0.31
Cocaine HCL and Base (mt)	10.39	9.95	8.19	7.46	5.61
Agua Rica** (ltrs)	1,149	2,275	16,874	16,874	14,255
Arrests/Detentions	1,766	995	600	1,469	1,045
Labs Destroyed					
Cocaine HCL	1	7	18	32	10
Base	1,022	2,033	2,226	1,891	1,300

*Includes Apolo, Chapare, and Yungas.

**Suspension of coca paste in a weak acid solution, 37 liters equal 1 kilogram of cocaine base.

Source: *International Counter-narcotics Strategy Report (INCSR) 2000* (Washington, D.C.: Department of State, 2001).

crossed an important threshold. It not only initiated the forceful eradication of coca fields in the Chapare, but the government admitted for the first time that the coca grown in the Chapare was exclusively for use by the cocaine industry.[24]

A second development under Sánchez de Lozada was the signing of an extradition treaty with the United States and the sending of a few Bolivians to the United States for trials and jail terms.[25] Extradition had been one of the most significant U.S. demands since the escalation of the War on Drugs in the mid-1980s. The Paz Zamora government (1989–1993) negotiated a treaty, but it refused to submit it to the Bolivian Senate for consideration, arguing that it feared the "Colombianization" of Bolivia. Sánchez de Lozada's team negotiated a new treaty and achieved Senate approval. The U.S. Senate approved it shortly thereafter.[26] The incoming Banzer administration was, therefore, under severe scrutiny to move forward and on U.S. terms.[27]

Changes in Public Opinion

A final factor in understanding the launching of Plan Dignidad was the general public mood in Bolivia. In many ways the strategy departs from previous Bolivian efforts at comprehensive drug control planning, which did not even make the pretense of broad social consultation. Members of the Banzer administration, however, claimed that Plan Dignidad was developed by a broad spectrum of society stemming from the October 1997 national dialogue. In the view of these officials, the strategy is firmly grounded in a national consensus that illicit crop cultivation and production actually hurt Bolivia's development prospects and international image.[28]

The notion of national consensus on Plan Dignidad is a very difficult factor to grasp for at least two reasons. First, although their opinions vary by class, ethnicity, and region, Bolivians have been largely supportive of a less aggressive approach against coca cultivation. Most have favored negotiations with coca growers and greater funding for alternative development projects.[29] At the same time, and although the available surveys do not provide an explanation, it appears that Bolivians have been largely shifting their views of the Chapare and of the role performed by coca growers and their leadership.

U.S. embassy officials argue that public opinion regarding the coca growers, especially concerning their periodic marches on urban centers, has shifted toward greater intolerance of the farmers. Although no survey data is yet available, the key appears to have been to convince urban dwellers that coca growers in the Chapare and narco-traffickers are related. The urban populations of La Paz and Cochabamba, which are the most affected by constant marches, road blockades, and the like, have welcomed the end of coca in the Chapare presumably because they believe that the daily disruptions may come to an end.[30]

The immense opposition in the coca-growing areas of the Chapare against Plan Dignidad is not surprising. It appears that outside these areas Plan Dignidad enjoys the tacit support of most Bolivians not directly involved in the conflict.[31]

A vice minister's quote to a UNDCP-sponsored 1999 video on the Chapare reflects a common official view: "Bolivia is tired of living under the stigma of narco-traffickers, we're tired of being considered a nation of narco-traffickers. Farmers are now realizing that it is not good to live pressured by repressive forces, pressured by narco-traffickers, pressured by the market and the general socioeconomic conditions of the country." Survey data confirms Bolivia's tiredness with the narco-trafficking stigma, but only anecdotal evidence supports the view that farmers are themselves tired of the narcotics link.[32] The sad fact was that coca growers who mobilized against government efforts to enforce eradication agreements with the United States unwittingly became linked to trafficking organizations, the most nefarious dimensions of the coca-cocaine complex. Moreover, in the mid- to late 1990s, it was widely recognized that the bulk of the coca leaf cultivated in the Chapare was for the refinement of cocaine. At the same time, it was also evident that in the 1990s many coca growers graduated to the production of cocaine.[33] Once this link was established, anti-narcotics policy based on interdiction and force was easier to sell to Bolivian public opinion.

The Results of Plan Dignidad

The early months of the Banzer administration were not easy. Facing the prospect of decertification from the United States, in 1997 the Banzer government set off on a race against time to meet the eradication targets. In mid-December 1997, the government announced that owing to its intensive and costly involuntary eradication program it had surpassed the 7,000-hectare goal. It also announced that narcotics-related arrests had increased considerably. After the launching of Plan Dignidad, between 1998 and 2000, the government achieved and surpassed even its most ambitious goals. And, has been noted earlier, in mid-2001, the government prematurely announced that it had met the goal of *coca cero* because only 600 hectares of coca were left to eradicate in the Chapare.[34]

The success of the Plan Dignidad strategy was well received internationally. The United Nations Drug Control Program in particular lavished praise on the program. And the U.S. annual certification statements have also praised the strategy in glowing terms. The overall statements praise Bolivia for successes in alternative development, in reducing the production and distribution of cocaine, in asset seizures, in extradition, and the like.[35]

In the 1999 International Counter-Narcotics Strategy Report (INCSR), Bolivia is praised in the following terms: "An extremely effective eradication program in the Chapare, Bolivia's principal coca-growing region, surpassed last year's record setting results, reducing the number of hectares of coca under cultivation by more than half, and by 43 percent overall. Even though Bolivia produced less cocaine hydrochloride (HCL) and cocaine base than in 1998, interdiction forces increased arrests and drug seizures (measured in terms of a percentage of potential production). A highly effective chemical interdiction program has forced Bolivian traffickers to continue to rely on substitutes for scarce and expensive chemicals smuggled in from neighboring countries and an inferior process to streamline base and HCL production. As a consequence, the purity of Bolivian cocaine has been greatly reduced and most foreign traffickers now prefer to purchase base in Bolivia and process it into HCL in Brazil, where essential chemicals are readily available. Alternative development initiatives in the Chapare continue to provide licit alternatives to coca, but demand for alternative development is exceeding the ability of the government of Bolivia to provide it."

And the 2000 INCSR report for the year 2000 stated: "Bolivia continues to be the model for the region in coca eradication. An extremely and effective eradication program in the Chapare, previously Bolivia's principal coca-growing region, has reduced the number of hectares of coca to fewer than 600."

Emboldened by the success in the Chapare, the Banzer government decided to strike also in the Yungas region of the Department of La Paz, where Bolivia's most traditional coca has been grown. Some government officials claimed that the success in the Chapare had resulted in the displacement of coca growers and their migration into areas such as La Asunta in the southern part of the Yungas region.[36] Fears were present that the Yungas coca growers were more closely aligned politically with Felipe Quispe (also known as Mallku), the controversial leader of the Confederación Sindical Unica de Trabajadores Campesinos de Bolivia, who on at least two occasions had mobilized hundreds of *campesinos* to blockade access roads to La Paz.

It is still a source of disagreement about who gave the orders to send eradication forces into the Yungas. U.S. embassy officials claim that they did not pressure the Bolivians into pursuing a Yungas strategy so soon after the Chapare, especially in the context of other social tensions in Bolivia.[37] Bolivian government officials argue that extensive U.S. pressure to take advantage of the momentum gained from the Chapare experience forced them to move decisively in the Yungas. Regardless of who led the charge, the results were almost catastrophic. When eradication forces moved into the Yungas in mid-June, they were immediately surrounded by coca growers. Government forces held their fire, and the coca growers controlled their lot. In the end, and much to the disappointment of U.S. embassy officials, an agreement was signed in which the government pledged never to forcefully eradicate coca in the Yungas. In retrospect, it is probably true that in signing the agreement the government averted a bloodbath. At the same time, however, it also signaled a turning of the tide against Plan Dignidad that would have an impact on the Chapare campaign.

Ambassador Rocha's support, however, was not enough to keep Banzer at the helm when the Bolivian president was diagnosed with cancer and rushed to the United States for treatment.[38] In August following all types of maneuvers by those most closely linked to Banzer to prevent a constitutional succession, Vice President Quiroga was sworn into office. Quiroga's ascension resulted in a three-month hiatus in the pattern of sociopolitical turmoil that had dominated the country for nearly two years. The problems facing the government in the economic front and with numerous groups, however, appeared to be insurmountable in the long term. None was more difficult than the conflict with the Chapare coca growers. This conflict intensified when in September 2001 Leopoldo Fernández, the new minister of interior, announced that a satellite error had resulted in the governments earlier claim that only 600 hectares remained to be eradicated in the Chapare. Instead he revealed that 6,000 hectares were in fact still left, and that the government would intensify its efforts to eradicate them.

As Bolivian efforts to target the remaining 6,000 hectares intensified so did *cocalero* resistance. By early October, the standoff between *cocaleros*—who surrounded military stations and alternative development offices—and eradication forces was serious. Evo Morales complained not only that coca production should remain, but that alternative development projects had been a complete failure. The Quiroga government appeared to backtrack on its earlier pledge to abandon compensated eradication programs when it announced a plan to provide 2,500 U.S. dollars in technical assistance to every *campesino* who abandoned coca cultivation. Ambassador Rocha, in turn, warned that U.S. assistance was tied to the political will of the Bolivian government to eradicate coca and that without it, approximately 120 million dollars in funding would disappear.

In the final analysis, Quiroga faced a dire scenario in late 2001. In ten months not only was he to resolve all of the social problems inherited from Banzer's four years, but he also had to resolve the economic crisis, preside over the 2002 national electoral round (which was fraught with problems), and close out the cycle of Plan Dignidad. As 2001 ended, it appeared that the task was too large even for Quiroga; the honeymoon with Washington ended with the release of the 2002 INCSR report. Although it notes overall praise for Bolivia's success, the report contains serious reservations about the will of the Bolivian government to push ahead with eradication of coca in the Chapare and Yungas regions. In particular, the INCSR notes that the Bolivian government has given in to pressure from coca growers in at least two critical areas:

restricting coca-leaf markets in the Chapare, and the speed of eradication. The INCSR report is also extremely critical of the agreement with coca growers in the Yungas that, in essence, prohibits forceful eradication in that region.

> Up to June 2001, the GOB seemed committed to implementing the 'Dignity Plan,' President Banzer's five-year initiative to remove Bolivia from the coca-cocaine production circuit by 2002. President Quiroga said he would continue to support the GOB's eradication, interdiction, alternative development, and demand reduction programs outlined in the Dignity Plan. However, the Quiroga administration has been reluctant to take certain measures, such as closing 15 illicit markets in the Chapare and prosecuting violators who continue to grow and sell illicit coca. In November 2001, the GOB issued a decree which authorized the seizure of illegal coca that is transported or dried in the Chapare and the arrest and prosecution of those involved. The decree came under heavy protest by cocaleros and those detained under the decree were soon released from custody. A series of violent confrontations with cocaleros protestors led to the GOB reversing its policy to pursue forced eradication in the Yungas region, and slowed eradication operations in the Chapare region. Despite the eradication of 9,395 hectares in the Chapare region during 2001, massive illegal replanting led to increased coca cultivation. Yungas coca cultivation above the 12,000 hectares allowed for traditional use also grew in 2001.

The official reasons for Washington's displeasure appear in the INCSR. Embassy officials interviewed for this project, however, noted two other related but nonquantifiable issues.[39] The first involved the naming of Leopoldo Fernández, a prominent ADN politician suspected of ties to the narcotics industry, to the post of minister of interior. Although Fernández had served under Banzer, Washington had expected Quiroga to purge him from his cabinet. Fernández had become an important negotiator with Evo Morales and the Chapare *cocaleros* and at one point was even considered a possible ADN presidential candidate. In President Quiroga's view, the U.S. accusation was unfounded, and it simply reflected the inability of Washington to understand the domestic constraints facing his interim government.[40] U.S. officials also argued that Quiroga's conciliatory policies were responsible for "resurrecting coca grower leader Evo Morales and CSTUCB secretary general Felipe Quispe." According to this view, Morales and Quispe were soundly defeated by the Banzer government and posed no threat to the government. President Quiroga argues, however, that this interpretation ratifies Washington's lack of clear analysis regarding the situation in Bolivia. An even more subjective reason for the falling out between Quiroga and Washington appears to be the

Table 2.3. Coca Cultivation and Eradication (in Hectares) per Region in Bolivia, 1996–2000

	2000	1999	1998	1997	1996
Chapare	600	7,500	23,500	31,500	33,000
Yungas	13,600	14,000	14,200	14,000	14,400
Apolo	300	300	300	300	700
Total Cultivation	22,253	38,799	49,621	52,826	55,612
Total Eradication	7,653	16,999	11,621	7,026	7,512
Net Total Cultivation	14,600	21,800	38,000	45,800	48,100

Source: INCSR Reports, 1996–2000.

Table 2.4. Coca Leaf, Coca Paste, and Cocaine Seizures in Bolivia, 1996–2001

Seizures	2001	2000	1999	1998	1997	1996
Coca Leaf (mt)	65.95	51.85	56.01	93.72	50.60	76.40
Coca Paste (mt)	—	—	—	—	0.008	—
Cocaine Base (mt)	3.95	4.54	5.48	6.20	6.57	6.78
Cocaine HCL (mt)	0.51	0.72	1.43	3.12	3.82	3.17
Combined HCL Base (mt)	4.46	5.26	6.91	9.32	10.39	9.95
Agua Rica* (ltrs)	20.240	15.920	30.120	44.560	1.149	2.275
Arrests and Detentions	1.674	2.017	2.050	1.926	1.766	995
Labs Destroyed						
Cocaine	1	2	1	1	1	7
Base	877	620	893	1,205	1.022	2.033

*Suspension of coca paste in a weak acid solution; according to the DEA, 37 liters of agua rica equal one kilogram of cocaine base.

Source: INCSR Report 2000

Table 2.5. Bolivia: Coca Cultivation and Eradication, 1993–2001

Coca	2001	2000	1999	1998	1997	1996	1995	1994	1993
Net Cultivation (ha)	19,900*	14,600	21,800	38,000	45,800	48,100	48,600	48,100	47,200
Eradication (ha)	—	7,653	16,999	11,621	7,026	7,512	5,493	1,058	2,397
Cultivation (ha)	19,900	22,253	38,799	49,621	52,826	55,612	54,093	49,158	49,597
Leaf: Potential (mt)	20,200	13,400	22,800	52,900	70,100	75,100	85,000	89,800	84,400
HCL: Potential (mt)	60**	43	70	150	200	215	240	255	240

*As of 6/01/01.

**The reported leaf to HCL conversion ratio is estimated to be 370 kg of leaf to 1 kg of cocaine in the Chapare. In the Yungas, the reported ratio is 315:1.

Source: INCSR Report 2001.

recurrent public and confidential statements by embassy officials about the key role played by General Banzer in Plan Dignidad's success. As noted earlier, evidence regarding Banzer's role in the design and/or implementation of the plan is scant.

Conclusion: Explaining Plan Dignidad's Success

The results of Plan Dignidad are indeed impressive from the standpoint of overall reduction in coca cultivation in the Chapare. The State Department's early praise was well placed from this perspective. A more balanced explanation of the factors that contributed to this success and which might lead to longer term prospects for Bolivia is required. Several factors appear important to understanding the policy's success. Of these, some were clearly intended, a few appear to be perversely serendipitous, and still others were unintended.

Policy design and implementation was an important dimension that contributed to the overall success. In this sense, achieving the political will and capacity to implement the program was a crucial first step. Whether one buys the notion that a national consensus was achieved, or whether one believes the national pride stories of President Quiroga, the government did muster enough political muscle to carry out the strategy. It is also very clear that U.S. pressure was an absolutely significant factor in 1997 that perhaps forced the hand of the incoming Banzer government. Without the pressures of Ambassador Kamman in 1997, perhaps Plan Dignidad would never have come to pass. With policy design came a number of very significant conceptual changes in Bolivian policy. The following changes are not mentioned in any rank order of importance; it is clear that all were important to the final outcome.

Reclaiming State Control of the Chapare through Militarization

Accurate or not, for at least two decades the Chapare had become known as an area in the control of drug traffickers and coca growers. Past policy failures were in large measure a result of the inability of the Bolivian state to enforce policy there in a sustainable manner. Earlier attempts at eradication, for example, were often routed even before they began as a result of organized coca-grower responses. While it would be farfetched to make a comparison to the Colombian situation where the state has surrendered control over a vast sector of its national territory, the Chapare in many ways became a territory where law enforcement activities could be carried out only exceptionally. Plan Dignidad appears to have provided territorial control of the Chapare, a key element of expanding the presence of the state. The problem in the long term is that the presence of the state is directly related to the militarization of the region. This factor must be placed in some context.

Until 1995, the notion that the armed forces could enter the Chapare was one of the most controversial subjects in Bolivia. Most analysts argued that militarizing the Chapare would inevitably lead to armed conflict in the region. The fact is that the presence of the armed forces and the police have led to increased tensions and to a number of shootings and deaths, but the doomsday predictions of some have not come to pass. The most serious incident occurred in October and November 2000 when farmers kidnapped, tortured, and murdered four policemen and the wife of one of the officers.[41] In the government's view, these attacks were the result of an alliance between coca growers and narco-traffickers bent on preventing the elimination of coca production. At the same time, accusations of human rights violations against members of the security forces became widespread.

In October 2001 tension in the Chapare increased as the new Quiroga government intensified its efforts to end all production in that region. The result was the death of two peasants and more than a dozen wounded, including four soldiers. As the government attempts to destroy the remaining 6,000 hectares, it is likely that greater casualties will result. Organized resistance by coca growers has added to the confrontation, especially after they surrounded military forts and alternative development offices.

The social tensions of 2000 and 2001 are illustrative of the unintended consequences of Plan Dignidad. In October, peasants surrounded the capital city of La Paz and the central city of Cochabamba among others in an attempt to force the government to revert certain policies and to give in to a series of economic demands. As one Bolivian politician described it, the country was on the brink of a racially based civil war between those who believed that the country was a shining example of democracy and economic reform and the vast majority who felt excluded completely from the benefits.

The Banzer government was correct in noting that Bolivia was deeply affected by the economic downturn of its neighbors, especially Brazil, and that the country was also affected by the significant increase in the price of hydrocarbons. But by far the most serious issue was the dramatic success of Plan Dignidad in curbing the cultivation of coca leaf.

According to Ronald MacLean, who was then the minister of planning, this success resulted in the sudden disappearance of 500–700 million U.S. dollars (one percentage point of GDP) from the Bolivian economy.[42] This figure is high for any country, but it is especially significant in a country such as Bolivia, where the long-term benefits of neoliberal reform will not be felt for several more years. It is also especially significant in a country where 70 percent of the population is poor, indigenous, and dependent mainly on informal market mechanisms.

The problem was that while the United States and the Bolivian government basked in the success of crop eradication, neither was capable of providing significant alternatives for farmers, nor could they inject economic resources to make up for the shortfall. Farmers in the coca-growing Chapare blocked roads and engaged in violent confrontations with government troops, demanding that the government give up its eradication campaign and halt the construction of three U.S. financed military bases. Moreover, they demanded the resignation of President Banzer.

Banzer's government was also trapped by the legacy of his past: he was the de facto military ruler of the 1970s whose murky human rights record was tainted by a bloody 1974 crackdown on striking peasants in the Cochabamba valley. Although he was democratically elected in 1997 (some even give him great credit for the country's nineteen-year-old democracy), few were willing to forget his authoritarian past. He also severely mishandled the April revolt, has been hesitant to crack down on the rebels, and has had little control over poorly trained soldiers eager to fire rounds at rock-throwing peasants. The government's principal source of support at one stage appeared to be coming from Manuel Rocha, the recently arrived U.S. ambassador, who is charged with enforcing the terms of U.S. counter-narcotics policy and for whom former General Banzer and Vice President Quiroga deserve to be recognized as the current Latin American heroes of the War on Drugs.[43]

In any event, the role of the armed forces in the success of Plan Dignidad is unquestionable. Sustaining the success of Plan Dignidad will also depend on the presence of the armed forces and the police in the Chapare for years to come. This is a role that may define the future long-term role of Bolivian security forces. More important to the long-term success of the policy will be the capacity to establish greater state presence in coca-growing regions beyond the armed forces. Generally referred to as nation and state building, the presence of nonmilitary state services for a population that now lacks the ability to support itself is directly linked to the long-term sustainability of Plan Dignidad.

The Elimination of Cash Compensation for Voluntary Eradication

A second significant factor in the success of Plan Dignidad was the phased out elimination of compensated voluntary eradication that paid farmers up to 2,500 U.S. dollars per hectare. As numerous studies have shown, this compensated payment provided an incentive for peasants to plant more coca rather than to accelerate eradication. As the 1999 INCSR states, coca eradication efforts were largely aided by field abandonment. Faced with no compensation for voluntarily eradicating crops and with no buyers for the excess production, farmers simply abandoned their fields.

Compensation for communities and then not in the form of cash payments but in technical assistance has been a significant improvement over the previous method. It is clear that this form of compensation has many supporters who believe that this is a way to secure community ownership of alternative development programs and an acceptance of forceful eradication efforts. Again, this form of compensation will depend greatly on the health of the Bolivian economy and the presence of foreign funding for the program.

Alternative Development Programs

This is not the place for an overall analysis of Bolivia's alternative development programs.[44] Suffice it to say that this dimension of Plan Dignidad appears to have worked well despite serious limitations in funding and problems with the way in which the program has been implemented. The success of Plan Dignidad has led to a significant increase in funding levels for Bolivia in 2001 with approximately 110 million dollars committed by the United States Congress and President George Bush's recently unveiled Andean Initiative.[45]

The results of alternative development are important although, according to the Ministry of Agriculture, Bolivia exports only 7 percent of the alternative crops, which results in an annual income of only 5.6 million U.S. dollars. Significantly, the Bolivian market for palm hearts, pineapple, banana, passion fruit, and orange crops planted to replace coca brought in a total of 73 million U.S. dollars. The Chapare's 116,000 hectares are said to be cultivated with bananas, pepper, yucca, orange, pineapple, mandarin oranges, rice, and hay. The government believes that in the future the area dedicated to non-coca crops could be expanded to 550,000 hectares.[46]

Other international donors have also become an important dimension of alternative development in Bolivia. The Spanish International Cooperation Agency (AECI), for example, is involved in a hearts-of-palm project in Chimore, which is deep within the Chapare. The Spanish project includes building and donating a processing plant and training workers to grow the palms, and market and sell the finished product.

Bolivia's experience with alternative development is important and many lessons could be derived from the last four years of Plan Dignidad. It is clear that these programs have provided some relief for former *cocaleros;* it is also clear that they may be insufficient to deal with the huge demand that massive eradication in such a short period of time has signified. Without significant international funding and without the opening of international markets for Bolivian products, this alternative development success could prove to be only a temporary diversion for unemployed coca growers in the Chapare.

Controlling Chemical Precursors

In 1999, Bolivian law enforcement officials claimed that as a result of Plan Dignidad the most profitable business in Bolivia was the smuggling of precursor chemicals.[47] It is perhaps most noteworthy that between 1996 and 2000, the entry of chemical precursors into Bolivia came to a dramatic end. As a

Table 2.6. Bolivia: Confiscated Precursor Chemicals, 1995–1999

Precursor	1995	1996	1997	1998	1999
Acetone (lt)	8,592	24,546	5,438	623	5,945
Hydrochloric Acid (lt)	2,770	3,477	9,946	1,408	5,001
Sulfuric Acid (lt)	15,242	33,793	9,881	8,970	7,583
Ethyl Alcohol (lt)	13,355	—	—	—	2,008
Ammonia	5,063	4,775	623	4,412	263
Sodium Bicarbonate (kg)	19,768	15,040	11,406	13,659	5,931
Lime (kg)	213,711	307,522	106,722	286,345	56,609
Diesel (lt)	230,854	350,383	159,832	481,826	171,855
Sulfuric Ether (lt)	8,830	24,619	3,152	28	3,484
Gasoline (lt)	10,652	9,764	12,371	46,839	110,858
Kerosene (lt)	42,331	72,843	16,074	10,815	7,499
Potassium Permanganate (kg)	22,137	740	128	36	82

Source: CICAD, Statistical Summary on Drugs (Washington, D.C., 2000).

result, the illicit drugs industry resorted to precursors such as cement to produce low-quality cocaine, which must inevitably be cleansed or whitened with traditional chemicals. Law enforcement officials in Bolivia believe that this dimension of Plan Dignidad was as important to the policy's success as was the forceful eradication of the leaf in the Chapare.

An analysis of CICAD data regarding precursor chemicals, however, reveals an important trend. The most significant year in precursor chemical interdiction appears to have been 1995, at least two years before the launching of Plan Dignidad. A more careful reading reveals the downward trend of traditional chemicals such as acetone and sulfuric acid and the increasing use of nontraditional chemicals such as gasoline and kerosene. Lime, an important component of cement, remains fairly constant throughout this period. In short, while the Banzer government boasts that its precursor interdiction policy was a key dimension of the plan, the data reveals that more chemicals were actually confiscated during the previous Sánchez de Lozada period.

External Factors and Plan Dignidad

As noted in the previous section, policy design, implementation, and political will were important ingredients in the much-lauded Plan Dignidad. Much of the plan's success, however, had to do with fortuitous timing and factors completely outside of the control of the Bolivian government. By the mid-1990s, several developments in Colombia and Peru were to have an important impact on the development of Bolivia's role in the international narcotics industry.

One of the more significant developments that had an impact on the plan's implementation was the intensification of Peru and Colombia's policy of shooting down airplanes suspected of carrying illicit coca paste and cocaine to Colombian laboratories. For many U.S. law enforcement officials, shutting down the "air bridge" effectively ended the capacity of drug-trafficking organizations to tap into Bolivian and/or Peruvian coca fields for the raw material.[48] The shoot-down policy has also apparently had an impact on the development of land and river routes into Colombia and has converted Ecuador into a player in the trafficking industry. In any case, the point is that Bolivian coca paste has been unable to reach Colombian laboratories, which for many years depended on the raw material produced in the Chapare. The recent accidental shooting down of a missionary plane has led to a serious questioning of this policy; however, it is unlikely that it will be reversed. Thus, the air bridge will be closed for the foreseeable future.

A second crucial external factor appears to be the concentration of all facets of cocaine production in Colombia since at least 1997. The concession of a huge tract of land to the FARC appears to be tied specifically to the concentration of production in Colombian territory. It is debatable whether the concentration of production in Colombia is the result of the effectiveness of the closing down of the air bridge or the effectiveness of Plan Dignidad; the more likely explanation is that the *zona de despeje* has made this vast zone a virtual free zone for the processing of coca cultivated in the Putumayo region of Colombia. As a result, the assertion that Bolivian cocaine is no longer available in U.S. markets is probably correct.[49]

A third international factor in this equation is the role of the United States. It is probably fair to argue that large-scale U.S. funding has been significant to the success of Plan Dignidad. It is also true, however, that U.S. funding was difficult to obtain and, at certain points in the last three years, even declined. Moreover, Bolivia's future U.S. funding will always be dependent not only on policy direction in Colombia, but also on competing bureaucratic priorities in Washington.

Consider, for example, the situation that occurred in 1998 when counternarcotics assistance to Bolivia was almost cut by nearly 70 percent. In part, the reduction reflected a lack of understanding by Bolivian government officials about the budget process, executive legislative relations, and bureaucratic politics in the United States. In 1997, the United States Congress ordered the Office of International Narcotics and Law Enforcement Matters to provide the means for Colombia to purchase Black Hawk and Hughey helicopters. At the same time the United States Congress approved a 17 million dollar increase in INL's budget. To complicate matters, former assistant secretary of state and also former ambassador to Bolivia, Robert S. Gelhard, who was then serving as President Clinton's special envoy to the Dayton Process, essentially raided the INL budget, taking 25 million dollars to provide assistance to the police in Bosnia. Gelhard's request for the same amount from Congress had apparently been denied. The long and the short of it is that to fund Colombia's needs, INL raided the Bolivia budget. Funds were eventually restored, although not at the level that Bolivia would have liked, only as a result of Vice President Jorge Quiroga's trip to Washington to plead with Congress to restore funds. Quiroga stating during a Washington press conference that Bolivia had adopted the "No thanks strategy" proved to be effective. In other words, it would seek international support for its strategy rather than accept the humiliating 12 million dollars. Moreover, he noted that it appeared that the message being sent by Washington was that a country must seriously misbehave if it is to obtain large doses of support. Quiroga's strategy worked in the long run as is evidenced by the support announced by Washington for the fiscal year 2001.

The unintended international consequence of the success of Plan Dignidad, the concentration of production in Colombia, and the success of the airplane shoot-down strategy has been that Bolivia has become a transit country for coca paste and cocaine produced in Peru. According to Bolivian law enforcement officials, the Department of Pando has become a virtual highway for Peruvian cocaine en route to the Brazilian and European markets. In Pando laboratories for cleansing cocaine produced by inferior chemicals such as cement appeared in the late 1990s. As a result of the chemical interdiction strategy, these are apparently giving way to Brazilian labs, which have easy access to chemicals.

The Altiplano region of western Bolivia is also becoming a significant transit zone for Yungas coca and for Peruvian base. The number of labs discovered in the Altiplano in 2001 is noteworthy. Again, as in the Pando region, these labs are used to cleanse low-grade coca paste produced by inferior chemicals used in the production phase. Perhaps the most noteworthy are Bolivian law enforcement officials' claims that some of the cocaine is being processed from Yungas coca. As noted earlier, the 14,000 hectares in the Yungas are sufficiently abundant to satisfy both the internal needs of the traditional market and those of the illicit drug industry.[50]

To conclude, Bolivia believes it is at the threshold of long-term success. However, the gains are fragile and are perhaps unsustainable unless more thoughtful nationwide policies are pursued to address issues of alternative employment for those who have lost jobs in the Chapare. National-level policies need to be pursued and not only those that continue to attract population into the Chapare. In the final analysis, Bolivia's democracy is facing serious challenges, and the paradox is that success in the Chapare has contributed to the fragility of the current government and the delegitimation of state institutions.

Bolivia elected a new president in late June 2002. The outcome was important in domestic political terms. Evo Morales and Felipe Quispe, the country's most significant indigenous leaders, mustered enough electoral support to control up to a couple of dozen seats in the lower house of the National Congress. Internationally the situation has also changed significantly after the September 11, 2001, terrorist events in New York and Washington, D.C. Ambassador Rocha's proclamation that Plan Dignidad is the equivalent of decree 21060, which led to the stabilization of Bolivia's economy in 1985, sends a very strong message that, no matter who takes office in La Paz, any deviation from the objectives of Plan Dignidad will not be tolerated by the United States. Bolivia's draconian approach to counter-narcotics policy may have paid off in short-term international praise and in some additional economic assistance. At the same time, however, Plan Dignidad established goals that will be hard to achieve and sustain over the long term. The problem is that the international community, especially the United States, will evaluate Bolivia using Plan Dignidad's own measures.

Notes

1. Bolivia's Dignity Plan has not undergone much academic scrutiny. At this stage only journalists and activists have written analyses of the policy. See, for example, GeorgeAnn Potter, "Is the War on Drugs Bringing Dignity to Bolivia?"; and GeorgeAnn Potter and Linda Farthing, "Bolivia Eradicating Democracy," *Foreign Policy in Focus* 5, no. 38 (2000), 34–48; *Albright Praises Bolivia's Drug Control Efforts, Increases United States Aid,* CCN.Com., August 18, 2000; Anthony Faiola, "In Bolivia's Drug War, Success Has Price; Farmers Victimized by Coca Eradication," *Washington Post,* March 4, 2001, sec. A, p. 1; Vanessa Arrington, *Bolivia Declares Victory in War against Cocaine,* Associated Press, February 23, 2001.

2. Rensselaer Lee notes: "An iron law of international drug control is that small enforcement successes often mask larger policy failures. The supposed achievements of the Andean Drug War, in fact, have spawned an array of unanticipated problems for the United States, Colombia and other countries in this hemisphere"; see chapter 10 in this volume. A contradictory viewpoint is offered by Luis Fernando Zamora, former minister of defense for Colombia, who argues that the concentration of production in Colombia has more to do with the vertical integration of the drug industry as a business decision of Colombian traffickers and less with the successes of the Bolivian and Peruvian eradication strategies; comments delivered at the seminar "El Impacto Regional del Conflicto Colombiano," presentation at the Latin American and Caribbean Center, Florida International University, June 23, 2001.

3. Author interviews with former U.S. ambassador Donna Hrinak (La Paz, Bolivia, July 2000) and with current ambassador Manuel Rocha (La Paz, Bolivia, October 2000, May 2001, and March 2002).

4. At the same time, however, some Bolivian officials complained about the lags in U.S. and international funding, especially for alternative development efforts in the Chapare.

5. In June 2001 the government claimed it had eradicated all but 600 hectares in the Chapare. In September the new government headed by President Jorge Quiroga admitted that a digital satellite error had led Bolivia to claim this early victory. In reality, the government claimed, the correct figure was 6,000 hectares. Earlier when the Bolivian government had boldly proclaimed that zero coca had been achieved, Evo Morales, the head of the coca-growers movement, questioned the government's assertion. Still under any measure, the eradication campaign far exceeded any original expectations about the plan.

6. According to Bolivian Law 1008, signed in 1988 under very close U.S. scrutiny, the Yungas may legally grow 12,000 hectares for traditional coca consumption. Thus, Bolivia will have to focus only on eradicating 2,000 hectares of Yungas coca. According to a U.S. study cited in the State Department's annual *International Counternarcotics Strategy Report* (INCSR), Bolivia needs only 5,000 hectares of coca for traditional consumption. If this is the case, then 9,000 hectares of coca are still available for the illicit drug market.

7. On August 6, 2001, owing to a severe bout with cancer, President Huga Banzer Suarez stepped down and was succeeded by Vice President Quiroga. Quiroga was scheduled to serve out Banzer's five year term, which ends in August 2002.

8. *!Por la Dignidad! Estrategia Boliviana de la Lucha Contra el Narcotráfico, 1998–2002* (La Paz: República de Bolivia, 1998).

9. One of the most arguable assertions of the plan is the idea that "a majority of coca growing peasants have joined the production of cocaine"; see page 8 of the plan.

10. Interviews with Jorge Quiroga (La Paz, Bolivia, July and October 2000, May 2001).

11. Quiroga delivers the same message nearly every time he is asked to speak in public about the plan. This repetitive theme played out very well in U.S. circles but was not very effective domestically.

12. These developments are analyzed in Eduardo A. Gamarra, *Entre la Droga y la Democracia* (La Paz: ILDIS, 1994). For an analysis of the Bolivian drug policy during this period see Eduardo A. Gamarra, "The United States and Bolivia: Fighting the Drug War," in Victor Bulmer Thomas and James Dunkerley, eds., *The United States and Latin America: The New Agenda* (London and Cambridge: Institute for Latin American Studies, University of London, and Harvard University Press, 1999); Eduardo A. Gamarra, "Las Relaciones entre Estados Unidos y Bolivia durante el Gobierno de Gonzalo Sánchez de Lozada," in Andres Franco, ed., *Estados Unidos y Los Países Andinos, 1993–1997: Poder y Desintegración* (Bogotá: Pontificia Universidad Javeriana, 1998).

13. In April 2001, the United States announced that it had restored Jaime Paz Zamora's visa. Paz Zamora promptly flew to New York. When asked about the factors that prompted the U.S. reversal on Paz Zamora's visa, Ambassador Rocha explained that access to the declassified cables that prompted the reversal would be available in thirty years or so (personal conversation, May 2001). Many in Bolivia believe that in returning the visa to Jaime Paz Zamora, the United States anointed the next president and also guaranteed a very cooperative future presidency from the formerly anti-American social democratic political leader. Off the record conversa-

tions with the U.S. State Department officials, however, suggest that rumors that circulated in Bolivia about the personal intervention of George Bush senior—whom Jaime Paz Zamora met during the Cartagena Summit—may have some credibility. According to a senior official who served in the Bureau of International Narcotics and Law Enforcement Matters (INL) at the time of the suspension of the visa, Bush senior developed a personal liking for Paz Zamora that prompted him to intercede on his behalf. It is also true, however, that the Bolivian government embarked on a lobbying effort with the new George W. Bush administration on Paz Zamora's behalf. In Bolivia, speculation had it that Marlene Fernandez, Bolivia's ambassador to the United States, had earned the vice presidential slot on the MIR's ticket as a result of her intense lobbying effort on behalf of Paz Zamora. Fernandez in fact became the vice presidential candidate of the Unidad Cívica Solidaridad (UCS) to contest the 2002 elections.

14. Telephone conversation, April 19, 2002.

15. Interviews with Robert S. Gelhard (La Paz, Bolivia, April 2002), Charles Bowers (La Paz, Bolivia, April 2002), Donna Hrinak (La Paz, Bolivia, July 2002), and Manuel Rocha (La Paz, Bolivia, October 2000 and March 2002).

16. Confidential interviews with current and former DEA agents in Bolivia and Miami. The most recent accusation surfaced in 1998 following the arrest of Marino Diodato, a member of the Santa Paola Sicilian crime organization. Vice President Quiroga often stressed in interviews that the Santa Paola crime family was one of the criminal organizations most wanted by the United States. According to Diodato's own sworn courtroom testimony, AND's 1997 campaign had received money from organized crime. This is not the place to analyze the Diodato case. It is very clear, however, that arresting and convicting Marino Diodato played a huge role in the U.S. government's support for the Bolivian government. It is also clear that former ambassador Hrinak chose to work with Quiroga because he was the only person in the government not tainted by the Diodato scandal. The Diodato case was so significant for the United States that once he was convicted, the secretary of state altered her South American itinerary to visit La Paz and bestow praise on the Bolivian government.

17. U.S. Embassy officials in the Narcotics Assistance Unit (NAU) disagree with this interpretation. In their view, it was General Banzer's decisive support and leadership that gave the policy its strength. A review of the record over the course of the implementation of Plan Dignidad reveals that Banzer was at best peripherally involved in the design and/or implementation of the policy.

18. The director of the NAS unit in the U.S. embassy in La Paz disagreed with this interpretation of Quiroga's role. In his view, Plan Dignidad's success was solely due to General Banzer's role. He argued in late 2001 that after Banzer's resignation coca was once again being planted and that the new Quiroga government lacked the will to press ahead with the goals of the plan. This interpretation would subsequently appear in the U.S. State Department's INCSR March 2002 report.

19. See Jorge Malamud Goti, *Smoke and Mirrors* (Boulder, Colo.: Westview Press, 1990) and Gamarra, *Entre la Droga y la Democracia* for a discussion of this event.

20. See Clare Hargraves, *Snow Fields* (New York: Holmes and Meier, 1992) for accounts of this incident.

21. This them has been recurrent in interviews with DEA and U.S. embassy officials in Bolivia since 1988.

22. On this point see Eduardo A. Gamarra, "Transnational Criminal Organizations in Bolivia," in Thomas Farer and Michael Shifter, eds., *Transnational Criminal Enterprise in the Americas* (Westbury, Conn.: Praeger Press, 1999).

23. This section has dealt mainly with the sins of past governments. The most significant problem facing the government of former general Banzer are allegations of family and other linkages with Marino Diodato, who was sentenced to twelve years in prison for narcotics trafficking in September 2000. Diodato became an important case, not only because of the alleged linkages to the current government, but also because of his presumed links to the Santa Paola crime family, which, according to Bolivian government officials, was so important that it was given the Rubicon priority security status in the United States.

24. According to Law 1008, in 1995 the Bolivian government had to initiate the forceful eradication of coca in the so-called transition zones.

25. See Gamarra, *The United States and Bolivia;* and Gamarra, *Las Relaciones entre Estados Unidos y Bolivia.*

26. United States Congress, *Extradition Treaty with Bolivia: Message from the President of the United States, 104th Congress,* 1st Session, October 10, 1995.

27. Shortly after the 1997 elections, Acting Assistant Secretary of State Jane Becker warned that Bolivia faced almost certain decertification if it did not meet its eradication targets. See *Jane Becker, Acting Secretary of State Office of International Narcotics and Law Enforcement Matters,* July 16, 1997.

28. Interviews with Vice President Jorge Quiroga (La Paz, Bolivia, July and October 2000, May 2001).

29. Public opinion polls in Bolivia have consistently demonstrated that drugs and narcotics trafficking are at best third on the scale of priorities of most Bolivians. Support for interdiction has rarely surpassed fourth place, well behind education, prevention, and alternative development. Moreover, Bolivians believe that *campesinos* have a right to defend the cultivation of coca, but they also believe that the government should do more to fight narcotics trafficking. See Roberto Laserna, Natalia Camacho, and Eduardo Córdova, eds., *Empujando la Concertación: Marchas Campesinos, Opinión Pública, y Coca* (Cochabamba: CERES y PIEB, 1999). Urban opinion about eradication of coca in the Yungas region largely favors the governments efforts to eradicate. Nevertheless, in a written accord, the government reversed its decision to pursue compensated eradication in the Yungas on June 22, 2000.

30. Interviews with U.S. ambassador Manuel Rocha (La Paz, Bolivia, October 2000, August 2001, and March 2002).

31. The decision by President Quiroga to order the military and police into the Chapare in October 2001, for example, appears to have been widely supported.

32. In casual conversations with coca growers they argued that they were willing to exchange piece and tranquility for the relatively higher income coca has provided. In other words, *cocaleros* are tired of the environment of repression that prevails in the Chapare with the presence of the armed forces and police.

33. See Roberto Laserna, *Twenty Misconceptions on Coca and Cocaine* (The Hague: Partners of Novib, 1998).

34. Evo Morales, the leader of the Chapare coca growers and a congressional deputy, claimed that the government figures were incorrect and that in fact more than 10,000 hectares were still available. In negotiations with the government, Morales insisted on allowing every *cocalero* family the right to keep one *cato* (88 sq. m.) of coca. Government officials noted that if thirty-five thousand families were allowed a *cato* each, this would result in another 6,000 hectares and the production of 60 tons per year of cocaine. The admission of a satellite error in mid-2001 proved Morales correct. Estimates in April 2002 placed the total hectarage under cultivation at 9,000.

35. According to the 1998 INCSR report, alternative development "has yielded significant results." Prior to 1992, coca was the principal crop grown in the Chapare. The hectarage in licit crops in the Chapare is now three times greater than coca cultivation, and 127 percent greater than in 1986. Licit agricultural production in the Chapare now represents 1.5 percent of Bolivia's gross domestic product. The success of this program has enabled the government of Bolivia to counter arguments effectively that coca eradication impoverishes poor farmers and makes the goal of total coca eradication politically unfeasible. See *International Counternarcotics Strategy Report* (Washington, D.C.: State Department, Office of International Narcotics and Law Enforcement Matters, 1998).

36. One sustainable development official told me that as many as seventy coca growers per day were leaving the Chapare and were showing up in the Yungas. No other source, however, confirmed this report. In fact, it appears that some displacement occurred but not to the extent that government officials feared.

37. Personal conversation with Ambassador Manuel Rocha, August 2001.

38. Apart from the historic ties that bound the Bolivian president to the U.S. military, Banzer's cancer treatment at Walter Reed Hospital was another sign of just how grateful the United States was for the results of Plan Dignidad.

39. Confidential interview, March 2002.

40. Interview with President Quiroga (La Paz, Bolivia, April 19, 2002).

41. See Theo Roncken, "The Conflicts Behind the Dignity," *Drugs and Development* 24, no. 4 (2000), 24–48.

42. Interview with author, October 2000.

43. For ambassador Rocha, Plan Dignidad represents the third most significant event in the history of Bolivia in the second half of the twentieth century. The other two are the 1952 Revolution and the 1985 New Economic Policy, which ended hyperinflation and set in motion the current market oriented development strategy (Interviews, October 2000 and May 2001). While there is no denying the success of eradication in the Chapare, to place it with the previous events reflects more the ambassador's enthusiasm than the real historical impact of Plan Dignidad.

44. Among the most cited concerns regarding alternative development programs in Bolivia are the lack of funds, the magnet effect of alternative development for rural populations throughout Bolivia, the absence of markets for products, the unsuitability of soils for large-scale agriculture, the unfeasibility of small-scale agriculture, and the conceptual links of alternative development to interdiction strategy.

45. According to the Bolivian government, the U.S. money and a considerable Bolivian investment will be used to prevent the sowing of new coca fields in the Chapare. The Bolivian government claimed it would invest 91 million U.S. dollars in

the region's development, which would benefit ten thousand rural families. The Agriculture Ministry also launched a so-called "Progress Plan" for the region aimed at improving roads, promoting alternative crops, and training farmers. Along with the 91 million U.S. dollars from Bolivia's government, the Chapare development project will receive 40 million of the 110 million dollars contributed by the United States. The government also announced that 20 million dollars would be invested in the region of Yungas to eradicate 2,500 hectares of illegal coca fields. Interviews with minister of agriculture Hugo Carvajal (La Paz, bolivia, October 2000).

46. Interview with Minister Carvajal (La Paz, Bolivia, October 2000).

47. Interviews with Guido Nayar, former minister of the interior, and Fernando Kieffer, former minister of defense (La Paz, Bolivia, July 1999).

48. Interviews with U.S. Southern Command officials and with DEA officials (Miami, July 2000).

49. This is Ambassador Rocha's claim (interview May 2001).

50. Interview with FELCN officials (La Paz and Miami, July 2000).

3

Questionable Alliances in the War on Drugs

Peru and the United States

Mariano Valderrama and Hugo Cabieses

The U.S. counter-narcotics policy has been characteristically defined in a unilateral way and with an input of a strong military perspective. In 1986, drug trafficking was declared a national security issue by President Reagan, requiring the firmest of actions on the part of the U.S. government. Three years later, President Bush defined an Andean strategy that included an active role of U.S. armed forces (Pentagon and Southern Command) and of those of the affected Andean countries in the combat against drug trafficking. Since then, all counter-narcotics strategies that have been presented annually at the White House have included an important military dimension. It was no coincidence that, following his retirement as chief of the U.S. Southern Command, General Barry McCaffrey was appointed director of the Office of National Drug Control Policy.

The predominant idea behind the U.S. anti-drug strategy is to impose bans in production areas by force. This implies military intervention (military advisors, equipment) and covert intelligence operations (conducted by the CIA and the DEA) with the support of local armed forces.[1]

Allies in the War on Drugs?

The United States has been the self-appointed judge of the efficiency of anti-drug policies in Latin America. It rules unilaterally on the certification of cooperation and good conduct for source countries and establishes which countries will be excluded from the benefits of USAID cooperation and other preferential treatment. Multilateral certification, possibly also including a qualification of American actions directed toward the control of trafficking and consumption in its own country, would be a more balanced procedure—

at least as viewed by the Andean countries—but has met with American resistance.[2]

Anti-drug policy is clearly subordinated to American geopolitical interests. Plan Colombia and the Andean Regional Initiative launched by the present administration show the readiness of the United States to intervene in the Andean countries in order to safeguard its interests in the region.[3]

The rationale of the American counter-narcotics policies has produced questionable results: The eradication policy has affected the peasant population but has left the drug-trafficking industry largely untouched. In doing so, it has exacerbated conflicts in producing areas and has become a factor generating violence. The alternative development programs—presented as the solution in supply-side control—have not worked. In general, the anti-drug operations have produced American interference in these countries' internal affairs, generating considerable irritation about perceived violations of sovereignty. However, one of the most openly questioned aspects of the U.S. policy rises from evidence that it has included—quite opportunistically— firm relations with prominent individuals in the governmental spheres of Latin America who have had ties to drug trafficking. National security interests dictated turning a blind eye toward drug-trafficking operations at the time of General Noriega's regime in Panama. A similar stance was taken toward the high-profit connections to drug cartels by the family of Mexican president Carlos Salinas de Gortari, not to mention the obscure relations existing between the United States and the Bolivia military in the 1980s, the contras in Central America, and the paramilitary forces in Colombia.

In reference to Peru, we should mention the strange alliances with Peruvian ex-president Fujimori and his advisor, Vladimiro Montesinos. Fujimori's Peru was perceived by the United States and the anti-drug agency (DEA) as an important ally in the War on Drugs and a participant in the operations that formed part of Plan Colombia. The Peruvian government was given official certificates of good conduct. The contacts between the office of the U.S. anti-drug czar and the political and military leadership that governed Peru were intense, even though it was well known that many among them had been involved in drug and arms trafficking.

In a revealing report entitled "Allies in Drug War in Disgrace," and published in May 2001 on the front page of the *Washington Post*, several generals, now imprisoned, presented testimony on the solid alliance established between the United States and themselves. General Juan Miguel del Aguila, who worked as head of security in the national police during the Fujimori regime, declared: "The United States was our partner in every respect, giving us intelligence, training, equipment and working with us closely in the field." Today, General del Aguila is in jail for having planned a terrorist attack that caused several deaths and that the government attempted to blame on the opposition. Similarly, an alliance was established between the United States and the ex-chief of the Armed Forces Joint Command, General Nicolás Hermoza Bari, also jailed as of now, who acknowledged having received 14 million U.S. dollars in bribes in arms purchases, and who was accused by several drug traffickers of having been involved in the drug trade.[4]

Faced with increasing accusations of corruption, authoritarianism, and anti-constitutional behavior by sections of the United States Congress, the Peruvian government sought closer relations with Washington's hardliners. During a visit to Washington in February 1999, President Fujimori made several declarations in public against Colombian president Pastrana's policy of dialog with the guerrillas and presented a proposal to resolve the problem through an intervention force assembled by all countries in the region.[5] On his return from Washington, Fujimori called a meeting of the National Defense Council, ordered troop movements, and established new control posts on the shores of the Putumayo river along the border with Colombia. The implicit message to Colombia was that it had to put its house in order or run the risk of a foreign intervention. The message to the Pentagon and the CIA was that they had a reliable ally in the region that supported the interventionist plans that the United States had been entertaining.

A Peruvian Narco-mafia?

As an ally of the United States, Montesinos had been providing arms to paramilitary forces in Colombia. However, he demonstrated the qualities of a double agent. U.S. intelligence services detected an arms transport operation from Jordan to the FARC in Colombia, which had been organized by Montesinos and his close collaborators in Peru.[6] Montesinos denied involvement but was undercut by subsequent statements from the governments of Jordan and Colombia, which produced evidence of the involvement at the highest levels of the Peruvian government and military. A well-known Jordanian arms trafficker even declared that he had taken part in the Jordanian arms purchase at Montesinos's explicit request.[7] The company in charge of transporting the arms was a supplier for the army and the presidential palace. This arms scandal was only one of a series of scandals involving Montesinos buying off many political and media figures, including leading officers of the Peruvian armed forces, as well as members of the parliament and the judiciary. The president of the Congressional Investigating Commission estimates that the funds accumulated by Montesinos and his collaborators amount to a total of 1 billion U.S. dollars.

Parliamentary inquests have shed light on transactions involving millions of dollars in the purchase of Russian armament of doubtful quality for which Montesinos and the military leadership have received lucrative commissions. According to a report by the Peruvian attorney general, a total of 150 million dollars has been frozen in bank accounts belonging to Montesinos and his collaborators. It is also suspected that part of the arms purchase operations may have been financed through drug deliveries to Russian gangs.

Research by the National Anti-Corruption Initiative (INA)[8] has indicated clearly that the drug trade is the main cause of the generalized corruption, next to the trade in arms and other illicit goods and influences. In the 1990s, corruption had become massive and systematic in that it was directed from the highest levels of government and formed a network including the electoral college, the judiciary, the legislature (parliament), the financial sector of business, and the military. As its height, this corruption scheme is estimated to have managed 264 million dollars annually. Its principal sources were illegal commissions, extortion, illicit financial and commercial operations, the public budget and—above all—drug trafficking. The funds have been found deposited in a wide range of banks and financial institutions in Switzerland, Luxembourg, the United States, the Cayman Islands, Mexico, Bolivia, Panama, and the Bahamas. In addition, monthly amounts of approximately 4 million dollars were used to oil the systems to bribe judges, TV stations, tabloids, politicians, and so forth. The funds originated from sources in the military, the intelligence service, and the ministry of the president and are suspected to have been provisioned by narco-trafficking. The corruption schemes and their relation to the activities of the drug industry have been subject of investigation by the INA. The study has concluded that in the 1990s all dimensions of the industry (production, trafficking, consumption, trade in precursor chemicals, money laundering, and the arms and explosives trade) had developed to previously unknown levels, had penetrated the principal state institutions, and had corrupted the most well-known representatives of civil society.

The principal dimensions of the development of the drug industry in Peru—in particular in the second half of the 1990s—were the following:

- a real increase in drug production, trade, and consumption, a phenomenon that has been underestimated at the national as well as the international level;
- a vertical integration of the coca-cocaine production complex;
- an incipient development of the production of other illicit drugs, such as poppy-heroin, marijuana, and synthetic drugs;
- an increasing involvement of wide sectors of the population in activities related to the drug industry;
- an increasing efficiency and sophistication in the function of the industry with—at times—an intense competition among groups of traffickers;
- the development of new foreign markets and new export routes for drugs;

- the restructuring of the industry through the disintegration of the cartels and a reintegration through smaller and more flexible organizations;
- the increasing involvement of public and private institutions and their representatives in the drug trade; and
- the generalized presence of defeatist attitudes with regard to the possibilities to control drug production and trafficking in the country.

The above-mentioned developments have been negated by the Peruvian government as well as by international organizations. Government agencies, involved in counter-narcotics action, glowingly reported on accomplishments in the War on Drugs that had no basis in fact. The cooperating international organizations have supported uncritically this smoke screen of "successes," this way contributing—involuntarily—to the maintenance of the extensive web of corruption that was pervading Peruvian society.

The resounding collapse of the Fujimori regime has unveiled the country's political and military leadership's part in the drug trade. It demonstrated the extent of influence peddling in the judiciary, the drug enforcement police, and parliament on the issue of drug trafficking, all of which has put the American support of that regime and the cooperation in fighting the drug trade and implementing Plan Colombia into question. Repeated accusations of corruption, drug trafficking, and involvement in serious crimes did not deter U.S. intelligence services from cooperating with the regime although "continuing allegations of misdeeds throughout the 1990s did raise concerns at the United States Embassy in Lima as well as in Washington. But the CIA argued that rumors of Montesinos's corruption were exaggerated and continued to consider him a vital asset."[9]

It has been suggested[10] that the support by the CIA for Montesinos, intended as a contribution to counter-narcotics action, in fact financed a drug operation that was to compete with Colombian organizations, cutting their access to sources of coca paste. This organization was connected with Mexican drug traffickers and with the Russia mafia while dealing in cocaine and armament, and laundering money.

As President Fujimori's omnipotent advisor, Montesinos exercised total control over the armed forces and the judiciary and had been accused of being connected to drug trafficking by the opposition press already at an early stage.[11] While working as a lawyer in the 1980s, he defended various drug traffickers. His links to the drug trade were exposed in 1983 in a report published in the Lima weekly *Caretas*. Following the 1985 explosion in Lima of a laboratory producing cocaine, high-ranking police officers were shown to be involved in the drug trade. With the help of Montesinos, they were absolved of all responsibility.[12]

Peru: A Narco-state?

The connection between Montesinos and the drug trade expanded when President Fujimori assumed the presidency of the republic in July 1990 and made him his trusted advisor. Pablo Escobar's brother even declared that the Colombian drug trafficker had contributed financially to Fujimori's presidential campaign and had maintained ties with Montesinos.[13] Radio communications by drug traffickers in the Amazon, intercepted and taped by the Peruvian Navy in 1991–1992, revealed the traffickers' links to the armed forces and the payments that were made. General Bellido, political and military chief of the Upper Huallaga area (epicenter of the drug trade) in 1992–1993, proved to have connections to drug trafficking but was promptly appointed military attaché in Israel and quickly dispatched out of the country to avoid any further investigation.[14]

Officers and subaltern personnel of the army, the navy, the air force, and the national police became increasingly involved in the drug trade. Among the armed forces, 588 officers have been prosecuted for drug trafficking in the 1990s. Among them, 330 were army officers and 240 were national police officers. Only a small number have actually been sentenced. The fact that the Geopolitical Monitoring Centre for Drugs (OGD) in Paris placed Peru, along with seven other countries of dubious reputation, on its list of "narco-states" should surprise no one.[15] On June 3, 1996, the Canadian police found 45 kilos of cocaine on board the navy steamer *Matarani* when it stopped in the port of Vancouver. On its return to Peru, 75 kilos were discovered. On July 5, the Callao port police found 17 kilos of cocaine on board another Peruvian navy ship, the *Ilo*. A few days later, two officers of the National Intelligence Service were detained owing to their relations with the gang of trafficker "Mosquita Loca." On February 2, 1999, the army's chief of staff, Tomas Marky Montero, was arrested for his part in the disappearance of a briefcase containing 1 million U.S. dollars in drug money. In May 1999, the police seized 383 pounds of cocaine on its way to Russia via Miami on board an armed forces aircraft. An Air Force commander and aide-de-camp to President Fujimori was implicated in the scandal. Another drug trafficker has already implicated the Air Force officer who was piloting the presidential plane and who was also Fujimori's close link to the drug trade.

In 1996, Demetrio Chávez Pena Herrera, alias "Vaticano," one of the most important drug traffickers in Peru, was arrested. In his testimony before the court on August 16, 1996, he revealed that he had bribed Army officers in order to use military helicopters and airports under military control to transport drugs. He also stated that in 1992 he organized 250 drug shipments and made monthly payments of 50,000 U.S. dollars to Montesinos. He had finally stopped paying when he was ordered to double the amount of his payments.[16] Immediately, and without the full course of an investigation, the attorney general herself defended Montesinos publicly, saying that these accusations were only a criminal's fabrication. After having been tortured to make him recant, Vaticano was sentenced to thirty years in jail by a military tribunal in a summary trial. He was then kept incommunicado for six years. Another trafficker, known as "El Negro," who was arrested in 1995, declared in the presence of a prosecutor that he had paid armed forces officers between 15,000 and 20,000 U.S. dollars per flight and that every two months he handed over 60,000 dollars to the military chief of the Mantaro area, in the central highlands of Peru.

Another trafficker, Lucio Tijero, pointed out that Montesinos was also connected to Perciles Sánchez, a drug trafficker linked to the Colombian cartels.[17] Yet another trafficker, Boris Foguel, also accused Montesinos of involvement in drug-trafficking operations. Various investigations have uncovered leads to operations directed by Montesinos to export to Mexico drugs that had been seized in Peru.[18]

In April 1997, the newspaper *Jornal do Brasil* reported the existence of a Brazilian federal police secret report on Vladimiro Montesinos's collaboration with the organization of Colombian drug trafficker Evaristo Porras. The former had facilitated operations involving aircraft that carried coca paste to Colombia, making stops in Brazil on their way. Peruvian justice had freed Evaristo Porras on June 17, 1978, thanks to the writ of habeas corpus filed by the then attorney Vladimiro Montesinos. The report pointed out that "given the protection surrounding Montesinos—current head of the Peruvian Intelligence Service and main advisor to President Fujimori—conducting official detention procedures against him is impossible."[19]

The videos of meetings filmed by Montesinos himself are now accounts of how he manipulated the judiciary. Various witnesses have testified that the presidential advisor, known as "doctor" or "doc," while using judges and attorneys close to him, negotiated with several defendants in drug-trafficking cases to lighten their sentences in exchange for lucrative payments. Javier Corrochano, a lawyer, was Montesinos's contact in widely talked about cases such as those of the "Los Camélidos" gang (he was the defending attorney of one its bosses, Bruno Chiappe) and of Jorge López Paredes.[20] The opposite also has taken place—as part of extortion schemes—when business owners were threatened with being implicated in drug trafficking if they did not make million dollar payments. The case of the "Hayduk" company in 1993 has been published and is well documented. Another video shows Montesinos himself accounting for secret funds used to promote the campaign of Fujimori's candidate to the post of mayor of Lima, saying that anti-drug resources covered campaign expenses, which is understood to be a euphemism for resources from obscure origins.[21]

Montesinos's influence and nerve were far reaching. In one of the videos that the intelligence service filmed, a conversation between media business-man Genaro Delgado Parker and Montesinos was taped in which Monte-sinos proposed setting up an international NGO directed toward counter-narcotics and alternative development issues as a front for other types of business. Montesinos suggested that Delgado Parker take advantage of his business contacts and his prestige as a man of the media to open an office in the United States. Through his solid contacts with individuals highly placed in the U.S. government—so it was suggested—he could find a way to obtain funds that would serve their business. In another example, a report prepared by Lima TV Channel 2 exposing the relations established by Montesinos and the commander in chief of the armed forces, General Bari Hermosa, caused the station owner to be stripped of his Peruvian nationality and dispossessed of his station.

In spite of these indications that there was "something rotten in the state," President Fujimori continued to defend Montesinos as his main advisor in issues of drug trafficking and terrorism. And so did the CIA. Enrique Ovando, a Peruvian expert on security and drug trafficking, reflects on the role of the United States in the fight against drug trafficking during the Fujimori govern-ment: "It would seem as though, in this case, an old far-West policy had been put in place, where in order to maintain law and order, a bandit was sought, given a sheriff's badge and put in charge of hanging other bandits."[22]

Cooperation against Trafficking: Results

At the beginning of the 1980s, the United States persuaded the government of President Belaunde to implement a program to fight drug trafficking.[23] Three initiatives were then set in motion. In 1981, a specialized police unit of four hundred officers in charge of controlling drug trafficking, the Rural Mobile Patrol Unit (UMOPAR), was created in Tingo Maria. Simultaneously, an orga-nization to eradicate the production of coca (CORAID) and a special project on long-term development (PEAR) were formed in the Upper Huallaga region. The amount of money assigned to these initiatives was minimal. Eradication actions caused widespread discontent and rejection among the peasant popu-lation and favored the growth of the Shining Path guerilla movement in the region. In 1984, the government decided to declare a state of emergency and sent in the armed forces to fight the subversion. Drug eradication actions were suspended since they motivated people to join the Shining Path in order to protect themselves against police action. Nevertheless, in 1985, the state of emergency was lifted and UMOPAR and CORAH resumed their eradi-cation operations. As a result, the presence of the Shining Path increased, leading to a new state of emergency, this time under police control. President Alan Garcia did not give in to American pressures for military intervention. U.S. support for the operations increased, but the Shining Path's control of the area made the presence of U.S. military personnel difficult. The guerrillas strengthened their control in the area, forcing local authorities to resign or flee, and demanding payments for drug processing and transport operations. Given the difficulties that the Shining Path's presence posed to eradication operations, the United States proposed the use of herbicides as an alternative.

In 1989, after the Shining Path had taken the town of Uchiza, the government decided to return control of the area to the armed forces. However, the military commander in charge of operations, General Alberto Arciniega, opted for the strategy of differentiating peasant farmers from drug traffickers. Eradication actions against coca-leaf-growing peasants were suspended and attempts were made to provide protection and incentives to growers, turning them into allies in the fight against terrorism. According to this new military strategy, the eradication of coca growing would only be viable if economically sound options were offered to the population. Forced eradication without alternatives would make people join the guerillas. The United States harshly questioned this approach and launched a campaign to discredit General Arciniega, accusing him of being an accomplice in the drug trade.

When Fujimori came to power, the U.S. government proposed an agreement similar to the one signed with Bolivia. It included the training of forty-five hundred Peruvian soldiers to eradicate coca crops. However, Fujimori did not accept the proposal and postponed the signing of an anti-drug agreement with the United States until May 1991. With the advice of Hernando de Soto, the so-called Fujimori Doctrine was drawn up, which recovered some of the ideas expressed by General Arciniega, in the sense that the difference between drug traffickers and producers had to be made and that offering support to producers for economically sound activities was essential.

In 1990, the Fujimori government created the Autonomous Authority for Alternative Development (AADA). De Soto suggested an alliance between the state, the armed forces, producers, international cooperation, and private investment, but he was forced to resign when the military torpedoed his proposal by murdering one of the best-known local leaders.[24]

In 1991, through Supreme Decree 137–91–PCM, the government gave in to American pressure and, faced with the expansion of terrorism in the area, it again put the armed forces and the National Intelligence Service in charge of the fight against terrorism and drug trafficking. In 1995, a new agreement concerning counter-narcotics action was signed between the United States and Peru. It involved a program of 35 million dollars for technical assistance and 19 million for interception of traffickers. Forced eradication was started in Alto Huallaga and the air force began intercepting drug flights. The results were not impressive: twenty-one flights were intercepted in 1995. Under previous arrangements this number had been higher (seventy in 1992 and sixty-seven in 1993). In early 1995, President Fujimori openly decided to place the task of fighting drug trafficking in the hands of his main advisor, Vladimiro Montesinos. From then on, from his office at the National Intelligence Service, Montesinos took on the initiative of formulating laws and policies, and control of institutional modifications and action in the fight against the drug trade. Such action was financed in part with funds from the CIA and the drug section (NAS) of the U.S. embassy in Lima. At the same time, an agreement was signed with the United States, which included the concept of coca crop eradication.[25] Under U.S. pressure, the Fujimori government accepted implementing the National Plan for the Eradication of Crops (Plan National de Erradicación de Cultivos). In 1996, the national commission for the fight against drugs, Contradrogas, was created and crop eradication actions began.[26] In October 1996, planes began spraying coca crops with defoliants.

Having donated 10 million U.S. dollars to alternative development through USAID from 1981 to 1994, the United States increased its contribution to 60.8 million for the 1995–1999 five-year period. Nonetheless, the effective use of these funds is questionable. A Peruvian expert has analyzed the impact of alternative development programs directed by Contradrogas in Peru, and funded by USAID, UNDCP, and several European countries. From 1985 to 1995, Contradrogas provided farming assistance covering no more than 20,000 hectares in priority areas and generating only 6,500 jobs or 3.2 percent of those jobs[27] that eradication had eliminated. It is estimated that between 1993 and 1998, at a time when a reduction in coca crops and a drop in prices were observed, farmers' gross incomes in coca-growing areas fell from a total of 514 million to 128 million U.S. dollars.[28]

The UNDCP acknowledged that "there are problems with the agricultural policy in the coca-growing valleys that need to be addressed. Current funding is a drop in the ocean."[29] In addition to the shortage of available resources in relation to the size of the problem, other deficiencies of alternative development programs are as follows:

 • Priority has been given to supporting traditional export products, the prices of which have declined, instead of promoting an increased diversification of agricultural production activities.
 • More emphasis has been put on coca crop substitution than on expanding the regional economy. Some farmers have sowed coca in order to benefit from the support of alternative development programs.
 • Producers have not been genuinely involved in the planning and monitoring of alternative development programs. Participatory

workshops organized by Contradrogas have allowed farmers to receive information on government plans, but they have not generated institutional mechanisms that would allow for participatory decision making.

• A heavy bureaucracy has emerged, which administers the programs and in doing so has absorbed a significant portion of the funds; this organization also has not been free from the scourge of corruption.

The national Anti-Corruption Initiative (INA) established in 2001 that 700 million U.S. dollars had been invested in counter-narcotics action in the 1990s by the Peruvian government and international donors. The INA concluded that:

• the funds that had been invested in projects of alternative development had been put to doubtful use with little result;
• the policy of counter-narcotics action had been directed mainly at secondary targets, leaving the principal drug lords and their interests in money laundering, the trade in chemical precursors, and the arms trade untouched;
• the investments in projects directed toward the prevention of drug use and rehabilitation have been minimal.

The various projects and programs that were undertaken suffered great problems in the administrative field and in the management of funds. Inefficiency and administrative incompetence, added to rampant corruption and malversation of funds and equipment, led to generalized failure.

Table 3.1. Peru: International Cooperation for Alternative Development, 1981–2000

Source	Period	U.S. $ in millions
PNUFID	1985–1998	54.8
U.S.A. (USAID)	1981–1994	10.0
U.S.A. (USAID)	1995–1999	81.1
Canada (ground Peru-Canada)	1989–1997	10.5
Germany (GTZ)	1993–1999	4.4
The Netherlands	1999–2000	4.4
Spain	2000	0.7
CIDAD	1999–2000	1.2
European Commission	1992–1996	0.7
Total	1981–1999	167.8

Source: Hugo Cabieses, July 2001; information and documentation against drugs, PNUFID, USAID, Fondo, Peru, Canada, GTZ, and European Commission.

Alternative development had been—at least on paper—a priority area of action for the government.[30] Through Contradrogas the government invested from its own budget 260 million U.S. dollars in the period 1992–2000. Foreign financing through bilateral and multilateral channels amounted to 440 million U.S. dollars in the same period.[31] There is no clear image about what happened with these funds, where they were invested and what have been the results of these actions. Those government agencies that have to supervise the use of public funds and of foreign loans and donations through international cooperation did not fulfill their obligations, leading to irregularities in many areas, such as

- the manipulation of data referring to the wide range of activities involved in counter-narcotics action;
- the abuse of public institutions and personnel on a national as well as on a local level in the process of justification of plans, programs, and projects while combating the drug problem;
- the repeated violation of technical procedures and administrative rules and regulations in the administration of funds;
- the malversation of funds and their use for party activities and personal projects;
- the "evaporation" of funds and the corresponding liquidation of plans, programs, and projects without technical reason.

The acreage under coca, an important issue directly related to the certification procedure, has been subject to endless discussions and calculations. In practice, the government accepts without debate the data that the U.S. embassy presents on the basis of satellite images, aerial photography, and inspections in the field.

Every year the pressure is on to show that the eradication policies are

Table 3.2. Peru: Net Production of Coca (in Hectares) According to the NAS, 1998–2000

Concepts	1998	1999	2000	Change in %
Coca cultivation beginning of period	68,800	51,000	38,700	
Abandoned	9,975	12,300	1,500	
Eradicated	7,825	13,800	6,200	
Newly planted	0	1,500	3,100	
Coca cultivated end of period	51,000	38,700	34,100	-33.2
Coca leaf production	95,600	69,200	61,000	-36.2
Potential cocaine production	240	175	154	-35.8

Source: Narcotics Affair Section (NAS), United States Embassy, Lima, Agro, Data-CEPES, July 2001; elaboration by Hugo Cabieses.

working, that the War on Drugs has been producing results and that the number of hectares under coca has been radically reduced. However, the methodology that has been used includes visiting the same areas every year, in a situation where coca is constantly "on the move." Various analysts[32] of the issue have pointed out that while trying to measure coca cultivation one has to consider the different situations in which the various production areas find themselves: present production, temporary abandonment, definitive abandonment, and the coca cultivations eradicated by force. Increases in coca cultivation relate to price developments of coca and to those of alternative products.

Since 1998, the price of coca has shown an upward tendency, while the prices of its alternatives have collapsed. As a result, the average acreage under coca production is estimated to have increased at an average of 20 percent annually, with most of the increased acreage in "new" areas deeper into the Amazon territory toward the frontier with Brazil. In the area of counter-narcotics action little positive can be reported. The projects of alternative development have suffered grave problems in their planning, the supporting infrastructure, the participation of the peasant population, and the organization of markets for the products other than coca. Law enforcement efforts toward the production of illicit drugs has led to the replacement of coca to more distant areas. Excessive focus on the interception of air transport left other means of transport unharmed. Moreover, action centered on the competitors of the corruption network of Montesinos and Fujimori.

It is also possible that the United States has used the Fujimori-Montesinos government to strike at competing groups and impose a crop-eradication policy. Coca producers have repeatedly denounced the way in which forced coca crop eradication is carried out, involving human rights abuses and the use of herbicides that are causing irreparable ecological damage and violate international agreements.

Table 3.3. Peru: Estimates on Coca Cultivation 1994 and 1998–2000

	1994	1998	1999	2000	Change in %
Area under coca	299,000	200,000	200,000	200,000	—
Temporary abandonment	100,000	60,000	57,000	55,000	—
Definite abandonment	59,700	59,000	47,100	44,700	—
Eradication	0	12,600	13,800	6,200	—
Presently in production	139,300	68,400	82,100	94,100	37.6
For traditional use	37,000	25,000	27,000	28,000	11.2
For illicit purposes	102,300	43,400	55,100	66,100	52.3

Source: Agro Data-CEPES, June 2001 by Hugo Cabieses.

Epilogue

After the fall of Fujimori's regime, forced eradication has continued. Faced with marches and protests from producers, the democratic transition government agreed to reinstate the Dialog and Consultation Group (Mesa de Diálogo y Concertación) in the Upper Huallaga in order to develop a concerted policy. However, strong pressure on Peru is still coming from the U.S. embassy to maintain the drug eradication policy. Additional aid in the amount of 25 million U.S. dollars was recently granted by USAID to Peru, on the understanding that it not relent in its efforts to reduce illicit crops.[33]

It is true that over the past few years coca-growing areas appear to have been reduced significantly, from 139,300 hectares in 1994 to 92,400 in 1997 and 68,500 in 1998.[34] According to U.S. figures (based on satellite information), which are accepted by the Peruvian government as its own, coca-growing areas were supposedly reduced to 29,700 hectares in 1999 and would currently stand at 34,200 hectares. The UNDCP does not share these views on estimates and maintains that the area is actually 20 percent more. It has expressed concern that "there seems to be a tendency to sow more coca and recover abandoned hectares."[35] U.S. numbers on the extent of coca crops are not exact because research has centered on traditional coca-growing areas, while new growing areas have not been explored. The eradication of coca crops in some areas leads to the production being moved to new growing areas (for example, in Ucayali, Loreto, and Madre de Dios).

There is a political undertone to the methods used in measuring crops, since U.S. organizations fighting drugs have a vested interest in elevating the success achieved through their work. The Peruvian government shares the same vested interest in demonstrating to the world and the country its determination to fight drug trafficking. A worrying element is that while acreage under coca has apparently been reduced since the mid-1990s, the industrialization of the product has advanced. In the past, coca paste was exported to Colombia to be processed and commercialized. However, in recent years, various laboratories producing cocaine have been discovered in Peru, and large shipments of cocaine, consigned by Peruvian gangs, have been seized. Moreover, the corrupting influence of drug trafficking on government and state spheres has significantly increased. It shows how difficult and often contradictory in its results counter-narcotics action is. We conclude with a quote from Gabriel García Márquez: "I think that the first step in reaching a definitive solution to the drug problem worldwide is to recognize the failure of the methods used to fight it. These methods, more than the drugs themselves, have caused, complicated, and aggravated the worse evils suffered by all producing as well as consuming countries."[36]

Notes

1. On this U.S. strategy toward Peru, see Julio Cotler, *Drogas y Política en el Perú: La Conexión Norteamericana* (Lima: Instituto de Estudios Peruvianos, 1999).

2. Within the framework of the inter-American system, a proposal for the creation of a Multilateral Evaluation Mechanism (Mecanismo de Evaluación Multilateral—MEM) was drawn up. According to the United States, it does not replace, but rather complements, certification.

3. The proposal, introduced to reporters on a State Department briefing on May 16, 2001, intends to pursue various objectives next to counter-narcotics action—liberalized trade, ecological preservation, and social stability.

4. See Anthony Faiola, "Allies in Drug War in Disgrace," *Washington Post,* May 15, 2001.

5. Talks given at the Inter-American Defense Committee/Junta Interamericana de Defensa (March 2, 1999), and at the Peace Institute/Instituto por La Paz (June 2, 1999). President Fujimori also made similar statements to the Colombian radio station Caracol, on February 2, in Caracas, during the inaugural ceremony of Hugo Chávez's government. More elaborate information is found in Carlos Reyna, *Plan Colombia y Plan Fujimori* (Lima: ALOP, 2001).

6. Information on this operation appeared in *La República,* Lima, August 22, 2000.

7. See related report in *La República,* Lima, December 28, 2000.

8. See Hugo Cabieses, *Informe sobre el Peru: Debate sobre las Drogas, Impacto de la Iniciativa Regional Andina, y los Resultados de las Políticas* (Lima: Centro de Estudios Políticas y Sociales, 2001).

9. Gustavo Gorriti in *Caretas,* Lima, September 12, 1993. On April 16, 1992, the *Miami Herald* published a report by Sam Dillon that described Montesinos's connections with the CIA. Secretary of State Madeline Albright acknowledged that Montesinos had worked for the American intelligence service. In 1998, a video was broadcast on Peruvian television showing a meeting between General Barry McCaffrey, Vladimiro Montesinos, and the political and military leadership in charge of the War on Drugs.

10. See Manuel Dammert, *Fujimori-Montesinos: El Estado Mafioso, el Poder Imagocrático en las Sociedades Globalizadas* (Lima: Ediciones El Virrey, 2001).

11. On these relations between Montesinos and the drug industry see Francisco Loayza, *Montesinos: El Rostro Oscuro del Poder* (Lima: Mosca Azul, 2001); Felipe MacGregor and Marcial Rubio, *Droga: Desinflando el Globo: Narcotráfico, Corrupción, y Opinión Pública en el Perú* (Lima: Universidad del Pacífico, 1998); Augusto Zimmerman, *El Espía de Fujimori* (Lima: Mosca Azul, 2001).

12. Cf. Evaristo Castillo Aste, *La Conjura de los Corruptos,* vol. 1 (Lima: Ediciones El Virrey, 2001).

13. Roberto Escobar Gaviria, *Mi Hermano Pablo* (Medellín: Quintero Editores, 1994).

14. See Castillo Aste, *La Conjura de los Corruptos,* passim.

15. Ibid.

16. Vaticano even specified that part of the payments were earmarked for the general commander of the armed forces and for the military chief of the Huallaga area, and that President Alberto Fujimori himself was aware of this. Testimony from army officers and other individuals involved corroborates that traffickers made payments to high-ranking army officers; see *El Comercio,* Lima, February 2, 2001, and *Liberación,* May 6, 2001.

17. *El Comercio,* Lima, March 12, 2001.

18. Further information appears in Reyna, *Plan Colombia y Plan Fujimori;* and in *El Comercio* and *La Republica* of April 30, 2001.

19. *Jornal do Brasil,* April 12, 1997.

20. López Paredes declared that Corrochano solicited payment for Montesinos, a fact later corroborated by the very attorney who testified that Montesinos had demanded 10 million U.S. dollars in order to settle legal problems. Corrochano declared that he had handed Montesinos 250,000 dollars in exchange for his interceding with Supreme Court justice Alejandro Rodríguez Medrano for a judgment to be issued in favor of a member of the "Norteños" gang. Reyna, *Plan Colombia y Plan Fujimori,* 52.

21. Ibid. and the Lima newspapers *Gestión* and *Liberación,* February 20, 2001.

22. Interview with Enrique Ovando (Lima, April 2002).

23. Cf. Michael Reid, "Una Región Amenázada por el Narcotráfico," in Diego García Sayán, ed., *Coca, Cocaine, y Narcotráfico: Laberinto en los Andes* (Lima: Comisión Andina de Juristas, 1990), 52–64.

24. As stated by Hernando de Soto in an interview with the authors, May 20, 2001.

25. *Operation Agreement between the Government of Peru and the Government of the United States on the Drug Control Program* (Acuerdo Operativo Entre el Gobierno de la República del Perú y el Gobierno de los Estados Unidos para el Proyecto de Control de Drogas), August 28, 1996.

26. Hugo Cabieses, *Plan Colombia: Seguridad National o Amenaza Regional* (Lima: ALOP, 2001).

27. It is estimated that with crop eradication resources, coca-growing wages have decreased, leading thereby to job losses for some two hundred thousand workers.

28. Hugo Cabieses, "Cooperación International, Lucha Contra el Narcotráfico, y Desarrollo Alternativo en el Perú," *Agro Cooperación,* bulletin no. 4 (July 1998), 36–54.

29. *El Comercio,* Lima, March 2, 2001.

30. Cabieses, *Plan Colombia,* passim; *Programas Integrales de Desarrollo Alternativo y de Prevención y Rehabilitación 1999–2003* (Brussels: Informe de Grupo Consultivo en Apoyo a la Lucha Contra las Drogas en el Peru, 1998).

31. Cabieses, *Informe sobre el Perú,* passim.

32. Ibid.

33. *El Comercio,* Lima, May 5, 2001.

34. A factor to be considered is that coca prices collapsed in 1995. Between the beginning and the end of that year, the price of an *arrabo* (between 11 and 12 kilos)

of coca went from 50 to 5 U.S. dollars (a kilo of coca paste went from 500 to 70 U.S. dollars), and even though it recovered slightly in 1997, the price only reached 10 U.S. dollars. There were several contributing reasons. One of them was the fall of the Cali cartel and the dismantling of the Colombian networks. But perhaps more importantly, the overproduction of coca leaves in Peru and Bolivia, as well as the significant expansion of coca crops, turned Bolivia into the world's main coca leaf producer, superseding Peru in that position.

35. *El Comercio,* Lima, April 28 and May 30, 2001.

36. Gabriel García Márquez, *Apuntas para un Debate Nuevo sobre las Drogas* (Bogotá: n.p., December 1993).

4

Illegal Drugs in Colombia

From Illegal Economic Boom to Social Crisis

Francisco E. Thoumi

At the turn of the twenty-first century, Colombian society finds itself in a profound crisis in which the illegal drug trade plays a very complex and important role. Colombia is the only country in the world where the three main plant-based illegal drugs are produced in significant amounts. Colombians are involved in illegal drug production, international smuggling, and marketing. In the 1980s Colombia became the largest cocaine producer in the world. During the 1990s it also became the largest coca grower. Furthermore, Colombia produces and supplies the lion's share of heroin consumed in the United States and also exports illegal marijuana.

Illegal drug production and trafficking in Colombia has dominated the last thirty years of the country's history. In no other country has the illegal drug industry had such dramatic social, political, and economic effects. Illegal drugs have contributed greatly to changes in institutions and values, have indirectly conditioned the country's economic performance, and have become a major element in the country's polity. Illegal drug revenues are a primary source of funds for left- and right-wing armed actors of the ambiguous war currently experienced in the country.

This chapter summarizes the development of the illegal drug industry, attempts to identify its main effects on Colombia, and analyzes the government's main reactions and policies in response to it.

Illegal Drug Industry Development

Marijuana

Illegal drug production and trafficking started to grow in Colombia in the mid-1960s when marijuana crops developed in response to increases in domestic demand, echoing developments in the United States. However, marijuana production and trafficking did not become important until the early 1970s. In the 1960s, the growth in marijuana consumption in the United States and Europe had triggered the development of large marijuana plantings in Mexico and Jamaica. Toward the end of the decade, the U.S. government promoted eradication programs in Mexico using paraquat, a herbicide known to have harmful health effects, which drew away U.S. consumers. This measure created strong incentives to find other marijuana growing sites and marijuana cultivation then moved to Colombia.[1]

Marijuana was grown mainly in the Sierra Nevada de Santa Marta on Colombia's Caribbean coast. At the beginning, U.S. smugglers sought Colombian suppliers. Some local and U.S. entrepreneurs provided seeds to poor peasants from whom they obtained the marijuana to be sold in the United States. After a short time, Colombian entrepreneurs seized the opportunity offered by this increasing demand and rapidly replaced the U.S. exporters to become marijuana exporters themselves, while the U.S. exporters retained marketing control.[2] News about the good marijuana business spread rapidly and by the late 1970s marijuana plantings had appeared in several other regions, particularly in isolated, recently settled areas of the country.[3]

Marijuana exporting organizations were relatively simple. The peasants produced for a local exporter who controlled and/or owned one or a few landing strips or a port and negotiated with the U.S. importer. Due to the lack of land titling and the very rudimentary and uncompetitive capital markets, the exporter frequently provided crop financing.[4] Most peasants in the Sierra Nevada de Santa Marta had roots in that area and many of them retired from the illegal business after a couple of successful crops had provided them with enough capital to maintain satisfactory levels of living while growing legal crops. The illegal marijuana boom started to decline in 1978 when it fell victim to several external forces. In late 1978 the U.S. government questioned President Turbays's anti-drug credentials, stating possible links between traffickers and some of his close political supporters. In response, the Colombian government engaged in an aggressive manual eradication campaign, confiscated boats and airplanes, and destroyed some of the marijuana processing equipment.[5] By that time, marijuana production in the United States had grown substantially after the development of the more potent "sin semilla" variety.

These developments made the marijuana business less attractive, but they did not destroy it. Moreover, marijuana had infused Colombian entrepreneurs with the awareness of other potential illegal sources of wealth. Methaqualone began to be produced or imported and then exported jointly with marijuana.[6]

Marijuana did not disappear but as the cocaine industry developed, the policy focus shifted away from it. This changed in May 1984 after minister of justice Rodrigo Lara-Bonilla was assassinated and President Betancur used aerial spraying against marijuana plantings. Traffickers' response to fumigation was to shift the location of marijuana plantings to locations with a weak state presence and a very high level of violence. In several of these regions guerrilla organizations rooted out the bullies, established order, and gained peasants' support.[7] Marijuana eradication campaigns continued during the 1980s with U.S. support, and by 1990 marijuana plantings were relatively marginal in Colombia.[8] Sergio Uribe concluded that in the mid-1990s there were about 6,000 hectares planted with marijuana concentrated in six regions of the country, mostly used to satisfy domestic demand.[9]

Coca and Cocaine

Cocaine trafficking is more appealing than the marijuana trade because it has much higher value to weight and volume ratios. Coca cannot be produced in Europe or the United States, except in a few areas in Puerto Rico, Hawaii, and Guam. Growing coca does not require special skills; the shrub is very strong and grows well on fragile tropical soils. Cocaine manufacturing is a simple process, not requiring much expertise.

In the mid-1970s, illegal entrepreneurs began to export small quantities of cocaine to the United States.[10] High profits allowed the business to become self-financing and expand, inducing Colombians to develop stable connections with coca-paste suppliers from Bolivia and Peru, and with suppliers of chemical inputs to refine cocaine. In addition, they developed transportation systems to make large shipments and organized distribution networks, especially in the United States. The large number of Colombian immigrants facilitated this organization downstream. The growth of the illegal business promoted the development of increasingly sophisticated money-laundering systems facilitated in part, by the large and complex contraband networks used to import many goods into Colombia.

The illegal traffic has been a strong incentive for the development of coca plantings in Colombia, which appeared as a backward linkage of the cocaine trade during the mid-1970s.[11] By 1987 Colombia was producing 11 percent of the world's coca crop.[12] Coca's production has had an upward, albeit unstable, long-term trend. Coca prices have fallen in the long run and at times, when the government has intensified its anti-drug fight against the cartels, they have collapsed, generating deep depressions in coca-growing regions because of the disruption of coca-leaf demand.

During the twentieth century Colombia suffered several episodes of internal conflict that forced significant displacements of peasants. Coca plantings in Colombia have developed almost exclusively in areas recently settled by displaced peasants where the state has a weak, if any, presence. These regions are isolated and distant from the main economic centers of the country.

During the 1990s coca plantings exploded in Colombia. In 1991, Colombia was the third largest coca-growing producer with 18.8 percent of the Andean countries' coca acreage while producing only 13.7 percent of the coca-leaf volume.[13] In 1995, Colombia counted 80,000 hectares of coca,[14] more than double the 1990 figure. The increase continued during the late 1990s, reaching some 120,000 to 150,000 hectares by 2000. This, coupled with substantial declines in the area cultivated in Peru and Bolivia, turned Colombia into the largest coca-producing country in the world. Furthermore, cocaine yields increased significantly as growers and refiners adopted important technological advances.[15]

Several factors should be mentioned as contributors to the 1990s coca boom. First, the Fujimori administration, with U.S. support, developed an illegal flight interdiction program that dried up coca-paste supply to Colombia. Second, the collapse of the Iron Curtain weakened the finances of FARC guerrillas, who subsequently sought alternative funding in the illegal industry. Third, paramilitary organizations and guerrillas have found it useful to promote illegal plantings to develop and keep peasant support in the areas they control.

The coca boom has incorporated a complex set of new actors to the illegal industry. In coca-growing areas guerrilla and paramilitary groups substitute for the state, imposing a very authoritarian regime, defining and applying their own laws and regulations, and providing education, police, and civil justice to solve conflicts among the population. In exchange, these groups charge coca production and cocaine export taxes.[16] Other actors include long-time settlers who moved to the region to follow their farmer vocations, produce mainly foodstuffs, and devote a small part of their land to coca; recent settlers who devote most of their efforts to produce coca paste but who also devote some of their land to coca; recent migrants who arrived in the region to grow coca;[17] and finally, commercial farmers with large plantings between 25 and 200 hectares who have direct links with traffickers. Many of these commercial farmers own laboratories and most workers in these farms are *raspachines* who pick coca leaves and help in the manufacturing process. José González-Arias argues that this is a heterogeneous group made up of displaced peasants, former rural hired workers, and pickers who came from regions that produce coffee or nontraditional crops and who expect to settle in coca-growing regions.[18] They include the transient *raspachines* who expect to make some money before returning to their places of origin.

Until recently coca was processed into paste by the peasants themselves and by *chichipatos*, who gather paste to sell in small quantities to *traquetos* and furnish the links to trafficking organizations.[19] An important role is played by the "parachuters," who do not live in the region, but who fly the small planes that bring the large amounts of cash (pesos or dollars) to buy big quantities of cocaine from the large "factories" and the *traquetos.*

In late 1998, the Pastrana administration granted the FARC guerrillas control over a large part of the country where coca plantings are widespread. To a large extent the guerrillas have replaced the *chichipatos* and *traquetos* and have profited from selling to trafficking organizations. A similar situation has developed in the coca regions controlled by the paramilitary. While illegal drugs are a main source of funds for these groups, the involvement in international drug trafficking is impossible to determine at this time.

The illegal industry has also generated a strong need for illicit chemical inputs and has promoted the arms trade. The trade in these products is extremely hard to control. Besides, once the industry has established export smuggling capabilities, it also can import many products by using many of the same smuggling systems.

Poppy, Opium, and Heroin

Poppy cultivation was first practiced in Colombia in 1986.[20] Available evidence indicates that traffickers who distributed seeds and guaranteed crop purchases to traditional peasants in small farms in high-altitude regions promoted poppy plantings. Many of these peasants belong to Indian communities. Poppy plantings have spread quickly over many areas of the Colombian Andes.[21] In traditional Indian areas poppy has increased peasants' incomes but has created conflicts over payments, misunderstandings about business transactions, and attracted undesirable outsiders to the growing areas, where violence has increased.[22] These developments have disrupted communities and have challenged their ancestral authority structures. In these communities many prominent elders support eradication negotiations.

Poppy has also attracted non-Indian migrants to high-altitude, unsettled regions and has been a main cause of high-altitude, old primary forest destruction. Guerrilla presence has also increased in poppy-growing regions. Poppy grows in "commercial" and "peasant" plantings.[23] The commercial plantings are generally in "vacant" government lands; their growers use modern techniques, fertilizers, herbicides and fungicides, which are mostly sold by drug buyers. These plantings generally do not exceed a total of 5 hectares, which are divided into several small plots to avoid detection. Commercial plantings employ hired labor while peasant plantings employ only family labor, use less sophisticated production techniques, and are less profitable.

Traffickers do not buy opium in Colombia because they cannot guarantee purity. Instead, morphine base is refined near poppy plantings where it is sold to traffickers.[24] Estimates of poppy, morphine, and heroin production are very weak partly because poppy is a short-cycle crop. Several estimates show poppy plantings between 6,000 and 20,000 hectares during the 1990s. [25] In any case, these are sufficient to supply most of the U.S. annual heroin demand of about 12 tons.

Cartels, Marketing Networks, Guerrillas, and the Paramilitary

Criminal networks are in constant flux to avoid detection. They continuously seek new routes, sources of chemical inputs, ways to disguise exports, and channels to influence politicians. High profits and low barriers to entry continuously attract independent operators, which spring up at various stages of the business.

Marijuana production did not require complex business enterprises. These emerged with cocaine, which started as a small-scale artisan activity but quickly became a sophisticated business activity. The development of large-scale smuggling methods increased potential gains dramatically and induced the formation of cartels or export syndicates.

These export syndicates were organized in order to minimize risk and maximize profits. They coordinated the Colombian cocaine industry. They bought coca paste and cocaine base in Bolivia and Peru, shipped it to Colombia, where they had established laboratories to refine cocaine, organized the illegal exports from Colombia, and sold the product to wholesalers in the United States and other markets. The extremely high profits of the cocaine business eventually induced Colombians to participate in all stages of the cocaine industry, including its distribution in the United States, where large numbers of Colombian immigrants facilitated the establishment of distribution networks.

The development of distribution networks in the United States has been also facilitated by the proclivity of Colombians to use violence against other smuggling organizations.[26] Violence has been also instrumental in deterring the development of export syndicates in Bolivia and Peru that would compete with Colombians.

The large profits generated by the illegal industry have required the development of sophisticated money-laundering systems. Rapid wealth acquisition, furthermore, has made it impossible for successful exporters not to be noticed. Their high notoriety has increased their need for a social support network to protect their businesses, illegal profits, and accumulated capital. One of the early strategies for social support was to let wealthy Colombians buy shares in a cocaine shipment, under a system known as *la apuntada*.[27]

The personnel involved in the drug industry comprised peasants; chemists; various types of suppliers, purchasers, and intermediaries; pilots; lawyers; financial and tax advisers; enforcers; bodyguards; front men *(testaferros)*; and smugglers who helped launder profits. They were tied to the central cartels in different ways. Some belonged directly to the cartels, but most of them were independent subcontractors loosely tied to them. The network also included politicians, police, guerrillas, paramilitaries, individual army members, public employees, bankers, loyal relatives, friends, childhood friends, and others. The social support network provides protection to the illegal industry, mostly at a price, and constitutes the main channel through which the illegal industry has penetrated and corrupted social institutions. Through this network, illegal income has been distributed to the rest of society, forging strong loyalties within the illegal industry.

During the 1980s, several export syndicates became important. The Medellín and Cali cartels gained notoriety in international cocaine markets. Smaller syndicates remained in the shadow of the big two. During the 1990s, the Colombian illegal drug industry experienced significant structural alterations in response to changes in demand and/or a turn around in government policies. First, cocaine demand in the United States stagnated while cocaine production increased. The resulting lower prices encouraged traffickers to search for new markets and products. Trafficking organizations became more internationally oriented and links were established between Colombian and European criminal organizations.[28] Second, the U.S. interdiction efforts in the Caribbean led to a routing shift through Mexico and the development of links between Colombian and Mexican traffickers. The latter increased their market share at the expense of the former. Third, after Galán's assassination, the Barco and Gaviria governments organized a "war against narcoterrorism" that eventually destroyed the Medellín cartel. The Samper government—under pressure by the United States—fought the Cali cartel and incarcerated all its leaders. Fourth, when the two large cartels were weakened, a large number of smaller trafficking organizations sprouted up. These have followed low profile strategies, are led by more educated Colombians, and are more difficult to track down. Fifth, these smaller organizations are also functional for heroin smuggling. Heroin has a substantially higher price per kilo than cocaine and its volume demand in the United States is much smaller (about 12 tons annually). These two factors make heroin an ideal trafficking drug for small criminal organizations. Sixth, coca and poppy planting boomed. This growth added new actors and complexity to the drug industry, particularly paramilitary and guerrilla organizations that use illegal drugs as their main source of funding.

The Size of the Illegal Industry and Its Economic Effects on the Country

Size is one of the determinants of an illegal activity's effects on a country. However, the illegality of the industry makes estimating its size quite difficult. Every estimate requires many assumptions about key variables such as cocaine content in coca leaves, chemists' skills, losses in transit, prices of each illegal transaction, transportation and smuggling costs, the share and penetration of the Colombians' international market, the percentage of profits obtained by Colombians abroad that are send back to Colombia, and so on. Not surprisingly, available estimates show a wide variation depending on the particular assumptions made.[29] The most rigorous estimates place total illegal drug value added in the range of 2 or 4 billion U.S. dollars in the early and mid-1980s and calculate slightly lower values in the later years. During the 1990s these estimates place total illegal drug value added at around 2.5 billion U.S. dollars per year but they do not include possible profits repatriated by Colombian traffickers abroad.

In the early and mid-1980s, Colombia's GNP was about 36 billion, measured in current dollars. It had grown substantially to 68.6 billion U.S. dollars in 1994 and 96.3 billion in 1997.[30] According to these estimates, the value added generated by the illegal drug industry in the early 1980s amounted to between 7 and 10 percent of GNP. By the late 1990s, however, it had dropped to between 3 and 4 percent of GNP. These estimates show that the relative importance of the illegal industry in the Colombian economy has been declining. One important issue concerns the effects of this illegal industry on the Colombian economy.

There is no doubt that this impact has been quite substantial. The capital formation by the private sector during the 1980s averaged 2.8 billion U.S. dollars a year.[31] Furthermore, any criminal organization exporting 50 or more tons of cocaine annually would have profits that compete with those of the largest financial conglomerates of the country.[32] Any estimate of the size and profits of the illegal drug industry, no matter how conservative, highlights the capacity of the illegal drug industry to change the economic power structure of the country.[33]

The effects of illegal revenues and profits on the Colombian economy have evolved through time. During the 1970s and 1980s they generated a real estate boom in a few cities and regions, revalued the Colombian peso, and encouraged contraband imports. The illegal export boom was welcomed by most Colombians who had lived under an economy that through the years continuously had to confront tight foreign exchange constraints.

It can be argued that the drug industry has penetrated many economic activities, particularly rural and urban real estate. However, a very large part of the Colombian economy, including its most modern enterprises, has been rather insulated from the power of the illegal industry. The modern Colombian economy has been controlled by a number of financial conglomerates that include financial organizations, manufacturing, modern agriculture, marketing, and the media. These groups tend to be self-contained and would have a lot to lose were they to develop partnerships with illicit entrepreneurs.

Furthermore, the stock market has been rather small and most companies traded are controlled by those financial conglomerates. Not surprisingly, there are few activities in which large sums of illicit funds can be laundered in Colombia. Indeed, the national "laundromat is quite small."[34]

While the illegal drug industry has been important, it cannot be argued that the performance of the Colombian economy has improved because of the drug income. Indeed, the rate of growth of Colombia's GNP during the cocaine era—from 1980 through 1997—was about 3.2 percent, while it averaged 5.5 percent during the thirty years before. This decline cannot be explained by the Latin American foreign debt crisis of the 1980s, which Colombia avoided, or by the worsening of the international terms of trade or other external conditions.[35] After 1995, the performance of the Colombian economy declined sharply and in 1999 it registered a decline of about 5 percent of GDP. This was the first year since the end of World War II in which national income fell. When the illegal industry began to grow, its short-term effects on the economy tended to be positive, but its medium- and long-terms effects have been highly negative. The drug industry has acted as a catalyst that accelerated a process of "delegitimation of the regime" that has contributed to the country's stagnation.[36] This process has produced a sharp decline in trust, increasing transaction costs; it has contributed to increased violence and impunity that has induced "clean" capital flight and larger security costs; and it has promoted expectations of very fast wealth accumulation that have produced highly speculative investments, and have increased bankruptcies, embezzlements, and so on. Increased criminality has had a significant declining effect on the country's income growth rate: "The cost of crime in terms of lost growth has exceeded two percent per year, without including its longer term effects on factor productivity and capital formation."[37]

During the 1990s the negative effects became sharply noticeable when illegal drugs became a main funding source for right- and left-wing guerrilla movements. Today a significant part of illicit revenues is used to buy weapons and pay guerrilla soldiers. This way, illegal drug funds are used to fund the ambiguous war in progress, and are also used to line the pockets of corrupt government officials and military officers. In both cases, the state and the licit economy are being greatly undermined. The illicit industry thus has become a main cause of the current Colombian social crisis. Presently, illicit moneys contribute to the destruction of productive activities and to capital flight.

The Illegal Industry's Effects on Politics

The political system has been more vulnerable to the power of the illegal industry than the country's economy. The illegal industry has had to develop social and political support networks to protect its investments and to prevent the government from jailing traffickers and, more importantly, extraditing them to the United States. The industry has used "carrot and stick" strategies to obtain these goals.

Extradition has been the main source of conflict between the government and drug traffickers, who have used all available resources to fight it. This was the main cause of the "narco-terrorism" that erupted in the late 1980s, which included the assassination of many prominent politicians, among them several presidential candidates.

In the early 1980s, members of the Medellín cartel tried to conquer political power and developed a strong support base while spending some of their wealth on public works. Pablo Escobar "bought" a politician and got himself elected to the Colombian Congress as a back-up.[38] Carlos Lehder established a small nationalist party that did not prosper. The Medellín cartel invested heavily in rural land and promoted the formation of self-protection paramilitary groups. It did not hesitate to use violence against anyone who opposed it or who simply tried to enforce laws as his or her duties required. The need to influence government policies also induced traffickers to develop links with politicians. Their wealth allowed them to make large political contributions. Together with the large financial conglomerates they became the main contributors to political campaigns.

By the late 1970s the illegal industry had already become a large election funding source and was contributing heavily to the 1982 election.[39] The 1986 and 1990 presidential campaigns and congressional elections were fairly free of funding by the drug industry because at the time the government was waging the war against narco-terrorism. However, in 1994 large amounts of illegal industry funds were received by the Samper campaign, causing a main political and international issue that crippled the government and produced an unprecedented political crisis.

The benefits that drug traffickers have obtained from their contributions to politicians are debatable. On the one hand, many drug traffickers, including the leaders of the old Medellín and Cali syndicates, were jailed or killed. Besides, despite large campaign funding, President Samper was forced by the U.S. government to take strong action against the illegal industry. This led Francisco Gutierréz-Sanín[40] to argue that traffickers did not get much for their money. On the other hand, most traffickers have avoided extradition and many among them may have continued to run their businesses from prison. A few points are worth mentioning with regard to this issue. While drug moneys can cover a very large share of the expenses of a political campaign, they are insignificant relative to total drug revenues. This means that traffickers are willing to spend money on politicians without a guarantee of any return. As noted by Lee and Thoumi, many traffickers simply use their contributions as a "joker" that they may need to use later on.[41] Also, many inconspicuous non-extraditable traffickers use their contributions just to gain social recognition.

Summing up, there is no question that the political party system has been thoroughly influenced by the illegal industry. Indeed, the illegal industry's political influence has substantially exceeded its economic one. As noted above, during the 1990s guerrilla and paramilitary groups became increasingly dependent on illegal drug funding. The illicit industry's effects on the country's ambiguous war have been notable. Its corruptive influence has weakened the state and delegitimized the establishment, in addition to funding the main actors of the conflict.

Colombian Policies and Attitudes

Colombia is in the midst of an institutional crisis characterized by extremely low levels of social capital and trust. It is a country where society imposes very few behavioral constraints on its members. Indeed, every Colombian has to develop his own ethical norms. Not surprisingly, Colombia is a country of "individual creativity and social indiscipline." This environment produces extreme behaviors and exceptional individuals, some of whom go to any extreme to comply with the law while others do the same to break it. Success in Colombia is individual but not collective. Loyalty is extended to those close to oneself, given the need to survive in a hostile institutional environment. "The net result is the abundance of antisocial conduct and the preponderance of private over collective rationality."[42]

Not surprisingly, during the last fifty years Colombia has been the country of "muddle through" policies. Policy changes were gradual and motivated by the individual interests of those in power. Social reforms deemed necessary by many intellectuals and foreign observers were at best enacted but weakly implemented so that they did not achieve their social goals. Major cases are those of rural land tenancy, access to education, and tax reform. The weak government confronted many policy issues: rapid urbanization; great pressures to provide education, housing, and health services to its population; and the need to promote food production, to create infrastructure, and so forth. Individual addiction to psychoactive drugs was (and is) a low priority issue in the government's agenda. Besides, individual addiction is perceived mainly as a personal problem. Most Colombians did not realistically expect to have the government take care of it. Indeed, "as long as it does not concern me directly, it is not my problem" has been the prevailing adage.

In Colombia impersonal norms are recognized but they are not taken seriously. There is a low law-breaking threshold, and many consider "my case to be an exceptional one" that requires breaking or dodging the law.

This constitutes a sort of democracy in which all are equal because they have the right to evade or avoid the law.[43]

Policies followed by the Colombian government at various times cover the full spectrum of repressive measures used against drug trafficking. These include jailing and extraditing traffickers; involuntary eradication of illicit crops and alternative development programs for affected peasants; import, production, and marketing controls of chemical inputs used to refine cocaine and heroin; interdiction of illicit drugs; anti-money-laundering measures in the financial system; and seizure and confiscation of assets. On the demand side there are also several addiction treatment policies.

The implementation of these policies has been affected by the government's priorities and weaknesses and the structural limitations of the policies themselves. Consider first eradication. Colombia is the only country where aerial spraying takes place. This is done because the government does not have a strong presence or control over the regions in question. This policy has generated a strong opposition from environmentalists and peasants and has not succeeded in limiting illegal crop acreage; rather, it has contributed to planting displacement around the country.

Alternative development programs have been attempted in Colombia. Unfortunately, it is difficult to think of a country where these are less likely to succeed. Coca plantings are in areas with very poor and fragile soils, inaccessible by road, far from any realistic market. Peasants are relatively recent settlers, have weak community institutions, and are armed. All this makes it difficult to negotiate any program and to find crops that may be a real alternative to coca. Indeed, whether there should be any agricultural activity at all in those areas is a big issue.

Traffickers have been imprisoned, but the state has very little control over what goes on inside jails and prisons. They are overcrowded and underfunded; prisoners have access to cellular phones, while weekly visitors smuggle arms, weapons, and other items. Jails are understaffed and personnel are poorly paid. Inmates organize themselves in gangs and many actually build facilities within the jail. Escapes are common and many traffickers have been able to continue running their businesses while in prison.

Expropriation of traffickers' assets has been presented as a key policy against organized crime and a source of funds for anti-drug policies. However, the government simply does not have the financial and managerial capacity to administer seized property and expropriation procedures are complex, costly, and difficult to implement successfully. The Colombian drug control office (Dirección Nacional de Estupefacientes) in charge of handling these properties is woefully inadequate to do the job. Only a handful of properties have been expropriated and lawyers have had a field day defending traffickers and their heirs against the state.[44]

When the illegal drug industry started it was very difficult to mobilize public opinion against something that was not perceived as a social threat. The first eradication campaigns in the late 1970s were pursued in response to U.S. pressures on the government. An extradition treaty was signed with the United States in the late 1970s and ratified in 1982 but the government did not enforce it until the assassination of a minister of justice by the drug traffickers. In other words, for many years anti-drug policies were reactive either to foreign pressures or to misdeeds by the illegal industry. The wave of terror that followed generated a strong anti-extradition sentiment among the population so that extradition was declared unconstitutional in the new 1991 constitution.[45]

Until the late 1980s most Colombians did not perceive the negative long-term effects of the illegal industry, and public support for anti-drug policies was weak. During the 1980s homicides and other violent crimes increased dramatically and by 1989 it was evident to most Colombians that the illegal industry's effects on the political system were perverse. During the 1990s it became clear that the illegal industry was funding both guerrillas and para-military groups. Contrary to what happened in some Central American countries and in Vietnam, guerrilla groups in Colombia do not have strong social support. Colombian guerrillas in many ways represent Colombia's past, not its future. They are rurally based in a country that is about 75 percent urban, their level of education is very low in a country where literacy rates have increased sharply, and they use violence and primitive conflict resolution methods in a society that aspires to modern social institutions. Furthermore, Colombia is subject to strong external pressures and Colombians are discriminated against around the world (Colombian profiling is legal and legitimate all over the world). Today, Colombians realize that the illegal industry has been a catalyst in a process of social decomposition but—in the short term—there is little that can be done about it.

Notes

1. Juan Tokatlian, "La Política Exterior de Colombia hacia Estados Unidos, 1978–1990: El Asunto de las Drogas y su Lugar en las Relaciones entre Bogotá y Washington," in C. G. Arrieta et al., eds., *Narcotráfico en Colombia: Dimensiones Políticas, Económicas, Jurídicas, e Internacionales* (Bogotá: Tercer Mundo Editores-Ediciones Uniandes, 1990), 300.

2. Francisco Thoumi, *Political Economy and Illegal Drugs in Colombia* (Boulder, Colo.: Lynne Rienner, 1995), 126.

3. Hernando Ruiz-Hernández, "Implicaciones Sociales y Económicas de la Producción de la Marihuana," in Asociación Nacional de Instituciones Financieras (ANIF), *Marihuana: Legalización o Represión* (Bogotá: Biblioteca ANIF de Economía, 1979), 124–56.

4. Ibid., 140.

5. Thoumi, *Political Economy and Illegal Drugs,* chapter 3.

6. Ruiz-Hernández, "Implicaciones Sociales y Económicas," 180.

7. Ricardo Vargas, "La Bonanza de la Marimba Empezó Aquí," in *La Verdad del '93: Paz, Derechos Humanos, y Violencia* (Bogotá: CINEP, 1994), 64–86.

8. United States Department of State, Bureau of International Narcotics Matters, *International Narcotics Control Strategy Report* (Washington, D.C., 1992).

9. Sergio Uribe, "Los Cultivos Ilícitos en Colombia. Evaluación: Extensión, Técnicas, y Tecnologías para la Producción y Rendimientos y Magnitud de la Industría," in Francesco E. Thoumi, ed., *Drogas Ilícitas en Colombia: Su Impacto Económico, Político, y Social, Dirección Nacional de Estupefacientes, y PNUD* (Bogotá: Editorial Planeta, 1997), 120–42.

10. Mario Arango and Jorge Child, *Narcotráfico: Imperio de la Cocaína* (Mexico City: Editorial Diana, 1987).

11. Thoumi, *Political Economy and Illegal Drugs,* chapter 3.

12. Eduardo Sarmiento, "Economía del Narcotráfico," in Arrieta et al., *Narcotráfico en Colombia,* 54–83.

13. Thoumi, *Political Economy and Illegal Drugs,* chapter 3.

14. Uribe, "Los Cultivos Ilícitos en Colombia," passim.

15. Ibid.

16. Ibid.; Vargas, "La Bonanza de la Marimba," passim.

17. José Jairo González-Arias, "Cultivos Ilícitos, Colonización, y Revuelta de Raspachines," *Revista Foro* 35 (1998), 48.

18. Ibid.

19. Ibid., 53.

20. Policía Nacional de Colombia, Dirección Antinarcóticos, "Amapola: Producción, Procesamiento, y Canales de Distribución" (presented at the International Technical Seminar on Illicit Poppy Cultivation in Latin America, Bogotá, UNDP, May 1993).

21. Maria Constanza Ramirez, "El Cultivo de la Amapola en Colombia" (presented at the International Technical Seminar on Illicit Poppy Cultivation in Latin America, Bogotá, UNDCP, May 1993); Ricardo Vargas and Jacqueline Barragán, "Amapola en Colombia: Economía Ilegal, Violencia y Impacto Regional," in Ricardo Vargas, ed., *Drogas, Poder, y Región en Colombia* (Bogotá: CINEP, 1995), 2:86–124.

22. Ibid.

23. Uribe, "Los Cultivos Ilícitos en Colombia," passim.

24. Ibid.

25. Ibid.; Vargas, *La Bonanza de la Marimba,* passim.

26. Guy Gugliotta and Jeff Leen, *Kings of Cocaine* (New York: Harper, 1990).

27. Ciro Krauthausen and Luis F. Sarmiento, *Cocaína & Co.: Un Mercado Ilegal por Dentro* (Bogotá: Tercer Mundo Editores, 1991), 74; Arango and Child, *Narcotráfico,* 130–31.

28. Patrick L. Clawson and Rensselaer W. Lee III, *The Andean Cocaine Industry* (New York: St. Martin Press, 1996), 62–90; Ciro Krauthausen, *Padrinos y Mercaderes: Crimen Organizado en Italia y Colombia* (Bogotá: Planeta Colombiana Editorial, 1998).

29. These have been surveyed by Thoumi, *Political Economy and Illegal Drugs;* Roberto Steiner, "Los Dólares del Narcotráfico," *Cuadernos de* FEDESAROLLO no. 2 (1997), 24–38; Ricardo Rocha, "Aspectos Económicos de las Drogas Ilegales en Colombia," in Thoumi, *Drogas Ilícitos en Colombia,* 78–92.

30. Data from Inter-American Development Bank (IADB).

31. Thoumi, *Political Economy and Illegal Drugs,* passim.

32. A back-of-the-envelope estimate can place export profit net of transportation costs at about 10,000 U.S. dollars per kilogram or 500 million per 50 tons. The weekly *Semana* in Bogotá estimates that in 1995 the four largest financial groups had profits of 530, 140, 480, and 190 million U.S. dollars respectively; "Los Cuatro Grandes," *Semana,* no. 731 (1996), 56–64.

33. Thoumi, *Political Economy and Illegal Drugs,* passim.

34. Francisco Thoumi, "La Relación entre Corrupción y Narcotráfico: Un Análisis General y Algunas Referencias a Colombia," *Revista de Economía del Rosario* 2, no. 1 (June 1999), 32–54.

35. Thoumi, *Political Economy and Illegal Drugs,* passim.

36. Ibid.

37. Mauricio Rubio, "Crimen y Crecimiento en Colombia," in Inter-American Development Bank (IADB), *Hacia un Enfoque Integrado del Desarrollo: Etica, Violencia, y Seguridad Ciudadana, Encuentro de Reflexión* (Washington, D.C.: IADB, 1996).

38. At the time every member of Congress had a backup who would replace the elected candidate when he or she was absent.

39. This issue has been studied in detail in Rensselaer W. Lee III and Francisco E. Thoumi, "The Criminal-Political Nexus in Colombia," *Trends in Organized Crime* 5, no. 2 (1999), 54–82.

40. Francisco Gutierréz-Sanín, "Organized Crime and the Political System in Colombia (1978–1998)" (presented at the Conference on Democracy, Human Rights, and Peace in Colombia, Kellogg Institute, University of Notre Dame, Indiana, March 26–27, 2001).

41. Lee and Thoumi, "The Criminal-Political Nexus in Colombia," passim.

42. Hernando Gómez-Buendía, "La Hipótesis del Almendrón," in H. Gómez-Buendía, ed., *¿Para Dónde Va Colombia?* (Bogotá: Tercer Mundo Editores-Colciencias, 1999), 20.

43. Ibid.

44. Only thirty-three thousand of thirty-four thousand seized properties have been expropriated as of May 2001; *El Tiempo,* May 9, 2001. The government does not have an inventory of seized assets, many looted and burned properties would be very costly to fix, and others continue to be exploited by their owners, who now do not pay taxes or maintain them. In some cases, armed paramilitary groups prevent the government from taking possession of seized assets. The potential cost to the government arising from litigation can be enormous.

45. A constitutional amendment has since changed this decree.

5

Mexico

Drugs and Politics

Luis Astorga

The close relationship between drug trafficking and politics in Mexico goes back to the second decade of the twentieth century during the Mexican Revolution. Historians and political analysts have never recognized the importance of this issue in their research on post-revolutionary developments in Mexico. They have preferred to ignore the presence of drug trafficking as a business, tolerated, promoted, and even controlled by prominent politicians at the local, regional, and national levels. First-hand documentation is often hard to come by. Criminal behavior is never included in a politician's autobiography, and the law of silence among the political class that came to power through the former state party (PRI) and among the drug lords themselves has never been broken. The protected witness program has not changed this situation. With the leading politicians, credibility is often at stake.

In this chapter, we will analyze the drug issue as it evolved during the most important and relevant periods in Mexican history since the prohibition era. Drug trafficking has become an increasingly important power base. In the last few years it has frequently been mentioned in connection with politics and the military, and with the activities of big entrepreneurs who maintain a special relationship with the former ruling party, the PRI. Short-term analyses, especially those that we find in the media, present the image of the Mexican state being infiltrated by drug traffickers. Long-term analyses show a different development and point to the political field, dominated for seven decades by the ruling party, as setting the rules of the game in the drug business. Changes in drug trafficking, in the past as well as in present times, have reflected changes in the political system. The relative autonomy of the drug-trafficking business in recent years should be understood in relation to the former ruling party elite's loss of power, and the cascade effect on the structural mediations between drug trafficking and the political sector. This structure, which has been in force throughout the years, has been shaken. However, it has not been completely destroyed, and its functioning has become more visible.

Antecedents

In the nineteenth century and the beginning of the twentieth century, drugs such as marijuana, opiates, and cocaine were commonly used in Mexico. Laudanum and other opium derivates, such as morphine and heroin, and pharmaceuticals, such as cocaine, coca wines, and marijuana cigarettes, were often prescribed by doctors. The products could easily be bought in pharmacies, popular markets, and even in hardware stores. There were attempts at quality control and consumer protection by the authorities. Addiction was viewed as a health problem and not as a criminal issue.[1] There were feeble efforts to control laudanum, poppy, and marijuana, without much success.[2]

In the first decade of the twentieth century, the U.S. government began its actions in the area of drug control, pressuring other countries to accept opium control and define legislation to back it up. The 1909 Shanghai Conference on opium control counts among the first international activities by the United States with regard to drug issues. The 1914 Harrison Narcotics Act on opium consumption control motivated the U.S. government to begin exporting its vision on drug control worldwide. At that time, the Mexican Revolution was in full swing. The revolutionary leaders were more interested in political power and survival than in controlling opium trafficking. This way, prohibition on one side of the U.S.-Mexican border and free trade on the other created ideal conditions for the drug trade. Most of the illicit drug trafficking was taking place through Ensenada, Mexicali, and Tijuana, in Baja California. The territory was governed by Colonel Esteban Cantú (1916–1920), who used his position to carry on an opium trafficking business that enabled him, among other things, to pay his troops, buy arms, and meet the expenses of his government. Prohibition had turned opium trafficking into such a profitable business that the governor himself had decided to take control of it.[3]

The cultivation and commercialization of marijuana was prohibited in Mexico in 1920; the prohibition of poppy followed in 1926.[4] Mexican officials pointed to the danger of "racial degeneration" that these and other drugs, such as cocaine, would produce. The ideas on these matters were inspired by the opinions that circulated among the social and political elites in the United States and Europe. Drug use and abuse in Mexico was not a widespread phenomenon and the number of people involved was reduced compared to the size of the drug scene of its northern neighbor. Marijuana use was limited to soldiers, criminals, and poor people; opium smoking was found among Chinese minorities; and morphine, heroin, and cocaine were used among artists, middle-class people, and bourgeois "drop outs." The main business of the drug traffickers was north of the border.

The manner in which illicit drug trafficking came into being in Mexico, namely as an economic activity, first penalized and than subordinated to political power, also determined its development, the impunity of the people involved and their protectors, and the nature of the violence that it generated. The foundation of a state party in 1929, with a virtual monopoly over political power and the military control of the national territory, made it practically impossible for any particular group of illicit drug traffickers to make it on their own. Those who tried met at some point with the representatives of a much stronger power structure who forced them to give up a substantial part of their profits.

Drugs and Politics: The Pattern Is Set

Several periods in the relationship between hegemonic political authority and the field of drug trafficking in Mexico can be defined that reflect changes in the machinery of control, mediation, and containment put in place over time. The first period runs from the prohibition days in the second and third decades of the twentieth century until the early postwar years. Depending on the strength of their particular ethical inclinations, governors entered the illicit trade, which they viewed as just an other business opportunity handed to them by their position of authority. Sanctions could only have arisen from a clash of interests within the same ruling class. Seldom did these become public knowledge.

Baja California was the first, and certainly not the last, example of the close cooperation between political power and drug-trafficking interests.[5] In the state of Coahuila, according to the investigation report sent by special agent Juan Requena to the Mexican Department of Public Health, the most important opium trafficker, the Chinese Antonio Wong Yin, was a *compadre* of governor Nazario Ortiz Garza. Other traffickers maintained a close relationship with General Jesús García Gutiérrez, who was in charge of military operations in the state.[6] Similar situations were reported about the governor of Chihuahua.[7] In this latter case, a famous trafficker from Ciudad Juárez, Enrique Fernández Puerta, who had begun his career by smuggling alcohol and counterfeiting dollars, but had taken up drug trafficking, "eventually controlled city hall and was a stepping stone toward wealth for many individuals who worked for the government of Chihuahua, including three governors."[8]

The second period in the development of the relationship between political power and drug trafficking began in 1947, when the national Department of Health ceased to be in charge of anti-drug policy in the country and the Office of the Attorney General of the Republic (PGR) was entrusted with the task. At the same time, the Federal Security Directorate (DFS) was set up as the political police of then president Miguel Alemán. It served as a counterpart to the CIA, providing surveillance of opposition groups, particularly those of "communist" orientation. The DFS was also given a say in anti-drug policy. The assistant military attaché of the U.S. embassy in Mexico City took it upon himself to disclose the link of the founders of the DFS with drug trafficking.[9] The most important among them, Colonel Carlos Serrano, was senator for the Federal District and very close to the president himself. At the time, in the United States, the fight against communism weighed more heavily than concern for the morality of Mexican police officers. With the establishment of the DFS, a structural connection was created between the ruling political class and the drug traffickers. Its work was to be twofold: first, it ensured that part of the profits of the trade were siphoned off in exchange for protection; second, it served as a mechanism for containing drug-generated violence and controlled any temptations traffickers may have had to translate economic power into political power.

For several decades the degree of violence was kept at socially acceptable levels. It remained limited to the area of the trade itself, only affecting clearly identified opposing groups while taking place in well-defined areas. A political scandal of huge proportions arose in 1947 when General Pablo Macias Valenzuela, ex-secretary of war and the navy and governor of the state of Sinaloa (1945–1950), was charged with leading a drug-trafficking ring and protecting opium traffickers. The information was published by national newspapers such as *Excelsior* and *El Universal*.[10] According to Jesús Lazcano Ochoa, attorney general of Sinaloa in Valenzuela's government, the governor had never even seen opium until Lazcano Ochoa showed him some samples seized from the traffickers.[11] The attorney general added that the accusations were inventions of his political enemies who suspected him of having masterminded the assassination of his predecessor, Colonel Rodolfo T. Loaiza (1941–1944), from the competing Lázaro Cárdenas group.[12] The scandal cooled down after a private meeting with President Miguel Alemán, when he was on an official visit in Mazatlán, Sinaloa, six days after the first note appeared in the press against Valenzuela. The governor finished his term and became commander of the First Military Zone (1951–1956).[13] Accusations against Valenzuela were never proven, but some doubts remained.

The scandal surrounding Valenzuela constituted the first time the drug-trafficking issue was used publicly and politically by one elite power group against another. It is important to note that since the beginning of the drug business, the best-known drug traffickers in Mexico have been mentioned in special official reports in Mexico and the United States as related to high-ranking politicians. These were politicians suspected of being directly involved in, even controlling, the illegal trade. In that scenario, freelancers or outsiders would not have had any chances to build up their own networks and succeed in their efforts at the same time. The political system that had emerged after the Mexican revolution was a state party system with a power structure resembling a social pyramid with the president at the top, concentrating powers over the legislative and the judicial branches. The loyalty of governors—most of them had been military officers formed on the battle-fields—was in many cases assured in exchange for the liberty to do business of a special nature. The limits were set by the president's permission, their own entrepreneurial capacity, and their ethical dispositions. In that context, drug trafficking was viewed as just another profitable business that could be run by powerful members of the "revolutionary family," while taking advantage of the political positions they occupied at a given moment. Controlled, tolerated, or regulated by mighty politicians in northern states, drug trafficking seems to have been a business that was developed from within the official political power structure. Drug traffickers appear to have emerged as a new class of outlaws that depended closely on political and police protection, had limited autonomy as a specialized social group, and was banned from political activity.

For many reasons, the state of Sinaloa has become a paradigmatic case in the study of drug trafficking in Mexico. Since the end of the nineteenth century, the state economy had been linked to the economies of California and Arizona in the United States. The opium that was produced in Sinaloa followed the same route as the agricultural products that were exported via the Pacific railroad. Chinese immigrants and local producers and traders, many of them from the mountains of Badiraguato (a municipal division of the State of Sinaloa) transported their merchandise to the border cities of Nogales, Mexicali, and Tijuana. Those operating on the other side of the law were merchants, some of them from wealthy families, but also peasants, adventurers, and middle-class people living in cities and towns where everybody knew each other, who had decided to tempt the devil, to make a quick profit to get rich, to capitalize their legal business, or to earn a living.[14] Those who continued in the business specialized in drug trafficking and became the professionals of the trade; most of the time they were people from the mountains where the poppy fields bloomed. They formed dynasties, passing their know-how on to successive generations and producing drug-trafficking leaders who would manage the business on a national level. In the long term, they have developed a situation resembling an oligopoly: most of them have been leading the important drug trafficking groups for decades; their exercise of power has not been limited to the normal six-year political cycles; and they have never shown any interest in organizing themselves in politics, as Carlos Lehder, Pablo Escobar, and the Extraditables did in Colombia. According to the Mexican authorities, successive counter-narcotics campaigns in the 1950s resulted in a "definitive elimination of drug trafficking" in Sinaloa,[15] statements—above all—designed to please the U.S. government and UN observers. The campaign led to the immediate expansion of illegal cultivation in the states of Jalisco, Nayarit, and Michoacán, following the pattern through which tough measures in one place provoke trafficking problems in another. Drug trafficking—mostly involving opium—using planes was so intense that the minister of communications and public works decided to suspend commercial flights in some airfields in Sinaloa, Sonora, Chihuahua, and Durango in 1953, and closed the aviation school in Culiacán. A former pilot and flight instructor at that time admitted having transported opium on his plane very often; however, he said, national airline companies (Aeronaves de Mexico) had done it on a bigger scale. The officially declared "successes" of the drug-control campaigns had no basis in fact.

In the 1960s and the 1970s, the structure of the international drug market began to change under the impact of external as well as internal factors. The balance of power between the principal social forces engaged in the trade and those engaged in the legal struggle against it changed equally. Marijuana became very popular among U.S. consumers, creating a growing demand. In the 1970s and, more clearly, from the 1980s onward, cocaine became a favorite choice of the most insatiable drug market in history. The U.S. government initiated the War on Drugs and intensified the prohibitionist policy that it had been advocating since the beginning of the century. Those countries producing drugs and those serving as transit points on the way to the United States were singled out for action. Political pressures on these countries were intensified and they were forced to cooperate with the United States in the area of drug control, following its strategy of increasing militarization of counter-narcotics action. Initially, this strategy produced a great deal of tension with the Mexican government, subsequently making place, however, for a complete dependency referred to, in the hygienic terminology of international diplomacy, as "bilateral cooperation."

In the mid-1970s, "Operation Condor" was set in motion in those states in northwest Mexico where most illicit crops were grown (Sinaloa, Chihuahua, and Durango). Most important in Sinaloa and in the country as a whole was an organization of traffickers that had begun to trade in cocaine from Colombia and could be regarded as the "mother of all modern gangs" that would emerge later: the one led by Miguel Angel Félix Gallardo. He had been a bodyguard of the family of the former governor of Sinaloa, Leopoldo Sánchez Celis, and had been his political protégé. Those hardest hit by Operation Condor, which had involved the deployment of ten thousand troops, were not the drug lords but large numbers of peasants in the region, who were tortured, sent to prison, or removed from their communities of origin. The big traffickers moved the headquarters of the trade to Jalisco and, subsequently, split up the organization into branches of equal or even greater power. No action was taken against them. They simply left their original home bases and moved their businesses to a much larger industrial, commercial, and financial center. The move gave them a better point of departure for the internationalization of their operations. According to a 1978 secret report from the Federal Security Directorate (DFS), officials very close to the head of the Office of the Attorney General of the Republic (PGR), Oscar Flores Sánchez, former governor of Chihuahua, had links with known traffickers such as Carmelo Avilés Pérez, the Herrera Nevarez family, Rafael Muñoz, Rafael Aguilar, and others. There was no hard evidence against the attorney general himself, said the report, although it was highly unlikely that Flores Sánchez would not have known about these activities of his subordinates.[16]

The U.S. authorities involved in drug control were convinced that DFS officials had assisted in the reorganization process and, subsequently, had ensured the protection of the new structures. These could have functioned successfully and without major problems for a prolonged period of time had it not been for an event that put an end to the complicit silence of several decades by the U.S. government. The assassination of the DEA agent Enrique Camarena at the hands of traffickers and police in 1985 meant the coup de grace for the DFS. At the same time, the structural connection between the ruling political elite and the drug trade suffered a serious setback, and the cover-up and containment policy that had operated for almost four decades came to an end.

The traffickers did not confront the state, as the Colombian drug lords did. They made increased use of violence in Sinaloa and Jalisco while settling their affairs, but the upper echelons of the police, the army, and the political class were not targeted. The traffickers had prospered thanks to the crisis in the machinery of mediation and control of official politics. Various law enforcement institutions had been given extraordinary powers, often on the fringes of the law, to contain opposition political forces and criminal groups. In exchange, they had allowed discretionary freedoms to power-holders in the political systems to share the spoils of the Drug War and to engage in shady deals while respecting the codes of silence that ensured the reproduction of the chain of institutional corruption. The DFS was dismantled by President De la Madrid in 1985. One arm was amputated but other limbs remained; one of them was the Federal Judiciary Police (PJF) in the PGR. This institution had been a key component of the mediation structures, with a long experience in crime organization and a reputation no better than the one the DFS had. The Camarena affair had triggered many arrests and even the assassination of police commanders. These phenomena have become part of everyday life in the criminal world of the country.

The year 1985 marked the beginning of the third period in the relationship between politics and drug trafficking. In 1989, with the presidency in the hands of Carlos Salinas de Gortari, the opposition party PAN won its first governorship in Baja California. During the six years of Salinas's presidency (1988–1994), several changes occurred in the relations among the big trafficking groups in the country. Power alternated among a group of traffickers from Tamaulipas, who first had taken control from Sinaloa traffickers, but later lost out to them again. The key operator in the reshuffling among these drug-trafficking groups—who was also involved in the arrest of drug lord Félix Gallardo—was the Tamaulipas-born commander of the PJF, Guillermo González Calderoni. He had been a friend and protector of drug lord García Abrego, who lives now, apparently officially protected, in the United States. When the Mexican government sought to have him extradited, he threatened to bring up sensitive matters and to reveal secrets connected with spying on the political opposition by order of Raúl Saunas, the brother of the president. The U.S. press reported on a possible connection between the president's elder brother and García Abrego. It was suggested that the traffickers had secured so much power that they could even afford to buy the president's brother, thus supporting the thesis of the "penetration" of the traffickers into the political power structure. However, another possibility would have been that the political clan to which Raúl belonged had used this connection and other organizations of traffickers for a variety of economic and extra-economic purposes. This would substantiate the thesis that the traffickers have remained subordinated to the political authorities despite the greater degree of relative independence they had achieved, in part as a result of the deadly conflicts within the ruling political elite itself.

It is no accident that the higher levels of violence connected with drug trafficking in the 1990s were observed mostly in those states where the political opposition had gained power. These are the same states, incidentally, where illegal crops are grown. At the same time, they share a tradition of trading and trafficking of drugs, have a presence of financial services that permit money laundering, and are located close to potential markets for the consumption of drugs. Examples are Baja California, Chihuahua, Jalisco, Nuevo León, and the Federal District. The mediation and control machinery that had been in place since World War II had assumed a dependent relationship between the local and federal police forces, and with state and federal government in the hands of one and the same party. The dismantling and weakening of the mediation bodies through international pressures and internal disintegration, in addition to clashes within the political elite itself, undermined the ability of the federal government to curtail the use of violence in the region. The increased violence in states governed by the opposition was capitalized on politically by the PRI, which tried to present the phenomenon as resulting from the political incompetence of the opposition. In reality of course, it was one of the effects downstream of the long-term process of weakening of the national power structures. At the same time, this gave the traffickers greater freedom of action locally since an opposition governor did not have the same strength and was not backed in the same way by the federation as one belonging to the same party as the president.

Drugs and Politics, the Impact of the War on Drugs

In 1986, President Reagan signed an important document concerning his War on Drugs policy,[17] the National Security Decision Directive, which considers drug trafficking a threat to U.S. national security, and permits the Department of Defense to get involved in a wide range of anti-drug activities, in particular in the Mexico-U.S. border area. Some analysts have regarded this policy as an important element of the Low Intensity Conflict doctrine,[18] a perspective also shared by the Mexican government. All presidents since Miguel de la Madrid (1982–1988) have been repeating Reagan's basic idea, although they have added the concern about the health issues involved.

The Bush administration continued Reagan's policy and intensified the pressure on the governments of the Latin American source countries—Colombia, Peru, and Bolivia—to militarize the War on Drugs.[19] Initially, Mexico was dealt with differently, but not for too long. On October 23, 1995, William Perry, the secretary of the Department of Defense, and General Barry McCaffrey, the commander-in-chief of the United States Armed Forces Southern Command, which coordinated all national security operations in Latin America at the time, and confirmed by the United States Senate as the director of the United States Office of National Drug Control Policy (ONDCP), visited the Mexican secretary of defense, General Enrique Cervantes Aguirre. The meeting concluded that Mexico and the United States shared political and economic ties, but lacked a connection in the military field. Subsequently five areas of cooperation were defined; one of them concerned anti-narcotics operations. By 1996, almost one thousand soldiers had received special training in counter-narcotics action in the United States. The first steps were set toward a militarization of drug control and the problem of public security.[20] Except for Operation Condor, mentioned earlier, the military had been used until then mainly in eradication campaigns. Traditionally, military tasks had concerned internal security, but as narcotics trafficking has taken on more ominous dimensions, the military's role has expanded to include the elimination of drug smuggling as a function serving national security.[21]

From November 1995 to September 1996, seventy-two soldiers were designated as PJF agents in a pilot project in Chihuahua.[22] When they failed in their mission to apprehend drug lord Amado Carrillo, they were sent to fight the EPR guerrilla group in Guerrero. Other military officers occupied leading positions in the PGR structure, as high-ranking officials, federal representatives in the states, and PJF agents. In December 1996, General Jesús Gutiérrez Rebollo was designated chief of the National Drug Control Institute (INCD). He had been commander of the Ninth Military Zone in Culiacán and of the Fifteenth Military Zone in Guadalajara, two cities with a presence of prominent drug traffickers. He lasted two months in the new position. On February 18, 1996, the secretary of the defense announced astonishing news: General Gutiérrez had been protecting Amado Carrillo, and had been apprehended.[23] He was sentenced to thirty-five years in prison on charges of drug and arms trafficking.[24] The twentieth century in Mexico ended with scandals involving the connection between politics and drug trafficking.

In January 1999, Raúl Salinas de Gortari, the ex-president's brother, was sentenced to fifty years in prison for masterminding the assassination of his brother-in-law,[25] then president of the ruling party (PRI), a sentence later reduced to twenty-seven and one-half years.[26] Charges for money laundering in Mexico remained pending.[27] Investigations into his Swiss bank accounts were able to trace 114.4 million U.S. dollars, the origins of which could not be established.[28] The case was passed to the PGR in 2002, which accused Raúl of receiving part of the money from a legal and secret account controlled by his brother Carlos while he was president. The investigation into the assassination had been conducted by Mario Ruiz Massieu, the deputy attorney general. Other members of the office accused him of protecting Raúl Salinas. When traveling to the United States, Ruiz Massieu was apprehended on charges of money laundering, but on September 17, 1999, two days before his trial, he committed suicide.[29] In one of the farewell letters he wrote, he blamed President Zedillo for his own death and that of his brother. Mexican and U.S. officials were certain about the extent of his knowledge regarding the secrets of the connections between drug trafficking and politics. They had expected some revelations at the trial, but rather than spilling the beans he decided to take the secrets to his grave. It was an example of the *omertà*, Mexican style.

On May 31, 1999, the Mexican newspaper *El Financiero* published a note based on a report by the National Drug Intelligence Center. The report had been classified as "law enforcement sensitive" and was requested by DEA and FBI offices in San Diego. In it, Carlos Hank Gonzalez—a powerful politician, ex-governor of the state of Mexico, and ex-minister of agriculture and tourism, who had died in 2001—and his clan were accused of being involved in drug trafficking and money laundering.[30] They were considered a "threat" to the U.S. government because of their relations with the Arellano brothers.

Jorge Hank Rohn, especially linked to them, was characterized as "more criminal than his father and brother," dangerous and violent. The report mentioned charges of money laundering, cocaine trafficking, and contacts with other drug-trafficking organizations. The Hank group was said to have tight relations with the Arellano and Amado Carillo organizations and had been able to operate with impunity for more than forty years. Its members considered themselves "above governments, their institutions, and the laws." Robert L. Tortoriello, lawyer of the Laredo National Bank, which was owned by Carlos Hank Rohn and suspected of laundering drug money, commented on the report, attributing its content to prejudices against Mexicans and Latinos among the police and intelligence agencies involved in the report's investigation.

That was not all. In September 1999, Liébano Sáenz, President Zedillo's private secretary, was described by the *New York Times* as being connected with drug traffickers.[31] Barry McCaffrey, the U.S. drug czar, Janet Reno, the attorney general, and Jeffrey Davidow, the U.S. ambassador in Mexico, denied having information on these accusations, and the Mexican authorities asked for a formal diplomatic note from the Department of State, clearing Liébano's name. At the same time, McCaffrey and Davidow denied having information concerning the accusations against Hank.[32] A spokesman from the Mexican minister of foreign affairs declared later that the U.S. Department of State had sent a note stating that Hank had not been accused of any crime. However, the note could not be shown to the press.[33] In Costa Rica, President Miguel Angel Rodríguez was criticized for having maintained a relationship with Hank, who allegedly donated a million dollars to his political campaign.[34] According to Hank himself, the accusations were "stupidities,"[35] and he succeeded in having government officials from Mexico and the United States describe him as an honorable man.

In 1995, Peter Lupsha, a U.S. investigator, reported to the U.S. Department of State information concerning a sum of 40 million U.S. dollars allegedly provisioned by Cali traffickers to be used in Zedillo's political campaign and related activities. The president's office denied the charges. In 1997, General Gutiérrez Rebollo declared in prison that the president's father-in-law had maintained a close relationship with the Amezcua brothers, a group of methamphetamine traffickers pursued by U.S. authorities.[36] The allegations were never investigated. Instead, the attorney general characterized General Gutiérrez Rebollo as a "traitor to his uniform, his institution, and Mexico" who had no other choice than lying and trying to discredit decent people like the president's father-in-law, and generals such as Cervantes (secretary of defense), Valencia (CENDRO), and Alvarez Nara (PJF). The latter two were mentioned by him as linked to Amado Carrillo.[37] This represents only one incident of the many mutual accusations of drug trafficking among generals that have generated public confusion, created suspicion, and have discredited the military's counter-drug activities. Furthermore, the publicity surrounding officers at the top level who have been found guilty will further undermine the moral fabric of the institution and may increase the chance of corruption at its other levels.

In early February 1998, the *Washington Times* published a note, leaked from a secret CIA report, accusing Francisco Labastida Ochoa, minister of government and former governor of Sinaloa, of maintaining links with drug trafficking while being governor.[38] Mexican officials rejected the charges. Some analysts related the issue and the time of its publication to the annual certification process that was taking place. Others pointed to Labastida's political enemies in Mexico who would have provided the information to the CIA with the purpose of damaging his image in view of his candidacy for the presidency in the year 2000. In response, the U.S. drug czar, General Barry McCaffrey, declared to have "personally no evidence of allegations of this nature that I would find compelling."[39] Editorials in the Sinaloa press defended Labastida's legacy as governor, remembering his actions against drug trafficking and the drug subculture: one of his bodyguards was killed in a shoot out with the Güero Palmas gang in the suburbs of Culiacán, Sinaloa's capital; during his mandate gang leaders changed their residences to Tijuana, Ciudad Juárez, Sonora, and Jalisco; and, while governor, he asked the radio stations and TV owners not to broadcast any drug traffickers' *corridos* (popular songs).[40] Mexican officials, among them the attorney general and the minister of foreign affairs, denied any investigation on the matter and the latter asked the Department of State for a diplomatic note.[41] The note came, but was never shown to the press, and was interpreted by Mexican officials as "incredible" and "useless."[42] James Rubin, the spokesman of the Department of State, confirmed the answer to the request, said he did not have any comment, and added that the U.S. government would continue to work normally with the Mexican minister.[43]

Governors from Sonora, Morelos, Puebla, Yucatán, and Campeche have also been mentioned in relation to drug trafficking.[44] Some of them (Sonora, Quintana Roo, and Morelos) have been under investigation since 1997. At the time, the attorney general denied any wrongdoing.[45] However, the general assumption is that the drug business cannot prosper without official protection from the top political levels in those regions where the drug bosses have decided to live, or where important transit and stocking zones have been established. Manuel Bartlett's home state is a case in point. He was governor and the minister of government when DEA agent Enrique Camarena was kidnapped and killed. He was a precandidate for the 2000 presidential elections, has been included on DEA's black list, and has been mentioned by protected witnesses in the Camarena affair.

During Salinas's presidency, Jorge Carrillo Olea headed the anti-drug apparatus (1991–1993) until his election as governor of the state of Morelos. Subsequently, Sinaloan drug lord Amado Carrillo established residence in the state and started operations from there. A Mexican military intelligence report mentioned Governor Carrillo, a military man himself, and his brother as protectors of drug trafficker. In 1997, the *New York Times* mentioned Governor Carrillo and Governor Beltrones from Sonora as drug lord protectors.[46] Both governors demanded a correction from the newspaper.

The governor of the state of Quintana Roo (1993–1999), Mario Villanueva, has been mentioned by U.S. sources as connected with drug trafficking since 1997. Subsequently, the U.S. consul in Cancún had to leave the country after receiving death threats by the local authorities. In November 1998, the *New York Times* reported on Villanueva and the investigation by PGR officials for drug trafficking. As a result of the federal investigations, some hotels were confiscated, and a private security service at Cancún airport was closed because of its links to drug-trafficking groups. A secret report, delivered in June 1997 to the *New York Times* by a political opponent of the governor, informed that approximately 4 tons of cocaine a week were being smuggled through the state of Quintana Roo.[47] The report mentioned Villanueva as implicated with the Juárez organization, together with a number of local authorities, police commanders, a chemist from the local PGR bureau, and a businessman from Chetumal who delivered the bribes to the governor. Villanueva disappeared a few days before the end of his administration and was a fugitive of justice. He has since been captured and incarcerated, and is fighting his extradition to the United States.

From the beginning to the end of the twentieth century, from the northern to the southern border of Mexico, from the governors to the president's family, what remains is the profound impression of an integration and articulation of interests between the political sector and drug trafficking, an impression supported by documentation from U.S. and Mexican government sources themselves. Yet, in the history of the relationship between drug trafficking and politics in Mexico, it is not always easy to establish the precise course of events and to separate facts from fiction. These activities have been going on for prolonged periods of time and are often unpunished by law enforcement. This impunity is not only due to failures of the Mexican justice system but also has to be attributed to the frequent use of the raison d'etat by the U.S. and Mexican governments alike.

Recent Developments

In the presidential elections of July 2000, the Mexican voters decided to put an end to the rule of the oldest state party in the world. A new period began in the relationship between the drug industry and the political sector. The new president, Vicente Fox, and his transition team on security and justice proposed the following measures in the area of drug control: first, to regard drug trafficking as a matter of public order rather than one of national security; second, to withdraw the army from the fight against drug trafficking; third, to abolish the PGR and to replace it by the Office of the Attorney General of the Nation and the Office of the Secretary for Security and Services to Justice; and fourth, to concentrate the police and the intelligence services in the latter office, removing control over the police corporations from the Department of the Interior.[48]

One of the main representatives of the transition team of President Vicente Fox in matters of security and justice was the former senator for Chihuahua, Francisco Molina, who was state attorney during the administration of Francisco Barrio (PAN). He headed the now defunct National Institute to Combat Drugs (INCD) in 1996, where he was replaced the following year by a military man (Jesús Gutiérrez Rebollo) as part of a more general change of policy that involved the appointment of military personnel to key executive and operational positions in the institutions engaged in anti-drug activities. Molina commented on this change of policy, describing it as a grave mistake. He emphasized the problems that had arisen within the INCD with the military because of their secretiveness, reluctance to share information, status aparte in legal matters, and claim to absolute control over crop eradication. He concluded: "The army took by assault the PGR, the INCD, CENDRO, 23 of the 35 national airports, and all the PGR delegations on the northern border."[49] Three years later, the senator summed up the result: "Today there are some 150 military officers who are under indictment and betrayed the confidence of their superiors by becoming connected with criminal organizations."[50]

The decision by the transition team to withdraw the army from the area of drug control has been turned back under pressure from the U.S. government, through its representative, drug czar Barry McCaffrey.[51] While underlining the autonomy of the Mexican government in these matters, he nonetheless emphasized the need for armed forces to become involved in the War on Drugs and expressed his doubts about the effectiveness of the reforms in the area of security and justice as proposed by the new government.[52] Within days, the proposed policy change had been annulled, clearly showing the limits of the maneuvering room of the Mexican government opposite the U.S. government in areas of drug control.[53]

President Fox later appointed a military man, General Rafael Macedo de la Concha, ex-attorney general of military justice, as head of the PGR. Upon taking office, the general declared himself against militarization of the PGR.[54] The most important posts would go to civilians. However, two months later, the PGR staff already contained fourteen generals.[55] In addition, lieutenant colonels, colonels, captains, and admirals were appointed to other posts. Despite denial by the president's office,[56] it is obvious that the PGR, in areas that have to do with the anti-drug campaign and the security apparatus involved, has come under increasing military control.[57]

In recent years, the armed forces have played an essential role in capturing important drug traffickers (Benjamín Arellano, "El Metro," Albino Quintero Meraz, "La Rana," "El June," for example) and their role with regard to civil society appears to have changed qualitatively. In fact, the civil authority (PGR) seems now to be under the command of the military security apparatus (SEDENA), although—legally—this should be the other way around. Beginning in 1947, the military is supposed to be subordinated to the PGR in matters concerning drug control. The separation between General Rafael Macedo de la Concha's responsibilities as a military officer and those that correspond to his position as attorney general has remained undefined. These developments have far-reaching consequences for the relationships between the presidency, the armed forces, and civil society as laid down in articles 89 and 129 of the Constitution.

Recent captures of important traffickers have been announced in the precincts of the SEDENA, not in those of the PGR. These are not mere symbolic acts: they show who really commands the drug-control policy. No date has been set for the return to the barracks of the military employed in operative posts in anti-drug activities, and those involved in police work in other security institutions. Internal vigilance about possible corruption and human rights violations in relation to the War on Drugs has been left in the hands of the armed forces authorities. The question remains, which institution will supervise the activities of the armed forces and, in case of violations of the law, will have the power to hold them accountable? The tradition of closeness and secrecy among the armed forces does not create much confidence. Handing back to civilians the control of the anti-drug policy and security matters does not seem to be on the political agenda, especially not after the September 11, 2001, terrorist attacks in the United States.

The new government will have to ensure the institutionalism of the armed forces and of the new military-dominated police structure. This will be all the more essential since the demand for drugs is not on the decline, and a change in the strategy of militarization of the War on Drugs by the U.S. government is not to be expected. Tensions between the Mexican government and the United States over drugs will surely continue since the Mexican army does not have a magic capability to control demand within its northern neighbor. Increasing involvement of the armed forces runs the risk of generating increasing levels of corruption among their ranks. In a nightmare scenario, this involvement may even serve as a stepping stone toward the joining of powerful interests connected with drug trafficking and a shift of the center of gravity of such interests from the old political structure to the armed forces and to other security institutions in which the military serve. An upward spiral of violence is to be expected in any case since the very logic of the repressive anti-drug policy inspired by the United States is in itself a dead-end street and will produce endless war. These developments have created a paradox: at the time when there are important changes toward the democratization of Mexican society, the presence of the military in the security apparatus has been increasing to previously unknown levels, suggesting a war-time scenario instead of one of advancing civilization.

Notes

1. Luis Astorga, *El Siglo de las Drogas* (Mexico City: Espasa-Calpe Mexicana, 1996), 15–28.

2. Ricardo Pérez Montfort, Alberto del Castillo, y Pablo Piccato, eds., *Hábitos, Normal y Escándala: Prensa, Criminalidad, y Drogas Durante el Porfiriato Tardio* (Mexico City: Ciesas-Plaza y Valdés, 1997), 152–54.

3. General Records of the Department of State, Record Group 59, 812.114 Narcotics 12–22, National Archives at College Park, Md.; see also Joseph Richard Werne, "Esteban Cantú y la Soberania Mexicana en Baja California," *Historia Mexicana* 30, no. 117 (July-September 1980), 1–32.

4. *Diario Oficial,* March 15, 1920; *La Farmacia,* June 1926.

5. Confidential memorandum, Department of Public Health, Mexico, DF., June 16, 1931, in Social Security Historical Archive (AHSS), Public Health Fund (FSP), Legal Service Section (SSJ), Box 28, File 6; Report of Juan Requena to the Public Health Department Chief, Mexico, DF., July 20, 1931, in AHSS, FSP, Box 28, File 6.

6. Report of Dr. Bernardo Bátiz B., Sanitary Delegate in Baja California, to Dr. Demetrio López, Chemistry and Pharmacy Service Chief, Department of Health, Mexicali, B.C., August 19, 1931, in AHSS, FSP, SSJ, Box 28, File 8.

7. Report of Juan N. Requena; *El Universal Gráfico,* December 16, 1937; *La Prensa,* May 9, 1936.

8. *El Universal Gráfico,* December 16, 1937.

9. General Records of the Department of State, "Report of the Assistant Military Attaché on the National Security Police of Mexico" (Confidential no. 4543), Embassy of the United States of America, Mexico City, September 4, 1947, Record Group 59, 812.105/9–447, National Archives at College Park, Md.

10. *Excélsior,* November, 14, 17, 19, 22, 23, and 25, 1947; *El Universal,* November 10–18, 1947.

11. Oral communication, Culiacán, Sinaloa, June 1998.

12. Neri Córdova, ed., *Una Vida en la Vida Sinaloense: Memorias de Manuel Lazcano Ochoa* (Los Mochis Sinaloa: Talleres Gráficos de la Universidad de Occidente, 1992), 113.

13. Roderic Al Camp, *Mexican Political Biographies, 1935–1975* (Tucson: University of Arizona Press, 1976), 195; *La Voz de Sinaloa,* March 31, 1951.

14. See Córdova, *Una Vida en la Vida Sinaloense,* 198–247.

15. *La Palabra,* April 19, 1956.

16. DFS, Exp. 17–0–78, H.155, L. 3, September 19, 1978, AGN. Thanks to Alejandra Xanic von Bertrab for giving me the transcript of this document.

17. Cf. Bruce Michel Bagley, "After San Antonio," in Bruce M. Bagley, William O. Walker III, eds., *Drug Trafficking in the Americas* (Miami: North-South Center Press, University of Miami, 1996), 61.

18. Timothy J. Dunn, *The Militarization of the U.S.-Mexico Border, 1978–1992: Low Intensity Conflict Comes Home* (Austin: Center for Mexican-American Studies, University of Texas at Austin, 1996), 25.

19. Bagley, "After San Antonio," 64.

20. Carlos Fazio, *El Tercer Vinculo: De la Teoria del Caos a la Teoria de la Militarización* (Mexico City: Joaquin Mortiz, 1996), 178–89.

21. CIA, "Operation Condor I: Mexican Military's Anti-Narcotics Campaign," in *Latin America: Regional and Political Analysis* (Washington, D.C.: Central Intelligence Agency, March 17, 1977).

22. *Proceso,* November 24, 1996.

23. *La Jornada,* February 19, 1997.

24. *El Financiero,* July 4, 1999.

25. *La Jornada,* January 22, 1999; *Miami Herald,* January 23, 1999.

26. *Proceso,* July 18, 1999.

27. *El Universal,* January, 21, 1999.

28. *Excelsior,* November 7, 1998, July 23, 1999; *El Financiero,* March 26, 1999.

29. The *New York Times,* September 17, 1999.

30. Dolia Estevez, "La Cuestión de las Drogas," *El Financiero,* May 31, 1999.

31. Tim Golden, "Mexico Clears a Top Official but Can't Convince the United States," *New York Times,* June 2, 1999.

32. *La Jornada,* June 4, 1999.

33. *El Universal,* July 10, 1999.

34. *La Jornada,* June 18–19, 1999; *Proceso,* June 20, 1999.

35. *Reforma,* June 24, 1999; *El Universal,* June 24, 1999; *La Jornada,* June 24, 1999.

36. *Procesa,* November 8, 1998.

37. *La Jornada,* September 20, 1997.

38. *La Jornada,* November 6, 1998; *Proceso,* November 8, 1998.

39. *Washington Post,* November 7, 1998.

40. *El Debate,* November 7, 1998.

41. *La Jornada,* November 7, 1998.

42. *La Jornada,* November 12, 1998.

43. *El Universal,* November 12, 1998.

44. *Proceso,* November 8, 1998.

45. *El Universal,* September 2, 1997.

46. *Proceso,* November 8,1998.

47. *El Universal,* November 26, 1999.

48. See: Jorge Alejandro Medellín, "El Narco es Sólo un Problema Policiaco," *El*

Universal, July 25, 2000; Daniel Lizárraga, "Buscan Unifícar Policía y Limpiarla de Corruptos," *Reforma,* July 25, 2000; Pablo César Carrillo, "Detallan Propuesta Foxista en Seguridad," *Reforma,* July 31, 2000; Reuters, "Fox to Pull Mexican Military Out of Drug Fight," July 31, 2000; Associated Press, "Fox Wants to Overhaul Mexico's Cops," July 31, 2000; Mayra Nidia Aguirre, "Planea Fox un FBI y Desmilitarizar Policía," *El Universal,* August 1, 2000; Jesús Aranda, "Fox, Por Desmilitarizar los Cuerpos Policiacos, Dicen Reyes y Molina," *La Jornada,* August 1, 2000.

49. See Alejandro Gutiérrez, "Francisco Molina, Exdirector del INCD, Diagnóstico: El Estado Mexicano, Contaminado por el Narcotráfico; Militares Corruptos Podrían Controlar los Cárteles," *Proceso,* August 3, 1997.

50. See Ricardo Ravelo, "El Narcotráfico, Invencible. En la PGR, los Enemigos en Casa," *Proceso,* May 14, 2000. On the army, General Luis Garfias Magaña (retired), who is affiliated with the Democratic Revolutionary Party (PRD) wrote: "Will the armed forces (both the army and the air force) continue to perform functions that are alien to their constitutional assignments in such matters as drug trafficking and public security? . . . Today the army is an institution that has lost prestige. There are almost a dozen generals in prison for a variety of offenses, particularly drug trafficking, and as many again are under suspicion but will never be punished since they are covered by the impunity afforded by power" (Luis Garfías Magaña, "¿Qué Pasará con la Secretaría de la Defensa Nacional?," *La Jornada,* August 23, 2000).

51. Abel Barajas, "Piden Continuidad en Próximos Gobiernos," *Reforma,* August 8, 2000.

52. Georgina Saldierna, Carolina Gómez, and Ciro Perez, "McCaffrey Apoya el Pedido del Presidente Electo," *La Jornada,* August 8, 2000.

53. Daniel Lizarraga, "Duda McCaffrey de Algunas Reformas," *Reforma,* August 8, 2000.

54. Esperanza Barajas and Abel Barajas, "Descarta Macedo Militarizar a la PGR," *Reforma,* December 10, 2000.

55. Abel Barajas, "Militariza la PGR Fiscalía Antinarco: Controlan Officiales Radares, Retenes, y Aeronaves," *Reforma,* February 7, 2001; Abel Barajas, "Llegan Más Militares a PGR: Suman 14 Generals los Adscritos a la Dependencia," *Reforma,* February 8, 2001.

56. Mayolo López, "Niega Presidencia Militarización en PGR," *Reforma,* February 7, 2001.

57. Luis Alegre and Abel Barajas, "Monopolizan Militares el Combate Antinarco," *Reforma,* March 18, 2001.

6

The Political Economy of Drugs in the Caribbean

Problems without Passports

Ivelaw L. Griffith

> Globalization offers the human race unprecedented opportunities. Unfortunately,
> it also enables many antisocial activities to become "problems without passports."
> Among these are drug abuse which beings misery to millions of families around the
> world every year, and drug trafficking which cynically promotes and exploits that
> misery for commercial gain.
>
> **Kofi A. Annan,** *World Drug Report 2000*

> Where political agendas used to consist of issues that governments could cope with
> on their own or through interstate bargaining, now these conventional issues are
> being joined by challenges that by their very nature do not fall exclusively within the
> jurisdiction of states and have rendered the Frontier increasingly porous. Six current
> challenges are illustrative: environmental pollution, currency crises, crime and the drug
> trade, terrorism, AIDS, and the flow of refugees. Since these challenges are fueled by
> shrinking social and geographic distances, such problems can appropriately be called
> "interdependence" issues. Given their diffuse, boundary-crossing structure, these types
> of issues are spawning a whole range of transnational associations that are further-
> ing the density of the multi-centric world and, as a result, are likely to serve as
> additional challenges to state authority.
>
> **James N. Rosenau,** *Along the Domestic-Foreign Frontier:*
> *Exploring Governance in a Turbulent World*

In differing ways, international statesman Kofi Annan and distinguished
political scientist Jim Rosenau capture most of the 3–M tripartite character
of the phenomenon of illegal drugs: it is multi-dimensional, multi-level, and
multi-actor. First, whether viewed in global, regional, or national terms, the
drug phenomenon is not a one-dimensional matter; it is not simply about
producing illegal drugs or trafficking them. Moreover, the multi-dimensionality exists in the problem element of the phenomenon, its consequences, and
in measures to deal with it. Production, trafficking, consumption-abuse, and
money laundering are among main problem elements; consequences include
corruption, economic distortion, arms trafficking, and crime; responses in-

clude eradication, rehabilitation, interdiction, chemical controls, crop substitution, and education.

Beyond multi-dimensionality, the phenomenon manifests itself at the national, subregional, regional, and international systemic levels, and is amenable to analysis at all levels, including cross-level assessments. This multidimensionality and multi-level manifestation combine partly to explain the phenomenon's interdependent character and truly global scope. Hence, no national boundary is beyond its reach; no region of the world escapes its impact.

These aspects of the drug phenomenon help to account for the mix of actors involved. Although looking at state actors is necessary, it is not sufficient, as the range of critical actors extends beyond them to include a variety of non-state actors, notably narco-cartels, drug kingpins, multinational corporations, and international nongovernmental organizations— some of which have more actual or mobilizable power than some states, which dramatizes the problems of coping capacity of some states.

This chapter addresses the Caribbean region, where problems of coping capacity are accentuated largely because of the scope of the challenges faced and the combined realities of Caribbean states being both small in terms of national power and weak in terms of institutional capacity for political and economic governance. My analysis does not deal with all the dimensions of drugs in the Caribbean. It also will not probe all the political economy aspects of the region's drug challenge, although it has been guided by a holistic approach to the issue. This approach underlines the importance of appreciating at least three things: the direct and indirect linkages between and among the various dimensions of the issue; how the pursuit of strategies to cope with them have direct and indirect implications for economic governance, political governance, and the nexus between the two; and the value of locating a regional level of analysis within a broader analytic discourse.

Of Society, but Not Just Sociological

In advocating the holistic approach to the response to the drugs issue and, by implication, to its content and consequences, one Caribbean scholar-statesman recently observed: "A drug community is a total society. It is not just a sociological phenomenon. It is [also] an economic phenomenon. But more than this too, it is a society that has carved out its own rules, including how it dispenses justice."[1]

This thinking resonates with my general approach. Thus, mine is the view that one is obliged to go beyond the confines of sociological perimeters even in examining the drug situation within a single country. Why? The answer is simple: while the drug phenomenon is "of society" it is not simply sociological. Adopting this contextual approach is even more important where the assessment seeks to address the interface between politics and economics.

Scholars and statesmen justifiably can condemn the drug phenomenon's precipitation or aggravation of crime, corruption, moral degradation, and other things that negatively affect sociopolitical intercourse. But they have to temper any inclination to level wholesale condemnation when it comes to the socioeconomic aspect, as they are faced with having to recognize—if not acknowledge—that drugs do have positive-sum aspects, including income generation, employment creation, and resource distribution, no matter how skewed.

Moreover, this mixed bag complicates matters when one turns to issues of global economic interdependence. As the first *World Drug Report* states: "The illicit drug phenomenon cannot be viewed outside the context of contemporary economic, social, and political development. Changes in the world political economy and advances in technology over the past three decades have had a significant impact on the scope and nature of the illicit drug problem. It is now recognized that rapid growth in the trade of goods and services has resulted in a more interdependent world. Yet, despite the positive implications which the increase in world trade has for prosperity and efficiency, sustained growth in international trade can complicate efforts to control the illicit problem."[2]

A harsh political economy reality of the phenomenon is that the drug market is fundamentally no different than any other commodity trade since it is driven by the basic economic forces of demand and supply. Where it does differ significantly, however, is in its legal status, which influences the market dynamics involved. Price, for example, is affected significantly. Paul Stares explains that supply is artificially constricted by the rules affecting which drugs can be legally produced, medically prescribed, and sold commercially, and by the many law enforcement barriers against illicit manufacturers and distributors.[3] Price and other demand-supply dynamics aside, perhaps the other single most important political economy concern of policy makers is about "cost." However, while critical, cost estimates are often imprecise partly because of the lack of empirical data, partly because the costs involved are not all economic costs, but include social costs not subject to easy economic estimation, and partly because there are both private and public costs involved. According to the United Nations experts, analysts have bypassed some of the cost estimation challenges by applying the concept of opportunity cost—calculating the benefits that would be derived from the best alternative use of a particular resource—which is based on the assumption that resources always have alternative uses.[4]

Understandably, irrespective of whether one looks at the political economy of drugs globally or in one region, much more than price and costs are involved. This much will become clear in relation to the Caribbean, to which we turn attention next.

The Caribbean Scenario

The Caribbean lies at what Cuban scholar and nationalist Jóse Martí once called "the Vortex of the Americas"; it is a bridge or front between North and South America. European actors recognized the strategic importance of this vortex soon after the 1492 encounter between Europe and the Americas.

This strategic importance has persisted over the centuries, and it was dramatized in geopolitical terms during the Cold War. However, the region's strategic value lies not only in its geopolitical significance as viewed by state actors engaged in conflict and cooperation. Over recent decades the region also has been viewed as strategic by non-state drug actors, also with conflict and cooperation in mind, not in terms of geo-politics, but geo-narcotics.

The concept of geo-narcotics captures the dynamics of three factors besides drugs: geography, power, and politics. It posits, first, that the narcotics phenomenon is multi-dimensional, with four main problem areas (drug production, consumption-abuse, trafficking, and money laundering); second, that these give rise to actual and potential threats to the security of states around the world; and third, that the drug operations and the activities they spawn precipitate both conflict and cooperation among various state and non-state actors in the international system.

Geography is a factor because of the global dispersion of drug operations and because certain physical, social, and political geography features of many countries facilitate drug operations. Power involves the ability of individuals and groups to secure compliant action. In the drug world, this power is both state and non-state in origin, and in some cases, non-state sources command relatively more power than states. Politics revolve around resource allocation in terms of the ability of power brokers to determine who gets what, how, and when. Since power in this milieu is not only state power, resource allocation is correspondingly not exclusively a function of state power-holders. Moreover, politics become perverted and and grow ever more perverted in the presence of drug operations.

The geo-narcotics milieu involves a variety of state and non-state actors, which differ in how they affect and are affected by the various problems and their countermeasures. Drug operations generate two basic kinds of interactions: cooperation and conflict. These are bilateral and multilateral, and do not all involve force. Some involve nonmilitary pressures, such as economic and political sanctions by the United States against countries that it considers not proactive enough in fighting drugs. Some actors engage simultaneously in both cooperation and conflict. The relationships between the United States and Colombia and Mexico over the last decade reveal this dual approach.

The geo-narcotics approach does not view the War on Drugs purely as a military matter. Hence, the application of military countermeasures alone is considered impractical. Moreover, international countermeasures are necessary, especially since all states—even rich and powerful ones—face resource constraints. However, collaboration among states may result in conflict over sovereignty and perception of the nature and severity of threats and, therefore, appropriate responses.[5]

The geo-narcotics relationship between the Caribbean and the rest of the world, especially North America, perhaps, is best known in relation to trafficking. However, the relationship entails more than the movement of drugs from and through the region; involved also are drug production, drug consumption and abuse, money laundering, organized crime, corruption, arms trafficking, and sovereignty conflicts, among other things. The following vignettes provide some relevant evidence.

- Operation Dinero, an international money-laundering sting operation conducted out of tiny Anguilla from January 1992 to December 1994, led to the seizure of 9 tons of cocaine and 90 million U.S. dollars worth of assets, including expensive paintings, Pablo Picasso's *Head of a Beggar* among them.
- Cocaine seizures in 1993 in just five Caribbean countries—the Bahamas, Belize, the Dominican Republic, Haiti, and Jamaica—totaled about 3,300 kilos. Seizures during 2000 for those same five countries amounted to almost 5,900 kilos, close to a 78 percent increase over the 1993 figure.
- In February 1997 the Dutch envoy in Suriname told Suriname's foreign minister that 195 couriers from Suriname had been arrested during 1996 at the Schiphol international airport, compared with 51 in 1995. Indeed, in 1999 Holland sentenced Desi Bouterse, former Suriname leader and later adviser to President Jules Wijdenbosch, following conviction on trafficking and other offenses.
- Between 1993 and 1998 more than 9,000 deportees were returned to Jamaica, most of them for drug-related crimes committed in the United States, Canada, and the United Kingdom. In 1993 the number was 923; in 1997 it was 1,647, with 1,213 being from the United States. In 1998, the figure was 2,161, with close to 1,500 coming from the United States.
- In a series of raids across Puerto Rico on December 17, 1997, the police and National Guard arrested 1,039 people and confiscated 1,356 bags of cocaine, 133 bags of heroin, 58 guns, 60 cars and vans, and 205,582 U.S. dollars.
- From December 7–15, 1998, Regional Security System (RSS) troops, U.S. Marines, and U.S. Drug Enforcement Administration

(DEA) officers joined the St. Vincent and the Grenadines Special Service Unit in conducting Operation Weedeater. They destroyed 1,162,496 marijuana plants in 314 marijuana fields, 1,400 pounds of cured marijuana, and 151 huts used to cure marijuana. Also, they seized weapons and ammunition.

• Operation Columbus, a counter-narcotics operation involving the United States and fifteen Caribbean Basin countries from September 29 to October 10, 1999, resulted in the seizure of 2,892 kilos of cocaine and 897 kilos of marijuana and the arrest of ninety-nine people in Trinidad and Tobago alone.

• Between November 24, 1999, and June 6, 2000, twelve cargo freighters were seized in Miami on arrival from one Caribbean location—Haiti—with a combined total of more than 6,000 pounds of cocaine in their freight.

• October 2000 saw the unfolding of a serious drug-related drama in Jamaica, involving (a) high-level police corruption, (b) illegal wire tapping of high government officials, including the prime minister, and (c) the attempted assassination of the head of the National Firearms and Drug Intelligence Center.

• On November 14, 2000, Jamaican police seized 782 kilos of cocaine worth 195 million Jamaican dollars (about 5 million U.S. dollars) in Manchester, in Southern Jamaica, and in early December 2000 police in the Dominican Republic seized 519 kilos of cocaine in Santo Domingo, the capital.

• On March 10, 2001, Cuban authorities arrested two Nigerians in Havana as they tried to smuggle 3 kilos of cocaine from Nicaragua, through Cuba, to France. Later that month (March 28) police in Grenada arrested one Kittian and one British citizen as they tried to smuggle 6 kilos of cocaine to Britain.

• Two hundred and twenty-two pounds of cocaine, worth 1.8 million U.S. dollars, were seized on April 21, 2001, on arrival in Miami from Curaçao aboard an ALM-Antillian Airlines flight.

• The United States Coast Guard seized a Belize flagged fishing vessel with 12 tons of cocaine off the eastern Pacific Ocean, 1,500 miles south of San Diego, California on May 3, 2001.[6]

A strict economic cost-benefit analysis of drugs in the Caribbean would require, at the very least, measurement of the opportunity costs of the factors of production used in the drug industry, and the income received by producers and traffickers, by money launderers, and by other economic activities that derive from narcotics-industry operations. For a variety of understandable methodological and data-related reasons, this is infeasible, and not only for the Caribbean.

However, it is useful to examine a few of the positive-sum and negative-sum aspects involved. This permits an appreciation of at least three things: first, some of the economic "positives" and negatives of drugs; second, some of the linkages between political governance and economic management; and third, some of the reasons why, consequently, policy management of drugs is intractable.

This positive-sum-negative-sum analysis is offered with full consciousness that the drug phenomenon also carries indirect economic costs and social costs not amenable to easy economic estimation. And although by itself such an assessment should reveal some of the political economy connections of the Caribbean drug business, the connections are better appreciated if examined against the backdrop of an economic snapshot of the region.

Economic Snapshot of the Caribbean

The Caribbean has some important natural resources, including oil, bauxite, gold, diamonds, and nickel. However, very few countries in the region have these resources. For instance, only Trinidad and Tobago, and Barbados, Cuba, and Suriname, to a much lesser extent, have oil industries, although exploration is underway in Guyana, and there are refining and transshipment operations in many countries. Bauxite is produced only in the Dominican Republic, Guyana, Jamaica, and Suriname. Diamonds are mined only in Guyana, and only Cuba, the Dominican Republic, Guyana, and Suriname produce gold. As for nickel, it is found only in Cuba and the Dominican Republic. This limited mineral resource availability partly explains why the region's gross domestic product (GDP) revolves around a narrow economic base: (a) agriculture—mainly sugar and bananas; (b) mining and manufacturing—notably bauxite, oil, nickel, gold, and apparel; and (c) services.

Off-shore financing and tourism are the two most critical industries in the service sector. The former has long been important to Aruba, the Bahamas, Curaçao, and to most of the British dependencies in the region, and it is becoming increasingly so to Antigua and Barbuda, Barbados, and Belize. But more important than this industry, both to these countries and the region as a whole, is tourism. Dennis Gayle has explained that tourism is the only industry in the Caribbean Basin that has grown progressively since 1973, generating some 96 billion U.S. dollars in gross expenditure annually. Indeed, "tourism generates more foreign exchange and tax revenues per dollar of investment than any other Industry."[7] The World Bank also reports that tourism is the largest export earner for the region, and one country—Cuba—where tourism had been playing second place to other economic sectors, notably agriculture, reported in 1997 that tourism had surpassed sugar as the single largest foreign exchange earner.[8]

Caribbean countries also are saddled with an economic albatross in the form of huge foreign debts, as Table 6.1 indicates. This albatross is not merely the size of the debt, but also its servicing, although various forms of debt relief have been granted to Haiti, Jamaica, Guyana, and other countries. Guyana provides the most dramatic case, with virtually everything it produces going toward debt servicing. Antigua and Barbuda, Jamaica, and St. Vincent and the Grenadines all devote more than 50 percent of their GDP to debt servicing, while Belize, Dominica, Grenada, St. Kitts and Nevis, and Trinidad and Tobago are in the more than 30 percent range.

At the same time, international economic developments have been affecting the availability of multilateral financing. As one report explains, for instance: "Multilateral non-concessional financing trends in the last two years have been driven by the international crisis, expanding considerably in 1998, when rescue packages were extended to various countries, and retrenching in 1999 when the crisis subsided. Averaging six billion U.S. dollars in 1990–1995, these net flows fell to four billion U.S. dollars in 1996 before rising to 13.4 billion U.S. dollars in 1997 and to 18.8 billion U.S. dollars in 1998. They fell back to 12.7 billion U.S. dollars in 1999."[9]

Compared with other parts of the developing world, the Caribbean has a

Table 6.1. Economic and Social Indicators of Caribbean Countries (United States Dollars in Millions; 1998 Unless Otherwise Noted)

Part A

Indicator	Antigua & Barbuda	Bahamas	Barbados	Belize	Dominica	Dominican Republic	Grenada
Population (thousands)	67	298	267	242	74	8,404	97
GNP per capita	8,450	12,863	7,890	2,660	3,150	1,770	3,250
GDP (1990 $)	518	3,507	1,957	567	201	11,714	287
1999	3.2	5.8	2.9	6.2	0.0	8.3	8.2
1998	3.9	3.0	4.8	1.5	3.5	7.3	4.8
1997	5.6	3.3	2.9	3.2	2.0	8.2	3.6
GPI % change	1.6	1.3	-1.3	-0.9	1.0	4.5	4.8
Pop. in poverty (%)	12	5	8	33	28	21	31
Unempl. rate (%)	7.0	15.0	16.4	11.1	10.0	30.0	16.0
Life expectancy years	75	74	76	75	76	71	72
Infant mortality (per 000 live births)	17	17	14	28	15	40	14
Literacy (% adult pop.)	89	95	97	93	94	83	96
Public sector overall bal. (% GDP)	-4.8	-2.3	-0.7	-2.0	1.5	-1.3	-3.3
External public debt (% GDP)	65.9	8.5	14.4	38.2	32.7	22.1	44.5
Debt service (% XGNFS)	95.1	15.3	45.4	88.1	80.0	57.6	85.7

Part B

Indicator	Guyana	Haiti	Jamaica	St. Kitts & Nevis	St. Lucia	St. Vincent & Grenadines	Surinam	Trinidad & Tobago
Population (thousands)	867	7,769	2,598	41	161	114	415	1,326
GNP per capita	780	410	1,740	6,190	3,660	2,560	1,660	4,520
GDP (1990 $)	642	2,332	4,277	219	516	251	2,453	6,276
1999	1.8	2.2	0.4	2 .0	3 .1	4.0	-1.0	4.2
1998	-1.5	3.1	-0.7	1.6	2.9	5.2	3.9	4.1
1997	6.2	1.4	-2.4	7.1	2.1	3.7	10.1	3.2
GPI % change	4.6	10.6	8.6	3.6	2.8	2.1	19	5.6
Pop. in poverty (%)	43	65	16	15	25	38	39	21
Unempl. rate (%)	11.0	—	16.2	12.0	16.0	20.0	16.0	16.0
Life expectancy years	64	54	75	72	70	73	70	73
Infant mortality (per 000 live births)	57	71	21	21	17	22	28	16
Literacy (% adult pop.)	98	48	86	90	82	82	93	93
Public sector overall bal. (% GDP)	-3.8	-1.3	-8.4	-6.3	-1.6	-2.1	-11.1	-2.5
External public debt (% GDP)	191.8	28.9	50.9	39.3	27.0	52.6	27.0	39.1
Debt service (% XGNFS)	237.6	7.3	119.4	41.0	37.4	132.3	32.1	76.5

Note: GNP—Gross National Product 1999; GDP—Gross Domestic Product; CPI—Consumer Price Index; XGNFS—Exports of Goods and Nonfactor Services.

Source: Caribbean Economic Overview 2000 (Washington, D.C.: Caribbean Group for Cooperation in Economic Development, World Bank, 2.

fairly good profile in areas of life expectancy, potable water supply, education, and GDP growth. One assessment notes, for example: "Most Caribbean countries have made substantial progress on macroeconomic stability in the 1990s. Inflation rates in 1994 and 1995 were below 20 percent annually in all countries except Jamaica and Suriname. . . . Exports as a share of GDP have increased in the last decade."[10] Yet the achievements do not mask a certain reality. In this respect, an observation by a Trinidadian economist in 1995 still holds true in 2001: the region is in crisis; poverty is rising in several states; Caribbean economies remain fragile and vulnerable.[11]

Moreover, an earlier characterization of the region's economic vulnerability is still accurate: the vulnerability is not only functional, but also structural, in that economies suffer from heavy reliance on foreign trade, limited production and export diversification, low savings, heavy dependence on foreign capital, and a dearth of economic and management skills, among other things.[12] Moreover, much of this vulnerability has been highlighted recently as some countries experienced setbacks in the garment and tourism industries and as others faced a threat to their banana market guarantees.[13]

Migration itself affects the economic landscape. Not only are many Caribbean migration rates high, but a significant proportion of those who migrate are skilled workers or managerial elites. In her 1997 study Judy Baker revealed, "In the Dominican Republic, Guyana, and Jamaica, about half of the skilled people graduating from local institutions emigrated between 1980 and 1986. Of emigrants from St. Lucia, and Guyana, 47 and 76 percent, respectively, had secondary education or higher."[14]

Although individuals who emigrate vacate jobs in labor markets with generally high employment rates, these positions are usually for highly skilled workers and are difficult to fill. This drain on skills has likely reduced the pace of economic growth and, thus, slowed the process of overall job creation and affected the long-run development potential in the region.[15] Aaron Segal noted that migration will continue to be a mostly positive factor for receiving countries, adding to their music, arts, and human (and economic) resources the talents of several million productive persons and their offspring.[16] Segal's remark is true, but it provides no consolation for sending countries.

All of these circumstances make credible the statement by one analyst for the Economic Commission for Latin America and the Caribbean that people in Cuba, the Dominican Republic, Haiti, Jamaica, Suriname (and I would add Guyana)—the biggest Caribbean countries—have become relatively poorer over the last decade.[17] Indeed, according to one report, "Approximately 38 percent of the total population in the Caribbean or more than seven million people can be classified as poor. . . . The incidence of poverty is highest in Belize, Dominica, Guyana, Haiti, Jamaica, and Suriname. . . . Poverty levels are lowest in Antigua-Barbuda, the Bahamas, Barbados, and St. Kitts-Nevis."[18] The decline in the countries concerned also has been affected by reduced government services, done to cope with budgetary difficulties generally, but also for debt servicing. Currency depreciation in some places has also aggravated the situation, affecting prices, purchasing power, savings, and investment. Reduced production and exports, economic mismanagement, and adverse global economic and financial conditions are also relevant factors. The drama of drugs also features prominently, and some of the connections have been captured poignantly.

The production, consumption, and trafficking of drugs (as well as drug money laundering) have increasingly affected most aspects of Caribbean society. This is turn has a debilitating effect on structural adjustment and development. First, there are adverse effects on economic activity. A country that develops a reputation as one that is unable or unwilling to confront its drug problem can find a chilling effect on efforts to attract new investment and promote tourism. Faced with the added costs of extra security for their shipments and potential embarrassment if their cargoes are used for drug-smuggling purposes, many multinational companies may simply opt to do business in countries that are less prone to narcotics transhipment. The net effect is a diversion in investment, a decline in export revenues, and a loss of legitimate jobs.[19]

The circumstances described above have led to several developments. For one thing, they have increased the importance of foreign remittances, both cash and in-kind, and both for the survival of individual families and the buoyancy of economies. According to Jamaica's deputy prime minister and minister of foreign trade, Seymour Mullings, the 2.5 million Jamaicans living in New York, Miami, Hartford, Washington, D.C., Toronto, London, and Philadelphia remitted 600 million U.S. dollars to Jamaica during 1994.[20] The September 27–October 2, 1996, edition of the *Santo Domingo News* reported that remittances to the Dominican Republic by Dominicans living abroad reach 1.2 billion U.S. dollars per year, the second largest source of foreign exchange after tourism. And, according to Poverty Reduction and Human Development in the Caribbean, on average for the region, remittances account for some 6 percent of the region's GNP, with about 36 percent of the households in Guyana, 11 percent in Jamaica, 13 percent in Trinidad and Tobago, and 17 percent in St. Lucia receiving remittances.

A more recent report shows remittances to be even more critical to the economies of the region. According to the Inter-American Development Bank study, *Remittances to Latin America and the Caribbean: Comparative Statistics,* remittances in 1999 represented 17 percent of the GDP of Haiti, 11.7 percent of that of Jamaica, and 10 percent of that of the Dominican Republic. Further, the 1.7 billion U.S. dollars in remittance flows to the Dominican Republic, the third highest volume in Latin American and the Caribbean (surpassed only by Mexico and Brazil), were triple the value of total agricultural exports. Perhaps of greater significance, remittances not only helped offset the country's trade deficit, but also accounted for more than eleven times the Official Development Assistance (ODA) the country received that year. In the case of Haiti, the 720 million U.S. dollars in remittances in 1999 amounted to twice the total revenues from exports and more than four times the ODA. Jamaica's 781 million U.S. dollars in remittances represented 50 percent of the country's export income and 63 percent of its earnings from tourism.[21]

The combined effects of the debt crisis, structural vulnerability, depressed exports, mismanagement, and other factors have been such that countries have been forced to seek foreign economic and financial support. One consequence has been the prescription by the World Bank and the International

Monetary Fund of strong doses of structural adjustment, central to which are privatization and deregulation. Structural adjustment programs are touted as beneficial in the long term, but they have some harmful short-term social and economic effects. One country study with region-wide relevance shows that the state's role in providing welfare has diminished, as social justice has become subordinated to market considerations. Both the quantity and quality of social services have been affected by cuts in public sector spending and reduced or removed subsidies for food, education, and health services, among other areas. All this has increased economic deprivation. Wages have lost the battle with persistent inflation, and prices have risen continually, partly because of the free market emphasis.[22]

In addition, and because of circumstances described above, the growth and importance of the informal economy have been stimulated, such that in the Dominican Republic, Guyana, Haiti, and Suriname it has become relatively more important than the formal economy to significant proportions of the citizens. All of this makes the engagement in illegal activities more palatable for some people and justifiable for others. It also makes some citizens both more susceptible and vulnerable to corruption.

Thus, the economic condition of the Caribbean makes the region hospitable to the conduct of drug operations and presents considerable institutional coping capacity challenges for state actors. A better appreciation of this twin reality is gained as we turn next to some of the positive-sum and negative-sum aspects of drugs in the region.

Positive-Sum Elements

Drug production, trafficking, and money laundering provide at least three areas of actual and potential economic value added: employment, income regeneration, and revenue enhancement. For obvious reasons, it is impossible to quantify the benefits from employment—or from any of the other areas for that matter—in terms of the number of people doing direct and indirect, and full-time and part-time work related to drugs. Categories and numbers of people employed vary from place to place and operation to operation. But generally, several different occupational areas are involved, including farmers, pilots, laborers, engineers, drivers, accountants, look-outs, and guards. This list does not include the variety of people in different public and private sector roles who are bribed to facilitate production, trafficking, and other operations. Moreover, in thinking of employment, account must be taken of the fact that narcotics countermeasures by governments also often boost employment in police, customs, coast guard, judicial, and other agencies.

A look at one area of operation—production—suggests that, given marijuana production and eradication levels in the Caribbean, especially in Jamaica, Guyana, Belize, and the eastern Caribbean, the number of people throughout the region "employed" directly and indirectly in this area would run into the tens of thousands. In regards to Jamaica, production is said to have generated employment and income for small farmers and wage workers in the context of declining jobs and income from traditional agricultural exports such as sugar and bananas.[23] Some six thousand Jamaican farmers alone are said to have been involved in marijuana production during the 1980s.[24]

Regarding income generation, production, trafficking, sale, and money-laundering transactions do generate income. For some of the people involved, the income is primary income; for others it is supplementary earnings. One Jamaican government study established clear linkages between marijuana production and income generation: "The Government's anti-drug eradication program has succeeded in destroying vast areas planted in marijuana, but the socio-economic problems remain. The small growers in these target communities have been experiencing a worsened situation in generating income or finding suitable employment. . . . The average disposable income was 84 percent above the national level, but since the [eradication] program it fell to 18 percent above the per capita disposable income."[25]

For some people the relative economic deprivation in the region is justification for engagement in drug activities. Paul Stares makes an observation that resonates with the Caribbean: "For most people involved in cultivating drugs, the motivation derives less from the promise of economic gain and more from the pressure of economic necessity."[26] As a matter of fact, some analysts see clear linkages between drug activities and contributors to the deprivation, particularly debt and structural adjustment.

University of the West Indies economics professor Dennis Pantin argues: "Amelioration of the drug trade is, [however,] impossible without a reduced burden of the so-called structural adjustment, which creates the fertile environment for drug activity."[27] Apart from poverty and deprivation, though, people are motivated by greed and acquisitive materialism. And considering the "big money" involved in drugs and the poor salaries for a wide cross-section of jobs in both the private and public sectors, one can understand—although not condone—the susceptibility to corruption, which itself could generate income.

While drug operators do not pay income, corporate, or other taxes into the formal economy, some of the income they generate does interface with the formal economy, contributing to government revenue. One way this happens is when income generated by drug transactions is used in a legal context where value added, property, or other taxes are paid. Moreover, countries that place a premium on offshore finance benefit from licensing and re-licensing fees for companies created expressly to launder drug money or that

undertake legitimate business but are also used for narcotics money laundering. Revenue enhancement is also a function of seizures of drug-related assets, fines levied by courts against people convicted of drug offenses, and
fines imposed by regulatory agencies, such as central banks and customs
departments, against companies that violate anti-trafficking and anti-money-
laundering regulations.

Understandably, much of the economic activity generated by drug operations becomes a part of the informal economy. However, as noted above, the
informal economy is crucial to economic survival in some countries. Moreover, there is always some interface between formal and informal economies
in all countries, which means that formal economies in the Caribbean benefit
from drug operations. Undoubtedly, then, employment, income generation,
and revenue enhancement owing to drugs affect the formal economy, and in
positive (as well as negative) ways.

The impact of drugs is also felt in more indirect ways. One area pertains to
savings. Although there is conspicuous consumption by many people who
profit from drug operations, money is also saved and invested in and through
formal financial institutions. This not only adds to the stock of savings, but
it affects, often positively, such things as investment capital and interest
rates.[28] As Stares has said in a general context, "Money gained from the drug
business also makes its way into the local economy with the purchase of
goods and services, the capitalization of banks and investment in real estate
and legitimate businesses."[29] In Jamaica, Carl Stone once noted: "The drug
trade provided access to capital and capital accumulation in an economy
dominated by a closely knit network of local white, Jewish, Lebanese, and
brown entrepreneurs, and [by] foreign capital. [It] served to open up opportunities for wealth accumulation for black middle class interests who found
themselves viable to break into the big business sector dominated by the
ethnic minorities."[30]

Foreign currency availability is also part of the picture. Given demand-
supply dynamics and the strength of the currency of the world's most significant narcotics market—the United States—drug operations generate U.S.
dollars, which are in high demand in both the formal and informal economies. Taking the Jamaica case again. Stone noted that in Jamaica's highly
dependent economy, imports represent some 50 percent of GDP. However,
the foreign exchange crisis of the 1970s reduced the formal economy's ability
to pay for imports, affecting negatively both production and consumption.
The government's response to the crisis involved tight foreign exchange controls and import restrictions. As a result, "Drug production and trafficking
were, however, immensely helpful to Jamaica. The illegal marijuana trade
emerged as the way business interests attempted to fill the growing gaps
between their demand for foreign exchange and the declining supply through

legitimate channels. In other words, the marijuana trade helped to sustain the flow of imports into this highly import dependent economy by providing a supplementary source of foreign exchange to importers, by way of a rapidly growing black market in U.S. dollars which was supplied mainly from the drug trade."[31]

Beyond all this, as is found in Latin America and elsewhere, Caribbean drug operators often engage in a form of social investment—Robin Hood-ism—by doing what governments are sometimes unable to do: They fulfill social welfare needs by providing medical and school supplies, funds for people to secure specialist medical care, sporting equipment and facilities, and church relief, among other things. They also bring business and work to some areas. Understandably, the beneficiaries of this benevolence do not see the drug operators as moral or legal reprobates; often they see them as heroes. This partly explains why some communities not only fail to aid in the apprehension or conviction of drug operators, but sometimes actually protect those operators from the law.

Negative-Sum Elements

Like the positive-sum entries, the negative-sum ones defy quantification. But they can be identified as including the impact on certain industries, fines imposed by foreign countries, and resource utilization.

The economic snapshot provided earlier revealed that tourism is critical to several countries. However, this industry is vulnerable to drug operations. The impact is largely indirect, and relates to crime. Indeed, Gordon "Butch" Stewart, one of the region's leading tourism entrepreneurs, has called crime "the evil of tourism."[32] The negative effect results from media reports that scare potential tourists away and the high incidence of drug-related crime in some places. Caribbean observers have known for some time what the New York Times once reported: drug-related crime has transformed the "paradise" character of the United States Virgin Islands and other Caribbean vacation spots, driving fear into locals and tourists alike, and depressing tourism.[33]

In the case of Jamaica, where tourism accounts for about 45 percent of the foreign exchange earnings, the alarmingly high rate of violent crime does not aid the image of the country. Nor does it inspire confidence on the part of potential tourists to risk jeopardizing their safety in the pursuit of rest and relaxation. In the murder category alone the portrait has been unwholesome, especially as most of the murders are drug related: 653 in 1993, and 690 in 1994. The number jumped in 1997 to 1,038, but was reduced the following year to 943, and still further in 1999 to 849, largely because the murders triggered both alarm and crisis reaction by the state and corporate actors.

This included the deployment of troops to tourist areas, which itself is not a positive tourism image.[34] The impact of drugs-driven crime on tourism is also of concern in Belize, Puerto Rico, Trinidad and Tobago, the Bahamas, and elsewhere in the region.[35]

The garment industry, which is used for trafficking, especially in Jamaica, the Dominican Republic, and the eastern Caribbean, is also affected. In one November 1998 case, Cupid Foundations, a U.S.-owned garment company that had been operating in Jamaica for twenty-two years, announced the closure of operations and relocation to Nicaragua. According to General Manager Ronald Josephs, the company could no longer afford the losses incurred with the seizure by U.S. Customs of its merchandise because of attempts to smuggle drugs into the United States among its clothing. Moreover, Jamaican law enforcement authorities could not provide assurance of drug-free shipping. The closure of the company put 550 people out of work.[36]

The second minus-side entry pertains to fines. It is related to the impact on the tourism and garment industries, but the effect goes beyond these areas. Heavy fines are often levied by U.S. Customs against the owners of carriers on which drugs are found. Under U.S. legislation—19 U.S. C. 1584, amended by PL 99–570—if a vessel found with drugs is not seized, there is a fine of 1,000 U.S. dollars per ounce for cocaine, heroin, morphine, and opiate. The fine for marijuana and opium used for smoking is 500 U.S. dollars per ounce.[37] Of all the countries affected by fines, notably Guyana, the Dominican Republic, Haiti, the Bahamas, Trinidad and Tobago, the Cayman Islands, and Jamaica, Haiti and Jamaica have suffered the heaviest toll.

On the issue of resource utilization, government and corporate and other nongovernmental agencies have been forced to adopt a wide range of narcotics countermeasures. Generally, the measures are costly, and even where there is external support, countermeasures have multiple economic-financial effects. In relation to government resource utilization, governments are obliged to devote considerable portions of already scarce financial resources to combat drugs. Moreover, because of economic difficulties generally and budgetary constraints specifically, governments are obliged to redirect resources away from health, education, housing, and other areas to meet the drug threat. Hence, there are significant opportunity costs at stake.

In addressing this issue recently, one Caribbean leader noted: "Over the past few years we have spent significant sums on interdiction. . . . But our donors need to understand that when a government decides to devote a significant percentage of its resources to fight drugs then it means that it is not giving attention to other social crimes throughout the community. When a police force like that of St. Lucia has to devote 40–60 percent of its resources to fight drugs then it means the community policing that we are talking about cannot be a reality."[38] The debit side entries discussed above are largely direct economic costs. But, as noted earlier, drugs also carry indirect economic costs, and social costs not amenable to easy economic estimation. For instance, providing public and private health care for drug users, for children exposed to drugs before and after birth, and for victims of drug-related crime also exact high social and economic costs. Moreover, there is lost or lower labor productivity (a) due to absenteeism, (b) because of the use of illegal drugs, (c) because of imprisonment for drug crimes, and (d) because of death from drug crime victimization, or drug-related work place or traffic accidents. Further, there is also a cost attached to having legitimate industrial production diverted to the production and distribution of illegal drugs. Also, one has to consider the diminished quality of life caused by illegal drug use, such as pain and suffering of families, friends, and crime victims.

The *1997 World Drug Report* notes an additional negative-sum aspect: large scale movements of illegal capital, particularly in small economies, can disable a government's ability to plan and control monetary policy. The report indicates that a traditional tool of macroeconomic stabilization is a central bank's ability to make credit—and, therefore, consumption and investment—more or less expensive by increasing or decreasing the money supply. However, "When the underground economy is large in relation to the legitimate one, these conditions no longer apply. Similarly, the two most important data sets governments use for planning—the balance of payments and national income accounts—become worthless when large international flows of liquidity, goods and services are unaccounted for." And, adds the report, "Decreased financial control undercuts financial credibility and as a result the benefits to a given country can be more than offset by reduced access to legitimate sources of finance. Small economies are more vulnerable to large amounts of illicitly derived capital flowing through the system because the relative proportion of illicit to licit capital is greater and, it could be argued, because small economies are more in need of accurate planning and policy."[39]

Beyond all this, there is what Paul Stares calls "the most pernicious effect" of the drug phenomenon: undermining the economic integrity and political legitimacy of the state. He argues correctly that "successful drug traffickers not only encourage others to imitate them, but they also contribute to the growth of an underground economy by visibly demonstrating the impotence of government authorities. Their ability to operate with impunity and avoid taxation infects other business practices, further corroding public confidence in the ability of state authorities to regulate economic activity equally for the common good. They deprive the government of revenues from untaxed business activity and makes its management of the economy more difficult."[40]

Conclusion

Settling the balance sheet of this interdependence issue is difficult for several reasons. Among other things, economic costs are both direct and indirect, and there are social costs. Yet, it is easy to sense that, in national and regional terms, although not always in individual terms, the costs involved far outweigh the benefits. More than this, though, the tripartite—multi-dimensional, multi-level, and multi-actor—character of the drug phenomenon dramatizes that the world is merely a global village, with the Caribbean being a small—albeit not unimportant—neighborhood. We are at the dawn of a new era in this village where problems without passports present challenges to neighborhoods both near and far, and clear and present dangers for our entire civilization.

A former Caribbean statesman called attention to some of these dangers more than a decade ago with the following assertion: "In a real sense, civilization is at a cross roads. There are many problems we face. Those of us in the Third World know that we cannot make progress, no matter how courageously we structurally readjust our economies, without paying some attention to debt relief. Equally we face the threat to our exports from protectionism."[41]

Both of these problems are wrongly seen as affecting developing countries more than the international community as a whole. No such myopia is possible with drugs. Ironically, it is through this evil that all of us may be led to understand that the world is today one global village. Interdependence is the hallmark of today's reality. The problem, therefore, is not only the kid in school who snorts coke, or the peasant who plants coca. These are but incidental victims in the game plan of the drug cartels. The problem is that we might have allowed ourselves as a world society to underrate and misunderstand this threat to our civilization. In a real sense, the twenty-first century with all its potential for human benefit, because of huge rapid technological advances, can either be one where we continue to progress, or one in which anarchy takes over as the criminal cartels seek to dominate the global political economy.

Notes

1. Address by Hon. Dr. Kenny Davis Anthony, prime minister of St. Lucia, to the 2001 Conference of the Association of the Caribbean Commissioners of Police, Castries, St. Lucia, May 21, 2001, p. 9. Before becoming prime minister in 1997, Kenny Anthony was a professor of law at the University of the West Indies School of Law and general counsel of the Caribbean Community and Common Market.

2. United Nations International Drug Control Program, *World Drug Report* (New York: Oxford University Press, 1997), 17.

3. Paul B. Stares, *Global Habit: The Drug Problem in a Borderless World* (Washington, D.C.: Brookings Institution, 1996), 47.

4. United Nations International Drug Control Program, *World Drug Report,* 103.

5. For an elaboration of this concept, see Ivelaw L. Griffith, "From Cold War Geopolitics to Post-Cold War Geonarcotics," *International Journal* 48 (1993–1994), 1–36; for an empirical study based on it, see Ivelaw L. Griffith, *Drugs and Security in the Caribbean: Sovereignty under Siege* (University Park: Pennsylvania State University Press, 1997).

6. These vignettes are culled from Douglas Farah, "Caribbean Cash Havens Arouse Unites States Suspicions," *Washington Post,* October 11, 1999, p. Al; Elaine De Valle, "Cargo of Cocaine Found in Freighter on Miami River," *Miami Herald,* June 7, 2000, p. 3B; Lloyd Williams, "Policeman Implicated in Drug-dealing," *Jamaica Gleaner,* October 29, 2000, p. l; "Big Cocaine Find: Police Seize over 700 Kilos in Alligator Pond," *Jamaica Gleaner,* November 16, 2000, p. 1; "Dominican Republic Police Seize Cocaine," *Nassau Tribune,* December 14, 2000, p. 9; United States Department of State, *International Narcotics Control Strategy Report, March 2001; Interpol Weekly Intelligence Message,* no. 7101, April 20, 2001; "Cocaine Seized on Flight from Curaçao," *Miami Herald,* April 20, 2001, p. 3B; and *Interpol Weekly Intelligence Message,* no. 10101, May 31, 2001.

7. Dennis J. Gayle, "The Evolving Caribbean Business Environment," in Anthony T. Bryan, ed., *The Caribbean: New Dynamics in Trade and Political Economy* (Miami: North-South Center, University of Miami, 1995), 144.

8. For the World Bank statement, see World Bank, *Caribbean Countries: Caribbean Economic Overview 1996, Report no. 15471–LAC,* May 1996, p. 12 and for the report on Cuba, see "Tourism Overtakes Sugar as Hard Currency Earner," *Canal News,* available at httpa/207.234.177.341cgi-binlsupersite.exe.news, September 2, 1997, p. 3.

9. World Bank, Caribbean Group for Cooperation in Economic Development, *Caribbean Economic Overview 2000, Report no. 20460–LAC,* June 2000, p. 7.

10. World Bank, *Caribbean Countries: Caribbean Economic Overview 1996,* p. 4.

11. Ramesh Ramsaran, "Challenges to Caribbean Economic Development in the 1990s," in Bryan, ed., *The Caribbean: New Dynamics in Trade and Political Economy,* 123, 125.

12. See Ivelaw L. Griffith, *The Quest for Security in the Caribbean: Problems and Promises in Subordinate States* (Armonk, N.Y.: M. E. Sharpe, 1993), chapter 3.

13. For more on this, see Hilbourne A. Watson, "The Globalization of Finance: Role and Status of the Caribbean," in Ivelaw L. Griffith, ed., *The Political Economy of Drugs in the Caribbean* (London: Macmillan, 2000), 29–57; Caribbean Development Bank, "Caribbean Development Bank Annual Report 2000," March 2001; and Emilio Pantojas-Garcia, "Trade Liberalization and Peripheral Post-Industrialization in the Caribbean," *Latin American Politics and Society* 43, no. 1 (2001), 57–77.

14. Judy L. Baker, "Poverty Reduction and Human Development in the Caribbean," *World Bank Development Discussion Paper,* no. 366 (July 1977), 25.

15. Ibid.

16. See Aaron Segal, "The Political Economy of Contemporary Migration," in

Thomas Klak, ed., *Globalization and Neoliberalism: The Caribbean Context* (London: Rowman and Littlefield, 1998), 225.

17. Trevor Harker, "Caribbean Economic Performance in the 1990s," Hilbourne A. Watson, ed., *The Caribbean in the Global Political Economy* (Boulder, Colo.: Lynne Rienner, 1994), 10–12.

18. Baker, "Poverty Reduction and Human Development in the Caribbean," 3.

19. Richard L. Bernal, Winsome J. Leslie, and Stephen E. Lamar, "Drugs, Debt, and Structural Adjustment in the Caribbean," in Griffith, *The Political Economy of Drugs in the Caribbean,* 73.

20. "Jamaicans Remitted 600 million US dollars," *New York Carib News,* November 7, 1995.

21. See Multilateral Investment Fund, Inter American Development Bank, *Remittances to Latin American and the Caribbean: Comparative Statistics,* May 2001. The report dealt with nine countries in Latin America (Brazil, Colombia, Ecuador, El Salvador, Guatemala, Honduras, Mexico, Nicaragua, and Peru) and three in the Caribbean (the Dominican Republic, Haiti, and Jamaica). Although the study did not deal with Cuba, it estimated that remittances to that Caribbean country were more than 800 million U.S. dollars in 1999.

22. See Dorith Grant-Wisdom, "Globalization, Structural Adjustment, and Democracy in Jamaica," in Ivelaw L. Griffith and Betty N. Sedoc-Dahlberg, eds., *Democracy and Human Rights in the Caribbean* (Boulder, Colo.: Westview Press, 1997), 193–211.

23. Carl Stone, "Crime and Violence," in Peter Phillips and Judith Wedderburg, eds., *Crime and Violence: Causes and Solutions, University of West Indies (Jamaica), Occasional Paper,* no. 2 (September 1998), 44.

24. See Scott B. MacDonald, *Dancing on a Volcano* (New York: Praeger, 1988), 90.

25. Government of Jamaica, Ministry of Agriculture, *Alternative Systems for an Illegal Crop,* September 1994, p. 8.

26. Stares, *Global Habit,* 50.

27. Dennis Pantin, "The Colombian Nightmare: Drugs and Structural Adjustment in the Caribbean," *Caribbean Affairs* 2 (October-November 1989), 145.

28. Some of these relationships were noted by a Trinidad and Tobago central bank official who requested anonymity.

29. Stares, *Global Habit,* 95.

30. Stone, "Crime and Violence," 45.

31. Ibid., 44.

32. Don Bohning, "For Resorts, Crime-Crisis," *Miami Herald,* April 10, 1995, pp. 43–44.

33. Larry Rohter, "Slaying in St. Thomas Stains Image," *New York Times,* April 19, 1994, p. 17.

34. See "Jamaica: Crime Triggers Alarm," *New York Carib News,* July 20, 1999, p. 3.

35. For recent reports on the impact of crime on tourism, see Leslie Casimir and Corky Siemaszko, "Sand, Sun and Siege: Rising Tide of Violence Hits Isles of Carib-

bean," *New York Daily News,* July 17, 1999, at http://www.nydailynews.com; Paula Szuchman, "Caribbean Cops Make Waves Against Crime," *Conde Nast Traveler* (August 1999), 25–30; Klaus de Albuquerque and Jerome McElroy, "Crime and Tourism in the Caribbean," *Annals of Tourism Research* 26, no. 1 (1999), 968–84; and Garwin Davis, "Crime Sinks Ugly Teeth into Tourism Insudtry: Decline in Sector Beginning to Bite Deeply," *Jamaica Gleaner,* August 28, 2000, p. 1.

36. "Firm Closes Factory over Drug Smuggling," *Miami Herald,* November 6, 1998, p. 6A.

37. I am grateful to Lt. Comdr. J. Chris Sinnett of the U.S. Coast Guard for this information.

38. Address by Hon. Dr. Kenny Davis Anthony, prime minister of St. Lucia, to the 2001 Conference of the Association of the Caribbean Commissioners of Police, Castries, St. Lucia, May 21, 2001, p. 9.

39. United Nations International Drug Control Program, *World Drug Report,* 144.

40. Stares, *Global Habit,* 96

41. "The Drug Menace," address by Michael Manley, prime minister of Jamaica, at the opening of the Inter-Ministerial Conference on Drugs, Kingston, Jamaica, October 2, 1989, 5.

III

Trafficking and Money Laundering

7

The Political Economy of Drug Smuggling

Peter Reuter

Illicit drugs, predominantly cocaine and heroin, now generate a substantial international trade. Production is concentrated in poor nations and the bulk of revenues, though not of consumption, is generated by users in wealthy countries. Earnings have an odd shape. Most of the money goes to a very large number of low-level retailers in wealthy countries while the fortunes are made by a small number of entrepreneurs, many of whom come from the producing countries. Actual producers and refiners receive less than 1 percent of the total.

It is not difficult to explain why production occurs primarily in poor countries and only a little harder to understand why the accounting profits are downstream.[1] Almost everything else about the trade presents a challenge, both descriptively and analytically. Why do only some poor nations export these drugs? How are the different sectors organized in terms of enterprise size and internal structure? What is the relationship of drug smuggling to other transnational and organized criminal activities? Why have international control efforts been so unsuccessful?

These questions serve to organize the chapter. It is focused primarily on the cocaine and heroin trades as transnational crime. Purely domestic aspects are introduced only as necessary. The trades in other drugs, such as cannabis and Ecstasy are not included. The chapter focuses mostly on the United States, which constitutes the largest market and the one for which more information is available. First, the existing knowledge about the scale of the international drug trade will be described. The following sections will examine where drug production and smuggling occurs and who is involved. Then, the evolution of the organization of the trade and the relationship to other criminal activities will be dealt with. We will conclude with a brief assessment of the consequences of enforcement.

The topic of transnational smuggling attracts a good deal of rhetoric but not much that could be called research. Few studies have specifically focused

on the international aspects of the trade, in contrast to the now almost volu-
minous empirical literature on retail markets, particularly street markets.
José Fuentes represents an important recent addition to the literature in the
United States.[2] Francisco Thoumi describes in analytic fashion the role of
cocaine production and distribution in Colombia.[3] Paul Stares synthesized
the research and official literature on global production, consumption, and
control programs.[4] In Western Europe the analytic literature appears slight,
though a number of descriptive studies have appeared since 1990. Official
reports provide some descriptive material but little use has been made of it.

The Scale and Distribution of the Drug Trade

The standard estimate of the international drug trade, thrown around with
ease even by publications as skeptical and numerate as the *Economist*, is 300
billion to 500 billion U.S. dollars.[5] This number is probably ten times the
actual figure for the trade flow.[6] Only for the United States have systematic
revenue estimates been documented.[7] The figures for 1988 to 1995 are presented in Table 7.1. They show a decline, primarily a consequence of the
continuing fall in the price of both cocaine and heroin, rather than in quantities purchased.[8]

For the rest of the world, only smatterings of data are available. Some of
the few available figures on numbers of dependent users and per addict expenditures are presented in Table 7.2. Roughly these figures suggest that
dependent users (who account for the vast bulk of total expenditures)[9] in rich
nations each spend about 20,000 U.S. dollars per annum on drugs (mostly
heroin and cocaine), fifteen to forty times per addict expenditures in poor
countries.

The total for the United States and western Europe is plausibly 120 billion
U.S. dollars, twice the official estimate from the United States.[10] Now assume
that the drug dependents in the rest of the world manage to spend 1,000
dollars each, the Thai figure; that is generous indeed, given that Thailand is

Table 7.1. U.S. Expenditures on Illicit Drugs (Selected Years, 1996 Billions
of Dollars)

	1988	1990	1992	1994	1995
Cocaine	61.2	51.5	41.7	37.4	38.0
Heroin	17.7	14.3	10.2	9.3	9.6
Marijuana	9.1	11.0	11.5	8.2	7.0
Other Drugs	3.3	2.2	2.0	2.6	2.7
Total	91.4	79.0	65.4	57.5	57.3

Source: What America's Users Spend on Illicit Drugs, 1988–1995 (Washington, D.C.: UNDCP,
1997).

substantially wealthier than most other Asian nations with large opiate dependent populations, such as Afghanistan, Myanmar, and Iran. Then literally hundreds of millions of such addicts would be needed to reach the global figure of 400 million U.S. dollars. Yet the numbers provided by the UNDCP are about 20 million (including the United States and western Europe) for heroin and cocaine, the only very expensive drugs in mass consumption. A total for the developing world of 30 billion U.S. dollars would seem extremely generous, giving a total of about 150 billion U.S. dollars in consumer expenditures on illicit drugs. The United Nations reaches its total by imputing to world consumption the low end of U.S. prices.[11]

The error is even more egregious than this because the figure is referred to as an international trade number. For example, the UNDCP describes it as "equivalent to eight percent of total international trade and larger than the international trade in iron and steel, and motor vehicles."[12] In fact, the international trade component of drug sales is quite small; the landed price, relevant for the international trade calculation, is only about 15 percent of the retail price, as shown in Table 7.3 for cocaine in the United States.

Thus, even if retail sales totaled 400 billion U.S. dollars, the international trade figure would be about 60 billion. If, in fact, the sales figure is only about 150 billion, then the trade flow is down to a mere 20–25 billion, a very small share of total trade, currently estimated at 5,000 billion U.S. dollars.

This is not mere pedantry about measurement. A certain amount of serious policy-making is dependent on the froth of international drug trade estimates. If 400 billion U.S. dollars in illegal drug revenues is flowing across borders, then the justification for stringent money-laundering regulations is clear. At 25 billion, one needs to look a lot more carefully as to whether the resulting impediments to the easy flow of capital are worthwhile. More germane to the current paper, the smaller figure points to something less than a behemoth among transnational criminal activities.

Table 7.2. Estimated Drug Expenditures by Nation, 1996

Nation	Dependent Users in Thousands (per 100,000 population)		Per capita Income (ca. 1994)	Drug Expenditures in Billions $ ($ per dependent user)	
Italy	179–420	(515)	$ 18,160	7–13	(33,898)
Sweden	17	(194)	$ 17,900	0.4	(23,529)
U.S.A.	2,700	(1,037)	$ 24,680	48.7	(18,037)
Australia	100–300	(1,121)	$ 18,530	2.0–4.4	(16,000)
Thailand	1,300	(2,203)	$ 6,350	1.1–1.9	(1,154)
Pakistan	3,000	(2,340)	$ 2,160	1.5	(500)

Source: UNDCP World Drug Report (Oxford: Oxford University Press, 1997).

Which Nations Produce and Transship and Why

A small number of nations account for the vast bulk of production of coca and opium. According to official estimates, Myanmar and Afghanistan account for 90 percent of global production of opium (3,100 tons out of 3,462 tons); Bolivia, Colombia, and Peru account for all of coca production.[13]

There is no technical reason for not producing cocaine or heroin in the United States. Hydroponic techniques could be used for both coca and opium poppies. However, the enforcement risks faced by producers in the United States are substantial and the risk compensation costs sufficiently high that, even with transportation costs and associated interdiction risks, local production of coca and heroin have never developed. Indeed, they are not even refined in the United States. It is useful to contrast this situation with that of cannabis. In that area, U.S. production accounts for a substantial share of U.S. consumption; apparently much of it is grown indoors. Cannabis's exceptional status probably rests on three factors: (a) the bulkiness per unit value, which raises smuggling costs substantially; (b) the existence of a boutique market of user/growers interested in developing better breeds of the plant; and (c) the ease of entry, since the seeds are widely available and there are probably few economies of scale beyond quite a small number of plants.

The principal costs of the international drug industry are associated with distribution rather than production; Table 7.3 provides approximate figures on the cost of cocaine at different points in the distribution system to the United States and generates three observations, which are also true for heroin and for western Europe: (a) The cost of production, as opposed to distribution, is a trivial share of the final price. That statement holds true even if one adds the cost of refining to leaf production; (b) The vast majority of costs are accounted for by domestic distribution in the consumer country. Smuggling, which is the principal transnational activity, accounts for a modest share but much more than production and refining; and c) Most of the domestic distribution revenues go to the lowest level of the distribution system. If the retailer and lowest level wholesaler each raise their purchase price by 75 percent,

Table 7.3. Prices of Cocaine through the Distribution System, 1992
(per Pure Kilogram Equivalent)

Leaf (Peru)	$650
Export (Colombia)	$1,050
Import (Miami)	$23,000
Wholesale-Kilo	$33,000
Wholesale-Oz	$52,000
Retail (100 mg pure)	$188,000

Source: Drug Enforcement Administration, Washington, D.C.

which until recently was a low estimate of the margin, they account for two-thirds of the final price. This is consistent with the enormous increase in price from the ounce level to retail observed in Table 7.3.

Production

Risks and the costs of bearing them provide a plausible, though still untested, explanation for all these observations.[14] Coca and opium are grown in countries characterized by labor and land that have low prices relative to those in Europe and North America.[15] The comparative advantage of these countries is reinforced by the reluctance or inability of governments to act aggressively against growers or early stage refiners. Low opportunity cost for factors of production plus low enforcement risks produce very modest prices for the refined product and also ensure that production does not move upstream geographically.

It is also useful to consider why neighboring countries, involved in transshipment, have not been major producers. Consider, for example, Thailand. In the early 1970s it was a major producer of opium. It also has, as listed in Table 7.2, a substantial addict population (predominantly heroin using). It continues to suffer from high levels of corruption, both in the powerful military and in the civilian government. It would seem to be a strong candidate for a large opium production sector.

Yet Thailand now produces little and serves primarily as a consuming and transshipment country for Myanmar. The explanation can probably be found in economic actors. Over the past twenty-five years Thailand has had high rates of growth, raising the opportunity cost of land and labor relative to impoverished Myanmar.[16] Thus, Thai farmers have not been able to compete in the opium growing sector, particularly since the illegality of the product has inhibited the development of more technologically advanced growing methods. The Thai government, despite the corruption of its border drug controls, has also been more willing to act aggressively against growers.

Until recently Colombia was the other anomaly. Though the principal source of refined exports to the United States, and an important source for western Europe, it was a distant third in coca production until the mid-1990s. The recent and rather sudden expansion of coca growing in Colombia, which has accompanied a decline in Peruvian and Bolivian production, may be the result of specific political factors.[17] The upturn in political violence in Colombia has led to a large internal migration from more settled agricultural regions, where the paramilitary are most active, to unsettled areas in which there are few economic opportunities other than coca growing and in which the guerrillas can provide effective protection. If political stability ever returns to Colombia, the coca trade may shift back to poorer Bolivia.

Smuggling

The modest share of costs associated with cocaine smuggling is easily explained.[18] Cocaine travels in large bundles at that stage; seizures suggest that shipments of 250–500 kilograms are quite common. Though large sums may be paid to pilots for flying small planes carrying cocaine or for Honduran colonels to ignore their landing, these costs are defrayed over a large quantity. A pilot who demands 500,000 U.S. dollars for flying a plane with 250 kilograms is generating costs of only 2,000 dollars per kilogram, about 2 percent of the retail price. Even if the plane has to be abandoned after one flight, that adds only another 2,000 dollars to the kilogram price. For shipments in container cargo, seizure constitutes little more than a random tax collection. The replacement cost of the seized drugs is substantially less than the landed price, so high seizure rates have modest effect even on wholesale prices.[19] This contrasts sharply with street level dealing, where the risks of arrest and incarceration can be spread over only the few grams that the dealer sells.

A large share of cocaine in the 1980s was smuggled in dedicated vessels, either small boats or planes. Intense interdiction has changed both routes and patterns. Small (and sometimes not so small) planes are still used to carry a substantial fraction of cocaine to Mexico, from where it enters the United States in regular cargo, either by truck or cargo vessel. Patterns of seizure also suggest that in recent years even shipments direct from Colombia have tended to travel in commercial traffic, both air and sea. The drug is found concealed in an enormous variety of cargoes; frozen fruit pulp containers, wooden furniture, and even suspended in other liquids.

Heroin smuggling appears to be less efficient, at least as measured in dollars per kilogram. Heroin that exits Myanmar at 1,000 U.S. dollars per kilogram (in bundles of 10 kilograms or more) sells on arrival in the United States for 50,000 dollars per kilogram. There have been a few multi-hundred kilogram shipments of heroin, but they are very rare compared to those for cocaine. The drug often travels in small bundles carried internally by individual couriers.[20] "Body-packing," where the couriers are low wage earners, produces per kilogram smuggling costs of less than 10,000 dollars. A body-packer can apparently carry about three-fourths of a kilogram. A payment of 5,000 dollars for incurring a one to ten risk in prison (perhaps acceptable for couriers whose legitimate wages are only about 2,000 dollars per annum), along with 3,000 dollars in travel expenses, produces a kilogram cost of just over 11,000 dollars compared to a retail price of 1 million dollars.[21] The remainder of the smugglers' margin is for assuming other kinds of risk.

Note, however, that as a share of the retail price, the ratio is actually less than for cocaine, about 5–10 percent compared to 15 percent for cocaine.

This is one of many unresolved puzzles about the relationship between cocaine and heroin prices, which maintain, in both Europe and the United States, a remarkably constant ratio of one to ten. Smuggling costs depend on the ability to conceal drugs in a flow of legitimate commerce and traffic. Colombia and Mexico serve as the principal smuggling platforms to the United States because they have large immigrant populations in the United States and maintain extensive air traffic and trade with that country. Though Mexico is a high cost producer, farm-gate prices for opium in Mexico being typically 2,000 to 5,000 U.S. dollars per kilo compared to a few hundred dollars in Myanmar, the low smuggling costs equalize total landed price. Colombia, a new source for heroin, also represents high farm-gate production with relatively low smuggling costs. Though Colombia and Mexico are minor producers of opium worldwide, accounting for perhaps 3 percent of the total, they are now the source of nearly two-thirds of U.S. heroin.

Nigeria is an interesting anomaly, a nation that seems to have little potential role in the international drug trade. It is isolated from the any of the principal producer or consumer countries and lacks a significant base of traditional domestic production or consumption. Nonetheless, Nigerian traffickers have come to play a significant role in the shipping of heroin between Southeast Asia and the United States and also Europe; recently these traffickers have even entered the cocaine business, though the production centers are still more remote from their home country.

The explanation is probably to be found in a complex of factors. Nigerians are highly entrepreneurial, they have been misruled by corrupt governments over a long time, have large overseas populations, a weak civil society, very low domestic wages, and moderate to good commercial links to the rest of the world. Thus, (a) it is relatively easy to buy protection for transactions in Nigerian airports (corruption and a weak governmental tradition); (b) to establish connections in both the source and consumption nations (large overseas populations) and to use existing commercial transportation;[22] (c) smuggling labor is cheap (low domestic wages); and (d) the entrepreneurial tradition produces many competent and enthusiastic smuggling organizers. Nigeria is not unique in most of these dimensions (except for size and connections with the rest of the world), and there is perhaps an accidental quality to its initiation into the trade, but these other factors plausibly play a major role.

One might more usefully ask whether the new republics of Central Asia are likely to become major players in the international heroin business. They certainly have low-cost land and labor, as well as apparently good ecological conditions for growing opium and a traditional expertise. Some governments, such as that of Uzbekistan, are desperate for foreign currency, have few alternative sources, and little concern about their standing in international organizations; they are unlikely to enforce aggressively prohibitions against growing opium poppies or to have the capability to do so even if they desired to. They are certain to be low-cost producers.

But are they advantaged, compared to current low-cost producers, notably Afghanistan and Myanmar? Though closer to Europe and with significant populations resident in Russia and perhaps even in western Europe, the commercial connections with western Europe are likely to be weak compared to those of Myanmar, which operate through established Thai and Chinese trafficking networks and are imbedded in growing legitimate traffic. The Central Asian republics will only become major players in the European opium markets if there are disruptions (including rapid economic development) in the current major supplier countries.

Increasingly the drug trade is taking more indirect paths for smuggling. Seizures in Germany frequently turn out to have traveled through Scandinavia into Russia and then exited through Poland to their final market. Ruggiero and South describe a joint Czech-Colombia venture to ship sugar rice and soybean to Czechoslovakia. This operation was used to smuggle cocaine, destined for western Europe. In 1991, police say that 440 pounds of cocaine were seized in Bohemia and at Gdansk in Poland, which would have been smuggled onward to the Netherlands and Britain.[23] Francisco Thoumi contrasts the distribution of illicit drug production across nations with that for legitimate agricultural products.[24] Coffee can be grown in many countries; in fact, a large number of those countries do have coffee producing and exporting industries. Many countries are capable of producing opium or coca; very few of them do. For example, opium has at various times been grown in Macedonia, Turkey, Lebanon, and India. However, none of these are currently active in the illicit markets.

Immigrants have advantages in exporting, with better knowledge of potential sellers and corruption opportunities. Few potential U.S. importers speak any of the languages of the Golden Triangle (Myanmar, Laos, and Thailand); English has more currency in Pakistan but not much in Afghanistan. Corrupt officials may be much more at ease in dealing with traffickers whose families they can hold in mutual hostage. Moreover, nonnative traffickers are likely to be conspicuous in the growing regions. Nor are the exporters merely agents for wealthy nations, in sharp contrast to the international trade in refined agricultural products. Khun Sa, an exotic figure associated with irredentist ethnic groups on the periphery of Myanmar, was the dominant figure in opium exports from the Golden Triangle for many years.[25] The Colombian cocaine trade has spawned some spectacular figures, such as Pablo Escobar and Carlos Lehder, all of them of Colombian descent. If there are major United States or European exporters in the source countries, they have managed to escape detection.

Immigrants and Trafficking in Consumer Countries

Dominance in the exporting sector does not imply dominance by the same nationalities in the smuggling business or in high-level distribution in the consuming countries. However, that seems to be the case.

Immigrant communities have substantial advantages in the consuming country as well as their own. For example, their communities are likely to provide less cooperation with the police. Even language can be a major asset; for example, few police departments are able to conduct effective wiretaps or other electronic surveillances involving various Chinese languages. Hence immigrants have better opportunities to hide and weaker licit market opportunities than most of the native population. Continuing immigration can serve as a source of new entrepreneurs and reduce the effectiveness of enforcement interventions, as may have been the case with organized crime and Italian immigration in the early part of the twentieth century. Many wealthy nations see foreign groups as critical to the import of drugs. Table 7.4 lists a few consumer countries and the immigrant groups thought to play a major role in the heroin or cocaine industries there.

Most of these associations are easily explicable, since the immigrant groups come from the producing regions. There are few Afghans in Britain but many immigrants from neighboring Pakistan. Morocco, a traditional producer and consumer of hashish, has sent many emigrants to France. The Balkans has long been a transshipment area for heroin entering Europe. The only one that is difficult to explain is the involvement of West Africans in the Scandinavian heroin trade.

The European literature is particularly rich and consistent on the role of immigrants. For example, Mats Killias reports the dominance of immigrants in every level of the drug trade in Zurich. "In 1992, in Zurich Canton, Swiss nationals were only 37 percent of suspected drug traffickers and 14 percent

Table 7.4. Immigrant Groups Involved in Drug Trafficking

Consuming Country	Drug	Immigrant Groups
Australia	Heroin	Chinese, Vietnamese
Denmark	Heroin	West African
Britain	Heroin	Pakistani
France	Marijuana	Moroccan
Switzerland	Heroin	Balkan, Lebanese
United States	Cocaine	Colombian

Note: These gross statements come from scrutiny of reports in the Foreign Broadcast Information Service (FBIS), a compilation of foreign media reports concerning narcotics, and from interviews with officials and researchers in these nations.

of suspected drug importers."[26] Interpol reports that seizures of heroin involving Turkish nationals accounted for 40 percent of the total 11.2 tons seized in 1996 in Europe. "The existence of Turkish communities, roughly totaling over three million in Western European countries, had given the opportunity among Turkish criminal groups to create a ready network for transport and redistribution of heroin in Western Europe."[27]

The variety of groups involved is impressive. Hans-Jörg Albrecht reports on the shift in the nationality of drug sellers in Frankfurt.[28] In the 1980s, there were many from sub-Saharan Africa; intense enforcement eliminated these nationalities from the trade, and they were then replaced by North Africans. Albanians are prominent in the Swiss market.[29] Vincenzo Ruggiero supplements this finding through his study of the Albanian population of source countries, finding that drug dealing and importation are important activities for immigrants, many of whom go to Italy.[30]

Even in the United States, where traffickers are forced to be much more discreet than in the source country, it appears that the high levels of the cocaine trade are primarily the province of immigrant groups. That is, the principal figures in the import sector are not U.S. nationals, but come from the producer or transshipment countries: China, Colombia, and Mexico for heroin; Colombia and Mexico for cocaine.

The Organization of the Trade

Some characteristics of smuggling organizations seem quite general. For example, smuggling is rarely integrated with downstream distribution activities. Organizations that import 250-kilogram shipments of cocaine do not distribute beyond the initial transaction, selling in loads of 10 kilograms or more. The explanation for this probably lies in risk management; lower level transactions are more visible and the purchasers less reliable. Integration thus increases risk of arrest. Only very small-scale importers are likely to operate close to the retail level. Markets for smuggling services contain many forms and sizes of organization. A credible case can be made that the 1990s U.S. cocaine market has been dominated by a few large organizations. For other eras, countries, and drugs, smaller and more ephemeral organizations may account for a significant share of the total. Monopoly control is rare. Prior to 1980, it was widely believed that the mafia had dominated the major illegal markets such as those for bookmaking and loan sharking, and even for heroin importation into New York City until the late 1960s.[31] Despite finding that some dealers within the United States have enormous incomes and traffic in large quantities, no researcher has found evidence, except on the local microlevel (e.g., a few blocks), that a dealer organization has the ability to exclude others or to set prices: the hallmarks of market power.[32]

Even at the trafficker level, market power seems elusive. Notwithstanding references to the Medellín and Cali cartels, these seem to be only loose syndicates of independent entrepreneurs, who sometimes collaborate but have to compete with other, smaller, Colombian smuggling enterprises.[33] The small share of the retail price accounted for by all activities up to import is strong but not conclusive, pointing at evidence of competition at this level.[34] The continuing decline of prices over a period of almost twenty years at all levels of the market suggests that, if market power ever existed, it has now been dissipated. Thus, there is no level at which policy makers need be worried that tough enforcement will lead to price declines because a cartel is broken, a matter raised thirty years ago by Tom Schelling in his classic paper on organized crime.[35] The explanation for the lack of market power may also be contained in Schelling's paper. The mafia may have been collecting rents on behalf of corrupt police departments that had exclusive jurisdiction and little external scrutiny, but those departments are less systemically corrupt and face substantial oversight from federal investigative agencies.

The different types of organizations that have functioned in the cocaine market as it has evolved in the United States over the last twenty-five years will be dealt with in the next few sections.

The Early Cocaine Market

Patricia A. Adler reported observations on sixty-five high-level dealers and smugglers in southern California whom she and her husband met through contacts while in graduate school. Her study notes considerable range in the closeness and stability of relationships among participants. Some formed close and enduring partnerships that were quite exclusive; for example, one pilot was constantly being recruited by a smuggler neighbor but refused to work for him because of his loyalty to his regular employer. Other dealers, characterized as "less reputable," existed in a network of shifting alliances.

The organizations Adler studied were micro-enterprises. Those of cocaine dealers typically consisted of only two or three people. Marijuana, because it is bulkier, required more elaborate transportation organizations. She concluded that "this is not an arena dominated by a criminal syndicate but an illicit market populated by individuals and small groups of wheeler-dealers who operate competitively and entrepreneurially."[36]

Peter Reuter and John Haaga interviewed mid- to high-level U.S. traffickers in cocaine and marijuana in the mid-1980s; the sample was recruited from low-security federal prisons. They found importers who were small, opportunistic, and niche-oriented. "All one needs is a good connection and a set of reliable customers." Though many of those interviewed regarded themselves as part of an organization, "[m]ost of the arrangements would be better described as small partnerships, in which each partner is also involved in trading on his own account, or as long-term, but not exclusive, supplier-customer relationships." Here is their account of one small-scale importing operation:[37]

> [O]ne couple residing in Florida would travel with another couple to South America, posing as tourists, and would then hand off their packages to the owner of a sailboat in a Caribbean port for delivery to a Florida location. The husband had a contact in Bolivia, whom he had met during a short stay in federal prison for a non-drug-related offense. The sailboat owner was a friend of a friend, also tracing back to a contact made in prison. The two couples would part company after each trip, each taking a share of the proceeds. Thanks to prison and his former life as a small businessman, the husband had enough contracts in different parts of the country to get his large quantities of cocaine and Quaaludes distributed within a short time after arrival. In some five years of operation about a dozen people had taken part.

Both Adler and Reuter and Haaga were describing the cocaine market in an early stage of its development. In 1978, cocaine consumption was estimated to be approximately 100 tons. By 1988 it had grown to approximately 200 tons.[38] Prices had plunged, the consequence of the emergence of more efficient distribution systems. It seems plausible that the generally amateur, small-scale smuggling operations described in the two studies, often involving well-educated principals with at least modestly successful legitimate careers, had been replaced by more professional and large-scale smuggling operations.

Colombian Smuggling Organizations

José Fuentes has recently provided the first fine-grained description of the operation of the high levels of the international drug trade since the shift to large-scale smuggling.[39] He relied on transcripts from court proceedings (including extensive wiretaps) on two major organizations and lengthy interviews with five senior traffickers, who have cooperated with federal agencies. These are accounts of organizations, and by participants, that were detected and punished. Thus, they might be atypical. In fact, both organizations had lasted for at least five years, while the informants had also been successful over an even longer period. Each trafficking organization accounted for non-trivial shares of the total cocaine market in the United States. On a monthly basis, a dozen or so customers brought in loads of hundreds of kilograms; a purchase of 250 kilograms at 20,000 U.S. dollars per kilo involves payment of 5 million dollars. There were a number of multi-ton shipments from Colombia; during the period August 1991 through April 1992 five shipments totaling 20 tons were warehoused by one warehouse operation.[40] In the context of a market delivering about 300 tons to final users, these are substantial quantities.

Fuentes described organizations that were durable, bureaucratic, violent, and strategic. For example, recruitment of new staff for U.S. operations was highly systematized with interviews by senior traffickers in Colombia, and the provision of collateral in the form of identification of family members who could be held hostage. References for prospective workers had to come from within the organization. Non-Colombians were considered higher risk employees because it was more difficult to threaten them if they defected with money or drugs. Providing familial details did help, though threats were harder to execute in the Dominican Republic than in Colombia. Recruitment was very selective. There was a strong preference for relatives in leadership positions, and cell managers were usually well educated with college degrees. Exit was allowed, provided the circumstances did not arouse suspicion that the agent had defected to the police. Colombians who were recruited to work in the United States were issued visas that expired shortly after entry, so as to limit their mobility.

The system was designed to move shipments very rapidly, since inventory in the United States represented risk. Twenty-four hours was the goal for getting rid of a shipment once it had reached the destination city. Stockpiles were held in Colombia, where the enforcement risk was vastly smaller. The organizations had their own domestic transportation systems, drivers who would carry shipments of 100 kilos or more for prices ranging from 300 to 1,000 U.S. dollars per kilo, depending on the length of the trip.[41]

The scale of the organization was impressive. One large cell was estimated to have three hundred workers in it, occupying at least six identifiable roles. It was estimated to have employed a total of twelve hundred individuals during its lifetime. Most of them received modest salaries: 7,000 U.S. dollars per month for a cell manager, 2,000 U.S. dollars for a stash-house sitter. Those incomes are rather moderate given the volume and margins for the organization that still generated annual incomes totaling millions of dollars for the principals.

M. Nataranjan describes an equally large organization.[42] She documents one surprising phenomenon, namely that the principal U.S. operative talks to numerous individuals, with twenty-four identified from wiretaps, including fifteen customers. This phenomenon is hardly consistent with maintaining low exposure, since any one of the fifteen could obtain relief from lengthy prison sentences by providing information about his supplier. Perhaps what we observe here is the end game of successful operations that have become increasingly confident of their own invulnerability.

European Smuggling

Smaller smuggling entities can still survive in the European market. Ruggiero and Smith describe opportunistic smugglers of less than a kilo of cocaine or hashish, concealing it in bicycles.[43] Disposal of smaller quantities requires less organizational capacity; a single domestic customer may be sufficient.

However, European heroin seizures of more than 25 kilograms are regularly reported. For example, Interpol reported in 1996 eight seizures of between 65 kilograms and 373 kilograms, totaling more than 1 ton, from truck traffic alone. Other large seizures were made at ports: seizures reported in May and June of 1996 included 217 kilos (Venice), 108 kilos (Madrid), and 134 kilos (Ipsala, Turkey).[44]

It is impossible to estimate systematically what share of total European heroin imports are accounted for by large shipments, that is, by groups with the financial, organizational, and personnel capacities to assemble, purchase, ship, and distribute large quantities. Large shipments appear to account for the majority of all heroin seized but that could reflect the higher per kilo risk associated with larger bundles.

Drug Smuggling and Legitimate Institutions

If drugs travel in legitimate commerce and traffic, then transportation companies, as well as financial institutions, may be active accomplices. For example, American Airlines has paid substantial fines in the past for inadequate monitoring; its planes were importing clandestine cocaine shipments. Recent investigations at Miami International Airport showed that employees of the airline have continued to find opportunities for large-scale smuggling. This time, the participating employees were baggage handlers at the U.S. landing point. Corruption in the consuming countries seems to be less central to the business, an assertion that arouses considerable skepticism in producer countries. Corruption, like scientific hypotheses, presents a problem of epistemological asymmetry. Scientific hypotheses can only be disproved, not proved; corruption can be found but its existence never disproved. Nonetheless, U.S. prosecutors pursue corrupt agents with considerable zeal when they find them. At the same time, the overlapping authority of enforcement agencies creates a situation in which any corrupt agent, no matter how well protected in his or her own department, has to be concerned with possible investigation by another agency. In such an environment, the market for corruption will shrink.

Organized Crime and Transnational Drug Traffic

The expansion of the drug trade in the last thirty years has presented opportunities for preexisting groups to build on their core capacities in other criminal activities, particularly those involving illicit markets (gambling, prostitution, loan sharking). One might also expect that success in the transnational drug business would lead new organizations to use their core capacities to enter other illegal markets and criminal activities. Though there has been a shift in specialization by experienced offenders (for example, in Britain many drug traffickers were previously active in other criminal pursuits, including armed robbery), generally that seems not to have happened at the organizational level.[45]

Particularly surprising is the minimal role of the U.S. mafia. Though apparently possessing some of the most important assets for this business, and having had a major role in heroin smuggling during the period 1935–1970, it has been marginalized in drug trafficking since then. Drug cases involving senior Mafiosi are almost unheard of, and the organizations themselves have not participated at all. Only in Italy has the mafia—a very different organization from its U.S. counterpart—played a significant role.[46]

Western European nations other than Italy had a less well-developed organized crime structure when the heroin market expanded. Western European organizations with international smuggling and distribution capacities appear to be a creation of post–Cold War developments. They are involved in the smuggling of cars into eastern Europe and of immigrants and prostitutes into western Europe.

The absence of the U.S. mafia from this trade, as well as the failure of the Colombian drug-smuggling organizations to develop a presence in other markets, may enable a better understanding of what is distinctive about the transnational drug market. In particular, it leads to consideration of the final topic, enforcement and its consequences.

The U.S. mafia, as a national alliance of predominantly Italian gangs based in various cities, emerged primarily through bootlegging, though the exigencies of the gambling business also played a role in its development.[47] It was characterized by highly developed networks of systemic corruption in local law enforcement, and until about 1950 or 1960, in city politics as well. Both bootlegging and numbers banking required large numbers of agents, geographically dispersed. Using its connections with the Italian mafia, the U.S. mafia imported heroin through the New York City docks, utilizing its control of the waterfront unions. The leaders were highly visible, as much reported on in the newspapers as prominent socialites. The names of the principal "families" were also well known throughout the nation. Membership in one of these families provided an important asset for an ambitious young criminal seeking to intimidate others without investing in extensive violence himself. The individual organizations endured in recognizable form for more than half a century at least. Leaders were occasionally incarcerated, but rarely for extended periods prior to the 1980s. The assets of the mafia families then were: a) reputation for control of contingent violence, both collective and individual; b) access to a network of agents; c) durability; d) access to capital; and e) control of corrupt police departments. Cocaine importing turned out not to require these assets. Most basic was that the drug originated in Latin America where other gangs had already established corruption relations with authorities. Moreover, the large Hispanic immigrant community in the United States was capable of providing the necessary networks and recruitment for operations in the United States. The Colombian organizations developed a reputation for violence that was comparable to, if not greater than, that of the mafia. In this area, they were building on the tradition of extreme violence that has characterized Colombia since the political troubles of the late 1940s. These organizations were willing to be less discriminating in their use of that violence, killing wives and children as well as principals. Perhaps most importantly, high-level participants in the United States were at great risk from enforcement agencies. Many agencies developed sophisticated and broad investigative capabilities, creating substantial risk of arrest. If arrested, leaders were likely to serve very long sentences. The mafia itself has shown signs of breaking down in the face of long sentences for other crimes that have generated high-level informants. The return here was not to broad reputation but to discretion. Ostentatious display of wealth and power might be an asset in Colombia where the corruption was systemic. It was a source of weakness in the United States where police corruption was only opportunistic and where enforcement agencies had strong incentives and tools for apprehending leaders.

The mafia, then, simply lacked useful assets for competing with Colombian and Mexican traffickers. But that may also explain why these drug-trafficking groups have not expanded their activities to other criminal markets in the United States. Their assets are not usable in many sectors. Discretion requires that they restrict the dissemination of information about their capacities. Similarly, their workforce is predominantly from their own community, limiting their capacity to operate in the general market place. The contacts with corrupt authorities are limited to source countries that play a minimal role in other smuggling, apart from illegal immigrants; in that market, only protection in the importing country has value.

Enforcement

Official estimates suggest that drug smuggling is a risky business, at least in terms of the drugs themselves. World cocaine production is estimated to total about 900 tons,[48] while total seizures may be as high as 400 tons. In western Europe, heroin seizures total 11 tons; a back-of-the-envelope calculation generates an estimate of heroin consumption of less than 30 tons.

Many seizures occur at the border and involve no offender other than the carrier, notwithstanding efforts in some countries to make "controlled deliveries," in which police follow the drugs to their final destination. Offenders carrying small amounts from one point to another across the border are called "mules," not merely for their physical roles; they also have minimal knowledge about who else is in the organization. When drugs are seized in container vessels, it can be very difficult to identify the responsible participants. Thus, though a high fraction of the quantity shipped is seized, risks to senior traffickers may be modest.

Fuentes's research does give some information on this subject.[49] The two trafficking organizations that he studied had operated successfully within the United States for a number of years: one from 1983 to 1992, the other at least from 1988 to 1992. The head of the first organization had been convicted in 1975, and then again in 1979, but after release in 1983, survived in the business for nine additional years without arrest. One other participant, a senior manager, also involved in money laundering, was said to have operated in the United States for almost ten years. The description of the cells and the organizations generally suggested an operation in more or less the same form for at least a few years.

As in other illegal markets, there is a constant interaction between enforcement agencies and drug smugglers, most conspicuously around routes and modes of trafficking. A concentration of interdiction resources around southern Florida in the early 1980s led to a shift in trafficking routes to the Caribbean. Pressure on those routes led to increased transshipment through Mexico. Increased focus on smuggling in TIR trucks (Trans International Router) in Europe may have led to a greater use of sea cargo.

Broader technological and social changes impinge on enforcement efforts. Ruggiero and Smith have noted that the growth of international personal mail has reduced the risk of sending small packages containing drugs through the regular international post. It is no longer a remarkable event for a household to receive a package from overseas.[50] The universal availability of cell phones makes electronic surveillance more complicated, though not necessarily less successful, once established. The same can be said for computers. They allow the organizations better control of their own activities, but once controlled and deciphered by enforcement agencies, provide more varied and detailed information for investigation and prosecution.

Money laundering is another component of drug enforcement specifically targeted at transnational trafficking. While no systematic measures are available as to the amount of money that is being laundered by drug traffickers, there are two reasons to believe that control may have had a substantial effect on drug trafficking. First, the absolute sums seized in a number of high-profile operations combating money laundering, occasionally amounting to more than 250 million U.S. dollars, constitute a non-trivial fraction of the total earnings generated by this level of trafficking. Second, there are reports that money launderers charge 5 to 10 percent for their services, a healthy tax on the revenues of high-level traffickers. Given the presence of many potential launderers, this may well represent a response to the risk of law enforcement.

Conclusion

Transnational drug trafficking has evolved in response to a variety of economic and social factors, next to the shifts in demand. Patterns of legitimate traffic, commerce, and migration have influenced the participation and organization of the trafficking. Modern communication technology has been an important factor, directly and indirectly influencing trade. In addition, the intensity and form of law enforcement have played a large role, driving up returns for successful traffickers to truly astonishing levels. This way, the principal figures in the Colombian cocaine trade have been able to accumulate fortunes in the hundreds of millions of dollars.

For cocaine as well as for heroin, growing efficiency appears to produce an industry in which a small number of enterprises account for a large share of total traffic, though without acquiring any market power. With their scale of operations, they have created great harm in producer and transshipment nations, exacerbating corruption and, in Colombia, Mexico, and Myanmar, undermining the power of the national state. Much research on the structural functioning of the drug industry and its effects on source and consumer countries remains to be done. A research agenda will require a specification of goals, sources, and methods. A basic research objective will be to assess the way in which alternative control methods do affect the harms from trafficking in both the producer/transshipment and consumer countries. Data sources are not likely to be found in official statistics. The information on seizures, arrests, or incarcerations will not provide much useful insight either. Price data, information on the mark-up between export and import prices and, if possible, on the prices charged by corrupt officials and various employee groups, would provide knowledge on the economic consequences of trafficking. Given the reluctance of enforcement agencies to enter this area, these data may have to be collected through interviews with participants, itself an expensive and difficult process.

Research may progress to the extent that it follows the national security research models that have been developed at organizations such as RAND and the Institute for Defense Analysis. Agency cooperation will be required if research is to be systematic and not driven by the erratic offering of opportunities. Agency cooperation, in turn, will be dependent on showing that what researchers produce can help the agencies perform better. The challenge is by no means impossible, as shown by how much official measurement of crime in recent years has been driven by researchers. A clear strategy, however, is required.

Notes

1. The distinction here is between true economic profits, which take account of shadow prices, and profits that appear as revenues in excess of actual payments for labor, transportation, rent, and so on. In very risky business, accounting profits may be high while true economic profits are low or even negative, once risk compensation is included in costs. See D. A. Boyum, "Reflections on Economic Theory and Drug Enforcement" (Ph.D. diss., Harvard University, 1992).

2. José R. Fuentes, "Life of a Cell: Managerial Practice and Strategy in Colombian Cocaine Distribution in the United States" (Ph.D. diss., City University of New York, 1998).

3. Francisco E. Thoumi, *Political Economy and Illegal Drugs in Colombia* (Boulder, Colo.: Lynne Rienner, 1995).

4. Paul Stares, *Global Habit* (Washington, D.C.: Brookings Institution, 1995).

5. United Nations International Drug Control Program (UNDCP), *Economic and Social Consequences of Drug Abuse and Illicit Trafficking,* Technical Series, no. 6 (Vienna: UNDCP, 1999).

6. Peter Reuter, "Book Review," *Journal of Policy Analysis and Management,* no. 17 (1998), 22–24.

7. Office of National Drug Control Policy, *What America's Users Spend on Illicit Drugs, 1988–1995* (Washington, D.C.: UNDCP, 1997).

8. John Caulkins and Peter Reuter, "What Can We Learn from Drug Prices?," *Journal of Drug Issues* 28, no. 3 (1998), 593–612.

9. Evringham and Rydell estimate that 22 percent of users accounted for 65 percent of total cocaine consumption in 1992; the figure can be higher, depending on the point in the epidemic. See Stuart Evringham and Charles P. Rydell, *The Demand for Cocaine* (Santa Monica, Calif.: RAND, 1994), 28.

10. This is a personal judgment developed from a host of speculative figures on the prevalence of heroin and cocaine addiction in the European Union; quantities consumed per addict; and the price of drugs (e.g., Pompidou Group, 1998). See European Monitoring Center on Drugs and Drug Abuse (EMCDDA), *Annual Report on the State of the Drugs Problem in the European Union* (Lisbon: EMCDDA, 1977); also Pompidou Group, *Heroin Seizures as an Indicator of Variation in Market Situations: Drugs Availability and Heroin Use in Europe* (Strassbourg: Council of Europe, 1998).

11. United Nations International Drug Control Program (UNDCP), *World Drug Report* (Oxford: Oxford University Press, 1999), passim.

12. Ibid., 124.

13. United States Department of State, *International Narcotics Control Strategy* (Washington, D.C.: Department of State Annual Report, 1999), passim.

14. Peter Reuter and Mark Kleiman, "Risks and Prices: An Economic Analysis of Drug Enforcement," in Michael H. Tonry and Norval Morris, eds., *Crime and Justice: An Annual Review of Research No. 7* (Chicago: University of Chicago Press, 1986), 62–98.

15. Michael Kennedy, Peter Reuter, and Kenneth J. Riley, *A Single Model of Cocaine Production* (Santa Monica, Calif.: RAND, 1992), passim.

16. The per capita GDP for Thailand is more than ten times that of Myanmar.

17. The decline in Peruvian production may also be the consequence of an extended blight, the first to hit the coca crop in recent decades, and a period of intense enforcement against air traffic of coca base between Peru and Colombia.

18. This analysis draws heavily on Peter Reuter, "Can the Borders Be Sealed?," in *Public Interest*, no. 92 (1988), 51–65.

19. This is not an argument for abandoning interdiction but for recognizing the limits of its effectiveness in making cocaine more expensive and less available in mature markets.

20. Nigerian traffickers seem to specialize in such smuggling. Mark Kleiman has estimated that Nigerian couriers body-packing heroin into New York in the early 1990s accounted for more than 500 kilograms per annum, 3 to 5 percent of estimated U.S. consumption. That requires only three body packers every two days. Kleiman, "Drugs and the Law," in *New York Review of Books* 40, no. 4 (February 11, 1993).

21. The risk and payment figures here are moderately informed guesses; the purpose is simply to provide a sense of the magnitudes involved.

22. Note that, as expected, the drugs travel with passengers rather than cargo, since Nigerian exports, apart from oil, are modest.

23. Vincenzo Ruggiero and Nigel Smith, *Eurodrugs: Drug Use, Markets, and Trafficking in Europe* (London: London University College Press, 1995), 75.

24. Francisco E. Thoumi, *The Political Economy of the Andean Drug Industry* (Washington, D.C.: Woodrow Wilson Center, 2001).

25. Michael Booth, *Opium: A History* (New York: St. Martin's Press, 1996), passim.

26. Mats Killias, "Immigrants, Crime, and Criminal Justice in Sweden," in Michael S. Tonry, ed., *Ethnicity, Crime, and Immigration* (Chicago: Chicago University Press, 1997), 386.

27. Interpol, *European Heroin Scene: Balkans—The Focus* (Lyon: Interpol, 1997), 18.

28. Hans-Jörg Albrecht, "Ethnic Minorities, Crime, and Criminal Justice in Germany," in Tonry, *Ethnicity, Crime, and Immigration*, 64–65.

29. Killias, "Immigrants, Crime, and Criminal Justice," passim.

30. Vincenzo Ruggiero, "Albanian Drug Trafficking in Europe," in M. Nataranjan and Peter Hough, eds., *Illegal Drug Markets: From Research to Policy*, Crime Prevention Studies, vol. 11 (Monsey, N.Y.: Criminal Justice Press, 2000), 224–49.

31. Donald Cressey, *Theft of the Nation* (New York: Harper and Row, 1969), passim.

32. The best evidence is simply the ease with which new sellers enter and the speed with which they depart. There may be rents for various capacities but certainly no

power to exclude; see M. Katz and H. Rosen, *Micro-Economics* (Burr Ridge Ill.: Irwin, 1994).

33. Patrick Clawson and Rensselaer W. Lee III, *The Andean Cocaine Industry* (New York: St. Martin's Press, 1998), epilogue, 134.

34. If demand is inelastic with respect to price, then a seller with market power can increase revenues and decrease costs by cutting production, until reaching a level at which the demand for cocaine and heroin may have elasticity of greater than one with respect to final price at current levels. It is very likely that elasticity is less than one with respect to high-level prices, though there are extreme models of price mark-up from import to trafficking that would yield a different result.

35. Tom Schelling, "Economic Analysis of Organized Crime," in *President's Commission on Law Enforcement and the Administration of Justice, Task Force Report Organized Crime* (Washington, D.C.: United States Government Printing Office, 1967), 48–61.

36. Patricia A. Adler, *Wheeling and Dealing: An Ethnography of an Upper-Level Drug Dealing and Smuggling Community* (New York: Columbia University Press, 1985), 66.

37. Peter Reuter and John Haaga, *The Organization of High-level Drug Markets: An Exploratory Study* (Santa Monica, Calif.: RAND, 1989), 39–40.

38. Evringham and Rydell, *The Demand for Cocaine,* passim.

39. Fuentes, "Life of a Cell," passim.

40. There is an ambiguity as to whether this total was for a single organization or a confederation associated with Miguel Rodriguez-Orejueta, a principal figure in the Cali Cartel.

41. This appeared not to be so much compensation for longer time as for the number of potential police encounters.

42. M. Nataranjan, "Understanding the Structure of a Drug Trafficking Organization: A Conversational Analysis," in Nataranjan and Hough, *Illegal Drug Markets,* passim.

43. Ruggiero and Smith, *Eurodrugs,* passim.

44. Interpol, *European Heroin Scene,* 10.

45. Adler, *Wheeling and Dealing,* passim.

46. Raimondo Cantanzaro, *Men of Respect: A Social History of the Sicilian Mafia* (New York: Free Press, 1988), passim.

47. Michael Halter, "The Changing Structure of American Gambling in the Twentieth Century," *Journal of Social Issues* 35, no. 3 (1979), 223–42.

48. United States Department of State, *International Narcotics Control Strategy,* passim.

49. Fuentes, "Life of a Cell," 19.

50. Ruggiero and Smith, *Eurodrugs,* passim.

8

Post-Fordist Cocaine

Labor and Business Relations among Colombian Dealers

Damián Zaitch

Colombian drug organizations that are active in Europe have been described either as mere representatives or cells of all-powerful Colombian enterprises, or as flexible criminal networks in which noncriminal roles and relations are, by definition, excluded from the analysis. These perspectives have produced distorted images of branches and professional businessmen or pictures of a chaotic web of international underground criminals. The analysis of drug enterprises and labor modalities within the drug economy,[1] in reference to Colombian dealers working in Europe, does produce a different image. Fieldwork among Colombian cocaine dealers in the Netherlands—a major entry port for drugs to the European market—does reveal very interesting forms of organization of the drug industry downstream.[2]

Branches, Criminal Networks, and Flexible Entrepreneurs

Although it is more or less agreed today that Colombian cocaine organizations have undergone a process of fragmentation and restructuring, most works mentioning Colombian groups or individuals involved in cocaine import and distribution in Europe still tend to describe them as branches, cells, representatives, or agents of the X Colombian cartel(s).[3] These descriptions are usually fed by a combination of economic and bureaucratic definitions of organized crime: Colombians are in business, and they belong to certain organizations. Whether the emphasis rests in highly organized and stable structures,[4] strict labor division, professionalism, or vertical integration,[5] the model in mind is that of a transnational corporation. Even when the notion of cartel is avoided, Colombian dealers abroad are thought to be integrated in large organizational structures. In an interesting attempt to compare the narco-business with any other large company, Sidney Zabludoff argues that "each cell is organized somewhat along the lines of its headquarters in Colombia. Cells vary in number of personnel according to their responsibilities and the size of the market they serve. Some employ as many as 50 Colombians including a cell leader and several 'vice-presidents' in charge of specific tasks. . . ."[6]

Others simply discuss the issue in terms of the activities of "Colombian cartels"[7] or "Colombian families"[8] in the Netherlands. Some versions of this picture also include an "alien conspiracy" dimension. For example, Johan van Doorn claims that "close family ties at the top and a cell-structure characterize the cartels. . . . Arrival and further distribution in western Europe is in the hands of high-placed Colombian cartel members who take up residence, either permanently or temporarily. . . . There is a very realistic possibility that the cartels will try to expand their influence in Europe over the next few years by setting up import corporations of their own."[9] Despite the fact that most economic roles and relations among Colombian dealers can indeed be compared with those of other legal markets, this perspective tends to institutionalize arrangements and businesses in a holistic way. Moreover, the exclusive stress on professional skilled managers and entrepreneurs simply ignores the reality of the mass of unskilled Colombian employees, often regarded as members and not as victims of the groups they supposedly belong to.

With a stronger accent in economic processes than in bureaucratic structures, Petrus van Duyne presents a less static picture of Colombian cocaine entrepreneurs and enterprises.[10] Even though he talks about "mother organizations" and mentions cartels holding sections of the European market, he pays more attention to business forms, as well as to symbiotic relations with the legal economy. He describes "commercial bridgeheads" and "pioneer firms," which are both flexible and not always a model of professionalism. He also identifies enterprises of different size related through intermediaries or brokers. Since only significant detected cases are analyzed (through police and judicial dossiers), Van Duyne does not deal with smaller units, more informal coalitions, and especially with the labor market of his "criminal enterprises."

With a strong entrepreneurial approach, Robin Naylor criticizes the misleading use of economic categories by drug enforcers, pointing out that cocaine trafficking proceeds through a complex of arms-length commercial transactions.[11] Other researchers have sustained the same stress on fragmentation as well.[12] The material presented by Frank Bovenkerk,[13] with a stronger focus on the socioeconomic and cultural context of those involved in large cocaine import operations, also reveals more fluid transactions, some levels of autonomy, and space for erratic behavior even among top *traquetos* (drug dealers).

A second popular paradigm to conceptualize Colombian cocaine traffickers spins around the notion of social network.[14] In the hands of crime analysts, this approach focuses on the social dynamics of criminal networks, trying to identify actors, connections, and the nature and intensity of criminal ties.[15] Despite these promising aims, the approach has often been reduced to a (potential) law enforcement instrument: how to hit on vulnerable spots in a criminal network and how to "remove" a significant actor. It is, therefore, no wonder that most sympathizers of this view are police investigators, policymakers, crime managers or consultants, and ministerial researchers.[16]

For example, in their study on serious organized crime in the Netherlands, Edward Kleemans et al. describe Colombian-related cases in terms of "criminal networks," both facilitated and hindered by the social context.[17] These researchers distance themselves from the economic view as theoretical departure, so they seldom talk about entrepreneurs or cartels. While they favor notions such as criminal networks or "cooperation agreements," they still refer to Colombian "groups" and "organizations." Their picture, sketched from some dossier-cases involving Colombian cocaine dealers, reveals flexible international cooperation, diversification to other illegal markets at distribution level, and, of course, different operational capabilities regarding contacts in Colombia and the Netherlands. Their view has the merit of recognizing flexible relations at the core of any drug transaction.

However, several risks and pitfalls are involved in the use of this approach for understanding drug economies and actors. Firstly, while some crime managers sacrifice relevant social questions about relations, they place all their emphasis on charting networks to present them as aesthetic devices in research appendixes or as tools in computer programs. Secondly, a tendency exists to view networks-as-things-in-themselves, and to refer to criminal networks as mere synonyms of criminal groups or organizations (coalitions, for network analysts). In these cases, the bureaucratic approach to organized crime is not challenged: flexibility is incorporated into the criminal organization paradigm as just another attribute of the structure. Thirdly, no attention is paid to the meaning that relations have for those involved in the "network." During my fieldwork, I met many people who, while knowing that they were engaged in illegal activities, did not consider themselves to be criminals. They saw themselves in first instance engaged in legal or informal activities, as workers, as adventurers acting under pressure, often blaming others for being the "true criminals." Illegality is a key factor, but should not be taken for granted when explaining the social behavior of *traquetos*. People engage in the drug economy because they are attracted by potentially large (illegal) profits, but are clearly conscious of the fact that cocaine is illegal. For example, during field research, many informants manifested the desire to end their illegal activities as soon as possible; they supported drug legalization, or planned to enter legal activities that provided greater symbolic rewards.

Further, a problem with this approach is the exclusive focus on a priori isolated "criminal" relations. "Noncriminal" relations are considered secondary or analyzed as an external social context—as "upper world," as corrupt officials, as spoiled legal businesses, and so on. For crime network analysts, flexible relations inside these networks mean flexible criminal relations. Other dimensions of social linkages (familial, commercial, ethnic, labor, class, religious, gendered, geographical, political, legitimate, and so on) are only considered as context, as facilitators, as risk factors, but are isolated from what really matters: the criminal suspect and his criminal network.[18] This view ignores that what is basically flexible around drug traffickers is the way in which money is made (flexible accumulation), the interactions among different types of legal and illegal economic units (businesses, enterprises, single entrepreneurs, brokers, facilitators, and financiers), and the way in which many sorts of employees work and divide tasks, risks, and responsibilities (flexible specialization). Behind flexible networks—whether they are criminal or not—there are flexible entrepreneurs, partners, brokers, and employees. Flexibility can be better explained—and compared—when the business and labor relations are the object of analysis.

Cocaine Distribution: Three Case Studies

We will discuss three cases of cocaine distributors working in the Netherlands. Their life stories give an interesting insight into the dynamics of the operations of the drug industry in consumer countries.

Riverito's Four Operations

At the time I visited him, Riverito was in his thirties and was serving four years in the Bijlmer prison of Amsterdam. Coming from a middle-class family living in Cali, he studied economics at the Universidad del Valle, where he graduated in 1992. After his studies he got a good job with a leading construction company in Cali, but found the work routine and boring. During his studies, he had been working as a waiter in a famous hotel in Cali, a place where top local cocaine entrepreneurs had been meeting for business and pleasure. In the hotel, Riverito got to know these people and their world of major cocaine producers and exporters. He learned their tastes, anticipated their wishes, and they invited him to more private events. "I was the private waiter of Pacho Herrera [a former major drug entrepreneur from Cali]. Once he gave me a 1,000 U.S. dollars tip at the end of a party. I had to share it with some other people."

Apart from this link and the fact that it gave him access to some cocaine to distribute among friends, he did not become involved in the cocaine trade. However, his closeness to the entrepreneurs had a tremendous impact. "Brother, you don't imagine how it is until you come close to them. So much money! They impress the people around them because they are not so different than you or me. They are not old rich bastards, no; they speak the same language as normal people do. Some are gentle and jointly liable. And you wonder: Why not me?"

Things were not going well for him in Colombia. He had a serious alcohol problem and went though a divorce. "Very rarely I took a joint or a coke line; no, my true nightmare is the drink: beer, and especially whisky and *aguardiente*. I don't get aggressive, but I lose control. I ruined my marriage in December 1994 due to the drink."

In 1995, he decided to go to the Netherlands where a sister was living. He went looking for work and soon came to participate in the cocaine business. He was less motivated by the opportunity to earn big money quickly or to create a path for social improvement than by the possibility to make a new start in life. When he became involved in the cocaine business he had not been sent by any one, nor did he belong to any group or organization in the business. He went to the Netherlands alone and established contact with local importers and distributors using his former contacts within the *Caleño* cocaine entrepreneurs.

Once in Amsterdam, Riverito shared a room with other Colombians. Some of them were already involved in the cocaine business. He was contracted by a Colombian importer, and he started to work as *encaletador:* the person responsible for safeguarding the cocaine loads before they are divided and delivered to wholesalers. After a couple of small operations through which he gained trust and demonstrated his competence, he was offered a more risky and profitable task: the unloading of several kilograms from a ship in Zeebrugge. He was rewarded with 30,000 U.S. dollars, an amount that he had to share with another Colombian who accompanied him.

Riverito's operation at Zeebrugge was successful. However, the 15,000 U.S. dollars that he was promised turned out to be just 10,000 U.S. dollars. He claimed the remaining amount for a while, but then settled and accepted. "I wasn't going to create problems, I wasn't in a position to ask for the rest. You see, after all they paid me well. I bought a house in Cali with that money, for my ex-wife and my son." The unloading operation at Zeebrugge reveals some interesting aspects regarding the labor relations involved. The actual operation involved at least two small independent units, contrary to the idea that a single, well-organized group was controlling import and distribution with a manager dividing the tasks and paying "his own" people.

The Colombian importer had bought the cocaine load from the exporter at 20,000 U.S. dollars per kilo. He sold at a wholesale price of 24,000 U.S.

dollars per kilo, making 200,000 U.S. dollars on the entire load. He operated with two informal helpers. Both of them were given several thousand dollars. The importer would receive information about the *cruce* (sending), but would not be responsible since he would buy from the exporter at the port of entry. He would unload the shipment, transport, stash, and divide it; often he would deliver it—in this case, in three packages—to wholesale distributors. He would not do this all by himself. For the most dangerous task, the unloading, he would contract somebody else at a pay of 10 percent of his own profits (20,000 U.S. dollars). The contracted person in this case was Riverito.

Riverito and his companion constituted a separate economic unit, independent from the importer. They were not responsible for the merchandise, and their contact would end as soon as the operation had been completed. Riverito and his partner would plan and execute their operation with considerable autonomy, although in a less strict way than in legal subcontracting, since Riverito was not in a position to guarantee a refund if the unloading operation were to fail. In practice, the importer would work close to Riverito, keeping an eye on him and providing him with ideas, information, and even with transportation, although Riverito and his friend had to arrange the many technical aspects of the unloading by themselves. They were contracted as external labor to assume the high risks involved in the unloading. To the importer, they offered a highly priced service to complete this particular operation. In contrast to what happens in legal business, this subcontracting relationship had little chance of being repeated in future operations. Riverito wanted more and would enter the trade on his own account.

After the Zeebrugge operation, a year after his arrival in the Netherlands, Riverito was joined by his older brother William. Together, they began looking for a possibility to import cocaine from Cali. They had no capital to invest, but knew many people in the trade. This time they intended to keep things in their own hands. "You see, I work no more with those *paisanos* [Colombians]. Everything is fine with them, but I just tried with other people in Colombia. I knew this man from before. He promised to send something, so we waited. We waited, and waited, and nothing happened. He kept giving stupid excuses; I think he liked to talk and tell things he really could not do. Pure bullshit!"

Riverito got what Colombians call a *línea muerta* (dead line), a nonexisting cocaine line or one that is failing. For this operation, he planned to buy in Colombia and sell in the Netherlands, dividing the profits with his brother. They phoned many traffickers in Colombia, but nothing worked out. People promised things and than just disappeared. The brothers survived with small jobs as load keepers and internal couriers.

Finally, a new operation appeared. It was small, but rather easy and it promised a good profit. They could expect a markup of 4,000 U.S. dollars on a kilo of cocaine that had been offered to Riverito by another Colombian. Riverito had become a wholesale distributor. He bought the cocaine, and his brother William and a *paisa*—a Colombian from Medellín—called Charley entered the deal as his helpers. Charley had just arrived and used to boast of his past as a bodyguard of Pablo Escobar. Charley told Riverito that a friend of his had a buyer for the cocaine kilo. This "friend," thought to be Colombian by Riverito, turned out to be an Aruban who gave Charley some money to ensure the deal. They went to meet the buyers, but things went wrong. Said Riverito, "Man, there was no buyer, there was only a gang of Antilleans who put two guns to our heads and stole the thing. It is a miracle we are alive. I know another *Caleño* who was almost killed in the same situation but still walks around with a bullet in his neck."

The man from Aruba did not disappear, but pretended to have been fooled as well. He appeared to be a trafficker avoiding prison by informing the police on "Colombian criminal organization" stories. After a failed attempt to recover the package from the Arubans, Riverito and his companions were detained by the police and convicted. In his last operation, Riverito was the boss.

Riverito's four operations, which took place in a two-year time span, reveal two interesting phenomena. First, instead of stable and large organizations, a mutating interconnection of small units seems to be involved in trafficking. Second, this connection changes with respect to people, positions, linkage nature, and tasks along the four operations in which Riverito was involved.

Miguel's Many Bosses

Although Miguel prefers to present himself as an "intellectual mainly interested in philosophy and criminology," he was rather open about his involvement in the cocaine business for more than a decade.[19] He almost made it as a criminal lawyer, but claimed having been expelled from the university. "I felt frustrated and I burned all the books. At that time, I was working in a small secondary school in Cartago as vice principal and philosophy teacher. I knew some people in Cali, but I did not enter this for the money, I suppose. I think it was out of bitterness."

He was first invited to work as a courier for a small organization in Bogotá, transporting small loads of between 3 kilos and 7 kilos. He made successful trips to the Netherlands, to France, and to a couple of Central American countries. After that, he made a trip to Portugal, where he was caught and he spent three years in jail. "It was terrible there, the law of the jungle, surrounded by 'garbage' that did not deserve anything. I survived because we have a name, I mean they think it is better not to mess with Colombians."

Back in Colombia, he tried unsuccessfully to resume his law studies. He began work in a cocaine kitchen near Cali, a job generally considered as very dangerous. "The chemicals are very inflammable, we had to wear rubber shoes because the slightest spark could provoke an explosion. Everything is very precarious, once a certain amount is cooked the kitchen is dismantled and you are moved to a new one. It is risky, but you get paid monthly."

After the capture of his *patrón* (boss), Miguel returned to Bogotá to resume his job as a drug courier, but this time for another organization. He already had experience and was no longer regarded as a simple courier. In 1993, he was sent to Frankfurt as a baby-sitter (professional courier and controller). Although he himself was not caught, the cocaine was seized, some Italian importers were detained, and the cocaine remained unpaid for. Shortly after this operation, Miguel attempted to smuggle a few kilos through Schiphol Airport in Amsterdam, where he was caught. The impression that he had been punished for the failure and "demoted" from baby-sitter to *mula* (unskilled courier) had to be corrected. Things were more simple than that: a new operation for a single courier had appeared, and he was happy to clinch the assignment. With a false passport and more than 3 kilos of cocaine, he was sent on a journey via Venezuela and Curaçao to Amsterdam, from where he would have traveled south to deliver the merchandise in Geneva, Switzerland. Miguel explains: "You see, I worked for many groups and I never saw anything like a cartel. I don't feel part of a cartel. Every group is more or less independent. Some people know each other, yes, and sometimes a couple of *patrones* could meet and work together. There are also informal rules and codes, but nothing like the mafia; people don't really respect them. I believe that the only rule is to survive and get rich."

When asked about his plans after having completed his jail sentence, Miguel suggested that he first had to settle things with his last boss in Bogotá. After that, he would go back to Cali to "see who is there." He was, however, very skeptical about finding his old employers after such a long period of time.

Traffickers like Miguel cannot be connected with a particular group or cartel in Colombia. They move rather easily from one employer to another and combine drug smuggling with other jobs as cook (chemist), bodyguard, or baby-sitter.

Joel's Loneliness

Joel is a Colombian cocaine wholesaler who has been active in Amsterdam, and can be called a truly "discreet professional."[20] He has been buying from importers in Cali, his hometown, and has been selling to Turkish, Italian, and German groups in particular. He arrived in the Netherlands in 1996, leaving his family behind in Colombia. Previously, he had been distributing cocaine in Chicago with varying fortunes, until an operation was busted and he had to "disappear." His brother, who had worked with him in the United States, had already settled in the Netherlands and convinced him to come. He introduced him to local and foreign buyers. These contacts at the import and export level helped him to do well in the business. "My family lives in Colombia and they tell others that I am on a 'business trip.' I really would like to see my sons. Here, you see, every day is the same. I miss playing football with them, or just a nice picnic. I think I will soon retire, so I go back."

He has tried to minimize risk by delegating cocaine collection and delivery, avoiding cash transfers or involvement in the actual transportation of the goods. He only negotiates the terms of the deals, handles the money, and stashes the cocaine. He usually buys and sells *escama de pescado* (fish scale) or *concha de nácar* (nacre shell), top quality cocaine known for its pink shining glints.

Joel has an excellent reputation for being just and jointly liable, not only with business partners, but also among close friends and subordinates. In the words of Tano, one of his former employees, "He is incapable of killing a fly, and he keeps his word. . . . He lends money, invites [people to] dinners, and always asks if everything is okay. Once he helped a friend with 19,000 U.S. dollars and he never saw it back. He even helps unknown people. Last week, for example, he gave accommodation to a Bolivian woman, just because she was illegal and had nowhere to go. . . . I don't think these are interested favors, he might have his reasons to help, but he is just like that."

He is usually the boss of his own illegal enterprise. He is clearly what Nicholas Dorn et al. refer to as a number 1, "cut out" from delicate operational matters such as cocaine transportation and money transfers, but "hands on" in others such as stashing cocaine.[21] In some cases, he will make Paisita, another Colombian, his partner. They will share a percentage of the profits but only when they sell to a couple of Paisita's clients. Joel has always been the investor, and he assumes the financial risk of the operations. His brother, who invited him to come to the Netherlands and gave him most of his initial business contacts, works independently from him, holding a different line. However, they used to work together in Chicago. Tano reveals: "Once he went to collect some money, I think a lot of money, and they told him that his brother had already received it. When Joel found him it was already too late, his brother had spent it all in Colombia. I believe they settled the score, but there is always some tension."

Joel only buys cocaine from other Colombians, but not always in the same way and from different people. He enters the game per operation. He may, for example, receive a message from exporter A from Cali, asking if he wants to play. Although Joel knows his nickname and a telephone number to contact him, he may never met have him personally. According to the price and the quantity involved, he will say yes or no. In practice, he will almost always agree to buy at least a part of the load. Exporter A will arrange the shipment with importer B, mainly through Rotterdam. Joel will also agree to share the financial risks with importer B, who is also from Cali. In the event that the shipment is lost or seized, he will pay for half of its value, and he will invite the exporter to provide proof that no rip-off has taken place.

The three partners in this *línea* (line) or *flecha* (arrow) share financial risk, but are operating with great autonomy. They seldom repeat the same scheme. Importer B and Joel also receive cocaine from exporter C, who has closed a deal with exporter A and has been using his contacts in the Netherlands. Importer B also sells to other Colombian and non-Colombian distributors.

Joel has been selling the cocaine to different groups including other local Colombians, some Turks and Italians in Amsterdam, and a number of re-tailers in Germany and Belgium. He will never deal with more than two or three clients at the same time. On one occasion, Joel was visibly irritated. He explained that "another group of *Caleños*, they sold the thing one point cheaper [a point, referring to the kilo price, is 500 dollars] but we had agreed to sell for 48. Therefore, they sold it and I didn't. I will speak with them."

These informal agreements appear to be common among two or three groups of distributors selling from the same bulk to the same groups. How-ever, even under these circumstances, it remains difficult to enforce these price accords when excluding the use of force. Agreements with the importer are in general tacit and may include a gray zone of misunderstandings, dis-cussions, and conflicts. For example, if the cocaine is not sold immediately, the importer can become rather impatient about the payment.

During the field research, I met six different Colombians working for or with Joel: Simona, Paisita, his brother, Tico, Chino, and Tano. Except for Paisita, who has been his business partner on some occasions, none of the others has engaged in any stable criminal activity in relation to him. They are only offered jobs in relation to specific operations, and Joel decides what the assignment will be. One of the secrets of the success of the business in this case is that Joel has been operating all by himself. He hires people to move the cocaine inside Amsterdam, to receive it and deliver it, and to transfer the money. People like Tano are delegated tasks in all these phases. Paisita and Tico are able to project the violent image that Joel has been lacking and are useful to enforce compliance with the deals. Finally, Simona generally cooks and cleans for him, and, of course, provides in her house a place to stash the merchandise.

The money transfers to Colombia are arranged in a rather simple way. Sometimes Joel prefers to go to the office by himself, but most of the time he sends somebody else. He is actually aware of the presence of videocameras and of the content of financial regulations. The transfers are made in uneven amounts of about 2,500 to 3,500 dollars by six different people, who will deposit the money through four or five well-known money transfer offices. For this work, peripheral people—for example, friends of Simona may be recruited—get between 100 and 150 dollars for the job. This way, an amount of around 90,000 U.S. dollars each time will be sent to different accounts in Colombia. People will not repeat visits to the same office. Occasionally, cash will be sent with trusted travelers. Far from being part of a group—that is, Joel's organization—these people are just friends or acquaintances who often will not necessarily know each other very well. Tano describes how he delivered the cocaine for Joel. "I put the stuff in a big suitcase and I just went alone to meet the buyers. Paisita met me there and we delivered it. Joel paid me 100 dollars for each kilo transported." Finally, Joel was participating in "projects"—one in Japan and another one in France—in which none of the people mentioned above were involved.

Ways of Doing Business in Cocaine Trafficking

The three cases analyzed above show Colombian dealers engaged in different kinds of business and labor relations. In the following paragraphs we will elaborate the most common ways of organizing these relations. They are defined as ideal types. In empirical situations, mixed forms will occur (for instance partnerships among relatives) and they may mutate (that is, traffickers changing from one method to another). The types show the diversity of business forms and serve to systematize the most important elements involved in Colombian cocaine trafficking.

Individual Enterprises

Self-employment, a paramount feature of immigrant economies,[22] is extremely rare among Colombian cocaine dealers. They usually tend to be employees of somebody else. The exceptions concern those involved in wholesale distribution. Joel, for example, acted in most of his operations as an individual entrepreneur hiring his assistants on an ad-hoc basis. Lupo, another distributor, combined in a rather erratic fashion cocaine dealing with a larger number of other informal or illegal activities in which he engaged alone.

Partnerships

Partnerships constitute the most common way of conducting business, especially at the level of import and distribution. Most partnerships concern no more than two people. Third parties tend to be non-Colombian associates providing local resources, infrastructure, or further marketing contacts. Some partnerships will last for several operations. Most of them, however, are temporary coalitions of two persons assisted by a number of helpers, employees, and other subcontracted personnel. Riverito would work with a partner when importing and unloading. His case, like that of some other adventurers or "opportunistic irregulars,"[23] was to combine or switch from partnerships to wage labor. The partnerships often involved family, especially brothers and brothers-in-law.

In terms of the typology of trafficking "firms" proposed by Dorn et al., none of these Colombian partnerships can be characterized as "trading charities" (ideologically committed to drugs) or "mutual societies" (drug exchange among users). Colombian *traquetos* combine characteristics of the other categories in a very flexible way.

In Colombia, "sideliners" (legal businesses that trade drugs as a sideline) are a common phenomenon. In the Netherlands, however, no traces of Colombian sideliners could be found. Legal Colombian entrepreneurship in the Netherlands has been lacking. Business in relation to the cocaine trade has always been an instrument designed to conceal trafficking. Colombians do associate at times with local sideliners, especially people with import or retail businesses suffering financial problems. In addition, a small number of Colombian prostitutes and ex-prostitutes also sidelined into cocaine through a relationship with a drug entrepreneur.

Dorn's category of "criminal diversifiers" (existing criminal business diversifying to include cocaine) is also uncommon in the Netherlands. Those Colombians who are active in burglary or shoplifting will enter the cocaine business as temporary workers, but never as entrepreneurs. For those Colombians who diversified to other criminal activities and markets in the Netherlands, cocaine was the first step and at the same time the most profitable activity. Many of these *traquetos*, engaged in partnerships with local entrepreneurs involved in illegal activities, have no criminal record in Colombia.

The categories of the opportunistic irregular (involved erratically in the illegal economy) and the "retail specialist" (with a boss employing people to distribute drugs to users) share a reference to retail levels in which Colombians are absent. Yet, these types are somewhat familiar to Colombian entrepreneurs. Most *traquetos* only manage two or three operations per year, and their involvement is more irregular than often thought. They react to short-term developments, acting as "jump-up merchants"[24] when a profitable business opportunity emerges. They will engage in temporary partnerships and recruit people for the project. The "groups" thus assembled in an ad hoc way will have a boss and employees or helpers performing specific tasks.

Finally, Colombian groups or partnerships, especially those involved in cocaine trafficking, run the risk of being approached by "state-sponsored traders," collaborating with enforcement agencies as informants, infiltrators, or undercover policemen. Our field research could not find one single Colombian willing to become a *sapo* (police informant), although many complained of making foolish mistakes by dealing with the "wrong" people.

Joint Ventures

Many partnerships involve people already active in other projects with other people. These joint ventures are usually between people with access to the different resources that are required to put the operation together. One, for example, provides the money to invest and owns a front-store business, while the other provides the supplier in Colombia and the people needed to complete the operation. Some of these coalitions are "virtual." Potential partners spend a great deal of time thinking and talking about projects that in the end never materialize.

Percentage Commission

The partnerships do not necessarily divide profits in an even way. Participation is negotiated. During these negotiations, the reliability and profitability of each party is subject to discussion, focusing on three basic issues: financial risk, personal risk, and the material/human resources that have to be employed. The first and third are the key factors. Personal risk is often difficult to assess as it could be shared or completely passed on to helpers and laborers. When Paisita shared profits with Joel, he would only get 30 percent for providing the customer, putting up some money, and arranging the deal. As the main investor, Joel kept the other 70 percent.

A different picture would result in cases where the partners are very different in size and power: the project's offer would be split with little or no discussion. The smaller party would receive a percentage commission either in cash from the general profits or in kind from the total amount of cocaine moved. This arrangement is typical in export-import operations involving "envoys" (import agents sent by Colombian exporters) such as Jairo. Although he organized the import for a certain group in Cali—that is, working for them in that particular operation—he became involved as a partner since he provided essential infrastructure, marketing opportunities, and assumed high personal risks. The percentage commission system should be distinguished from the "sales on commission" method widely used among small wholesale distributors. As I will explain below, this contracting arrangement applies to a flexible labor force rather than to entrepreneurial partnerships.

Family Business

None of the cocaine enterprises found are structured along family lines in the style of the "crime families" or "family businesses"[25] discussed by the vast literature on middleman minorities and ethnic economies. Local family firms[26] are rare for obvious reasons: many Colombian *traquetos* are not "locals" and have no family in the Netherlands. Of course, kinship relations are often involved in partnerships and in labor recruitment and provide the basis for solidarity and trust. Joel and Riverito sometimes worked with their respective brothers, and some couples cooperated in export-import operations. However, most of them have relatives who do not participate in the business. They most commonly deal with and employ nonrelatives. The idea of "family labor" is absent. As one trafficker explained: "Here in The Hague I met many family members: blood brothers and relatives-in-law. But also close friends, that can be almost the same. . . . I see here many Arabs and they look like one big family, they are close and help each other. But Colombians are more individualistic, I don't know why. . . . Yes, family is important, but money makes them blind."

Jairo, who was sent by the Grajales family from Cali, was not related to them. The Grajales family business was in fact a conglomerate of legal and illegal businesses run by different members of a large family and did not have a unified structure. Joel and his brother also ran separated businesses. In some cases, a relative would provide the know-how, human and financial capital, or infrastructure. This has been the case with "mixed couples" or Colombian couples in which the woman had a Dutch passport and provided local contacts. Tano emphatically denied that family ties were important amongst *traquetos* in the Netherlands. "Look, you can not do this for many years, so some people try to keep their relatives out of this." Paisita also insisted on Colombian over family ties: "We work with other *Calichanos* [Colombianos]. They won't do silly things, you know for sure because everybody has a family in Colombia. . . ."

The Centrality of Intermediaries and Brokers

This system of small and changing coalitions is certainly invigorated by the intervention of a specific type of entrepreneur: the broker. Social brokers connect people, either directly or indirectly, for profit.[27] The usual role of brokers in the cocaine business—also referred to as "go-betweens," "intermediaries," "criminal brokers," and so forth—is to link potential partners, potential buyers and sellers, and potential employees and employers. In this informal way, cocaine brokers combine some of the tasks usually performed by chambers of commerce, employment agencies, social clubs, or legal businesses. They also reproduce other linkages—among friends, relatives, colleagues, co-nationals, and so forth—participants in monetary or nonmonetary transactions.

Brokers tend to belong to the very social networks that are being connected. They are neither necessarily cocaine entrepreneurs or employees themselves, nor external powerful actors such as local politicians, *mafiosi*, or migrant community leaders.[28] Brokers among Colombian *traquetos* include people occupying intersections of very different networks: illegal immigrants, musicians, frequent travelers, local dealers, local entrepreneurs, prostitutes, undercover police officers, and so on. Tico, for example, introduced Tano and Chino to Joel, who later helped them in many ways. Tano acknowledged, "Yes, I can work with Tico. He isn't selfish, he didn't know me very well, but he told Joel to trust me."

Silvio, a musician himself, indicated that some salsa musicians in Amsterdam will act as brokers, exchanging sales to their broad network of potential cocaine users for regular free cocaine supplies to their inner circle of friends. In The Hague, some Latino DJs also knew how to use their contacts with established *traquetos* and "second generation" Colombians. Additional cases of brokerage are to be found among telephone operators, restaurant workers and bartenders, coffee-shop owners, doormen in salsa discotheques, and non-Colombian inmates. Some members of these groups facilitate new contacts and transactions, earning a profit.

A broker's tariff (profit) is rarely defined directly in terms of money.[29] Cocaine brokers will obtain material as well as immaterial benefits. The most common among the latter are credit with *traquetos;* reputation and status; expectation to enter the business in the future; future possible favors or services; more clients; cocaine for consumption; and moral leadership. Credit and reputation are very important since they are key credentials for business success.

Many Colombians refused to perform as brokers when asked by non-Colombian drug dealers to connect them with the "big guys." They did not see any clear benefit in it. When Cabeza, a Colombian migrant, was learning Dutch, two Moroccans approached him at the language school. They wanted to get in touch with Colombian cocaine suppliers, and wondered if he could help them. Said Cabeza, "I thought why not, so I found a Colombian and I did the *cruce* [favor]. The Moroccans were real *desprolijos* [lit., sloppy, amateurs], and after two failed meetings I said: You know what? I cancel the thing and I step out." Manipulating *traquetos* with hopes and promises—recommending unreliable people, lying about their skills, making them wait, and so on—is for many the only way of getting close to a business with such large profits. Instead of focusing on building a career, cocaine brokers tend to rely on short-term thinking. The temporary status of cocaine enterprises—in terms of organization and staff—is reinforced continuously by the circulation and replacement of brokers when they run out of credit.

While explaining the diversification of markets and activities among Colombian drug entrepreneurs, Michel Koutouzis from the former Observatoire Geopolitique des Drogues (OGD) in Paris concludes that cocaine importing has become a part of a huge broker operation: "It is not the product (cocaine), but the very network that is really at stake, that is the real merchandise. The present and future tendency is to buy and sell lines, routes, and networks. Internationalized criminal organizations will be able to provide any illegal product."[30] This process reminds us of the trends toward horizontal integration and flexible accumulation and consumption that we find in late capitalism.

Labor Relations

Most of the people contacted during the field research were selling a service to some *traqueto* or working for him. Both import and distribution activities can be organized as an enterprise, with cocaine entrepreneurs assisted by a wide range of helpers and employees. In the following paragraphs we will analyze this specific labor market, showing the most common contractual arrangements found and the logic behind them. When analyzing drug economies, too much emphasis on professionalism has obscured the fact that the "crime industry also needs a large number of unskilled criminal employees,"[31] who at the same time pose a major threat to their employers. Peter Reuter argues that "the entrepreneur aims to structure his relationship with employees so as to reduce the amount of information available to them concerning his own participation and to ensure that they have minimal incentive to inform against him."[32]

Traquetos try to solve this problem by segmenting units, subcontracting, using friends and relatives, avoiding fixed employees, relying on brokers, passing minimal information, providing personal incentives, and replacing, intimidating, or lowering the number of employees. In sum, they become flexible and relatively unorganized. When reviewing the specific labor market on which Colombian *traquetos* operate, it becomes clear that these solutions are part of a wider picture that goes beyond illegal markets. While illegality tends to intensify them, they touch core developments of current capital and labor markets under "disorganized capitalism,"[33] "flexible specialisation,"[34] or "post-Fordist" economies.[35]

Skilled Subcontractors

Colombian cocaine entrepreneurs rely heavily on subcontracting to a variety of individuals and enterprises that provide infrastructure, knowledge, or skills for a particular operational aspect. These contractors are usually paid either in cash or kind per individual project. In this way, relatively small economic units are able to operate rapidly and efficiently, integrating flexible layers of contractors and subcontractors.

Subcontracting other illegal enterprises is a rare phenomenon in the Netherlands. It is very common though in Colombia. Cocaine exporters will contract the services of organizations—some with two or three people—specializing in the recruitment and loading of small couriers, or in large scale transportation, or in the exercise of violence, the organization of private armies, the recruitment of *sicarios* (hired gunmen), and so on. Other subcontracted businesses have a much better reputation. Whether subcontracting concerned single corrupted employees inside a firm (import-export, freight or transport companies, chauffeurs, bank employees and managers, and so on) or small businesses (retail and distribution shops, restaurant owners, and so on), all had in common that they were paid to provide essential infrastructural services beyond mere know-how or labor power. Most operations will at a certain stage need services from legal companies. These so-called "facilitators" are essential for the cocaine business.

Much subcontracting takes place at an individual level, and at times the divide between wage labor and entrepreneurship is blurred. It concerns the more simple tasks, requiring a particular skill and a material resource not provided by the employer. I have explained, for example, how Riverito was contracted to unload cocaine, for which he had to arrange many things for himself. Some infrastructural services were subcontracted on a more permanent basis. Simona was regularly paid by Joel to stash cocaine in her flat. Some individuals will regard the contract as an extra-income, next to more stable sources of income from jobs or social benefits.

Professionals

Professional skilled workers also tend to be externally hired or recruited. Again, small and temporary enterprises do not allow for stable departments with specialized personnel. Some of these services come from legitimate professionals, who are often paid salaries or fees well above the average. A pool of local or Colombian lawyers specializing in cocaine cases has remarkable job stability compared to their clients. Travel and real estate agents are paid excellent prices and commissions. In contrast with Colombia and with local legal and illegal entrepreneurial circles, local accountants are not involved in laundering money. This professional service is directly provided by the institutions or the employees involved. In some cases, people with know-how in import-export bureaucracy and in information technologies are also involved, in particular when organizing large importing operations. Professional truck drivers were also hired or paid off to transport cocaine in their trucks.

Traquetos also will hire people with particular skills acquired by virtue of their full-time involvement in some illegal activity. They include professional smugglers of all sorts, routine burglars (for operations that involve breaking into warehouses, containers, or flats) or individual *sicarios* (though rare in the Netherlands). The trend for these professional criminals is to diversify skills and become polyvalent multi-skilled workers. In due time, they may replace bosses or become their bosses' closest employees.

Managerial Bodies

The heavy use of subcontractors and external professionals discourages the organization of stable managerial bodies. In many cases, the *patrón* himself will directly control the performance of the contracted unskilled workers. When people are sent to the Netherlands to organize the import (envoys), they will combine the functions of managers and entrepreneurs. More specific organizers—sent, for example, to supervise a delivery, to assess risk, to make a collection, or "fix" a problem—are often focused on one particular operational aspect. They follow orders from the boss closely and are more busy with external relations and arrangements than with internal labor organization. These people, although highly trusted by the cocaine entrepreneur, do not behave so much as white-collar "company men" or "vice presidents." They will often identify with subordinates in their expectations of taking over, changing *patrones,* or quitting the job altogether. Hierarchies are understood in terms of authority and leadership rather than as compartmentalized, vertical bodies of delegation and control. Superiors and chiefs are often respected for past events or deeds instead of present positions and current developments. In some cases, more horizontal relations may have developed as in the style of project crimes or crimes in association,[36] which involve mutuality beyond the business or labor relationship. Says Miguel, "It is not just pure business and cold contracts. Within the group you discuss your personal life, your problems with others or with women, you have fun together."

This trafficking alternated between performing as a supervisor (babysitter) and as a worker *(mula).* There are also cases in which outsiders such as overseas partners, who recruit and deal with employees, have taken managerial functions. Sometimes tasks and arrangements were simply abandoned by those hired to execute them, with the bosses not having the will or the power to supervise while the task was being carried out. Finally, some cocaine entrepreneurs suggested that managers are important but also dangerous, since they know many things that could easily be used against them. Mary McIntosh made the point in her classic work *The Organization of Crime:* "In fact it is not easy to distinguish control over subordinates from control over rivals. A subordinate may at any point cut loose and become a rival; a rival may become a boss, or a subordinate."[37] The use of relatives may offer only a partial solution. The pressures to be in charge will often be greater among close relations, regardless of the ability to manage people.

Unskilled Part-Time Employees

Unskilled irregulars, people who will perform multiple tasks with differing levels of complexity, form the final and extremely important category of employees. Their type of work and the absence of promotion prospects do not guarantee a high degree of job satisfaction. For some, the job means an extra income next to other legal or illegal occupations. For others, it is a last resort solution to tackle economic hardship, desperate conjunctures, or the absence of any other promising job perspective. Also, some employees dream of becoming a *traqueto* some day.

The category of unskilled irregulars includes people performing the tasks of body packers or small air couriers, local chauffeurs, divers, unloaders, load keepers, informal bodyguards, internal couriers, cash remitters and smugglers, flat hosts, helpers, and peddlers. These workers have no job security. As a protection buffer to the business, they are placed in the front line, and easily replaced when targeted by law enforcement agencies. Continual replacement not only restricts the flow of sensible information—weakening their bargain position—but also keeps labor costs lower than those cases with a need to construct stronger loyalties over time. Many people are waiting to be called by a *traqueto*. Others had done some job for the boss, and had been put on hold until the next operation. Waiting could take months. People often rotate through different tasks in one or several operations. They do "a little bit of everything" and are called *toderos*. Their occupational prestige is low. The workers are preferably not recruited from among established criminal milieus, such as relatives of cocaine entrepreneurs, illegal migrants, or local drug dealers. They tend to be drawn from external labor markets.[38] Only a few employees will receive a salary on a regular or irregular basis. Most of them, however, are given a flexible personal payment for each task performed. Load keepers, for example, are paid by the day. International unskilled couriers are either paid a fixed amount or an amount per kilo transported, depending on their experience and the financial resources of the exporter. This way, the payment may vary between 1,000 U.S. dollars and 10,000 U.S. dollars per trip. Internal couriers and cash remitters or smugglers are commonly paid a percentage of the amounts handled. Finally, the helpers of wholesale distributors are given a few kilos of cocaine, under the agreement that they can keep the difference above a certain price. Many of these salespersons on commission belong to this type of unskilled, interchangeable labor force.

Post-Fordist Arrangements

For the past twenty years, the Fordist-organization[39] of capitalist production has experienced a serious crisis, leading to significant changes. The Fordist system basically implied, in the realm of production and work, the following (well-known) features: mass production and consumption of uniform and standardized goods; vertical integration; displacement of knowledge from labor to managerial bodies; disciplining of the labor force; "Taylorist" segmentation of tasks performed by single workers in a repetitive and alienating way; job specialization; payment by rate; little or no on the job training and learning; and functional as well as spatial division of labor.

The causes, the extent, and the prospects of this transformation have remained a matter of debate. However, the main characteristics of so-called post-Fordist conditions of accumulation are pretty well agreed upon.[40] Paul Hirsch argues that post-Fordist firms are "increasingly conceived as a 'bundle of contracts,' none of which requires elaborate headquarters, overhead, staff, hierarchy, slack, or much in the way of organizational memory. These organizational attributes are seen as irrelevant, if not unnecessary and wasteful. Managers are conceived of as interchangeable; specialized skills, if not available in house, can be purchased outside at market prices. . . ."[41]

Contrary to Vincenzo Ruggiero, who conducted research on drug economies in Italy and Britain,[42] I find the way in which Colombian *traquetos* organize cocaine trafficking, from export to wholesale distribution, to represent a good example of such a post-Fordist firm. Ruggiero found their labor markets reproducing the Fordist model, in which "assembly-line delinquents" had clearly divided roles and tasks within a vertically integrated industry. He recognizes that the overwhelming presence of flexible work does not agree with his hypothesis, and that the industry is competitive rather than monopolistic. Strangely enough, he does not explain why such a dynamic business should follow a trend—that is, Fordist—contrary to other legal markets of the same kind that are comparable in terms of business organization and labor relations. Other authors have shown convincingly how developments in contemporary crime are shaped by ongoing processes of globalization, market liberalization, late modernity, and post-Fordism.[43] Table 8.1 shows how most of the characteristics of the cocaine business run parallel to more general trends of post-Fordist or flexible accumulation.

The illegal nature of the cocaine business gives an even greater impulse to post-Fordist trends. No taxes, large profits, no labor regulations and unions, no training costs, not even a company building: the utopia of the propagandists of market flexibility. The lack of a stable workforce, the massive use of subcontracting, or the reliance on brokers are obviously also risk-minimizing strategies to neutralize the effects of repression. The illegality of trafficking decreases the possibility that the actors involved will develop a stable business or labor relationship. It even will make it unlikely for them to be operating on the same deals more than once. The following factors will add to this effect:

Table 8.1. Post-Fordism and Cocaine Business Compared

Post-Fordism	Cocaine Business
Decline of hierarchical management and corporate structure.	No "branches." Small firms with arms length transactions. Flexible cocaine brokers.
Technical innovation.	New smuggling and packing methods. New communication technology.
No stocks.	No cocaine stocks.
Economy of scope in a global market. Flexible and small batch production and distribution.	No "pipe-lines" but specific operations. European market as a unity.
Differential, nonstandardized consumption. Demand driven.	New products (crack). Heterogeneous consumers. New markets.
Dual segmentation toward professionalization and de-skilling.	Criminal lawyers, legal businessmen, professional smugglers and unloaders versus *mulas, boleros, toderos, encaleradores,* and helpers.
More horizontal labor organization.	Despite clear *patrones* (bosses) and separation of planning and execution: weak managerial structures, many project crimes, little supervision, vertical clashes, workers become bosses.
Worker's co-responsibility.	Workers take more risks and are expected to solve problems. Little information exchange.
No job security, poor labor conditions, temporary workers, hire-and-fire.	People hired per operation. Many unfulfilled promises. People "waiting" for an operation. Many alternating with legal and illegal jobs. Many arrests. Risk of hopeless imprisonment or death.
Dispersal, diversification of the spatial-territorial division of labor.	Cocaine consumers in Colombia and Colombian capitalists in the Netherlands. Less regional specialization.
(Quasi-)vertical integration through increased subcontracting and outsourcing.	Many skilled tasks subcontracted by *traquetos:* transport, unloading, legal aid and protection, violence, and so on.
Decline of blue-collar working class.	No stable employees, no bureaucracy.

Post-Fordism	Cocaine Business
Elimination of job demarcation. Multiple and rotating tasks.	*Toderos.* Entrepreneurs also "hands on." Polyvalent multi-skilled promoted.
Revival of domestic and family no labor systems.	Kinship and ethnic bonds important, but "family business."
Personal payment (bonus, on flexi-wage, on commission).	Conditional payment if success. Kg sales commission. Courier's wages very flexible. Bonus after successfully completing the deal.
On the job learning and training.	Many people with no "criminal record." Improvization and imitation.

- Changes in volumes and prices, production or consumption levels; marketing routes; smuggling methods; and developments in the legal business around the cocaine trade.
- Death of important actors or their need to move; imprisonment; bankruptcy; changes in expectations, interests, ambitions, or reputation.
- Disagreement on terms of the deal; "dirty play"; or dissatisfaction from the first transaction.
- Police intervention and undercover operations, creating mutual distrust and paranoia.
- Possibilities to corrupt law enforcement authorities; the room for new partners and alliances.

This "wild" flexibility may threaten individual entrepreneurs, increase their transaction costs, and expel first-time losers from the game. However, it also provides the overall cocaine business with a superb incentive and a competitive advantage. Although illegality shapes internal business and labor relations, these relations can also be found in other highly competitive legal markets that are struggling to survive under post-Fordist conditions.

Conclusion

Our research on the organization of Colombian cocaine enterprises operating in the Netherlands questions two dominant frameworks addressing the issue: the "economic-bureaucratic" and the "criminal network" approaches.

The economic-bureaucratic model tends to see the drug industry as operating through fixed branches of cocaine cartels. It has facilitated comparative analysis and research on the interwovenness of legal and illegal economies.

The model has not been able, however, to provide convincing evidence for the presence of Fordist organizational structures and monopolizing transnational corporations with rigid organizational hierarchies and a strict division of labor. Further, it does not agree with the reality of very competitive markets, and seems to underestimate the impact of illegality upon the cocaine business. Within this bureaucratic model, the notion of cells is often used. The drug industry and participating actors are viewed in terms of hyper-organized international conspiracies, feeding the rhetoric of the War on Drugs crusaders. These notions are in total contradiction with drug traffickers' daily practice of operations and their dealing with the broader socioeconomic context.

The criminal networks approach has the merit of capturing the flexible and dynamic nature of interpersonal interaction on the micro-level. However, it only relates the flexibility of trafficking to the illegal dimensions of the industry, isolating the cocaine business and its actors from the overall economy. It does not allow cocaine dealing to be understood within the broader picture of economic logic and profit making, and neglects the non-criminal aspects of social relations within the industry, such as internal conflict and collusion with legal structures.

The study of the internal business—and labor relations of cocaine trafficking—has given us good knowledge of the economic dimensions of these enterprises and the factors that determine their dynamics. We found Colombian cocaine firms to be informal, small, mutating, and decentralized. Some are individual enterprises; others function through temporary partnerships among two or three people. These arrangements are often formed solely for a single project. Some of the people involved may also be engaged in other partnerships or in activities in the legal economy. Often, a percentage system is used to divide profits, and payments in kind commonly happen. Despite the importance of kinship ties and the frequent use of relatives in business operations, none of the enterprises that we researched can be characterized as family businesses. Brokers (people with contacts) play a central role in bringing about the partnerships and transactions.

Labor relations are very flexible. Most people continuously change or switch tasks and employers. Many tasks are subcontracted in order to share financial risk and allow for (quasi-)vertical integration while keeping the business small. Subcontractors range from skilled professionals or legal enterprises selling their specialized services, to multi-skilled cocaine entrepreneurs who delegate particular risky operational tasks to unskilled, easily replaceable workers. These are hired, for specific or for multi-task operations *(toderos)* and are paid with some sort of flexi-wage. They have poor skills, no promotion perspectives, and face death or imprisonment with no security for them or their families. They are irregulars; some combine their work with other legal, informal, or illegal activities. Many of them had no criminal record, and learned their tasks on the job.

These enterprises do not develop stable managerial bodies, contrary to what is commonly thought. Bosses often work "hand in hand" with their helpers, some of whom may have their own businesses or envision eventually replacing the boss in case he is caught. The division of labor is not rigid and compartmentalized along vertical lines. It has a more horizontal fragmented structure, despite a clear division between capital and labor, between bosses and subordinates with different power and status. Some people, especially subordinates, brokers, and subcontractors, switched roles in an ad hoc way between what Mike Davis has called "lumpen capitalists" and "outlaw proletarians."[44] Finally, the system of payments is very flexible and includes commission and bonus systems, gifts, or other incentives if things go as planned. Failure to comply with the job, conflicts, or even business delays or seizures usually mean payment cuts or no payment at all.

We conclude that these characteristics of the enterprise structure and labor relations resemble those among post-Fordist businesses in the legal sphere. Illegality only accentuates the flexibility regarding production, labor and service contracts, and capital accumulation. This, in fact, would be a normal feature of any other highly competitive market under contemporary forms of capitalism. These shared characteristics contribute to the overlap that we observe in the areas of organizational structure and labor relations between legal and illegal businesses.

Notes

1. Ethnographic studies on so-called "organized crime" with a focus on business and labor relations can be illuminating for several reasons. They can shed light on the reasons behind internal interaction, changing arrangements, conflicting interests, and risk transfer inside the illegal business. They can further help to understand the meaning of violence, secrecy, and trust for the actors involved. Finally, they can expose both similarities to and interconnections with broader social and economic arrangements—other labor markets, other legal and illegal businesses or entrepreneurs, and so forth. For studies with a focus on business and labor relations, see Petrus van Duyne et al., *Misdaadondernemingen* (The Hague: WODC-Gouda Quint bv, 1990); Nicholas Dorn et al., *Traffickers: Drug Markets and Law Enforcement* (London: Routledge, 1992); Dirk Korf and Hans Verbraeck, *Dealers en Dienders* (Amsterdam: Criminologisch Instituut Bonger, 1993); Vincenzo Ruggiero, "Drug Economics: A Fordist Model of Criminal Capital?" *Capital and Class* 55 (1995), 131–50; Dick Hobbs, "The Firm: Organizational Logic and Criminal Culture on a Shifting Terrain," *The British Journal of Criminology* 41 (2001), 549–60.

2. For a complete report, see Damián Zaitch, *Traquetos: Colombians Involved in the Cocaine Business in the Netherlands* (Dordrecht: Kluwer Academic Publishers, 2001).

3. The notion of cocaine "cartel" was always a matter of controversy. Many scholars rejected or criticized the concept. See Francisco Thoumi, *Political Economy and Illegal Drugs in Colombia* (London: Lynne Rienner Publishers, 1995); Rosa del Olmo, "Drogas: Discursos, Percepciones, y Políticas," in Xavier Arana and Rosa del Olmo, eds., *Normal y Culturas en la Construcción de la "Cuestión Droga"* (Barcelona: Editorial Hater, 1996), 124–38; Alvaro Camacho Guizado, "Empresarios Ilegales y Región: La Gestación de Clases Dominantes Locales," *Delito y Sociedad* 4/5 (1994), 163–82; Dario Betancourt and Martha Luz García, *Contrabandistas, Marimberos, y Mafiosos: Historia Social de la Mafia Colombiana* (Bogotá: Tercer Mundo Editores, 1994); Pierre Kopp, "Colombie: Traffic de Drogue et Organisations Criminelles," *Problèmes d'Amérique Latine* 18 (1995), 21–39; Ciro Krauthausen and Luis F. Sarmiento, *Cocaína & Co.* (Bogotá: Coediciones Tercer Mundo—Instituto de Estudios Políticos de la Universidad Nacional de Colombia, 1991); Ciro Krauthausen, *Padrinos y Mercaderes: Crimen Organizado en Italia y Colombia* (Bogotá: Planeta Colombiana Editorial, 1998); R. Thomas Naylor, "Mafias, Myths, and Markets: On the Theory and Practice of Enterprise Crime," *Transnational Organized Crime* 3 (1997), 1–45; Hermes Tovar Pinzón, "La Economía de la Coca en América Latina: El Paradigma Colombiano," *Revista Nueva Sociedad,* no. 130 (1994), 86–111; Rodrigo Uprimny, "Notas sobre el Fenómeno del Narcotráfico en Colombia y las Reacciones a Su Control," *Comisión Andina de Juristas, Drogas, y Control Penal en los Andes* (Lima: CAJ, 1994). Others have worked with the notion of cartel but with explicit reservations. See Alain Labrousse, *La Droga, el Dinero, y las Armas* (Mexico City: Siglo Veintiuno Editores, 1993); Rensselaer Lee III, "Colombia's Cocaine Syndicates," *Crime, Law, and Social Change* 16, no. 1 (1991), 339; Patrick Clawson and Rensselaer Lee III, *The Andean Cocaine Industry* (New York: St. Martin's Press, 1996); Umberto Santino and Giovanni La Fiura, *Dietro la Droga* (Turin: CISS-Centro Giuseppe Impastato-Edizioni Gruppo Abele, 1993); Frank Bovenkerk, *La Bella Bettien* (Amsterdam: Meulenhoff, 1995); and Petrus van Duyne, *Het Spook en de Dreiging van de Georganiseerde Misdaad* (The Hague: SDU, 1995).

4. Carl P. Florez and Bernadette Boyce, "Colombian Organized Crime," *Police Studies* 13, no. 2 (1990), 54–68.

5. Lee, "Colombia's Cocaine Syndicates," passim.

6. Sidney Zabludoff, "Colombian Narcotics Organizations as Business Enterprises," *Transnational Organized Crime* 3, no. 2 (1997), 20–49.

7. Ernesto Savona, *European Money Trails* (Singapore: Harwood Academic Publishers, 1999); Observatoire Geopolitique des Drogues (OGD), *Où va la Cocaïne en Europe?* (Paris: OGD, 1997).

8. OGD, *The Geopolitics of Drugs,* 1996 ed. (Boston: Northeastern University Press, 1996), 67.

9. Johan van Doorn, "Drug Trafficking Networks in Europe," *European Journal on Criminal Policy and Research* 1, no. 2 (1993), 101.

10. Van Duyne, *Misdaadondernemingen,* 55; Petrus van Duyne, "Organized Crime in a Turbulent Europe," *European Journal on Criminal Policy and Research* 1, no. 3 (1993), 15, 80–85.

11. Robin T. Naylor, "Mafias, Myths, and Markets," 20.

12. Krauthausen and Sarmiento, *Cocaína & Co.*, passim; Thoumi, *Political Economy and Illegal Drugs*, passim; Kopp, "Colombie: Traffic de Drogue," passim.

13. Bovenkerk, *La Bella Bettien*, passim.

14. Jeremy Boissevain, *Friends of Friends: Networks, Manipulators, and Coalitions* (Oxford: Basil Blackwell, 1974), passim.

15. Nigel Coles, "It's Not What You Know—It's Who You Know That Counts: Analyzing Serious Crime Groups as Social Networks," *The British Journal of Criminology* 41 (2001), 580–94.

16. See Van Doorn, "Drug Trafficking Networks," passim; Janet Jackson et al., "Examining Criminal Organizations: Possible Methodologies," *Transnational Organized Crime* 2, no. 4 (1996), 83–105; Peter Klerks, *Ondergrondse Organisaties in Vergelijkend Perspectief* (Rotterdam: Erasmus Universiteit Rotterdam, 1996); Edward Kleemans et al., *Georganiseerde Criminaliteit in Nederland: Rapportage op basis van de woDC-monitor* (The Hague: WODC, 1998); Edward Kleemans and Marius Kruissink, "Korte Klappen of Lange Halen? Wat Werkt bij de Aanpak van de Georganiseerde Criminaliteit?," *Justitiële Verkenningen* 25, no. 6 (1999), 99–111.

17. Kleemans, *Georganiseerde Criminaliteit*, passim.

18. Ibid., and Klerks, *Ondergrondse Organisaties*, passim.

19. During our encounters in the prison of Veenhuizen, he commented upon Hegel, Kant, Russell, Bentham, and Foucault. He also referred to social utopists such as Owen, Fourier, Saint Simon, and Comte, and to authors such as Huxley and Orwell. Quoting Kundera, he finally thanked me for the unique opportunity to share thoughts about these thinkers, implying that he was an exception in that "criminal subculture." Upon this intimacy he also based his willingness to tell me his story.

20. Zaitch, *Traquetos*, 157.

21. Nicholas Dorn et al., "Drugs Importation and the Bifurcation of Risk," *The British Journal of Criminology* 38, no. 4 (1998), 537–60.

22. Alejandro Portes, "Economic Sociology and the Sociology of Immigration: A Conceptual Overview," Alejandro Portes, ed., *The Economic Sociology of Immigration* (New York: Russell Sage Foundation, 1995), 64–82.

23. Dorn et al., "Drugs Importation," 540.

24. Dick Hobbs, *Doing the Business: Entrepreneurship, the Working Class, and Detectives in the East End of London* (Oxford: Clarendon, 1988), passim.

25. Francis Ianni, *A Family Business: Kinship and Social Control in Organized Crime* (New York: Russell Sage Basic Books, 1972), passim.

26. Hobbs, *Doing the Business*, passim.

27. Boissevain, *Friends of Friends*, 148.

28. Bovenkerk, *La Bella Bettien*, passim.

29. Boissevain, *Friends of Friends*, 158.

30. Interview with Michel Koutouzis, Paris, April 1997.

31. Vincenzo Ruggiero, "Organized Crime in Italy: Testing Alternative Definitions," *Social and Legal Studies* 2, no. 2 (1993), 137.

32. Peter Reuter, *Disorganized Crime: The Economics of the Visible Hand* (Cambridge, Mass.: MIT Press, 1983), 115.

33. Scott Lash and John Urry, *The End of Organized Capitalism* (Cambridge: Polity Press, 1987), passim.

34. David Harvey, *The Condition of Postmodernity* (Oxford: Basil Blackwell, 1989), passim.

35. Andrew Amin, "Post-Fordism: Models, Fantasies, and Phantoms of Transition," in Andrew Amin, ed., *Post-Fordism: A Reader* (London: Basil Blackwell, 1994), 210–42.

36. Mary McIntosh, *The Organization of Crime* (London: MacMillan, 1975), passim.

37. Ibid., 54.

38. Chris Tilly and Charles Tilly, "Capitalist Work and Labor Markets," in Neil J. Smelser and Robert Swedberg, eds., *The Handbook of Economic Sociology* (Princeton: Princeton University Press, 1995), 287.

39. For an extensive analysis on capital and labor organization under Fordism, see Henry Braverman, *Labor and Monopoly Capital: The Degradation of Work in the Twentieth Century* (New York: Monthly Review Press, 1974); and Harvey, *The Condition of Postmodernity,* passim.

40. See Amin, "Post-Fordism," passim; Harvey, *The Condition of Postmodernity,* passim; Lash and Urry, *The End of Organized Capitalism,* passim; Bob Jessop et al., eds., *The Politics of Flexibility* (Hants: Edward Elgar, 1991); Stuart Wood, ed., *The Transformation of Work?* (London: Unwin Hyman Ltd., 1989); and Paul Hirsch, "Undoing the Material Revolution? Needed Research of the Decline of Middle Management and Internal Labor Markets," in Robert Swedberg, ed., *Explorations in Economic Sociology* (New York: Russell Sage Foundation, 1993), 158–84. It is beyond the scope of this chapter to analyze thoroughly the nature and implications of post-Fordism. I do not intend to compare businesses at an empirical level. I regard this theoretical exercise, inspired by the work of Vincenzo Ruggiero, as a provisional hypothesis that is worth exploring in further research.

41. Hirsch, "Undoing the Material Revolution," 160.

42. Ruggiero, "Drug Economics," 140.

43. Most notably Manuel Castells, *The End of Millennium: The Information Age: Economy, Society, and Culture* (London: Blackwell, 1996); Ian Taylor, *Crime in Context* (Oxford: Polity, 1999); Jock Young, *The Exclusive Society* (London: Sage, 1999); and John Lea, "Post-Fordism and Criminality," in Neil Jewson and Stefan MacGregor, eds., *Transforming the City* (London: Routledge, 1997).

44. Mike Davis, *City of Quartz: Excavating the Future in Los Angeles* (London: Vintage, 1990), 310.

9

Follow the Money

Anti-Money-Laundering Policies and Financial Investigations

Ernesto Savona

Drugs and terrorism are two poles of the path through which the international anti-money-laundering regime has developed in the last fifteen years. Combating drug barons was the initial reason for the first anti-money-laundering legislation in the United States in 1986. Drugs were the focal point again at the 1988 Vienna Convention, which made money laundering a criminal offense in the legislation of the 165 countries that have subscribed to this convention. Since the events of September 11, 2001, terrorism has become the prime subject of attention of anti-money-laundering legislation. All international and national initiatives against terrorism call for cooperation between countries in identifying, freezing, and confiscating assets that finance terrorist groups. These policies against drugs and terrorism share the assumption that the trail of the money that has been generated by criminal activity, or that serves to finance it, can help to identify criminals, leading to the confiscation of their assets and the disruption of their organizations. In the case of terrorism, the "traditional" direction of the money trail has been reversed. With drug trafficking the proceeds are derived directly from this crime, while with terrorism the assets are mostly criminally generated and continue to finance criminal activity. In both situations, the main question concerns the effectiveness of the anti-money-laundering policies and in particular those directed to the identification, freezing, and confiscation of the proceeds that come from or go to the financing of crime.

Anti-Money-Laundering Policies and Their Effectiveness

After almost seventeen years of anti-money-laundering policies, we have built a sound knowledge of how criminals launder their proceeds. We know the ways they try to avoid the controls that anti-money-laundering legislation has put into place. However, we know much less about the effectiveness of the various anti-money-laundering policies. We are not in a position yet from which we can establish the effectiveness of these policies in achieving the end result for which they originally had been designed. The usual assessment has used two general parameters: the amount of anti-money-laundering legislation that has been created; and the number of institutions that are supposed to implement this legislation. Little to nothing is known, however, about the direct impact of these policies and the activities of these institutions upon the launderers' behavior. There has been a lack of reliable data that would help measure this impact. Also, the political interest in knowing the extent of this impact has been low for a long time. The current argument, which has weakened research efforts in the field, has maintained that new money-laundering methods developed by criminals result from the effectiveness of existing anti-money-laundering controls. However, the fact that launderers are elaborating new methods does not automatically prove the effectiveness of present policies. The main response to those who question the effectiveness of these policies had always been: "What would happen if this or these policies did not exist?"

It is clear that criminals try to beat the controls because they want to minimize risk. In this chapter, we will focus on anti-money-laundering controls and their effectiveness, emphasizing a crucial aspect of the whole mechanism: the financial investigation. This procedure appears to be the Achilles' heel of anti-money-laundering policies. In practice, their effectiveness depends on the capability of financial investigations to trace the proceeds from drug trafficking or those directed toward terrorism and to freeze and confiscate them. This capability was limited when the drug trade producing illicit money was the only predicate offense to the crime of money laundering. It is even more limited in the case of terrorist financing when investigators have to trace the illicit financial resources sustaining terrorist activities.

Money-Laundering Investigations

Historically the proceeds from drug offenses have been the origins of the money-laundering business and, consequently, of national and international anti-money-laundering regimes. The demand for them to be more effective has produced a progressive enlargement of the categories of crime considered as a predicate offense to the crime of money laundering. They have moved from only drug crimes to serious crimes, or to an even larger category including all crimes. This extension has been necessary because the investigation of the laundering process cannot be limited to drug trafficking only, as the process also entails many other crimes, such as corruption and fraud. Limiting the predicate offense to drug trafficking was making anti-money-laundering prevention almost impossible. Money does not smell and the employees at financial institutions charged with reporting suspicious transactions had difficulty in distinguishing whether the criminal proceeds entering a financial institution were derived from drugs or from other crimes. The enlargement of the predicate offense has made it easier to establish the connection between the crime committed and its proceeds, thereby allowing the prosecution of money laundering to develop its full potential. However, reconstructing the money trails remains extremely complicated. The effectiveness of the investigation phase in the search for the link between the proceeds from crime and the criminal activity is the Achilles' heel of any prosecution. Discovering the location of the illicit funds makes it possible not only to convict the criminals, but also to confiscate the proceeds from their crime. This is the challenge, whether the proceeds are linked to drug trafficking or to any other crime.

This chapter will analyze this problem in a regional framework (the European Union member states), drawing on the results of research carried out by Transcrime, Research Centre on Transnational Crime at the University of Trento, under the 2000 Falcone Programme of the European Commission. It describes how the European Union has been confronting this issue and indicates the variables that define the effectiveness of a financial investigation into the laundering of illicit funds. We will compare the various strategies followed by the European Union member states and will conclude with some policy implications.

The Importance of Financial Investigations

The tool used by law enforcement agencies to trace the proceeds from criminal activity is the financial investigation. It can be defined as "the tracing of profits directed toward (organized) crime-enterprises by means of the analyses and examination of their management (the flow of goods, payments and spending)."[1] A financial investigation may include a wide range of investigative strategies, such as an asset search for real property, the screening of bank, brokerage, and mutual fund accounts, credit analysis, a review of business relationships, bankruptcy, liens, and judgments, and the use of other financial instruments.

Whatever the case, a financial investigation has one objective: to reconstruct, by following the movement of dirty money through paper and computerized records, "the link between where the money comes from, who gets it, when it is received and where it is stored or deposited."[2] The reconstruction of such a link can obviously provide proof of criminal activity, proof that may contribute to the conviction of criminals and lead to the seizure and confiscation of the proceeds from crime. This implies that the financial investigation represents the necessary starting point for an effective proceeds-oriented strategy against criminal groups.

While defining their policies against cross-border crime, European Union institutions are paying greater attention to the importance of financial investigations as an essential part of a proceeds-oriented strategy against criminal organizations. In fact, financial investigations are considered as a condition sine qua non for the effectiveness of legislation dealing with money laundering and the confiscation of criminal proceeds.[3] They are considered necessary for several reasons: "the gathering of intelligence regarding the behavior of suspects; the gathering of evidence against them; the calculation of the criminal proceeds; the identification and seizure of assets; the identification of the origins and structures of organized crime; the identification of those controlling organized crime, and the possibility to confiscate their working capital."[4] The consequence is that "in principle, all criminal investigations, and in particular those concerned with organized crime, should include a financial part," thus, representing "an integrated part of each (complex) criminal investigation. . . . ."[5]

Financial Investigations in the European Union Member States

Financial investigations are regarded as effective if they achieve their objective, that is, when they succeed in locating the proceeds from crime. How can this effectiveness be measured? An impact evaluation will not suffice. Indeed, it will not be possible to use the ratio between the assets owned by the criminal and the part detected and later seized as a measure of the effectiveness of the financial investigation (that is, the greater the ratio, the more effective the financial investigation). The volume of capital accumulated by criminals is not known. Also, the data on proceeds seized are scare and, when produced, are often not very reliable.

We have accumulated data about the practice of tracing the proceeds from crime through financial investigations in the fifteen European member states.[6] The effectiveness of this operation in the various countries of the European Union was established through indirect measurement. The presence of rules, actors involved, and the procedures that contribute to the success or the failure of a financial investigation have been established in each case. Two kinds of general indicators have been used in establishing their effectiveness: (a) those that refer to the existence or absence of a legal framework that will permit the tracing of the proceeds from crime; (b) those having to do with the actions of law enforcement agencies in addition to other institutions and people cooperating in locating criminal proceeds. The indicators that were selected on the basis of their relevance and potential contribution to the effectiveness of tracing the proceeds from crime have been listed below.

They have been defined for research in a regional European context, but—obviously—have a much wider applicability.

1. The presence of special financial investigative units for locating the proceeds from crime. The constantly changing techniques used by criminal organizations to conceal their illicit wealth require greater specialization by law enforcement agencies. Hence, the presence of such investigative units may be assumed to increase the effectiveness of financial investigations.

2. The use of special means of investigation that help locate the proceeds from crime. The access to special investigative devices (for example, electronic surveillance, undercover operations) to find unlawful gains will improve the investigators' ability to locate proceeds and may be assumed to increase the effectiveness of tracing the illicitly accumulated assets.

3. The presence of legal provisions that allow for the investigation of third parties (that is, persons not themselves defendants in the proceedings). To conceal the illicit origin of their wealth, criminal organizations frequently use "dummies" (that is, persons with apparent, not effective, power over the criminal members' assets). Consequently, the existence of legal provisions that permit law enforcement to investigate third parties may be assumed to result in a greater effectiveness of the investigative phase.

4. The possibility to subject categories of third parties to investigations. If investigations can involve third parties, and if the category of persons other than the defendant liable to investigation can be broadened, the more effective the investigative phase may be assumed to be.

5. The types of assets and/or activities investigated. For example, the more varied these are the more effective the investigative phase may be assume to be.

6. The level of cooperation in the investigative phase provided by banks, other financial institutions, and nonfinancial institutions. The more intensive the cooperation by each of these institutions (where criminal proceeds are invested), the greater the amount of illicit wealth that potentially can be discovered by investigators, and consequently the more effective the phase may be assumed to be.

7. The level of investigation training. Effectively fighting organized crime requires the regular updating of investigative techniques to adapt them to the changing methods used by criminals to conceal their assets. The level of investigative training, therefore, contributes to the effectiveness of the investigative phase: a higher level of investigation training may be assumed to produce more effective investigations.

8. The level of cooperation in investigations. The closer this cooperation, and the more intensive the sharing of experience, knowledge, and competencies among different law enforcement offices, the more effective this investigation phase may be assumed to be.

9. The frequency with which investigators have been consulting private experts. The private financial and accountancy sectors hold a considerable body of financial investigation expertise. The more frequently these experts share their knowledge and expertise with investigators, the more effective the investigative phase may be assumed to be.

10.   The presence of legal provisions that permit the cooperation with law enforcement by "super grasses" who assist in tracing the location of the proceeds from crime as a prerequisite for admission into a special protection program. Because they have been involved in the activities of criminal organizations themselves, super grasses will have inside knowledge about the location of the profits accumulated through illicit activities.

11.   The types of assets seized by law enforcement. These are indicative of the effectiveness of the investigative phase, given the close connection between investigations and the contents of seizure orders. Seizure is usually ordered on the basis of the evidence from the investigative phase provided by the public prosecutor and before the defendant is able to assert his rights. Tangible assets such as real and personal property are usually easy to locate. By contrast, assets such as stocks—in which significant amounts of criminal proceeds are invested—are more difficult to uncover due to their intangibility. Their location will require a well-developed investigative system. Consequently, the higher the percentage of intangible assets seized compared to tangible assets (that is, personal and real property), the more effective the investigative phase may be assumed to be.

The indicators mentioned above were incorporated into two questionnaires. In each European Union member state the questionnaires were scored by two national experts.[7] The results were discussed by the experts during a two-day seminar organized to improve the effectiveness of the financial investigation and to increase the understanding of the whole process. Subsequently, the data were quantified and assembled in an effectiveness index for each of the indicators mentioned above.[8] The index expressed, on a scale from 0 to 100, the degree of effectiveness of financial investigations with reference to the specific indicator.[9] Subsequently, the various indexes were combined into a general effectiveness index, which indicated, also on a scale from 0 to 100, the degree of effectiveness of financial investigations in a general sense. The results indicated two main groups of countries: (a) countries where financial investigations work (that is, countries that achieved a score between 80 and

100), and (b) countries where financial investigations do not work properly (that is, countries that achieved a score between 40 and 79).

Two countries achieved a high financial investigation effectiveness score: Ireland and Denmark. The elements that had made financial investigations work in these countries can be summarized as follows:

- A high level of cooperation from both financial and nonfinancial institutions. In the two countries investigations can count on excellent assistance, not only from the financial system, but also from nonfinancial institutions.
- A well-developed multidisciplinary approach. Both countries maximize the effectiveness of financial investigations by putting together the information, experience, and abilities of different offices. In Ireland, the Criminal Assets Bureau traces the proceeds from crime by combining the experience, knowledge, and information of members of the Ministry for Social Welfare, the police, and the revenue commisioners;[10] furthermore, the bureau "works in close cooperation with a large number of institutions and agencies, in particular the An Gárda Síochána (both national and local units), the Customs and Excise Enforcement and Administration Branches, the Office of the Chief Inspector of Taxes and the Department of Social, Community and Family Affairs."[11] In Denmark, there is close cooperation among the various law enforcement agencies involved in the location of criminal assets;[12] furthermore, financial inquiries are quite frequently conducted in collaboration with private experts whose knowledge has proven very useful in the search for criminal proceeds.
- A high level of training for financial investigators. Significant investments have been made in training investigators and in updating investigative techniques directed to break the money-laundering schemes used by criminals while concealing their wealth.

In the remaining countries, financial investigations have been only partially effective. In these countries, the establishment of specialized units to conduct financial investigations has not been enough, as many obstacles hamper their effectiveness. The elements responsible for making financial investigations less effective in these countries can be summarized as follows:

- A low level of cooperation from nonfinancial institutions. With the exception of Luxembourg, collaboration in financial inquiries by nonfinancial institutions is usually inadequate, despite the generally good cooperation from financial systems.
- The absence of a systematic use of financial investigations. Greater importance is usually given to the arrest of the perpetrators of a crime over efforts to locate the proceeds of their criminal activity. In

countries such as the Netherlands, Luxembourg, Portugal, and Spain financial investigations are not practiced in all cases that concern organized crime; in addition, they are often initiated at a late stage of the game, after the defendant has been charged and has had ample possibilities to conceal his illicit profits.

• Inadequate training of financial investigators. Few material resources are generally allocated to financial investigation. Because of this underfunding, and also because of a lack of awareness of the importance of financial inquiries, the creation of investigative units has not been accompanied by the necessary training. This situation concerns in particular Austria, Belgium, France, Greece, Italy, the Netherlands, Portugal, Sweden, and the United Kingdom.

• A lack of a multidisciplinary approach. In a number of countries —Austria, France, Italy, Luxembourg, Portugal, and Spain—the exchange of information and the cooperation between the agencies involved in the investigative phase is unsatisfactory.

• A rare use of the expertise of the private investigative sector. In countries such as Belgium, Finland, France, Greece, Italy, and Spain, this sector has become well developed, but at the same time has remained underused because of the high costs involved.

These investigations into the phenomenon of money laundering in countries of the European Union have—as we said earlier—a wider application, and the indicators of the effectiveness of anti-money-laundering policies have a more general relevance, although source countries—in the light of the generalized institutional weaknesses of their societies—would have a long way to go before these policies could be put to work with any chance of success. The complexity of tracing the proceeds from drug trafficking and other illicit activities requires extensive institutional support. In their absence, following the money will resemble a tour through a labyrinth without exit.

Policy Implications

Understanding the reasons for the failure of financial investigations is the starting point for making them more effective. In the very same way, understanding the reasons for the success of such investigations in some countries means a learning experience that, eventually, can serve a successful implementation in other countries. This way, the experience within the European Union framework will help the definition of policies that will serve the tracing of ill-gotten gains in other parts of the world.

The legislative framework governing financial investigations in the European Union can be regarded as basically sound. Investigative units organized to locate the proceeds from crime are active in most European Union countries and they have been developing special investigative techniques. In addition, in all European Union member states, legal provisions permit financial investigations not only into the activities of those suspected of a crime, but also into the activities of third parties that have a personal or business relationship with the suspects. Such provisions will make it possible to trace the illicit funds generated by criminal activity to dummy persons or institutions. However, the cooperation among law enforcement agencies (specialized investigative units, police, tax authorities, and so on) and the sharing of information regarding money-laundering issues have left much to be desired. The same can be concluded with regard to private institutions (financial as well as nonfinancial institutions plus the private investigation sector). The material resources that are allocated to financial investigations are generally few in number. The area has been chronically underfunded. Investigation units have been created, but they often lack adequate training. Collaboration in the investigation phase between nonbanking financial institutions and nonfinancial institutions has been usually inadequate, as our research has shown. Furthermore, despite the growth of a well-developed private investigation sector, exploitation of its expertise is rare, largely because of the high costs involved. Therefore, in order to improve the ability to trace the proceeds from crime, it is imperative to redefine the way in which the information network involving the public and private actors has been operating.

In order to meet these problems, both the human investment and the material support for financial investigations have to be increased. The level of training of financial investigators and their capability to locate the proceeds from crime should be improved. Finally, new ways should be defined to make the relevant information concerning the tracing of the proceeds from crime accessible to the different law enforcement agencies.

The level of cooperation with financial institutions and, above all, with nonfinancial institutions, while tracing money-laundering schemes, needs to be improved. A lot could be gained already by simplifying the means of their collaboration. The skills of private investigators should not be left untapped and more financial resources should be budgeted for this purpose.

Money-laundering practices have grown in numbers and complexity with the growth in the importance of transnational crime, among which the activities of the drug industry play such an important part. The financial investigations in those countries affected by these activities are involved in a game of catch-up with the daring entrepreneurs of the criminal sector. Recently, the activities of the off-shore banking sector have come under pressure, but in those cases a financial investigation is even more complicated. Only extensive international action along the lines explained above may begin to bring effective control of money-laundering practices within reach.

Notes

1. European Committee of Crime Problems (CDPC), Committee of Experts on Criminal Law and Criminological Aspects of Organized Crime (PC-CO), Criminal Financial Investigation, "A Strategic and Tactical Approach in the European Union Dimension" (Strasbourg, May 21, 1997), 2.

2. See the Internet-site at the following address: http://www.ustreas.gov/irs/ci/re-cruit/mission.htm.

3. This terminology is used in the Council of the European Union, "Proposal Regarding the Implementation of Recommendation 8.6 of CRIMORG 17399–Dealing with the Expertise Required for Applying Sophisticated Investigative Techniques," CRIMORG 51 (Brussels, May 4, 1999).

4. See Informal Money-laundering Experts Group, "Draft Report," CRIMORG 173, (Brussels, November 6, 1999).

5. Ibid.

6. The content of this section is based on the final report of the study: "The Seizure and Confiscation of the Proceeds from Crime in the European Union Member States: What Works, What Does Not, and What Is Promising." The study was awarded by the European Commission on Transcrime, Research Centre on Transnational Crime at the University of Trento (Italy), in collaboration with the University of Palermo (Italy) and the Italian Ministry of Justice under the Falcone 2000 Annual Programme.

7. The first questionnaire (questionnaire for public prosecutors) was addressed to public prosecutors with considerable experience in the field of seizure and confiscation of the proceeds from crime. The second questionnaire (questionnaire for public officials) was addressed to public officials, preferably employed at the Ministry of Justice. The national experts were selected with the assistance of the permanent representatives of the Ministries of Justice of the European Union member states. The final report gives a descriptive analysis of each of the fifteen member states. This analysis helps explain the problems, which in this article is left only to the indicators.

8. It has to be said that some of the variables initially selected were excluded from the calculation, namely, (1) Variable 4—Categories of third parties subject to investigations, because this is a specification of Variable 3, and (2) Variable 11—Types of assets seized, because of the scarcity of data and nonreliability.

9. For the values used in the calculation of the effectiveness indexes, see Ernesto Savona and Bruno Vettori, *The Seizure and Confiscation of the Proceeds from Crime in the European Member States: What Works, What Does Not, and What Is Promising* (Trento: University of Trento, 2001), 158–60.

10. According to the F.A.T.F., the Criminal Assets Bureau "is a well-organized group which has achieved some excellent results by taking a robust 'proactive approach' against major criminals. The strengths of the Bureau are that it is a new, multi-agency, intelligence driven body, with all its staff located in one place." See *Financial Action Task Force on Money-laundering, Second Mutual Evaluation Report on Ireland* (Brussels: European Union, 1999).

11. Ibid., 7.

12. See *Financial Action Task Force on Money-laundering, Annual Report 1996–1997* (Paris: OECD, 1997), 15.

IV

The Drug Industry
and the War on Drugs

10

Perversely Harmful Effects of Counter-Narcotics Policy in the Andes

Rensselaer Lee

The U.S. international drug-fighting strategy as it has evolved in recent years comprises two related but distinct imperatives. The primary imperative is simply to limit the availability of illicit drugs in U.S. markets. The standard fare of supply-reduction measures has included eradicating coca and opium poppy fields, destroying processing laboratories, and seizing illegal drug shipments en route to the United States. Latin America has been the venue for most such source-control efforts, especially the Andean countries, which supply 100 percent of the cocaine and (now) as much as 75 percent of the heroin consumed in U.S. markets. For instance, much of the recent 1.27 billion U.S. dollars contributed to Plan Colombia is earmarked for supply-control purposes: helicopters, planes, and training to support a massive coca-spraying effort in southern Colombia, as well as electronic surveillance technology to help detect the northward flow of drugs from coca-growing areas of that country.[1]

An additional imperative, one that has acquired increasing prominence in the 1990s, is to attack and disrupt large aggregations of criminal power. In practice, this has meant breaking up so-called cocaine cartels, immobilizing their top leaders, and severing drug traffickers' links to the economy and the power structure. As initially conceived, counter-organization strategies were supposed to contribute to the goal of supply reduction—for instance, by making it harder for traffickers to direct and coordinate major shipments. Nevertheless, the fundamental rationale for counterorganization has been political—to limit the power and reach of trafficking establishments. As an unpublished 1995 World Bank study noted, "Even if drug flows cannot be stopped completely, it may be better for the country to have [them] originate from a large number of small producers, each of whom has less power and influence, than from a small group of traffickers able and willing to use their economic power to intervene in the political/judicial process."[2]

The War on Drugs

The entire U.S. international drug control effort, including source-country programs and border interdiction, has consumed more than 30 billion U.S dollars since the early 1980s. Globally and regionally the results have been unimpressive, at least in supply reduction terms. South American production of coca leaf, for instance, reached an all-time high of 650,800 tons in the year 2000—a 30 percent increase over five years earlier—despite aggressive eradication programs in the Andean countries. The total amount of cocaine potentially available from Andean leaf could exceed 900 tons if realistic conversion figures are used (see Table 10.1). At the U.S. end, cocaine, heroin, and other dangerous substances are becoming more rather than less available to consumers. According to the U.S. drug czar's office, retail prices (adjusted for purity) of cocaine and heroin declined more than 70 percent from the early 1980s to the late 1990s. For the period 1991 to 1998 the decrease was 35 percent and 63 percent respectively for the two drugs. In 1999, a gram of cocaine could be bought for as little as 20 U.S dollars in Miami and 24 U.S. dollars in New York City according to DEA price statistics.[3]

While failing to stem the flow of drugs, U.S. drug policy has had major consequences for the organization of the cocaine trade in the hemisphere. Certain of these changes might be counted as success stories. In the early and mid-1990s Colombia—with extensive logistical and intelligence support from the United States—effectively dismantled the Medellín and Cali cartels—among the most powerful criminal enterprises the world has ever known. The collapse of the cartel system resulted in the apparent fragmentation or "atomization" of the Colombian cocaine industry into as many as eighty to three hundred—according to widely varying official estimates—distinct exporting organizations.[4] This structural transformation hardly affected cocaine exports at all, but the smaller and (presumably) weaker successor groups seemed to pose less of a threat to Colombian governing institutions than did the Medellín and Cali coalitions. Moreover, in the late 1990s a combination of intensified aerial interdiction, alternative development incentives, and some forcible eradication brought about major reductions in coca cultivation in Peru and Bolivia—declines of approximately 70 percent in the period from 1995 to 2000 (see Table 10.2). Bolivia, according to the U.S. State Department, is on its way to becoming a marginal producer of cocaine and—because chemicals essential in refining are in short supply— the purity of that country's product has been sharply reduced. Such positive achievements, though, have come at a substantial cost. In Colombia, for example, in one of the more grotesque sagas of the Drug War, hundreds of lives were lost and hundreds of millions of dollars spent in a protracted hunt for a single Medellín drug kingpin, Pablo Escobar Gaviria. That pursuit was the product of a de facto unholy alliance linking the U.S. Embassy, the DEA, CIA, an elite military espionage unit (Centra Spike), an army strike team (Delta Force), and the Colombian police Search Bloc responsible for tracking Escobar with a consortium of Pablo Escobar's enemies within the Colombian cocaine establishments.[5] Among these were the so-called People Persecuted by Pablo Escobar (PEPES) group, assorted paramilitary figures, and the godfathers of the rival Cali coalition, who reportedly paid the Search Bloc a reward of 10 million U.S. dollars for its ultimately successful operation against Escobar.[6] Of course, Cali's collaboration in the operation simply allowed that group to cement its relationship with the Colombian government and (for a time) to supplant Medellín as the dominant player in the cocaine business. A Colombian crackdown on the Cali cartel in the mid-1990s again changed the configuration of actors in the industry; yet the industry—now decentralized and essentially leaderless—is in certain respects a more difficult target for U.S. and Colombian authorities than were the cartels.

Elsewhere in the Andes, deep reductions in coca cultivation—considered an almost unattainable goal a decade ago—are a palpable achievement of drug policy. Nevertheless, they may have clouded short-run prospects for economic growth, especially in Bolivia. For instance, a recent UNDCP-funded study by a Colombian economist estimated that "repatriable" cocaine income in Bolivia amounted to 714 million U.S. dollars, or almost 11 percent of GDP, in 1995.[7] The disappearance of 70 percent of these revenues, albeit over a five-year period, inevitably would have some macroeconomic impact. Indeed, average GDP growth in 1999–2000 (1.6 percent) was less than half the average growth in 1994–1998. Of course, factors other than reduced cocaine exports could have contributed to this drop. Sales of so-called alternative development crops—approximately 125 million U.S. dollars in Bolivia in 1999–2000—hardly compensate for the loss of cocaine-related income.[8] Unsurprisingly, coca-farming communities are not happy; they have responded to eradication with violent demonstrations and protests against the government in both Bolivia and Peru. In Bolivia, where less than half of eradicated farming families have received assistance in cultivating legal crops, ongoing protests by disaffected growers have created a crisis atmosphere that itself has depressed legal economic growth in the country.[9]

The goals of the U.S. anti-drug policy seemed reasonable enough. The Medellín and Cali cartels possessed the ability to inflict economic damage on governing institutions; few people would mourn their passing. Escobar's self-described war against the Colombian oligarchy in the late 1980s and early 1990s and Cali's apparently successful attempt to subvert the democratic process in Colombia's 1994 elections are obvious cases in point.[10] The elimination of coca plants—the raw material for cocaine—is central to the concept of supply reduction. The experience of eradication was disruptive—especially in Bolivia—but whatever economic distress occurred could eventually be compensated for by positive growth in national economies, helped along by "structural adjustment" loans and other forms of assistance from the international community.

Unfortunately, the story does not end here. An "iron law" of international drug control is that small enforcement successes often mask larger policy failures. The supposed achievements of the Andean Drug War, in fact, have spawned an array of unanticipated problems for the United States, Colombia, and other countries in this hemisphere. Recent statistics show, for example, that cultivation of coca has ballooned in Colombia, largely negating the eradication achievements elsewhere in the Andes (see Tables 10.1 and 10.2). Colombian syndicates reportedly also have succeeded in improving leaf yields and alkaloid content to compensate for lost Peruvian and Bolivian supplies. These developments in turn have had dreadful implications for Colombian internal stability; the increased concentration of upstream coca production in Colombia has fueled that country's ongoing civil conflict by vastly increasing the resources available to antistate groups. The disintegration of the cartel structure has had a similar result, if for different reasons. The cartels had provided a degree of order and control in the industry, but their demise allowed or emboldened Colombia's various guerrilla organizations to integrate forward into refining, trading, and even exporting drugs.[11] Since these groups seem to contemplate the violent overthrow of the government or (minimally) a permanent partition of the country, they may represent a greater threat to Colombia's survival than did the classic criminal coalitions of the 1980s and 1990s.

Other unfavorable consequences have ensued from the counter-organization strategy pursued in Colombia. One has been an apparent shift of trafficking resources from cocaine to heroin. Heroin is not a new phenomenon—factions of the Cali cartel were involved in processing or distributing the drug—and the extent of the shift cannot be precisely determined. Nevertheless, the breakup of the cartels appears to have encouraged diversification. Heroin, which has a much higher value-to-weight ratio than cocaine—at least where the U.S. market is concerned—is an ideal illicit product for micro-enterprises that have limited reach and resources. Colombian heroin is capturing an increasing share of the U.S. market, although overall U.S. consumption of that drug has not increased significantly in the 1990s.[12]

Another consequence relates to overall drug-trafficking patterns in the hemisphere. Pressure on the cartels (and the subsequent breakup of these aggregates) caused major modification of these patterns. Since the early 1990s,

Colombians have increasingly relied on intermediate organizations in transit countries—Jamaica, Haiti, the Dominican Republic, Mexico, and the like—to transport cocaine to the continental United States or (in the case of the Caribbean) to Puerto Rico. Recently the smaller Colombian exporting organizations have been selling cocaine outright to traffickers in these countries. Also, these traffickers over time have been establishing their own distribution networks in the United States, in some cases supplanting those of the Colombians. The bottom line here is that groups in Mexico and the Caribbean are acquiring an increasing share of the income stream generated by the international drug trade. The results have been calamitous. Drugs have widely infiltrated and corrupted the economies and political systems of these transit states; in certain Caribbean countries local drug lords and their money-laundering henchmen can manipulate elections and virtually dictate political outcomes. Closer to the United States, Mexican traffickers—newly flush with cocaine cash—have succeeded in corrupting not just Mexico's top police and judicial officials, but U.S. federal and local authorities across the border, as well.[13] To ascribe the above-mentioned trends entirely to the pathologies of international drug policy, of course, would be unfair. The United States did not invent Colombia's modern-day guerrilla problem. Colombian diversification into heroin was partly a response to growing saturation of the U.S. cocaine market, a trend already apparent in the early 1990s. Criminals, rogues, and scoundrels in various guises have perennially flourished throughout the Caribbean and Mexico. Nevertheless, the so-called Drug War in some countries—while solving absolutely nothing from a supply-reduction standpoint—has in some instances exacerbated these problems. The deteriorating political-military situation in Colombia in particular poses a major threat to U.S. security interests in the hemisphere. For these reasons, alternatives to the current failed supply-side approaches to fighting drugs must urgently be found.

Table 10.1. Andean Coca-Leaf (and Potential Cocaine) Production, 1995 and 2000 (in Metric Tons)

	1995	2000
Colombia*	229,300 (80)	583,000 (580'-7292)
Bolivia	80,000 (240)	13,400 (43)
Peru	183,600 (460)	54,400 (145)
Total	497,900 (780)	650,800 (768–917)

Notes: Assumes a more than 1,000:1 leaf to cocaine HCL conversion ratio, reported in INCSR 2001.

*Assumes an 800:1 ratio, based on recent field estimates in Colombia.

Sources: Elaboration Data, International Narcotics Control Strategy Report 1995–2000 (INCSRs); Sergio Uribe in Bogotá.

Table 10.2. Cultivation Trends in the Andes, 1995–2000, in Hectares (and Percent)

	1995		2000	
Colombia	50,900	(24)	136,200	(74)
Bolivia	48,600	(23)	14,600	(8)
Peru	115,300	(54)	34,200	(18)
Total	214,800		185,000	

Source: Elaboration Data International Narcotics Control Strategy Report (INCSR), 2000.

The Crop Reduction Debacle

The U.S. cocaine-control efforts in source countries in the 1990s effectively redrew the map of coca cultivation in the Andes. As Tables 10.1 and 10.2 show, Bolivia and Peru accounted for more than three-quarters of the coca cultivated in the region in 1995, and Colombia for less than one-quarter. By the year 2000, these proportions had been reversed, although the total area devoted to coca had decreased somewhat. Similarly, reported production of cocaine from Colombian leaf was only 10 percent of combined Andean production in 1995, but 75 percent in 2000. According to unofficial Colombian field estimates, the proportion may have reached close to 80 percent in that year. To accomplish its targets in Peru and Bolivia, Washington used both the carrot of alternative development—mainly assistance in developing and marketing legal agricultural commodities—and the stick of forcible manual eradication or the threat of it. In addition, in Peru especially, an aggressive air interdiction effort limited illegal drug flights to Colombia, causing local coca prices to fall and inducing farmers to switch to other activities. In recent years, though, prices have risen again, which would spur new planting of coca. In Colombia, aerial spraying of coca has been underway since 1994, but the effort so far has been an utter failure. According to the U.S. State Department, farmers planted one new hectare for each of the approximately 124,000 hectares eradicated in the period 1995 to 2000.[14]

The shifting pattern of coca cultivation in the Andes turned out to be a windfall for Colombia's various outlaw groups, especially for the Revolutionary Armed Forces of Colombia, or FARC. As a 2001 U.S. State Department report notes, "The Colombian syndicates, witnessing the vulnerability of Peruvian and Bolivian coca supply to joint interdiction operations in the late 1990s, decided to move most of the cultivation to Colombia's southwest corner, an area controlled by FARC, the country's oldest insurgent group."[15] The resultant expansion of drug revenues benefited other outlaw organizations such as the Army of National Liberation (ELN) and the rightist United Self-Defense Forces of Colombia (AUC); however, FARC appeared to be the biggest winner. As a former Colombian defense minister, Rafael Pardo observed in a recent *Foreign Affairs* article, "FARC is both a narco-trafficking operation and an insurgent group seeking political power. Its strongholds are the areas that grow 90 percent of the country's cocaine."[16] Truly, the coca-cocaine trade is the lifeblood of FARC's operations and of Colombia's armed conflict generally.

The critical fact in all of this is that Andean coca leaf is now mostly processed in Colombia. Colombia had always produced three-quarters or more of the world's finished cocaine, but traffickers until the mid-1990s had relied mostly on Peru and Bolivia for intermediate coca products to supply Colombia's cocaine refineries. In 1995, Colombian refineries imported an estimated 90 percent of their cocaine base requirements from Peru and Bolivia; by the year 2000 they were able to obtain 75 percent of this product domestically.[17]

The result of these trends was a huge expansion in the guerrillas' revenue base. Consider that every large coca plantation, every kilo of base, every kilo of cocaine HCL, every fifty-five gallons of processing chemicals (ether, acetone, sulfuric acid, and the like), and every incoming or outgoing truck or aircraft in guerrilla-held zones is subject to a protection fee. The quid pro quo (at least in theory) is that the guerrillas' presence deters intervention by the authorities in trafficking operations. The funds generated from such taxes are doubtless substantial; however, in recent years guerrillas have opportunistically gone deeper into the cocaine trade—expanding beyond taxation into refining, and even into trafficking and sales. For example, they apparently have cornered the market for cocaine base and possibly also for poppy latex in Colombia—buying these products from farmers and selling them to traffickers at a huge markup. According to a recent report from Colombia, FARC's profit margin on each base transaction is approximately 200 U.S. dollars per kilogram. Assuming that approximately 1.3 kilograms of base convert to 1 kilogram of cocaine, that potential production from Colombian leaf is 580 tons in 2000, and that insurgents control 90 percent of the coca-growing area in Colombia, the total income from base turnovers could be as high as 140 million U.S. dollars—representing a significant part of guerrillas' total earnings from criminal activities.[18]

Traffickers also have benefited from these arrangements. Even considering the guerrillas' control of the cocaine base market, Colombian base appears to be cheaper and of more even quality than base purchased in Peru or Bolivia. Some recent statistics on price trends seem to bear this out. According to the above-cited UNDCP study, the ratio of the cost of a kilogram of base to the (low-end) U.S. wholesale price of a kilogram of cocaine rose from 2.3 to 1 in the 1981–1985 period, to 5.15 to 1 in 1986–1990, to 9.35 to one in 1991–1995, and to 13.9 to 1 in 1996–1998.[19] Such numbers suggest the possibility

of a growing modus vivendi between drug traffickers and Marxist guerrillas—in contrast to a relationship that was characterized by frequent conflict
in the era of the Medellín and Cali cartels. Military-strategic considerations
or perhaps purely mercenary ones have prompted FARC to expand further
downstream in the narcotics business. Certain fronts are said to operate
small cocaine laboratories; alternatively, guerrillas pay independent refineries a per-kilo fee to convert base to CHCL, subsequently marketing that product in Colombia or abroad. Evidence has surfaced recently that links FARC
fairly definitively to exports of Colombian cocaine to Brazil and to Mexico.[20]
Fairly sizeable shipments seem to be involved in these cases. Participation in
the classic trafficking functions of refining and (especially) exporting obviously will increase FARC's overall share of revenues from illicit drug sales.
This new and ominous development is reciprocally related to the increased
fragmentation of the cocaine business since the mid-1990s and to the loss of
the integrated marketing structure for cocaine that the cartels had developed
and perfected. This point will be discussed in more detail in the following
section.

Cartels, De-Cartelization, and Colombia's Civil Conflict

Colombia's cartels were essentially regionally based groupings of different
trafficking organizations that coalesced to rationalize the system of smuggling and marketing cocaine. The aim was to maximize export volumes and
profits while reducing the risk to each participant. This included curious co-
financing and co-insurance schemes, as well as the pooling of certain business
services—for instance, financial advisors, lawyers, counterintelligence and
security operatives, and assassins. The larger participating organization either owned trafficking assets such as cocaine laboratories and shipping companies outright or enjoyed exclusive access to them.[21] Some fusion of administrative structures seems to have occurred to oversee certain functions—for
instance, laboratory production, the handling of shipments in transit countries, distribution in major markets, and the recycling of proceeds from drug
sales. The core of the Cali cartel comprised approximately sixty such admin-
istrators according to one authoritative study.[22] In other words, the cartel
system implied a degree of vertical integration to ensure predictability in
flows of product and money; also, it was designed to protect the component
organizations against their natural enemies, which included the Colombian
and U.S. authorities, rival traffickers, and predatory guerrilla groups. The
principal coalitions centered in Medellín and Cali at one time controlled 80
percent or more of the cocaine exported from Colombia. Other quasi-inde-
pendent groupings centered in Bogotá or the Atlantic coast maintained loose
associations with Medellín and Cali and tended to follow their lead on policy

issues. The cartels commanded significant financial and human resources. At their zenith—approximately the end of the 1980s—the cartels earned combined annual revenues of at least 6 billion U.S. dollars, of which 3 billion to 4 billion was profit. Also, they coordinated a vast trafficking infrastructure of perhaps eight thousand to ten thousand skilled workers and professionals, most of whom—admittedly—were contract help rather than full-time employees.[23] By any standard this represented an enormous concentration of economic power in criminal hands. To some extent this was directed power; a leadership structure of sorts existed within Colombia's cocaine establishment, exercised by the heads of the dominant trafficking organizations in each coalition. This included the Rodriguez Orejuela brothers (Gilberto and Miguel) in Cali and Pablo Escobar Gaviria in Medellín. Leaders played a vital role in setting overall strategy for the cartels, particularly perhaps in noneconomic realms. For example, the leaders were able to channel resources from member organizations to joint industry purposes. These included influencing national election campaigns—the Cali cartel's donation of 6 million U.S. dollars to Ernesto Samper's 1994 presidential bid is a notorious case in point—delivering bribes to senior police officials and legislators, underwriting the activities of self-defense and paramilitary forces, and unleashing narco-terrorist violence against the state. The cartels, in other words, were not amorphous patterns of collaboration among like-minded criminal entities; rather, they possessed a malevolent purpose and direction.[24]

The cartel system implied considerable coordination and control of cocaine-trafficking functions. Member organizations imported cocaine base from the southern Andes, processed it in dedicated laboratories, and exported the finished product along painstakingly developed routes to transit points and then to the country of destination. Control, in turn, signified the capacity to maintain functioning of vital supply lines and income of production. The cartels, or the larger member organizations, financed elaborate security systems to protect key facilities and to ensure an uninterrupted flow of product. These security forces may have been a pooled resource. These networks comprised a combination of perimeter guards, surveillance teams, paramilitary-style forces or other organized thugs, and (in some cases) local military units willing to supply weaponry or intelligence information.

These arrangements were directed partly against rapacious guerrilla forces that roamed the Colombian country in search of taxable sources of wealth. As a whole, Colombia's trafficking establishment was strongly anti-Communist. Although some drug warriors in the Reagan and (first) Bush administration liked to float the idea of a "narco-guerrilla alliance," this relationship in the cartel era was characterized more by conflict than by cooperation. From the traffickers' perspective, the guerrillas were at best an economic nuisance—a threat to the smooth functioning of the system—and at worst potential competitors in the cocaine business. The FARC and the ELN admittedly taxed a percentage of cocaine HCL and base production with the acquiescence of the cartels, but this was in the areas in which the insurgents exercised a preponderance of military and political control.[25] The demise of the cartel system radically altered the cocaine-trafficking landscape in Colombia. The industry became fragmented—cocaine shipments were smaller and were handled by a larger number of traffickers. A power vacuum or sorts emerged in the industry; there was no clear leadership or articulated common strategy. Moreover, the successor organizations—individually smaller, weaker, and less wealthy—could not maintain the same degree of control over trafficking functions and assets. Pieces of the cartels' former empire were, practically speaking, up for grabs. One Colombian source knowledgeable about the drug trade relates that in mid-1996, Cali-based trafficking organizations, under pressure from FARC, simply "abandoned" some seven to ten cocaine laboratories located in the Caguan region of Caqueta Department. The FARC also inherited a cache of 5 to 6 tons of cocaine that had been stored by the departing traffickers.[26]

In any event, the stage was set for the entry of new actors into the narcotics business. Significantly, the new entrants were criminalized political actors that competed for control over territory and wealth and (in the case of the armed leftist groups) that directly challenged the authority of the Colombian state. As Colombian narcotics expert Sergio Uribe observed in a recent paper: "As the large cartels fell to the pressures of the authorities, the paramilitary, the FARC and the ELN all began slowly to move into the market. . . . Today they buy the cocaine base from the farmers and sell it to the traffickers. The level of their involvement in the business is increasing and there are credible accounts that the FARC are running their own HCL and heroin labs and are attempting to form a new cartel exchanging guns for drugs."[27] The FARC, like classic trafficking organizations, appears to maintain a dedicated inventory of CHCL refineries. Guerrillas typically contract with the laboratory owner to process quantities of cocaine base, paying a fee (100 U.S. dollars according to a recent found document) for each kilogram of refined product.[28] However, FARC by now probably has commandeered the skills to manage labs on its own; for years, according to a Colombian army colonel, FARC had "insisted that its members be allowed to work in laboratories' operating in areas under the organization's control, so the guerrillas are at least broadly familiar with the processing technology."[29]

Of special interest, perhaps, are FARC's recent forays into exporting cocaine. Rafael Pardo called FARC "a criminal organization which compares favorably with any of the international drug mafias." This is an exaggeration, but the organization's ability to move cocaine beyond the borders of Colombia in exchange for money or weapons is cause for concern. One recent case involved the Sixteenth FARC Front, which reputedly controlled a gigantic "cocaine complex" of eighty HCL laboratories spread out over an area of 17,000 in two eastern departments (Guainia and Vichada). The FARC evidently had arranged to sell much of the product to a Brazilian drug king-pin, "Fernandinho." Fernandinho, captured last April by Colombian authorities, assumed responsibility for transporting the drugs from Colombia to Brazil. The police found documentary evidence that the guerrillas and the Brazilian had realized seven separate shipments totaling 1,900 kilos at an average price of approximately 2,100 U.S. dollars per kilo. Some other documents indicated that Fernandinho had bartered some 2,200 pistols and 500 assault rifles to FARC for cocaine. Alarmingly, the trafficker, in separate statements to the minister of defense and to the commander of the armed forces, claimed that he had paid FARC an average of 10 million U.S. dollars per month in connection with the drug trade and that he had taken monthly amounts of 20 to 25 tons of cocaine out of "the south of the country." This estimate seems inflated, but it suggests that the Sixteenth Front and the Brazilian were doing a thriving business. The Colombian government, finally convinced of the reality of the relationship, issued an arrest warrant in April against the commander of the Sixteenth Front, Tomas Medina, on drug-trafficking charges.[30]

Information also has surfaced that seems to tie FARC to criminal organizations in Mexico. In August 2000, a Colombian doctor, Carlos Ariel Charry Guzman, was arrested by Mexican authorities and accused of acting as a go-between between FARC and the Arellano Felix gang based in Tijuana. The idea was to exchange cocaine for cash and possibly arms. Charry's contacts with the gang reportedly resulted in at least one successful shipment of 800 kilograms of cocaine to Mexico. According to one account, Charry had even engaged a former money launderer for the Cali cartel to manage the proceeds of his deals with the Tijuana group. Other evidence suggested that FARC had developed a maritime smuggling route to Mexico from Colombia's Pacific coast. For instance, in a November 2000 incident the United States Navy intercepted two go-fast boats carrying 4 tons of cocaine to Mexico from the Colombian port of Buenaventura; documents and insignia found aboard the craft and testimony of the crew indicated that the Thirtieth FARC Front, based in southwestern Colombia, had organized the shipment.[31] The Mexican connection, it should be noted, is potentially a lucrative one for the guerrillas. Cocaine transported to that country could fetch a price of 7,000 to 7,500 U.S. dollars per kilo, considerably more than FARC received from its documented transaction with the Brazilian.

Such reports, of course, should be placed in perspective. So far, at least, FARC has opted for a limited export strategy. Representatives of FARC are not dealing drugs in New York, Miami, or Los Angeles, nor has the organization been able to smuggle shipments directly from Colombia to the United States or Europe. Nevertheless, a capacity to move drugs into neighboring or transit countries implies a significantly larger revenue stream than do the sales of cocaine products to Colombian middlemen and exporters. As the guerrillas' revenue base and their war-fighting capacity both expand, the chances for a successful settlement of Colombia's civil war become correspondingly more remote. Of course, narco-funded guerrillas are not the sole source of Colombia's current problems. As a U.S. ambassador to Colombia remarked, "The FARC and the paramilitary groups are functioning in Colombia like the grand cartels that existed previously."[32] But the paramilitary movement has always been interwoven with international drug trafficking; indeed, its leader, Carlos Castaño—himself identified by the DEA as a small-time narco-trafficker—once remarked that 70 percent of the movement's revenue derived from the drug trade.[33] Also, the paramilitaries are not waging war against the Colombian state and the military. The FARC, meanwhile, insists that it is merely taxing the trade in coca products, a claim that only a few of the movement's most politically correct supporters in journalism and academia still seem prepared to believe.[34]

The economic and strategic dimensions of the post-cartel guerrilla threat are not known with certainty. Colombian government estimates of annual guerrilla income from all illegal activities typically range from 500 million to 1 billion U.S. dollars. (Revelation of FARC's recent exporting activities might favor the upper end of the range.) If FARC, ELN, and the Army of Popular Liberation (EPL), a smaller splinter group, together have twenty thousand people under arms, earnings could reach 25,000 to 50,000 U.S. dollars per guerrilla fighter.[35] It is generally believed that FARC—the largest insurgent group—accounts for most of this income and that, in contrast to the other groups, most of FARC's earnings come from narcotics-related activities. (A representative breakdown is shown in Table 10.3.) The guerrillas are not in the same economic league as the former cocaine cartels; however, they probably generate a substantial surplus over what it takes to maintain an army in the field and to administer the guerrillas' various political fiefdoms. One detailed study by an intra-agency Colombian group placed FARC's surplus at 310 million U.S. dollars in 1998. Even if certain business-related costs are factored in (such as outlays for cocaine base or processing services), the estimated surplus is likely to exceed 200 million U.S. dollars annually. According to the above-mentioned study, some of these funds are invested in various legal enterprises—banks, security firms, transport companies, real estate, ranching, and the like—some in sophisticated weaponry such as surface-to-air missiles, and some in imported machinery for arms manufacture. The FARC, in sum, is well positioned to carry on the war in Colombia indefinitely or to escalate hostilities if need be.[36] Various wider scenarios also should be

Table 10.3. Colombian Guerrillas Earnings from Illegal Businesses, 1997 (in Million U.S. Dollars)

	FARC	ELN*	EPL	Total
Narcotics	381	35	—	416
Kidnapping	78	122	5	205
Extortion	84	243	10	337
Total	543	400	15	958

*Army of Popular Liberation 1998.
Source: Colombian Government report, cited in Maria Cristina Caballero, "La Guerrilla Billonaria," Cambio 16 (July 6, 1998), 28–31.

contemplated, including threats to Venezuela's oil fields or to shipping in the Panama Canal and possible flows of money or weapons to revitalize moribund revolutionary movements elsewhere in Latin America.

Other Unintended Effects

As argued here, U.S. supply reduction and counter-organization policies in the Andes resulted in a significant repositioning and restructuring of the Andean cocaine industry. Major consequences of these developments were the strengthening of Colombia's various insurgent groups and the deepening of that country's internal crisis. Other consequences occurring specifically from the assault on the cartels can be cited. One of these is the growing economic significance of the heroin industry in Colombia and the increased penetration of Colombian heroin into the U.S. market. A second consequence, reflecting the diminished strategic reach of successor organizations to the cartels, is the changing dynamic of drug smuggling in the Western Hemisphere; this has meant a greater participation of trafficking groups in transit countries in the value-added sector from Colombian narcotics exports. Heroin is not a new industry in Colombia. Small-scale opium cultivation and heroin processing have been taking place in Colombia for upward of thirty years. However, marijuana and later cocaine were the commercially significant narcotics products. (Cocaine, of course, still is the dominant drug export.) By the late 1980s or early 1990s, though, Colombian traffickers—especially those associated with the Cali coalition—began to view heroin as an alternative source of income to the established cocaine trade. One Cali faction—the Ivan Urdinola group—acquired a measure of control over cultivation and processing, and the dominant Rodriguez-Orejuela organization within the cartel undertook to distribute heroin to the United States.[37] Law enforcement pressure on the cartels seems to have increased traffickers' propensity to diversify into heroin. It is not hard to see why; the per gram price of the drug averaged almost ten times that of cocaine during the 1990s.[38] For independent trafficking enterprises—those that succeeded the cartels—the drug offered exceptionally attractive commercial possibilities. Storage and handling of large quantities of heroin is not an issue as it is with large cocaine loads. Transport by human couriers, or mules, the preferred pre-cartel mode of smuggling (at a time when cocaine prices were several times higher), again allowed the small operator to realize a substantial return.[39] For these reasons, the heroin business took off in Colombia during the 1990s. Estimated repatriable heroin revenues increased from 45 million U.S. dollars per year in 1991 to 323 million U.S. dollars in 1998, according to the above-mentioned UNDCP study, making heroin Colombia's second most important narcotics export. In the United States, according to DEA figures, 23 percent of the heroin seized in 1994 was of "South American" origin; by 1999 this proportion had risen to 75 percent. Currently, approximately 85 percent of the heroin seized in the northeastern United States by federal authorities originates in Colombia.[40] Also, heroin prices have declined somewhat compared to cocaine prices—in the 1990s from thirteen to one in 1990–1991 to four to one in 1997–1998, indicating possibly a higher relative availability of that drug in U.S. markets—not exactly a positive development from a U.S. drug policy perspective.[41]

The decline and fall of the cartels also had a significant effect on the distribution of drug-smuggling revenues within the hemisphere. Since the early 1990s, risk-averse Colombian exporters—cognizant of the dangers of shipping cocaine directly to the United States—have relied increasingly on transportation groups in transit countries to make the final delivery to customers based in the United States. Initially, arrangements took different forms—such as payment in cash per kilogram or in a share of the load—and the smugglers undertook to transfer the drugs to Colombian wholesaling organizations or cells in different U.S. cities. With the progressive "de-cartelization" of the cocaine business, Colombians became more inclined to sell cocaine outright to the intermediaries themselves (such as Mexicans, Jamaicans, or Dominicans), receiving somewhat less than the port-of-entry U.S. price (6,000 to 7,500 U.S. dollars per kilo compared to 11,000 to 12,000 U.S. dollars) and exiting from the transaction at that point. Correspondingly, as Francisco Thoumi points out, the Colombian "cell" structure began to atrophy as the intermediaries established their own distribution networks in the United States.[42] By 1997, for example, Mexican-based trafficking groups had practically supplanted Colombian distributors throughout the western and midwestern United States (in such major cities as Chicago, Houston, Dallas, Denver, and Los Angeles), although the Colombians continued to be the dominant player in the Northeast.[43]

The results have been predictable. In Mexico the profitability of the cocaine business greatly augmented the economic resources of trafficking groups; by the late 1990s traffickers' net earnings from drug smuggling approached 7 billion U.S. dollars per year, or about 2 percent of GDP.[44] In the Caribbean federation of St. Kitts-Nevis, cocaine's share of the islands' GDP was estimated at 20 to 30 million U.S. dollars, or 10 to 15 percent of GDP, according to a 1998 British study. With respect to the Dominican Republic—the most important transit country outside of Mexico—a recent United Nations study calculated that half of the country's 7 to 8 percent annual growth in the 1990s was attributable to the repatriated proceeds of criminal activity, especially drug trafficking. Possibly reflecting such transfers, assets of Dominican Republic commercial banks grew at almost double the rate of GDP growth from 1995 to 2000; over the same period, the Dominican Republic's largest commercial bank, Banco Intercontinental, increased nearly a phenomenal 1,000 percent. In Haiti, what is left of the floundering economy is being kept afloat principally by net aid flows from the international community and by revenues from the 40 to 70 tons of cocaine that pass through the island annually.[45] The inflows of cocaine wealth have spawned powerful and well-connected narco-mafias in Caribbean states such as the Dominican Republic, Jamaica, Haiti, and St. Kitts, as well as in Mexico. The resulting corruption of political and economic elites and of government institutions is almost unbelievable.

In some Caribbean countries drug money has become the lifeblood of party-building activities and electoral campaigns. For example, the St. Kitts' Labor Party and the Dominican Revolutionary Party (PRD) have received substantial backing from local drug kingpins and, in the case of the latter, from the party's network of drug distributors in the northeastern United States.[46] Lines between the upper world and underworld are becoming increasingly blurred. In one Caribbean country, a leading organizer for the ruling party in the capital city is also a master strategist of the cocaine trade, establishing ties with Colombian suppliers and handling payoffs to senior politicians and police officials. In another, the head of a prominent financial institution invests the institution's capital in cocaine futures—that is, in smuggling ventures that offer large returns and high odds of success. In another, the superintendent of banks reputedly manages a thriving money-courier-cum-laundering business between that country and the United States. In a smuggling operation uncovered in the Mexican state of Quintana Roo, police commanders reportedly were "coordinating the drug shipments," while the staff chemist of the local office of the federal attorney general was employed by the traffickers to analyze the purity of the cocaine. Also, the fugitive former governor of the same state was recently arrested on charges of taking millions of dollars in bribes from cocaine traffickers.[47] Many more such depressing examples can be cited.

Significantly, the countries in which these newly rich narco-traffickers have entrenched themselves are geographically close to the United States and maintain extensive economic, cultural, and demographic links to this country. For example, annual U.S.-Mexican trade is approximately 130 billion U.S. dollars, almost twenty times U.S. trade with Colombia. Obviously the massive yearly flow of people and goods across the U.S. southwestern border (approximately 3.5 million commercial vehicles enter the United States from Mexico annually) creates a ready pipeline for movements of illicit drugs. Moreover, the stain of Mexican corruption has reached out to federal and local agencies on the U.S. side of the border, so the problem is no longer confined just to Mexico. Similarly, the machinations of Mexican, Dominican, or Jamaican drug distributors in the United States seem likely to influence the flow of money to political parties and campaigns, at least in some states and cities. Such unwelcome developments present new enforcement challenges and political complications for U.S. Drug War strategists at the start of the new millennium.

Counter-Drug Strategies: Pros and Cons

America's international drug problems have produced a difficult legacy. More than a quarter century of fighting the Andean cocaine industry—the main drug threat to the United States—has done essentially nothing to reduce the availability of cocaine in U.S. markets. Apparent achievements such as curtailing illicit crops in the southern Andes and dismantling Colombia's cartels have entailed significant indirect costs. As detailed in the preceding sections, these include a growing insurgency threat in Colombia (which threatens to metastasize to neighboring countries), a buoyant South American heroin industry, and—reflecting shifts in narco-wealth and power—the increased "Colombianization" of criminal and political structures in a number of drug transit states.[48]

Such adverse consequences raise the obvious question of whether the benefits of international drug control are commensurate with the costs. Certainly the goal of supply reduction has been elusive. As we have seen, eradication of drug crops merely shifts the locus of upstream production from region to region and country to country. Another unanticipated consequence has been unwanted crop diversification, the expanded cultivation of opium poppy in Colombia and (according to recent reports) in Peru, as well.[49] Even the intensified aerial spraying effort envisaged under Plan Colombia is unlikely to succeed in its objective; farmers probably will respond by pushing the coca frontier (and the attendant polluting effects of the cocaine industry) further into the Amazonian jungle with little or no decrease in net cultivation. Indeed, recent reports from Colombia suggest that this is already happening.

More importantly, the spraying campaign exacerbates the government's problems of political control in coca-growing areas, alienating large rural populations who stand to lose their main source of income. In the southern Department of Putumayo, according to a recent RAND corporation study, 135,000 of the department's 314,000 inhabitants depend directly on coca growing for a livelihood.[50] Since FARC poses as advocates for growers, spraying widens their base of support, contradicting the objectives of the government's counter-insurgency efforts in Putumayo and other affected zones. The United States and Colombia need to rethink the logic of the spraying program. Perhaps they could learn from the example of Peru, which suspended eradication of coca altogether at the end of the 1980s to counteract the influence of Sendero Luminoso and to improve the image of the Peruvian government locally. Possibly Colombia's enforcement priorities should shift to targeting critical nodes in transportation and refining and (to the extent possible) sealing off traffic routes to and from the main coca-producing zones. Interdiction can disrupt internal markets for coca derivatives, and compared to eradication it imposes fewer direct costs on peasant producers and generates less political unrest.

Even relatively benign or noncoercive strategies for crop control have some disadvantages, at least in the conditions prevailing in South America. Alternative farming, for example, has little intrinsic appeal to farmers because coca and opium poppy offer a more attractive cash flow picture than do most licit crops. An element of compulsion, therefore, is always present in alternative development programs. Also, typical conditions of drug crop zones—geographical remoteness, marginal soils, and (in Colombia) extreme insecurity—tend to limit prospects for legal commercial agriculture. Of course, the mix of constraints differs from country to country: in Bolivia, where decent roads connect the main coca-growing areas to major markets, farmers have achieved some success in cultivating nontraditional crops such as pineapples and export-grade bananas; in Colombia, where most such areas are effectively cut off from markets and lie largely outside of government control, crop substitution projects have made relatively little headway. To be sure, substitution-in-place can temporarily alleviate the effects of enforcement measures such as spraying. A more promising strategy overall, though, is to foster development of the legal economy in other locales, including urban areas, in order to attract people away from areas that have a comparative advantage principally in coca or opium cultivation.

By any reckoning, though, the outlook for supply control in Colombia—now the epicenter of Andean coca cultivation—is dim for the foreseeable future. Even if drug policies can be improved at the margins, Colombia's current instability as well as a poorly performing economy (growth averaged only 1.3 percent annually between 1994 and 2000) virtually rule out large-scale reduction of illegal crops. In any event, the government's top priority at present is to combat insurgency and to assert control over the national territory, imperatives that conflict at certain points with the requirements of fighting drugs. For the United States, the best course is to support state-building in Colombia while tolerating for the time being the tactical compromises (including "hearts and minds" efforts vis-à-vis small drug producers) that this process would necessarily entail.

The counter-organization imperative of international drug policy requires a somewhat different interpretation. Few would disagree that the structure of criminal power and criminals' corrupt accomplices within governments are legitimate targets for law enforcement. Furthermore, the often-articulated national security justification for counter-organization—that large and wealthy criminal aggregates pose threats to fragile democratic institutions around the hemisphere—contains a kernel of truth. Even if criminal actors are not hostile to democracy, at least in the procedural sense, their participatory style (relying heavily on bribery and intimidation) tends to distort political outcomes and, over time, to erode the legitimacy of the system. In this hemisphere, Colombia has been the principal laboratory for Washington's counter-organization initiatives. Unfortunately, U.S. Drug War strategists—obsessed with chasing Medellín and Cali kingpins—never evolved a conception or vision of what the post-cartel trafficking environment might look like. Such a lack of foresight proved costly. Now this environment has become hopelessly politicized, and Colombia's democratic survival is threatened by armed political criminals of all stripes, though most directly by FARC.[51] Conceivably the United States can target FARC and other guerrilla formations qua criminal organizations and there are signs that Washington is moving in this direction. (For instance, the U.S. ambassador to Colombia talks of extraditing FARC and paramilitary leaders to the United States on drug trafficking and money-laundering charges.)[52] There are risks in such a course, though, and rules of engagement must be carefully drawn to limit direct U.S. involvement in Colombia's civil war, and especially to rule out the possibility of U.S. engagement with guerrilla armies on the ground.

Other challenges for U.S. policy also lurk in Colombia's treacherous and ever-changing trafficking environment. Physical evidence of a new configuration in the narcotics underworld was discovered recently in an industrial warehouse outside of Bogotá—a half built, 100-foot-long submarine capable of transporting 10 tons of cocaine to the United States "while remaining at snorkel depth the entire trip." Construction of the vessel, which may or may not be the first of its kind, was estimated to cost 20 million U.S. dollars. Such a complex and expensive undertaking could not have been managed by a single "mom-and-pop" trafficking organization; some larger entity must have been coordinating the project. Are new drug cartels emerging in Colombia, one wonders, or are the old ones really dead as advertised?

Conclusion

Efforts to scale back the huge Andean cocaine industry, which supplies 500 or more tons of cocaine each year to international customers, have been an embarrassing failure. The outlook for current supply-reduction policies in Colombia, the epicenter of that business, is dismal at best. Outlaw armies control directly or intermittently most of the coca-growing areas as well as a significant piece of the cocaine and heroin action, which increases the attendant risks and complexities of drug fighting in that country. Both supply-reduction and counter-organization policies need to be tailored to fit that reality. The recommendation here is to shift to an interdiction-based strategy vis-à-vis peasant producers and—in a careful and limited fashion—to try to disrupt the criminal side of FARC activities (especially, perhaps, its drugs-for-arms deals and money-laundering networks outside Colombia). The United States also must be alert to new organizational threats of a more conventional kind, such as tendencies to recombination and re-cartelization. But these are really minimalist prescriptions for carrying on the drug fight in the volatile and highly unstable circumstances of a country that is rapidly going downhill politically.

Past mistakes and failures of strategy (announced as "successes") have led to the current U.S. predicament in Colombia. But the United States cannot easily extricate itself from its anti-drug commitments there; certainly to do so now would simply provide inspiration and comfort to the violent narco-based groups and new-age "boutique" traffickers that now populate the Colombian trafficking scene. With Colombia's national future increasingly in jeopardy, the United States can no longer afford just to muddle through on drugs; new concepts and approaches are desperately needed.

This writer's view is that Colombia's drug agonies—and those of the United States—will not be much alleviated by actions that the United States takes inside Colombia. Actions taken closer to home are likely to have more lasting effects. One necessary measure, widely advocated in the wake of the events of September 11, 2001, is to revamp and upgrade the entire U.S. system of border defenses, increasing significantly patrols, checks, and searches along U.S. borders and at main U.S. ports of entry. In the current crisis atmosphere in the United States, this seems a sensible precaution, whether the aim is to stop smugglers of drugs, illegal immigrants, or terrorists toting nuclear weapons or other lethal objects.[53] The Bush administration plans to spend 10.6 billion dollars in fiscal year 2003, 20 percent above base fiscal year 2002 levels, bolstering the capabilities of the U.S. Customs Service, the Immigration and Naturalization Service, and the Coast Guard. Conceivably this new preoccupation with defending the homeland against outside threats can shield the United States more effectively against inflows of illicit drugs and even encourage some cocaine or heroin exporters to seek other markets or shift to a different line of work. Drug prices in major U.S. cities could be expected to rise with increased border security although traffickers may have enough cocaine and heroin stockpiled to keep a lid on them for the time being.

Improved surveillance of U.S. borders also should be coupled with a forward defense strategy encompassing U.S. neighbors, principally Mexico and the Caribbean countries. As argued earlier, entrenched criminal formations in Mexico and parts of the Caribbean acquired increased power and influence partly as a result of weakening and disintegration of the cartel system in Colombia. The United States must collaborate more closely with these countries to apprehend and prosecute the leaders of such organizations, to shut down land and maritime smuggling routes, and to disrupt money-laundering channels. Unfortunately, U.S. drug policy has been overly focused on and obsessed with Colombia; responses to the growing Mexican and Caribbean drug connections have been weak and ambivalent. Political pressure from immigrant communities in the United States, as well as concerns that crackdowns on smuggling could hurt Mexican exports and the U.S.-Mexican border economy, incur a U.S. "bully" image in the Caribbean, and alienate immigrant voting blocs at home have blunted the thrust of U.S. enforcement policies in these countries. Perhaps these concerns will fade as a new national security consensus takes shape in the United States; this of course remains to be seen.

In addition, as part of a Caribbean-wide defense shield against drugs, Washington should widen cooperation with the Castro regime against drugs, even in the absence of normal diplomatic and economic relations with Cuba. The most direct routes for Colombian cocaine and heroin en route to the United States pass through Cuba. Cuba lacks the resources to patrol its 3,700-kilometer coastline effectively and—in the sunset years of the Castroite order—the island appears increasingly vulnerable to penetration by organized drug mafias. Substantive forms of cooperation—such as U.S. technical assistance and training for Cuba's border guard—should receive serious consideration in Washington despite likely resistance from anti-Castro groups and their allies in Congress.

Finally, it goes almost without saying that the supply-side architecture that the United States is constructing in the Andes and elsewhere can serve little useful purpose unless the two million-odd chronic users of cocaine and heroin in the United States can be induced to cut their intake of these substances. Recent comments by administration officials pay at least lip service to the need for greater attentiveness to the demand side of the trafficking equation. President Bush, for instance, recently remarked that the administration would continue to "work with other nations to eradicate drugs at their source and to stop the flow of drugs into America. However, the most effective way to reduce the supply of drugs in America is to reduce the demand for drugs in America."[54] Still, treatment, prevention, and related research account for less than one-third of the 20 billion U.S. dollars budgeted by the federal government for drug control. Much more money is needed for these purposes. If such increases can be coupled with substantive changes on the supply-side—such as tighter border controls and more sensible and humane drug policies in the Andes—so much the better.

Notes

1. Office of National Drug Control Policy (ONDCP), *National Drug Control Strategy 2001: Budget Summary* (Washington, D.C.: U.S Government Printing Office, 2000), 14–22.

2. The World Bank, *Illegal Drugs in Latin America: Implications for Economic Development,* Report No. 15004 (Washington, D.C.: World Bank, 1995).

3. Office of National Drug Control Policy (ONDCP), *National Drug Control Strategy 1999* (Washington, D.C.: U.S. Government Printing Office, 1999), 131; Drug Enforcement Agency (DEA); *Annual Price Data for Cocaine and Heroin* (Washington, D.C.: Drug Enforcement Agency, 2001).

4. Author interview with Alvaro Camacho, Bogotá, April 26, 2001. "Los Nuevos Narcos," *Semana,* May 8, 2000, 71.

5. Mark Bowden, *Killing Pablo* (New York: Atlantic Monthly Press, 2001), 73–98, 203–49.

6. Patrick Clawson and Rensselaer W. Lee, *The Andean Cocaine Industry* (New York: St. Martin's Press, 1996), 114–15, 177.

7. Ricardo Rocha Garcia, *La Economía Colombiana tras 25 Años de Narcotráfico* (Bogotá: Siglo del Hombre Editorial, 2000), Statistical Annex, Table 12. This is admittedly a high figure. The above-mentioned World Bank report estimated the export value of Bolivian cocaine in 1994 to be in the range of 190 to 260 million U.S. dollars. See World Bank, *Illegal Drugs in Latin America,* 39.

8. Department of State, *International Narcotics Control Strategy Report (INCSR)* (Washington, D.C.: Department of State, March 2001), iv–7. The estimate is an extrapolation from a September 1993 figure.

9. Anthony Faiola, "In Bolivia Drug War Success Has Its Price: Farmers Victimized by Coca Eradication," *Washington Post,* March 4, 2001, A1, A15.

10. On these points, see Clawson and Lee, *The Andean Cocaine Industry,* 37–61.

11. There is a wealth of evidence that this is happening. See, for example, "Golpe Maestro," *Semana,* March 12, 2001, 36, 38; "La Prueba Reina," *Semana,* April 2, 2001, 26–29; "De Su Puño y Letra," *Revista Cambio,* April 23, 2001; and Steve Salisbury, "Raid Shows Colombian Rebels Are Also Drug Lords," *Washington Times,* March 20, 2001, A1, A15.

12. National Drug Intelligence Center, United States Department of Justice, *Colombian Heroin: A Baseline Assessment* (Johnstown, Penn.: National Drug Intelligence Center, 1994), 1–18; "Los Nuevos Narcos," 72; National Narcotics Intelli-

gence Consumers' Committee (NNICC), *The NNICC Report 1997* (Washington, D.C: DEA, 1998), 40.

13. For example, see NNICC *Report 1997,* 11–20; National Drug Intelligence Center, *The Dominican Threat: A Strategic Assessment of Dominican Drug Trafficking* (Johnstown, Penn.: National Drug Intelligence Center, 1997), 1–14; Alvaro Camacho Guizado, et al., *Las Drogas: Una Guerra Fallida* (Bogotá: Ediciones Tercer Mundo, 1999), 93–114.

14. *INCSR 2001,* iv–26.

15. Ibid., ii–3, 4.

16. Rafael Pardo, "Colombia's Two-Front War," *Foreign Affairs* (July-August 2000), 71.

17. Estimates are based on figures for potential cocaine production in Table 10.1.

18. "Alerta Maxima," *Revista Cambio,* December 11, 2000, 23. Author telephone interview with Sergio Uribe in Bogotá, May 10, 2001.

19. Rocha, *La Economía Colombiana,* Statistical Annex, Table 8.

20. "Alerta Maxima," "Golpe Maestro," "La Prueba Reina."

21. See, for example, Clawson and Lee, *The Andean Cocaine Industry,* 37–69.

22. Fabio Castillo, *Los Nuevos Jinetes de la Cocaína* (Bogotá: Editorial Oveja Negra, 1996), 29–35. Relations among the participating organizations and leaders were highly complex. For example, according to Castillo, Cali's Helmer Herrera Buitrago managed the Rodriguez Orejuela distribution network in New York; at the same time he entrusted his brothers with running Herrera organization cells in Houston, Miami, and New York.

23. Clawson and Lee, *The Andean Cocaine Industry,* chapter 2; Castillo, *Los Nuevos Jinetes,* 30; "Los Nuevos Narcos"; Sidney J. Zabludoff, "Colombian Narcotics Organizations as Business Enterprises," *Transnational Organized Crime* 3, no. 2 (1997), 48.

24. The corruptive influence of these enterprises extended well beyond Colombia. Pablo Escobar's brother Roberto reports that Escobar delivered a cash contribution of 1 million U.S. dollars to Alberto Fujimori's 1992 election bid in Peru; the money was channeled via Fujimori's close associate and later intelligence chief Vladimiro Montesinos. Escobar also paid Montesinos 300 U.S. dollars per kilo for each drug flight that successfully took off from Peru and ended in Colombia, according to Roberto. According to U.S. political scientist Peter Lupsha, Miguel Rodriguez of Cali fame sent 40 million U.S. dollars in two shipments to Mexico as a donation to support Ernesto Zedillo's election in that year. In the following year, unnamed Cali organizations reportedly channeled 1 million U.S. dollars to now-Prime Minister Lester Bird's election campaign in Antigua; the middleman for the transaction was Santiago Medina, who had served as treasurer for Ernesto Samper's campaign in Colombia the year before. See Roberto Escobar, *Mi Hermano Pablo* (Bogotá: Quintero Editores, 2000), 139–46; Peter Lupsha, "Transnational Narco-Corruption and Narco-Investment: A Focus on Mexico," *Transnational Organized Crime* 1, no. 1 (1995), 93, and "Did the Lester Bird Regime Get One Million U.S. Dollars from the Cali Cartel?" *The Outlet,* August 26, 1997, 1, 3.

25. Clawson and Lee, *The Andean Cocaine Industry,* 191.

26. Author interview with a former official of the Colombian Department of Administrative Security (DAS), Bogotá, May 8, 1998.

27. Sergio Uribe, "Crime, Drugs, and Justice in Colombia" (Unpublished manuscript, February 2001), 15.

28. Salisbury, "Raid Shows Colombian Rebels Are Also Drug Lords," A1, A12.

29. Luis Alberto Villamarin Pulido, *The FARC Cartel* (Bogotá: Editiones The Pharaoh, 1996), 23.

30. "La Prueba Reina"; Claudia Rocío Vasquez, "Cada Mes Entregaba Diez Milliones de Dólares a las FARC," *El Tiempo*, April 23, 2001, 1–12. If the 10 million U.S. dollars had been payment for the 20–22 tons, the per kilo price would have been unreasonably low: 500 U.S. dollars per kilo. Some inflow of arms must, therefore, have been involved. Alternatively, Fernandinho was exaggerating the scale of his transactions with FARC to ingratiate himself with his military captors.

31. "De Su Puño y Letra"; "EE.UU. Acusa," *Revista Cambio,* December 11, 2000, 21–26; "Los Contactos de Cuevas," *Revista Cambio,* April 23, 2001 (Internet communication).

32. "EE.UU. Acusa."

33. "And Death Shall Have Its Dominion," *Harpers*, October 2000, 16; "Narco-Castaño," *Semana*, April 26, 1999, 42–43.

34. For a typical account, based on meetings with FARC spokesmen, see Alma Guillermoprieto, *Las Guerras en Colombia* (Bogotá: Aguilar, 2000), 34–35.

35. See, for example, "El Costo de la Paz," *Revista Cambio*, July 17, 2000, 25; Maria Cristina Caballero, "La Guerrilla Billionaria," *Cambio-16*, July 6, 1998, 28–31.

36. For example, by deploying missiles against the new Black Hawk helicopters introduced under Plan Colombia. On FARC's balance sheet, see "Los Negocios de las FARC," *Semana*, March 8, 1999, 38–40.

37. National Drug Intelligence Center, *Colombian Heroin*, 1–2.

38. Office of National Drug Control Policy, *National Drug Control Strategy 1999*, 131.

39. National Drug Intelligence Center, *Colombian Heroin*, Tables 12 and 16.

40. National Narcotics Intelligence Consumers' Committee (NNICC), *The NNICC Report 1994* (Washington, D.C.: DEA, 1995), 23; NNICC, *The NNICC Report 1997*, 40.

41. National Drug Intelligence Center, *Colombian Heroin*, 1–2.

42. Camacho Guizado, et al., *Las Drogas*, 111–12.

43. NNICC, *The NNICC Report 1997*, 11. Colombian organizations still control exports to the lucrative European market, however.

44. Peter Smith, "Semi-Organized International Crime: Drug Trafficking in Mexico," in Tom Farer, ed., *Transnational Organized Crime in the Americas* (New York: Routledge, 1999), 196.

45. Author interviews with British law enforcement officials and St. Kitts economic leaders, Basseterre, November 10–20, 1998; author interviews with UNDCP officials and Dominican Republic bankers and police officials, Santo Domingo, March 15–20, 2001.

46. The PRD fundraising activities by Dominican Republic drug dealers resident in

the United States are the subject of a current lawsuit in Pennsylvania. See U.S. District Court for the Middle District of Pennsylvania, Civil Action—Law. I-CV-97–1555, October 11, 1997, 1–36.

47. Rensselaer Lee, "Transnational Organized Crime: An Overview," in Tom Farer, ed., *Transnational Organized Crime in the Americas,* 24. Tim Weaver, "Ex-Mexico Governor Arrested and Linked to Cocaine Traffic," *New York Times,* May 26, 2001, A4.

48. Of course, many other factors contribute to Colombia's current crisis, among them the Colombian government's failed strategy of negotiating with the guerillas. See, for example, the excellent analysis by Michael Radu, "The Perilous Appeasement of Guerillas," *Orbis* 44, no. 3 (2000), 363–79.

49. *INCSR 2001,* iv–38.

50. Angel Rabasa and Peter Chalk, *Colombian Labyrinth* (Santa Monica, Calif.: RAND, 2001), 66.

51. Tolerance of drug crime with a political face has a long history in U.S. foreign policy. For instance, in Southeast Asia during the 1950s and 1960s the CIA provided financial and logistical support for various anti-Communist armies that supported themselves principally from the traffic in opium and heroin. In late 1998–early 1999 the U.S. State Department conducted talks with representatives of FARC in Costa Rica, despite evidence of FARC's growing participation in the cocaine trade. In the 1999 Balkan War, Washington's spin masters made every attempt to conceal or suppress information concerning the Kosovo Liberation Army's (KLA) well-established ties to the European heroin trade. Of course, the KLA was Washington's de facto ally against Serbia at the time. One person's drug dealer, it seems, is another person's freedom fighter.

52. Vadira Ferrer, "United States Cracks Down on Rebels," Bogotá, Inter Press Service, October 30, 2001.

53. Fox Butterfield, "Officials Say Increased Security Has Slowed Drug Smuggling," *New York Times,* September 28, 2001, A14.

54. Mike Allen, "Bush Suggests Shift in Drug Strategy," *New York Times,* May 11, 2001, A6.

11

Diverging Trends in Global Drug Policy

Martin Jelsma

In the 1980s, policy debates within the United Nations Commission on Narcotic Drugs (CND) acknowledged a "shared responsibility" between North and South America in reference to the drug problem. It was recognized that the agricultural crisis in the developing countries had contributed to the expansion of the illegal economy and that development assistance was needed to provide viable alternatives to the peasant communities concerned. In addition, the debate emphasized northern responsibility with respect to demand, the production and trade in chemical precursors used in cocaine and heroin production, money laundering, and the production of synthetic drugs. In keeping with this discourse of "shared responsibility," the United Nations International Drug Control Programme (UNDCP), founded in 1990, developed policies in two areas: demand reduction and alternative development.

Since then, drug control policies have diverged into two different strategies: one, supported by European countries, and emphasizing a certain degree of tolerance and pragmatism, and the other, supported by the United States, and defending zero-tolerance with a strongly repressive orientation. Both, however, share the same point of departure: the recognition that all counter-narcotics action, combining eradication, crop substitution, drug seizures, disruption of traffickers' organizations, as well as various forms of demand reduction, have failed to have an impact. There have been interesting projects on the local level, but these have remained isolated attempts with little influence on the more general supply or demand for illicit drugs. All through the years, wholesale and retail prices of cocaine and heroin have shown a downward trend while purity has been increasing, which would indicate ample supply. Preferences in drug use are changing with changes in consumption patterns and culture fashions. However, there is no indication that the overall levels of consumption of illicit drugs have been decreasing. The Inter-American Drug Abuse Control Commission (CICAD) reports about cocaine: "The overall conclusion is that, notwithstanding efforts to reduce crops in producing countries and cocaine seizures, production and availability of this drug for consumption have not been reduced."[1]

After such a conclusion, one would expect some soul searching leading to a profound evaluation of relevant policies, a reassessment of the applied principles, and a debate on the appropriateness of alternative approaches guided by more realistic objectives of counter-narcotics action. However, the international establishment involved in the War on Drugs has maintained that the "medicine" has not worked because not enough of it has been applied and that a stronger dose should be administered. In short, according to the establishment's perspective, the political commitment to a zero-drugs situation should be reaffirmed, any tolerance should be opposed, the ranks behind a "get-serious" approach should be closed, deadlines should be set and—when necessary—one should not be afraid to get one's hands dirty in order to achieve concrete results.

At the multilateral level, the differences in strategy have paralyzed political action. The UNDCP has taken a hard line. Countries defending a more moderate view have maintained a low profile and have been careful to avoid controversy on issues of policy strategy within the CND.

The 1998 UNGASS on Drugs

The differences between the two major drug control approaches became pronounced at the United Nations General Assembly Special Session (UNGASS) on Drugs, which took place in June 1998, ten years after the adoption of the 1988 Vienna Convention. The 1988 convention meant a turn toward a more repressive approach, already criminalizing all aspects of cultivation, production, trafficking, and distribution of illicit drugs, including the possession for personal consumption. The UNGASS motto, "A Drug Free World—We Can Do It!" expressed the conviction that with a strong commitment to this bold strategy, it would be possible to eliminate illicit drugs from the planet within a limited time frame. The UNDCP voiced wholehearted support for this position and, during the months preceding UNGASS, elaborated the ambitious Strategy for Coca and Opium Poppy Elimination (SCOPE), which was defined as a mixture of alternative development projects and eradication operations meant to wipe out by 2008 illicit crops in Colombia, Bolivia, Peru, Burma, Laos, Vietnam, Afghanistan, and Pakistan, the eight countries where coca and opium production have been concentrated.[2]

The Strategy for Coca and Opium Poppy Elimination was pursuing the "zero-option" rhetoric of total elimination, which also meant shifting the major burden back to the traditional producing countries: "After three decades of experience, the international community is now equipped with tested methodologies and the know-how to tackle the problem in the producing areas. The strengthening of the drug control mechanisms in the regions concerned has paved the way for full-scale interventions and most producing countries have adopted well-defined national strategies and action plans that are ready for implementation."[3]

However, the SCOPE plan has never been implemented. The proposal was harshly criticized by several member states, and did not enter the UNGASS agenda, although some of its principles made their way to the Political Declaration from UNGASS.[4] The opportunity to reassess current anti-drug policies was lost. However, owing to action by Mexico, several European countries, Australia, and Canada, the concept of "shared responsibility," which had been developed in the 1980s, was saved. The same countries also succeeded in having the principles of "non-intervention in internal affairs," and "full respect for all human rights" included in the final declaration in addition to the mentioning of "the special importance of cooperation in alternative development" and "special attention to be paid to the protection of the environment." They also supported an action plan for demand reduction aiming at measurable results by 2003, explaining that if demand for illicit drugs clearly can not be reduced within a reasonable time span, it would be an illusion to think about an elimination of supply. Still, the Political Declaration embraced "strategies with a view to eliminating or reducing significantly the illicit cultivators of coca bush, the cannabis plant and the opium poppy by the year 2008."[5]

The Chemical and Biological War on Drugs

In the years 1997–1999, the United States underlined its position of zero-tolerance. In 1998, Congress passed the "Western Hemisphere Drug Elimination Act," in fact a prelude to the Plan Colombia two years later. Pressure increased in 1998–1999 to intensify the chemical War on Drugs worldwide. In addition, the U.S. Congress allocated resources in support of a new front, which would use biological means. At that point, only Colombia and Mexico had a program of aerial spraying of coca, opium poppy, and cannabis crops. In 1998, the United States Drug Enforcement Administration (DEA) proposed a massive herbicide spraying program across the United States to combat cannabis cultivation. A project to develop a fungus to destroy opium poppy fields began in 1998 in Uzbekistan. By 2000, arrangements had been made for field experiments to test the effectiveness of a bio-engineered fungus to kill poppy in Central Asia. However, Kazakhstan and Turkmenistan refused to carry out the experiment, stating that the small illicit plots of poppy on their territory could better be eradicated by hand.[6] Afghanistan was clearly the target of this UNDCP project funded by the United States and the United Kingdom. The United Nations had reported a record harvest of 4,000 tons of opium from Afghanistan in 2000, or approximately 75 percent of the world supply.[7]

In that same year, the Taliban regime did impose a ban on growing opium poppy and, combined with the effects of a severe drought, production was reduced by 90 percent in 2001.[8] By the autumn of 2001, the research and development stage of the Uzbek project was concluded, awaiting a final scientific review before considering further steps. Early 2002 UNDCP estimates revealed that, since the downfall of the Taliban regime, cultivation of opium poppy has resumed massively to between 40,000 and 60,000 hectares. Suggestions made by the United States to apply chemical or biological means aerially to eradicate opium poppy crops so far have met with strong objections. Manual eradication, in return for a financial compensation to the farmers, has led to stiff resistance.

In 1999, top drug officials in the United States proposed using the Fusarium fungus for coca eradication. Fusarium was considered the "silver bullet" that would stop coca production in Colombia and sabotage the war economy of FARC and ELN guerrillas at the same time. The idea was incorporated in a multilateral initiative, involving UNDCP, which presented the Colombian government with a blueprint for action in this area.[9] The project generated harsh criticism from scientists, environmentalists, drug policy experts, and indigenous movements, who argued that the intentional release of a plague of this nature could trigger grave environmental consequences, endanger the health of the population, threaten food security, and—at the end of the day—would cause further displacement of people and illicit crops deeper into the Amazon forest. The Colombian government responded positively to the criticism and rejected the proposal. Concern about this strategy spread across the region. Peru banned the use of any chemical or biological means for coca eradication.[10] Ecuador,[11] in conjunction with the Andean Committee of Environmental Authorities,[12] banned the use of Fusarium. As a result, UNDCP withdrew from the project.

Plan Colombia and Plan Dignidad

The SCOPE vision of total eradication, combined with the UNGASS objective of "a drug free world" in 2008, and the aggressive approach contained in the "Western Hemisphere Drug Elimination Act," were integrated into a grand master plan for the Andean region. In Peru at that point coca production had decreased significantly from a peak of 129,000 hectares in 1992 to 38,000 hectares in 1999. So the offensive centered on Bolivia and Colombia.

Plan Dignidad, the Bolivian Strategy for the Fight against Drug Trafficking 1998–2002, adopted an even tighter schedule than the one proposed by UNGASS. In his chapter in this book, Eduardo Gamarra explains the motives behind the decision. With this plan involving 952 million U.S. dollars, Bolivia's government announced that it would have the country leaving the "coca cocaine circuit" by 2002. The greater part of the budget—a total of 700 million U.S. dollars—was earmarked for alternative development projects, largely to be funded by the international donor community. The elimination of coca production was to take place through voluntary eradication. Soon, however, violence broke out, and the Chapare region has been in turmoil ever since. Crop substitution efforts in the Chapare have been underway since 1983 and since that year more than 180 million U.S. dollars have been invested. However, the program has a history of failure and has not been able to reduce net coca production. New donor commitments for alternative development have been slow in coming. In response, the government decided to move and to force eradication of all illegal coca in the Chapare. Some five thousand troops of specialized military and police units moved into the region, converting it into a "war zone."

Early in 2001, victory was declared in what was presented as a drug-free Chapare region. However, the admittedly impressive reduction of the coca-cultivated area had been achieved with a heavy loss of human life, social tension, and livelihood destruction. Plan Dignidad showed that a reduction of coca-cultivated areas could be achieved, at least temporarily, and through application of great force. It is very questionable, however, whether this situation can be sustained. The point of "zero coca" was never reached and official sources later acknowledged that some 7,000 hectares of illegal coca still remained in the Chapare region at the end of 2001.[13]

The other master plan in the Andean region, Plan Colombia, originally had been conceived as a strategy that would accompany the peace process negotiations with the FARC guerrillas, initiated by the Pastrana government in 1998. However, after negotiations between the United States and the Colombian government, the original plan was turned into an anti-drugs strategy primarily aimed at denying the guerrillas the income from the opium and coca-paste economies in areas under their control. Its objective was to reduce the cultivated area by 50 percent over a period of six years. In 2000, the plan was supported by an aid package of 1.3 billion U.S. dollars financed by the United States. Plan Colombia came to include massive aerial spraying operations, the creation of a counter-narcotics operations army battalion, and the provision of dozens of helicopters to support a "Push into Southern Colombia," where coca cultivation had been concentrating. Action began in December 2000. In the first two months, 29,000 hectares of coca fields in the Putumayo Department were sprayed. In the process, food crops and licit crops forming part of alternative development projects were destroyed next to the coca. In the course of 2001, an additional 90,000 hectares were sprayed with an aggressive herbicide. Plan Colombia has been facing harsh criticism from broad sectors within Colombian society, as well as from the international community. Next to the controversy about the environmental and health problems associated with the chemical spraying, the effectiveness of the operations was questioned since the operations appeared to result in a further displacement of people and illicit crops deeper into the Amazon.[14] Increased spraying efforts proved to be unable to prevent a further expansion of coca cultivation. In addition, the U.S. aid package and the military operations in southern Colombia were contributing to an escalation of the armed conflict, pushing a negotiated settlement between the Colombian government and FARC guerrillas beyond reach.

Europe Distances Itself

At the international donor conferences in support of Plan Colombia held in 2000 and 2001, the differences in strategy between the American and European positions proved to be irreconcilable. Europe, expected to contribute the alternative development components of the plan, distanced itself from the carrot and stick approach defended by the United States. With the differences between development and eradication evaporating and with a growing emphasis on force and military might, European donors became very critical of the program. Officials of the United States expressed their disappointment: "Everyone was looking for the rest of the world, particularly the Europeans, to do the soft side. We have done the military side. You can't do one without the other."[15] But, as the Austrian ambassador to Colombia explained, "The military aid has been like putting a blue stocking in the wash with white clothes—everything comes out blue."[16] A resolution adopted in the European Parliament in February 2001 against Plan Colombia received almost unanimous support, a vote of 474 to 1. The resolution stated: "Plan Colombia contains aspects that run counter to the cooperation strategies and projects to which the European Union has already committed itself and jeopardize its cooperation programs." The resolution is crystal clear on the chemical spraying and the threat of a biological war stating that the European Union "must take the necessary steps to secure an end to the large-scale use of chemical herbicides and prevent the introduction of biological agents . . . , given the dangers of their use to human health and the environment alike."[17]

It is clear that the political agendas of the United States and the European Union are largely incompatible in this area. As a result, the alternative development dimension of Plan Colombia never got off the ground while the law enforcement and military dimensions have been creating havoc around the country. The U.S. and Colombian governments have been addressing concerns by the opposition, presenting "voluntary eradication agreements" with small coca growers, which were concluded in coordination with local authorities and communities in the Putumayo Department. However, these agreements were negotiated under the threat of pending fumigations. To avoid spraying, no less than thirty-four people signed an agreement to eliminate all coca within twelve months, in return for roughly 900 U.S. dollars compensation and promises of infrastructure improvements in the area.

In response to concerns in the Andean-Amazon region, in 2001 the United States defined an aid package that would serve as a follow-up to Plan Colombia: the Andean Regional Initiative. The new package has increased funding for alternative development and includes wider assistance to the other countries in the region as well. The initiative, however, was debated in a post–September 11th context where the War on Drugs has become identified with the War on Terrorism. The latest additions to the package intend "to elevate the fast-escalating Colombian crisis from a regional counter-narcotics problem to formal inclusion in the war on terrorism, according to administration officials."[18]

Harm Reduction

On the demand side, the differences in drug control strategy between the United States and the European Union are also becoming more pronounced. During the 1990s, a record number of people have been arrested in the United States for consumption or for possession of small quantities of illicit drugs. Organizations such as Human Rights Watch call for "the need to move beyond the war on drugs and to begin to dismantle the racially unjust 'drug gulag' it has spawned."[19] "Human Rights Watch does not challenge the public's decision to use criminal sanctions in its effort to curtail drug abuse and drug trafficking. But the use of the criminal sentences is subject to important human rights constraints. To be consistent with internationally recognized human rights standards, criminal sanctions must be both humane and proportional to the gravity of the offense."[20]

The extremely repressive counter-narcotics policy approach, with especially negative effects for the black community, has been receiving increasingly negative comments by broad social sectors. In Europe—as Tim Boekhout van Solinge has explained in his chapter to this book—a different approach has been gaining ground. The core idea of this strategy is "harm reduction." The concept has gained wide acceptance in recent years and has become the basis for a rational and pragmatic drug policy in most European Union member states, next to Australia, New Zealand, Canada, and Brazil. In addition, practices including the decriminalization of consumption, leniency in law enforcement toward soft drugs and toward possession of other drugs for personal use, heroin maintenance programs, needle exchange, and Ecstasy testing, have become accepted in several European Union member countries.

Room for Maneuver

There is no question that sooner or later the tolerance trend guided by the harm reduction philosophy will collide with the limits imposed by the UN conventions. It already touches the very edges of the letter and spirit of some articles. All steps taken so far can be defended in reference to the 1961 Single Convention and even to the stricter obligations agreed to in the 1988 Vienna Convention.[21] Still, the International Narcotics Control Board (INCB) warns in its 2001 report of an increasing tension between expanding tolerance practices and strict adherence.[22] The INCB notes "some shifting towards a more liberal cannabis policy in several developed countries," specifying that in Italy, Luxembourg, Portugal, and Spain, "possession of cannabis is not considered a criminal offence, and acts preparatory to personal consumption, such as acquisition, transportation and possession of cannabis are not penalized." The report worries that Belgium and the United Kingdom are considering legislative changes toward liberalization and has negative comments for the Netherlands and Switzerland, where cannabis policy developments are moving in the direction of de facto legalization.

For those countries committed to the search for pragmatic solutions to the drug problem, the conventions are functioning as a straitjacket. The consensus-driven functioning of the CND has been killing any innovative idea, and it is unlikely that agreement might be reached on the possibility of increasing the space for member states to redefine their own drug policies.

Among the fervent defenders of the prohibitionist regime, considerable differences exist as to the cultural and political roots of their zero-tolerance position. In Sweden, for example, this position is rooted in its social democratic tradition, which includes a special role for the state in protecting its citizenry against the threat of alcohol and drug abuse. The rise of Islamic fundamentalism and the accompanying strong religious laws against any drugs, including alcohol, have resulted within the CDN in a stronger opposition by Islamic states against any deviation from zero-tolerance. The United States has been the principal force promoting a global prohibitionist regime with a zero-tolerance position rooted in Christian fundamentalism, although its position as a world power often leads it to combine the drugs issue with other foreign policy and security considerations.

With this blend of motives dominating the zero-tolerance camp, there is little possibility of negotiating a new consensus on the basis of rationality and pragmatism. There may still be a possibility, however, to break the impasse at the UN level and create space for policy diversity while avoiding the necessity to reach a new consensus. Established procedures can be followed in order to change the scope of control for specific drugs. In principle, it will only take a simple CND majority to ratify a recommendation by the World Health Organization (WHO) to reschedule substances under the 1961 convention and there is no formal rule that prohibits voting procedures. The CND practice of proceeding by consensus was adopted only when the United States lost its voting power for not having paid its UN dues. Resolutions of the CND do not necessarily require consensus. They can be helpful to clarify the interpretation of provisions of the conventions and to stretch the latitude countries have to develop their own national drug policies.

With regard to formal amendments to the conventions themselves, beyond the scheduling of substances, basically all parties have to agree. Ultimately, the only formal escape route out of the consensus stalemate here would be for countries to write a statement of denunciation to the UN secretary-general, specifying why they can no longer abide by the obligations of specific articles of a convention. Politically this is a very difficult step to take and would only be possible where a strong alliance between like-minded countries has been constructed on the basis of a shared reform agenda.

Informally, a number of countries could choose to test the boundaries of UN conventions by adopting an approach of tolerance of drug use beyond the point where it still could be justified under the internationally agreed upon drug control principles, and then "just take the heat." The legal complications such a move would generate would have to be defended on the basis of constitutional obligations or tensions with other international agreements, for example, in the field of HIV/AIDS prevention or within the framework of human rights protection. Clearly, only few countries can afford to play with those margins. The INCB may not have the mandate or power to impose any sanctions, but the United States still maintains its disciplinary system of annual drug control certification, the main instrument of pressure that can be brought to bear on any country that is dependent on U.S. aid or that has to negotiate with international financial institutions.

Harm Reduction in Source Countries

The polarization between drug policy trends has produced serious inconsistencies. There is a contradiction between liberalization on the consumption side while maintaining or even increasing international pressure to eradicate drug crops in the traditional production regions of South America. These source countries are allowed less political space to reassess their national policy and enter a path toward pragmatic solutions. Moreover, the international conventions allow less flexibility for the production side as compared to the consumption side when it comes to national policymaking.

If the narrowness of the margins for policy intervention regarding global supply reduction are duly recognized, and the fact accepted that the phenomenon of drug-linked crop cultivation is here to stay as long as demand exists, then alternative development donors and illicit crop producing countries could be relieved of the pressure to comply with unrealistic reduction targets and deadlines. More flexible time frames, allowing for a gradual reduction over a period of several years in conjuncture with realistic possibilities for demand reduction, could be agreed on. The "participatory approach" advocated in alternative development could become more than just a community consulting mechanism and could evolve toward a serious dialogue in which the communities involved in drug crop cultivation would have room for negotiation. Mutual trust could be created through arrangements allowing a continued presence of an established maximum of illicit crops per family for subsistence purposes, in case developments in the target period would not guarantee dignified conditions of life.

This strategy would isolate alternative development from the conditionality embedded in the "balanced approach" that combines developmental investments with law enforcement and forced eradication measures. It would also mean turning the burden of proof around. Communities would no longer have to "prove their willingness to substitute," but the government and the international community would have to "prove the viability of alternatives" before demanding that peasant and indigenous communities place the fragile foundations of their survival economy at risk. From the perspective of a more rational and pragmatic approach, several ideas could be put forward on how harm reduction concepts may be applied to the production side:

- Shifting away from the current obsession with counting and reducing the numbers of hectares toward prioritizing the policy goal of reducing the harm associated with the existence of illicit crops, including measures to reduce the harm done to the environment and attempts to reduce their importance in fueling armed conflict.
- Opening up spaces for dialogue with involved communities—free of deadline and "zero-option" thinking—about their own problems with drug-linked crops, allowing flexible, gradual reduction processes.
- Defining small growers more as economic victims that have become "addicted" to illicit crops for survival. Similarly to the harm reduction approach to drug addicts, this means trying to provide conditions that allow them to leave their situations; if that doesn't work, assisting them in a way that reduces the harm to themselves and to society at large rather than spraying, incarcerating, or killing them.
- Supporting the option of de-penalization or law enforcement leniency toward small illicit cultivation similar to the tolerance trend in several European countries toward individual consumption of soft drugs or the possession of small quantities for personal use.

• Exploring options of direct linkages between harm reduction interventions on the supply side and on the demand side in order to stimulate the global debate on alternative measures of counter-narcotics action.
• "De-demonizing" certain aspects of illicit drugs by differentiating more between specific substances and their potential harms and benefits on the basis of scientific studies.

Conclusion

The UNDCP is the leading multilateral agency for drug issues. It has been implementing UN programs and advising many governments on drug policy matters and, in these areas, it has been a crucial institution. The agency went through a deep crisis these past few years, triggering a reform process starting in mid-2001 at UNDCP's Vienna headquarters. Donors lost confidence and the UN Office of Internal Oversight Services (OIOS) was called in to investigate mismanagement. The combination of a strong zero-tolerance position and bad management has meant that UNDCP has not been able to play a role of moderation amid the growing polarization in the field of drug control strategy. The organizational improvements based on the recommendations of the OIOS are already well underway. But the question remains as to whether the UNDCP will be able to transcend its politicized position and develop toward a center of expertise on drug policies and the problems involved in their implementation A useful guiding principle can be found in the conclusions reached by the New York County Lawyers' Association: "The appropriate goal of any drug policy must be to decrease the prevalence and spread of harmful drug use and substance abuse, and to minimize the harms associated with such problems where they are found to exist. Additionally, any policy which creates more harmful results than the societal problems it proposes to solve must be re-evaluated in terms of the advisability of further pursuit of such policy. Further, to justify continuation of any public policy, the costs incurred must always be weighed against the benefits derived. It is within this context, and with these criteria in mind, that present approaches to drug policy must be objectively assessed and, where appropriate, alternative models for future policy evaluated and considered."[23]

Meanwhile, in Europe and among several like-minded countries, the pragmatic approach of harm reduction has gained ground in domestic drug policymaking, creating distance from the U.S. approach of indiscriminate repression and zero-tolerance. In these countries the trend toward more leniency has become irreversible, and rational thinking has been gradually replacing the dogmas of the past.

Notes

1. Organizations of American States, Executive Secretariat of the Inter-American Drug Abuse Control Commission, *Statistical Summary on Drugs 2001* (Washington, D.C.: Inter-American Drug Abuse Control Commission, 2002), 34.

2. For a detailed critique of SCOPE, see Tom Blickman, "Estrategia Mundial Antidrogas: Barniz de un Colapso," *Revista Acción Andina,* no. 2 (1998), 26–48.

3. *An International Strategy to Eliminate the Illicit Cultivation of Coca Bush and Opium Poppy: Progress Report,* United Nations Commission on Narcotic Drugs, Document E/CN, 7/1998/PC/CRP.4, Vienna, March 3, 1998.

4. *Political Declaration,* United Nations General Assembly Session, 9th Plenary Meeting, June 10, 1998, A/RES/S-20/2, Article 19.

5. *Political Declaration,* UNGASS, art. 18; and *United Nations General Assembly Resolution International Cooperation against the World Drug Problem,* 85th Plenary Meeting, December 9, 1998, A/RES/53/115, Article 1.

6. UNDCP *Situation Reports-Uzbekistan,* January 2000.

7. *Britain's Secret War on Drugs,* BBC 1, Panorama, October 2, 2000.

8. *Afghanistan Annual Opium Poppy Survey 2001* (Vienna: UNDCP), passim; and *Global Illicit Drug Trends 2001* (Vienna: ODCCP, 2001), passim.

9. For a detailed account on the draft Fusarium contract, see Martin Jelsma, "Un Hongo Contra la Coca: UNDCP y la Guerra Biológica Contra las Drogas en Colombia," *Boletín Internacional Acción Andina 9,* no. 1 (2000), 76–90.

10. *Decreto Supremo nrs. 004–2000–AG,* Perú, Ministerio de Agricultura, 24 de Marzo del 2000, "Articulo 1°, Prohíbase el Uso de Plaguicidas Químicos de Uso Agrícola, Sustancias Afines, Productos y Agentes Biológicos en Plantaciones de Coca (Erythroxylum Coca)."

11. *Registro Official N. 140,* Ecuador, Acuerdo Ministerial, 14 de Agosto del 2000, Ministerio de Agriculture y Ganadería, Articulo 1°, "Prohibir el Ingreso y la Utilización del Patógeno Fusarium Oxysporum, en Todo el Territorio Nacional, A Efecto de Preserver la Salud Pública, de los Animales y el Ecosistema en General."

12. *Declaration released in Lima, Peru,* September 7, 2000, of the Second Ordinary Meeting of the Andean Committee of Environmental Authorities (CAAAM), held in the city of Lima, September 5–6, 2000. Original quote in Spanish, "Las autoridades ambientales presenter en la II Reunión Ordinaria del Comité Andino de Autoridades Ambientales (CAAAM), celebrada en la Ciudad de Lima, Los Días 5 y 6 de Septiembre de 2000, DECLARAN: Su rechazo a la utilización del hongo Fusarium Oxysporum, como herramienta pare la eradicación de cultivos ilícitos en el territorio de la países miembros de la Comunidad Andina."

13. "Conflict Flares in the Bolivian Tropics," *Drug Policy Briefing,* no. 2, Amsterdam, Transnational Institute, January 2002.

14. The spraying program shifted from Monsanto's normal Roundup to Roundup Ultra and a new ingredient, Cosmoflux, was added to enhance penetration into the coca leaf. See for more details Martin Jelsma, *Vicious Circle: The Chemical and Biological War on Drugs* (Amsterdam: Transnational Institute, 2001); and Transnational Institute, "In the Heat of the Debate: Fumigation and Conflict in Colombia," *Drugs and Conflict Papers,* no. 2 (Amsterdam: Transnational Institute, 2001).

15. "Europe's Aid Plan for Colombia Falls Short of Drug War's Goals," *New York Times,* October 25, 2000.

16. Marianne de Costa de Moraes, quoted in "Europeans Scale Back Colombian Drug Aid," *Washington Post,* October 19, 2000.

17. *European Parliament Resolution on Plan Colombia and Support for the Peace Process in Colombia,* B-5–0087/2001, February 1, 2001.

18. "Pentagon Officials Urged Expanded United States Role against Rebels," *Washington Post,* February 28, 2002.

19. Human Rights Watch, *Punishment and Prejudice: Racial Disparities in the War on Drugs* (Washington, D.C.: Human Rights Watch, 2002), 24.

20. Human Rights Watch, *Reforming the Rockfeller Drug Laws* (Washington, D.C.: Human Rights Watch, 2002), 18.

21. See Nicholas Dorn and Alison Jamieson, eds., *European Drug Laws: The Room for Manoeuvre* (London: Drug Scope, 2001); Brice de Ruyter, et al., *Multidisciplinary Drug Policies and the UN Drug Treaties* (Antwerp/Apeldoorn: IRCP/Maklus, 2002).

22. *International Narcotics Control Board, Report 2001* (New York: United Nations, 2002).

23. *Report and Recommendation of the Drug Policy Task Force* (New York: County Lawyers' Association, October 1996).

12

Multilateral Drug Control

Sandeep Chawla

Much contemporary discourse on the drug problem falls into one of three
categories: a) sensationalism; b) the call for an intensification of present control efforts; or c) the call for new approaches because the current ones have
failed. The first one, sensationalism, can be dismissed at the outset, not because it cannot be explained, but because however justifiable its reasons, it
still impedes serious inquiry. The two latter categories, while often posited as
discrete and mutually exclusive, are in fact not necessarily so. In this chapter,
I will argue that they can be combined to mutual benefit. The necessary
condition for securing the combination, however, is to give multilateral drug
control the credibility it deserves, but seldom gets.

The multilateral drug control system spans the twentieth century. Its history is full of insights. They are seldom seen, or appreciated, because there is
a certain immediacy to the drug problem. The concern with the here and the
now usually displaces reflection about how things came to be what they are.
The dictum that "those who forget the past are condemned to repeat it" is
particularly appropriate here. The only corrective is to remember the past
and use it as a means to understand the present. Such a process could begin
by considering the proposition that if it were not for the multilateral control
system, the drug problem would be much worse than it is today.

It Could Be Worse

In 1909, when the international control system began, world opium production was at least 25,000 metric tons.[1] In 2000, nearly one hundred years later,
it was more than four times less: about 6,000 tons, which includes 1,300 tons
of licit opium and 4,700 tons of illicit opium production.[2] The population of
the world, by contrast, is today nearly four times more than it was in 1910,
having grown from 1.75 billion to 6.1 billion.

The opium trade with China provides another good example.[3] Until the middle of the eighteenth century, opium imports into China amounted to less than 100 tons a year. During the mercantile era, and following the British East India Company's monopolization of the opium trade, Chinese imports began to increase. At the time of the first opium war, China imported 2,600 tons of opium. The second opium war inaugurated the imperial opium trade, and China had to accept opium imports as legal. By 1880, China was importing about 6,500 tons, more than total world production, licit and illicit, today. After the 1880s, opium cultivation within China began to grow. At the time of the Shanghai Conference of 1909, opium production in the country amounted to some 20,000 tons,[4] more than three-fourths of world production in that year, and more than three times as large as world production today.

A similar picture emerges if we consider the consumption of opium. At the beginning of the twentieth century, China apparently had about 100 million opium users: between 15 and 20 million of these were supposed to be addicted.[5] Estimating the number of users is not a very exact science. It was even less exact one hundred years ago. Some measure of magnitude can nonetheless be established. The United Nations' most recent estimate is 13 million opiate users worldwide, which includes 9 million heroin users.[6] This means that there are less consumers of opiates in the world today than there were in only one country a century ago. While there may be many explanations for the phenomenon that global production and consumption of the world's most dangerous drug are both lower than they were a century ago, the multilateral control system has to be one of them. The argument presented above may not be able to bear a great deal of weight, but it can certainly carry the proposition that the drug problem would have been worse if the multilateral control system had not been established.

The Origins of the "International System"

Global control regimes, such as those to control piracy, slavery, and indeed drugs, have long historical antecedents. Their appearance was predicated upon the creation of what has come to be called the "international society."[7] This developed over the last five hundred years as a result of two separate and quite distinct historical processes, one within Europe, the other without. The internal European process happened from about the fifteenth to the eighteenth centuries, during which Europe integrated internally and developed a system that by the middle of the seventeenth century was already being called the "diplomatic commonwealth of Europe."

This system was built essentially upon two principles that are at the root of our international society and of our whole system of international law. By the time of the Congress of Westphalia in 1648, these two principles were generally accepted. The first was the principle that all member states of the system were judiciously equal. The second was the principle that every member state of the system had absolute sovereignty. These two principles are fundamental to our international multistate system today. Were they to be removed, the whole edifice of an international society, and indeed of international law, would collapse.

This internal European system was developed through a range of techniques and means, all of which are still the heart of our international system. The first of these was the principle of anti-hegemonialism and the balance of power: never letting one power become powerful enough to dominate the rest. The second was the principle of congresses, carefully prepared meetings of the powerful states that came together to settle the most important affairs of the day: the famous Congresses of Westphalia in 1648, of Utrecht in 1713, and, of course, of Vienna in 1815, which set many of the borders of our contemporary world. To draw a parallel between the Congress system and the Security Council of the United Nations is not far-fetched. There was also the invention of the system of diplomacy, of diplomatic exchanges that implied not only the idea of resident embassies in each country, but also the very novel idea in the seventeenth century of actually exchanging professional staff from particular ministries among the countries, so that a permanent and informed dialogue was maintained. This, of course, is the ancestry of our public international organizations today. Finally, there was the system of international law: this was the codification of the actual practice of states into a set of regulatory rules of war and peace. The practice of states, the way in which they conducted their relationships—that is, international relations —was based upon the two principles noted earlier: judicious equality and absolute sovereignty. From these international relations grew international law. It was limited, however, by the very principles upon which it was based: the equality and sovereignty of member states in the international system.

When member states that are sovereign and equal come together there is always an open question: Who will adjudicate between them? Who, apart from God, can rule between two sovereigns? The situation is not all bleak and grim real politik, however. There is another dimension to soften this picture. International law not only codified the practice of states but also assumed—gradually and incrementally—undertones of morality and overtones of obligation. The pace of this process has increased gradually since the adoption of the Universal Declaration on Human Rights in 1948 and the supplementary instruments of international law (including the drug conventions) through the last five decades. The Cold War took some of the teeth out of these instruments, but now that it is over it looks as though the obligations of international law are becoming more powerful.

The second, extra-European process, which created the international system, happened simultaneously with the internal European one, also from the fifteenth to the eighteenth centuries. In simple terms, it is called colonialism. It was a process by which Europe went out and dominated the world through migration, the creation of extension states, direct colonialism, or informal empires. The system was operational in the seventeenth century and the European dominion over the rest of the world was basically effective by the eighteenth century. The irony in contrasting the internal European process with the extra-European one was that the rules that were developed within Europe for the diplomatic commonwealth were not applied outside Europe.

There emerged, thus, a very odd dichotomy between an internal arena within Europe, where the new rules of war and peace were being applied, and the arena outside Europe, the rest of the world, where it was all anarchy, where the rules were evaded regularly, where European states very often indulged in actions among themselves, and among other states, which violated the rules that were applied within Europe. From this experience of colonialism grew one of the first paradoxes of the international system: the fact that in theory all states were equal, but in practice some states were more equal, and more sovereign, than others. Expressed another way, this is the paradox between national sovereignty, which means order, and no international sovereignty, which means anarchy and disorder.

The principle of nationalism cannot escape mention because any discussion of "international" presupposes a prior conception of the "national." With nationalism, a very interesting inversion took place. In Europe, nationalism appeared in a particular way: the political entity (the state) was already there, like a shell, and a cultural entity (the nation) was developed to fill the shell (the nation-state). In the rest of the world, nationalism came in exactly the inverse way.[8] The rest of the world was under European colonial domination. Here, the nation was postulated as existing prior to the state because the anti-colonial movements had to legitimate their objective to get rid of the colonizer and the colonial state. When the national liberation movements were successful, and the colonial states were gone, the consequences of the inversion became evident. The new states inherited the colonial frontiers, but they were not really nation-states. The nations that they had postulated as existing prior to the states only existed in the imaginations of the new national leaders. The nations did not exist in reality. They had to be built. Thus began an internal process of nation-building that continues in many parts of the world to this day. Another way of describing this situation is to see it as the building of sovereignty internally, to balance the sovereignty externally guaranteed by the multi-state international system. All global regimes that developed in the paradoxical situation between national order and international disorder, to regulate some of that disorder, grew up through several stages.[9]

The first stage was the one characterized by the ambiguity between the "national" and the "international"; this ambiguity is evident if one looks at any of the historical movements, for instance the slave trade. The state that virtually monopolized the slave trade, and made the most profits out of it, was also the state that eventually condemned the trade, and stopped it—the British Empire. This was in the early period of global regimes, during the seventeenth and the eighteenth centuries.

The second stage in the development of a global regime is a time of moral redefinition. It usually happens as a result of the efforts of "moral entrepreneurs," a very useful concept drawn from Howard Becker's famous sociology of deviance.[10] These moral entrepreneurs—we have lots of parallels in our world today—spearhead movements of moral redefinition so that moral consensus is formed in the society against the problem: for instance, abolitionist forces in the anti-slavery movement. It is no coincidence that the anti-slavery movement in Britain was also the source of some of the first public diatribes against the opium trade. The next stage comes when some kind of open international convention is eventually adopted against the problem in question: this happened with slavery, this happened with piracy and privateering, but it never happened against alcohol and prostitution, two of the several problem areas for which international conventions were never developed.

The final stage is the adoption of global regimes against the particular activity that needs to be controlled, regulated, banned, or prohibited. In a regime of this nature, where all member states become the signatories to an international convention, the paradox between national sovereignty and international lack-of sovereignty, or anarchy, is still present. The accession to the convention does make a difference, but there are still four weaknesses in any international regime, even the ones we have today.

The first weakness is the problem of deviant states: if a sovereign state violates the regime to which it has subscribed, explicitly or implicitly, then the only answer, the only way to stop it, is with force—the law of the jungle. The second weakness is the problem of weak states: those that are willing to accede to an international convention or an international regime, but unfortunately have not the means or the resources to enforce the law within their own frontiers. They have external sovereignty, but their internal sovereignty, or nation-building, is not complete. The third weakness is the problem of powerful states: those that may go ahead and pursue any policy or action they please because they are "more equal than others," and others do not have the power to stop them.

These three kinds of states—the deviant, the weak, and the powerful—have at least one thing in common. They can each violate the integrity of a multilateral system by taking unilateral action. Such an option is of course open to any sovereign state, but the three types described above clearly have more incentives to choose it.

The fourth weakness of the international system has not to do with the kind of state, but rather with the fact that the importance of the state is clearly diminishing in our contemporary world. It is a world in which the state is no longer able to lead society effectively, and civil society comes to its own defense, either because it wants to or because it has to. It is a world in which capital (financial markets), trade, information (the Internet), and transnational organizations (profit and nonprofit) perpetually slip out of the controls that the state may seek to impose on them; common discourse refers to this process as globalization. There seems to be a gray area where the control of the state stops and where the control of the international regime does not quite begin. This is something of a no-man's-land. It has become much smaller over the last few hundred years because most international control regimes are recent. But as these regimes have grown, the control of the state has diminished. The no-man's-land is still there and groups that inhabit it can often continue to do so with impunity. The shorthand for these groups is to call them transnational organizations. They include a whole variety of commercial, charity, and voluntary organizations. Unfortunately, they also include increasingly transnational and sophisticated criminal networks.

The Development of the Multilateral Drug Control System

The specific elements of the multilateral drug control system can now be slotted into the general framework of the international system sketched above. Though every society, since time immemorial, has had its psychoactive plant or plants of choice, there was no real drug "problem" until the nineteenth century. Technology and organic chemistry unleashed both the positive and the negative potential of drugs. The psychoactive ingredients of plants were extracted in their pure, and vastly more potent, forms: morphine was isolated early in the century; cocaine in 1860; diacetylmorphine in 1874—this became better known as heroin when the pharmaceutical company Bayer introduced it in 1898. There is an interesting irony here: at Bayer, it was the same research team that isolated aspirin (a widely used medicine) and heroin (a widely abused "poison") within one month of each other.[11] The invention of the hypodermic syringe made it possible to deliver these newly extracted drugs more efficiently to the body. The public health potential of all this was enormous; so also, was the abuse potential. It is no surprise that the first drug epidemics appeared in the late nineteenth century. Expanding, dynamic, market-oriented societies took well to drugs that induced euphoria, relieved pain, and enhanced performance through stimulation of the central nervous system. The nineteenth-century epidemics were not confined to the then rapidly industrializing countries. There was one in China, too, and some of its implications were discussed at the outset of this chapter. The Chinese epidemic, however, was not driven by industrialization. It was the result, rather, of the colonial trade, which was the face of European industrialization in the non-European world. A discussion of the Asian opium trade is beyond the ambit of this chapter, but a recent reappraisal of it shows how crucial it was in both the building and the consolidation of the British, French, and Dutch colonial empires in South and Southeast Asia.[12]

The switch in the drug problem, from a number of national problems into one international problem, happened at the beginning of the twentieth century.[13] In February 1909, the United States convened a meeting of thirteen nations at Shanghai. The meeting came to be known as the International Opium Commission. The United States was moved by domestic concerns about drug abuse; drug smuggling in the Philippines, which it had acquired in 1898; the need to secure a commercial opening in China; and the need to appease Chinese anger about the treatment of Chinese labor in America. In a now-familiar form of scapegoating minorities, the Chinese migrant labor was blamed for the spread of opium abuse.[14] The Chinese minority was, somewhat ironically, also blamed for the spread of cocaine in London in the 1920s.[15] For their part, the Chinese regarded opium as a symbol and an instrument of Western domination throughout the nineteenth century.

The Shanghai Commission—since it was not a "conference," it could not adopt a treaty binding upon the countries attending—adopted a resolution about the serious nature of the opium problem. The United States, convinced that controlling crops and trafficking in producer countries would help solve its domestic problem, now pursued a conference to give some teeth to the Shanghai agreements. This happened at The Hague in 1911. Twelve countries signed a convention on January 12, 1912. It required each signatory to enact domestic legislation controlling narcotic drugs so they could be restricted to medical use. This led to the Harrison Act of 1914 in the United States. The act set an interesting precedent for American policy.[16] Since prescribing narcotic drugs concerned states' rights, the federal government could only use its taxation powers to impose the law. Thus, a tax had to be paid at each stage from the entry of the drugs into the country till their final dispensing to the patient. A similar method was used to control cannabis with the Marijuana Tax Act of 1937. This peculiar character of American arrangements for drug control, which criminalized illicit use by means of the tax code, still survives. The shaky legal ground underpinning the early statutes such as the Harrison Act compelled the federal government to try and buttress them by means of international agreement.[17] The use of international agreements to legitimate domestic policy is one of several explanations for American championship of international drug control in the twentieth century.[18]

The First World War prevented The Hague Convention from coming into effect. It finally did, in 1920, when it was added to the peace treaties ending the war. At the first assembly of the League of Nations, the Advisory Committee on Traffic in Opium and other Dangerous Drugs was created. Ratification of The Hague Convention then led to a spate of domestic legislation in several countries—for instance, the British Dangerous Drugs Act of 1920. From this time until 1964, when the 1961 Single Convention came into effect, the essential elements of the international control system were brought together. The Hague Convention had already tried to control consumption and retail sales of narcotic drugs by restricting access to physicians and pharmacists. Then, in 1925, the Geneva Convention on Opium regulated international trade in narcotic drugs. Now, cannabis was added to cocaine and opiates, at the insistence of Egypt, which had a domestic problem with it. The 1925 Convention set up a system of export and import certificates, which were monitored by the Permanent Central Narcotics Board at the League of Nations. The 1931 Convention for the limitation of production then sought to solve the problem of diversions for illicit use, since pharmaceutical production regularly exceeded the amount estimated for consumption. States agreed to limit this production, and to report annual estimates of narcotic drugs for medical needs to the Drug Supervisory Body at the League. The carefully negotiated 1953 Protocol on cultivation never came into effect because pharmaceutical companies resisted it. Through the 1930s and the Second World War, they enjoyed the benefits of low raw material prices as a result of competition between opium and coca suppliers.[19]

The 1953 Protocol was, in the event, superseded by the 1961 Single Convention, which unified all these control elements under one regime, for cocaine, cannabis, and the opiates. The League's Advisory Committee on Opium became the United Nations Commission on Narcotic Drugs, still the governing body of the United Nations International Drug Control Programme (UNDCP). The Central Narcotics Board and the Drug Supervisory Body were incorporated into the International Narcotics Control Board (INCB), whose secretariat is a part of UNDCP. The control system was then further extended in the 1971 Convention, to control psychotropic substances, and the 1988 Convention against trafficking, which also tried to regulate the beginning (precursor control) and the end (money laundering) of the complex production-to-consumption chain. At least three conclusions emerge from this survey of the evolution of the international system.

First, its history is not yet fully and properly written. There are a few works, but most have national focus and do not cover the uniqueness of this international system.[20]

Second, this international system is unique because it has a mandatory nature. It requires countries to enact complementary legislation, and makes them measure their own policies against international standards. It makes drug control into a subject within which the national and the international are not easily separated.

Third, there is a great, but often hidden, success story here. It concerns the licit drugs. The international control system is meant not only to limit abuse of drugs, but equally to ensure their availability for medical and scientific purposes. Many of the "narcotic drugs and psychotropic substances"—this is UN shorthand to describe all the drugs that are controlled under the 1961 and 1971 Conventions—are still essential drugs to treat a large number of diseases. Chronic pain, much of it related to cancer, affects about one in every ten people in the world. About one in every seven people suffer from chronic anxiety. Insomnia affects 20 to 30 percent of the adult population in the industrialized countries. About 40 million people suffer from epilepsy. Anywhere from 0.3 to 6 percent of the school-age population could be affected by attention deficit disorder. The incidence of obesity is estimated at 30 to 50 percent of the middle-aged population in many countries.[21]

For all of these conditions, several narcotic drugs and psychotropic substances are still the best available treatment and most rational choice: for instance, morphine and the opiates for pain; the benzodiazepines for anxiety; some amphetamine-type drugs for attention deficit disorder and obesity. More than half of prescription drugs worldwide are narcotic drugs and psychotropic substances. The fact that these drugs are available and delivered to patients as medicines under a carefully regulated system is a success story. The success is not unqualified. There are tendencies toward both oversupply and undersupply, which need to be corrected whenever they occur. Oversupply is the result of many different factors: performance pressures in modern society; affluence; consumer drives toward self-medication; the increasing use of drugs as "cosmetics" to alter the mood; and ever more aggressive marketing techniques that capitalize on the new medium of electronic communication. Undersupply is the result of the familiar developmental problems of poverty, lack of resources, and know-how. About half of the population of the world lacks access to essential medicines. But undersupply has another reason: the fear of drug abuse. For example, even in as affluent a part of the world as Europe, only 25 to 30 percent of physicians prescribe morphine for cancer pain, even though the opiates are known to have the highest success rate in this area. Surveys in Germany in 1990 and 1992 showed that only 11 to 16 percent of physicians ever prescribed opiate analgesics for pain relief.[22]

The Incremental and Progressive Nature of Multilateral Drug Control

The multilateral drug control system is incremental and progressive in nature, and it has been adapted and refined over the years. Thus, the scope of control began with international trade and then grew to cover the whole supply side, from cultivation to production. Now, it is beginning to extend to the demand side of the drug problem as well. It began with opium and was extended to cover other botanical drugs such as cocaine and cannabis. With the 1971 Convention, the control over the botanical drugs was extended to cover psychotropic substances. The 1988 Convention was directed against trafficking, but also attempted to regulate at the beginning of the production-trafficking-consumption chain by introducing precursor control, and at the end of the chain by setting the basis for controlling money laundering.

Though demand reduction is now an integral part of the international drug control regime, one could argue that—at least until recently—there has been a certain bias in favor of supply control. This has been criticized for a long time, notably by developing countries. Demand for drugs in the developed countries was seen as the ultimate cause for production in the developing countries. By concentrating on supply reduction, the burden was put on developing countries.

The critique is justified, though a remedy is not easy to find or apply. There are obviously limits to the degree to which international standards on approaches to reducing drug demand will be acceptable in an individual sovereign country, developed or developing. Practical examples of very broad interpretations that come close to de facto violations of the international drug conventions are, for instance, the permission—by domestic law—of coca-leaf chewing in some of the Andean countries, or the Netherlands' approach of de facto decriminalization (though dejure it remains forbidden) of cannabis consumption on the grounds of a national strategy to split the market between "hard" and "soft" drugs. Other examples are testing of Ecstasy pills for consumers, the establishment of shooting galleries, and the provision of heroin for drug addicts as part of harm reduction policies. In all of these cases, legal constructs exist that can be used to argue that the policies adopted do not violate the drug control conventions; however, they definitely go to the limits of interpretation of those conventions.

At the same time, there may be perfectly valid reasons for policies on the demand side to differ from one country to another. The mild reaction of the international community to apparent violations of the international drug conventions on the demand side can be seen in this context. In other words, demand control is, to a large extent, left de facto to individual countries for good reasons. Social and cultural realities differ from country to country and they cannot simply be disregarded in the formulation and implementation of drug policies.

All of this, however, is a difficult and complex argument. Why should there be a difference if an apparent violation of the multilateral control system concerns the demand or the supply side? Should not peasants have the same "right" to cultivate crops considered to be illicit as users who can buy their illicit cannabis more or less freely in coffee shops in the Netherlands? Why should governments—if they have an electorate that wishes it—forgo possible income from taxing narcotic plantation and trafficking, instead of investing public resources in fighting such phenomena? There are no simple answers to such questions. There is, however, one simple criterion, drawn from the multilateral principle, that can help: the impact on another country, or countries. Unlimited production will, almost unavoidably, affect other countries. The problem is exported. Domestic consumption, if not checked by appropriate demand reduction efforts, will primarily affect the country concerned. If the problem gets out of hand, the government of the country in question will be compromised. In other words, in the first case of the producing country that reneges on its international commitments, it becomes a free-rider, benefiting financially while other countries are burdened with the resulting problem. In the second case of the consuming country, even if domestic opinion finds the situation acceptable, the problems of "drug tourism" as well of demand creating incentives for supply are exacerbated. It looks as though the paradox of national sovereignty and international anarchy, elaborated in the earlier part of this chapter, will just not go away. The only possible resolution of this paradox is the multilateral system. If, as the popular adage goes, a chain is no stronger than its weakest link, then the weak links of the multilateral system are those states—weak, deviant, dysfunctional, or simply free-riding—that, for one reason or another, pursue unilateral policies. If the multilateral system is to be changed, it should be changed by precisely the same means as those by which it was developed—collective action of its contracting parties or member states.

Balancing Supply and Demand Reduction

There are several other positive elements of the multilateral drug control system that have evolved in response to a perpetually changing situation. Controlling precursors and money laundering are two recent examples, starting with the 1988 Convention, which have been mentioned earlier. Another interesting illustration of the pioneering role of the multilateral system is that the first time action against money laundering was embodied in international law was in a drug control instrument, the 1988 Convention. Money laundering, of course, involves the proceeds of crime, of which illicit drugs are only one part. Thus, the multilateral drug control system becomes the foundation for launching a much wider international regulation to control the proceeds of crime.

Measures such as these reflect another positive dimension: balancing supply and demand reduction in the control system. Though lip service has been paid to the "balanced approach" for a long time, it was only at the recent

Special Session of the General Assembly that the balance was redressed and demand reduction put on par with supply side interventions.[23] While this may seem like a platitude for many countries, a number of countries, notably developing ones, have—until recently—relied almost exclusively on supply reduction (that is, law enforcement), to deal with the drug problem. For these countries, the obligation to follow a balanced approach is certainly a step forward.

Treatment as an Alternative to Incarceration/Punishment

The common misrepresentation of the multilateral drug control system as a simplistic prohibitionist regime, discussed earlier, is particularly unhelpful because it draws attention away from many positive elements in the system. Advocates of reforming the system, for instance those that coalesce under the rubric of harm reduction, often argue that treating drug users is better than incarcerating or punishing them. When the argument becomes a platform for reform, the implication is that the system to be reformed does not allow for treatment as an alternative. Nothing could be further from the truth.

The 1961 Convention as amended by the 1972 Protocol, for instance, under the heading of Penal Provisions (Article 36) states: "when abusers of drugs have committed such offences, the Parties may provide, either as an alternative to conviction or punishment or in addition to conviction or punishment, that such abusers shall undergo measures of treatment, education, after-care, rehabilitation and social reintegration . . ." (para 1[b]).[24] The same idea also appears in the 1998 Convention. Article 3, on Offences and Sanctions, states: "Notwithstanding the preceding subparagraphs, in appropriate cases of minor nature, the Parties may provide, as alternatives to conviction or punishment, measures such as education, rehabilitation or social reintegration, as well as, when the offender is a drug abuser, treatment and after-care" (para 4[c]).[25] The 1998 Guiding Principles of Demand Reduction (adopted at the Special Session of the General Assembly) go one step further: "In order to promote the social reintegration of drug-abusing offenders, where appropriate and consistent with the national laws and policies of Member States, Governments should consider providing, either as an alternative to conviction or punishment, or in addition to punishment, that abusers of drugs should undergo treatment, education, aftercare, rehabilitation and social reintegration" (para 14).[26]

Supporting Cultivators: From Crop Substitution to Alternative Development

Another interesting concept that has evolved over the years and appears in the 1988 Convention is the promotion of integrated rural development, which is now known in the trade as alternative development. In contrast to the 1961 Convention (and its predecessors), which simply contained an obligation for countries to "seize any plants illicitly cultivated and to destroy them" (Article 22), the 1988 Convention states: "The parties may co-operate to increase the effectiveness of eradication efforts. Such co-operation may, inter alia, include support, when appropriate, for integrated rural development leading to economically viable alternatives to illicit cultivation. Factors such as access to markets, the availability of resources and prevailing socio-economic conditions should be taken into account before such rural development programs are implemented" (Article 14, para 3[a]).

The Political Declaration and the Action Plan on International Cooperation on the Eradication of Illicit Drug Crops and on Alternative Development, both passed by the 1998 Special Session of the General Assembly, go further, refining the role of alternative development as a drug control strategy. The Political Declaration conceives alternative development as part of a comprehensive approach for the elimination of illicit narcotic crops, stressing "the special importance of cooperation in alternative development"[27] (Article 18). In the Action Plan on International Cooperation on the Eradication of Illicit Drug Crops and on Alternative Development, the preamble recognizes that "effective crop control strategies can encompass a variety of approaches, including alternative development, law enforcement and eradication."[28] The Action Plan categorically states that "in cases of low-income production structures among peasants, alternative development is more sustainable and socially and economically more appropriate than forced eradication" (para 7), and introduces the concept of "shared responsibility" to fund alternative development efforts (para 8). It then elaborates the conditions for successful alternative development interventions, such as a strong political will of the governments concerned (para 10), encourages international financial institutions to assist, underlines the catalytic role of UNDCP to make funding available (para 13), and calls upon the international community to provide greater access to domestic and international markets for alternative development products (para 15). A large number of additional benefits are spelled out: alternative development programs should, among others, "contribute to the promotion of democratic values to encourage community participation, and promote social responsibility to develop a civic culture that rejects the illicit cultivation of crops" (para 18, c).

Dilemmas of Drug Policy

One of the biggest dilemmas in drug policy today is that it is difficult to establish a clear-cut relationship between the type and form of a drug policy and the level of drug use or drug problems in any particular country. It is widely believed that there is such a relationship. Common sense dictates that there should be one. Yet it is very difficult to document such relationships in empirically verifiable terms. History can help us resolve this dilemma: not the history we have, but the history that still needs to be written. There is thus a need for historical research on the political, economic, social, and cultural contexts of drug policy, national and international. In a thoughtful paper on the need for historical perspectives in assessing different national, international, and European drug policies, Virginia Berridge proposes several ways in which historical work could be advanced.[29] Drawing on this work, and the arguments presented above, there seem to be three themes that will be particularly important for further investigation: first, drug policy histories; second, social history of epidemics and anti-drug laws; and third, the historical development of different drug control models.

Drug Policy History

A recent survey of European drug research pointed out that it had become more and more policy led. Yet there were few policy studies available.[30] There is a manifest need for drug policy histories that are informed by the national culture, and explain why different countries developed such different forms of control and regulation. This would also explain why different drugs, and different routes of administration of the drugs, took root in different places. Why did a cocaine epidemic not happen in Europe in the 1980s and early 1990s, even though it was so widely predicted? Of the synthetic drugs, why is methamphetamine preferred in both America and the Far East, and amphetamine in Europe? Even though initial conditions were available for both, why did Japan suffer an epidemic with methamphetamine, but not with cocaine?

If we look within Europe, the explanatory power of this kind of history can be shown even more clearly. Contrast the liberal Dutch policy after 1976 with the firm adherence to the abstinence model in Sweden. The origins of the 1976 act in the Netherlands, which introduced the famous distinction between hard and soft drugs, have been attributed to at least three different things: the colonial experience of the Dutch in Indonesia, where they instituted a maintenance-prescribing system for opium; the economic experience of the Dutch in the era of declining colonial empires, when the Netherlands remained an important production center and trading route for drugs, even after the international export/import certificate system was introduced in the 1920s; and the desire in the Netherlands to avoid what were perceived as the failures of U.S. prohibition policies and British heroin maintenance policies.[31]

Another area that such national policy histories could illuminate is how, in the different relationships between state and society, voluntary organizations and professional associations come to play a crucial role in drug control.[32]

The overlapping histories of the slave abolition movements, the temperance societies, and the anti-opium movement are well known. Much less studied are the specific directions given to drug policies by particular groups of professionals and voluntary (or today, nongovernmental) organizations. In the United Kingdom, for instance, the drug control model at the beginning of the century was to control supply through the pharmacy profession, and to control the user through the medical profession. After the First World War, medical control became the dominant one, and has remained so, throughout this century. In the last decade, however, new "public health" professionals have begun to be heard as much as medical doctors. To take another example, it has been argued that countries with more liberal drug policies, such as the Netherlands and Spain, have policy makers with sociological backgrounds. The voluntary sector also needs to be understood in this context. Some countries have strong traditions of voluntary service provision. It often has a religious basis, for instance the therapeutic communities for drug addicts in Italy.[33] All of these things will become clearer if we set drug policies into the context of the historically determined relationship between state and society.

The Social History of Drug Epidemics and Anti-Drug Strategies

The history of the illicit drug problem is the only way to explain the fear of drug abuse. The experience of illicit drug epidemics in the past, in Europe, America, and China, in the last two centuries, has had a paradoxical consequence. The very success of anti-drug strategies makes it more difficult to deal with the problem when it reappears. Strong anti-drug laws are usually enacted when there is widespread public concern about an epidemic of drug abuse. This is what happened in the first two decades of the twentieth century. But social histories of some drug epidemics have shown us that there are three other responses that accompany strong laws: public "fear," official "silence," and media "exaggeration."

- Fear grows out of widely experienced encounters with the damage of addiction.
- Silence, often well-intentioned, means that no information is available, because providing that information might encourage new users —such as young people—to try the drugs.
- Exaggeration about the effects of the drugs and the extent of their use may also begin with the good intention of steering people away from the nonmedical use of drugs.[34]

Unfortunately, fear, silence, and exaggeration feed upon each other, and the main casualty of this is public memory. The essential context of strong drug laws is forgotten because the epidemic is over and the anti-drug strategy has been successful. But then those very laws begin to look unnecessarily severe because the public memory of their context is gone. Public opinion turns hostile to the control structures. Scapegoating, associating a drug with a particular racial or ethnic group, or a political cause, becomes widespread. Complex phenomena need complex explanations. These are hard to provide in our age, which is so obsessed with current information and messages reduced to mere headlines. Public opinion is thus ignorant of the complexity of drug use. History could provide a solution: it is, after all, the public memory of a society. In an age when the politician, policy maker, and practitioner are all grappling with increasing complexity, the historian can offer some guidance. He or she can unravel the complexity by showing how we got to our present situation, and how a particular policy choice is likely to have a certain outcome.

We need, therefore, to look at why drug epidemics happen in the countries and localities they do; what impact socially instituted fear and anxiety have on subsequent drug abuse patterns; how silence and exaggeration stop epidemics but also breed conditions for new epidemics to occur; and why scapegoating and finger-pointing continue to be enduring themes in public discourse on drugs.

The History of Drug Control Models

Historical investigation is also needed to illuminate the different models of drug control that have been tried in the past. This will inform current policy choices and decisions about what is the most appropriate model, or mix of models, in a given situation. There are at least four models that bear investigation. Each one can be historically located. There is, first, the open availability model, which is not really control at all but which prevailed throughout the world in the nineteenth century. In the beginning of the twentieth century, two new models appeared, closely linked to the evolving international control system: penal control and medical regulation. These held the field, though there were often tensions between them, throughout much of the century. In the last decade or so, particularly in the wake of the AIDS epidemic, a fourth model has appeared: public health regulation.

With regard to open availability, we need much more careful history than we have at present. The nineteenth-century experience, particularly with opium, is used by both sides in present debates about legalization: one side uses it to show that open availability can work; the other side uses it to illustrate the necessity of control and regulation. Just as drugs can be used or misused, history can also be used or misused. There is a small literature on nineteenth-century drug availability; some of these national histories are very good.[35] But the literature is by no means extensive enough to enable us to generalize confidently about the real impact of open availability. Even more difficult, the progress of science, technology, and development make the drugs much more potent than they were in the nineteenth century; routes of delivery to the body are much more effective; and distribution chains linking producer and consumer are far more complex. Historical evidence has to be considered in the light of these changing conditions.

If we go further back than the nineteenth century, the need for rigorous history becomes even more evident. Open availability is not even an appropriate description here because most societies had some form of regulating the use of psychoactive plants and materials. These traditional forms of regulation are a fertile area of anthropological and ethnographic investigation, but we still have no real sociology, or history, of drug use.[36] Until we do, odd bits of historical evidence will continue to be used selectively to fuel ideological battles in the present.

Coming back to more recent history, the legal and medical control models appeared at the end of the nineteenth and the beginning of the twentieth centuries. It has already been noted how the history of the international system that incorporated them is yet to be written. Their national histories are also incomplete. Because there was often tension between the penal and medical models, we need to look carefully at which particular model came to prevail in a given country, and why this happened. Policy history will help answer crucial questions about which particular ministry of government was given central responsibility for drug control.[37] In the United Kingdom, the Home Office (the Ministry of Justice, or the Interior) was given control, and keeps it, even though a new Ministry of Health was created in the 1920s. In the Netherlands, the Ministry of Health has played a leading role in drug control.

Such divisions reflect national attitudes about which we could learn from the social and cultural history mentioned earlier. Is the drug addict a sick person who has to be treated, or a criminal who has to be incarcerated? Even the terms we use to describe the condition of drug abuse change with the times.[38] "Addiction" was fashionable for a long time. The etiology of addiction was frequently debated: was its origin physical or social/psychological? In the 1960s and 1970s, the term addiction was largely displaced by the term "dependence" in an attempt to merge physical and psychological explanations. Now, in the 1990s and the twenty-first century, both these terms have given way to yet another: "problem drug use." This reflects the emergence of what was described as the model of public health regulation.

Traditionally, the health issue was divided into prevention and cure/treatment. Prevention implied public health approaches to limit the conditions within which a particular disease would thrive; cure implied the clinical or medical approach to treat the disease. Social historians of the impact of AIDS are now showing that there is a new public health response to drugs. Prevention is as important as cure. Treatment and cure are not easy to separate. For example, given one of the ways in which AIDS is transmitted, methadone maintenance, which is a medical treatment, is now considered in some countries to be a prevention strategy. This new notion of public health, in which treatment and prevention merge, has other consequences. For instance, the language of prevention has entered the criminal justice system. There are more interactions between the health and criminal justice systems, not least because treatment is more frequently used as an alternative to incarceration or punishment. All of these relationships can be better understood through the different kinds of historical investigation suggested above. History will not only enrich our understanding of the present, but can thereby also show us which way to go in the future.

Conclusion: The Future of Multilateral Drug Control

This chapter has argued, and tried to demonstrate, that the multilateral drug control system is progressive and incremental and has evolved in response to changing conditions. The system has its weaknesses—deviant, dysfunctional, and free-rider states, and the paradox of national sovereignty and international lack-of-sovereignty—but these are common to the whole international multi-state system, and not peculiar to drug control.

In the specific area of drug control, it appears that we can go forward in at least three different ways. First, the positive and progressive elements of the system, some of which were discussed above, should continue being developed. Second, the drug issue is badly in need of both demystification and desensationalization. The debate on drug policies needs to be taken beyond narrow ideological concerns and grounded in empirical evidence-based discussion. One of several ways of doing this was suggested and documented in this chapter: to revive the history of the drug issue as a way to guide present practice. Finally, unilateral action, however well intentioned and progressive it may be, is hard to legitimate in the context of drug control. If the system needs adjustment or reform, then it must be done by precisely the same means with which the system was created in the first place—multilateral consultation and action.[39]

Notes

1. These figures are derived from the *Report of the International Opium Commission*, Shanghai, February 1–26, 1909; other estimates, for instance, Alfred W. McCoy, *The Politics of Heroin* (New York: Lawrence Hill Books, 1991), put the figure as high as 41,600 tons.

2. *Report of the International Narcotics Control Board, 2001* (New York: United Nations, 2002) and UNDCP, *Global Illicit Drug Trends, 2001* (New York: United Nations, 2001).

242 / Sandeep Chawla

3. There is an extensive literature on this subject, cf. the bibliographic essay "The Literature of the Opium Trade," Appendix 1 in Carl A. Trocki, *Opium, Empire, and the Global Political Economy: A Study of the Asian Opium Trade 1750–1950* (London: MacMillan, 1999).

4. *Report of the International Opium Commission,* passim.

5. There are many scattered references in the literature to these figures, but I have not found any systematic treatment of how they were derived. The two following citations are merely indicative: *Report of the International Narcotics Control Board, 1998* (New York: United Nations, 1999), 1, 58; and Rensselaer W. Lee III, "Drugs in Communist States and Former Communist States," *Transactional Organized Crime* 1, no. 2 (1995), 193–205.

6. Annual prevalence of opiate use; UNDCP, *Global Illicit Drug Trends, 2001,* 225.

7. Hedley Bull and Adam Watson, eds., *The Expansion of International Society* (Oxford: Oxford University Press, 1988) provides a good survey of the issues discussed in this section.

8. There are vast literatures on nationalism and colonialism, and the two citations are only meant to be indicative: on the conceptual question, cf. Ernest Gellner, *Nations and Nationalism* (Oxford: Oxford University Press, 1992); and on non-European nationalism and anti-colonial movements, cf. Geoffrey Barraclough, *An Introduction to Contemporary History* (Harmondsworth: Penguin, 1988).

9. The following discussion of stages in the development of global regimes draws on a useful survey by Ethan Nadelmann, "Global Prohibition Regimes: The Evolution of Norms in International Society," *International Organization* 44, no. 4 (1990), 480–526. The only problem with an otherwise excellent article is that it fails to draw clear distinctions between "control," "regulation," and "prohibition," thereby perpetuating the erroneous categorization of the multilateral drug control regime as a prohibition regime, and fostering a debate that, at least on the international level, is increasingly sterile, vacuous, and unhelpful.

10. Howard Becker, *Outsiders: Studies in the Sociology of Deviance* (New York: Free Press, 1963).

11. Walter Sneader, "The Discovery of Heroin," *The Lancet* 352 (1998), 1697–99.

12. Trocki, *Opium, Empire, and the Global Political Economy,* passim.

13. The best, and most up-to-date history of the multilateral drug control system, based on primary sources, is William B. McAllister, *Drug Diplomacy in the Twentieth Century: An International History* (London: Routledge, 2000).

14. David F. Musto, "Opium, Cocaine, and Marijuana in American History," *Scientific American* 265 (1991), 40–48.

15. Marek Kohn, *Dope Girls: The Birth of the British Drug Underground* (London: Granta, 1992), passim.

16. Musto, "Opium, Cocaine, and Marijuana," 43–44.

17. McAllister, *Drug Diplomacy,* 27–36; David F. Musto, *The American Disease: Origins of Narcotics Control* (Oxford: Books on Demand, 1987), 54–68; and Arnold H. Taylor, *American Diplomacy and the Narcotics Traffic* (Durham, N.C.: Duke University Press, 1969), 182–86.

18. In contemporary debates, this is sometimes cited to support the argument that

the United States is the principal champion of the global drug prohibition regime. Quite apart from the misrepresentation of a control regime as a prohibitionist one (see note 9 above), it is almost a truism to state that the major power of a particular age is the champion of the international status quo at that time: the British Empire was the pioneer of the slave trade in the eighteenth century; it was also the champion of abolition and suppression of that same slave trade in the nineteenth century.

19. The interwar period is full of unexplored avenues, all awaiting historical investigation. For instance, coca cultivation was not confined to the three Andean countries in Latin America. The British tried to introduce it in Ceylon (Sri Lanka) and India. The Germans tried to grow it in Cameroon. The Dutch grew it, quite successfully and in fairly large quantities, in Java. Coca-leaf exports from Java even outstripped exports from Peru in 1912. Japan grew coca in its colonial territory, Formosa (now Taiwan). Japan even had a problem with domestic consumption of cocaine, and is alleged to have diverted its cocaine to other markets. New historical work is beginning appear, cf. Paul Gootenberg, ed., *Cocaine: Global Histories* (London: Routledge, 1999), but the literature is still overwhelmingly skewed in favor of "official" accounts by drug control "experts."

20. Particular mention should be made of Karl Brunn, I. Pan, and I. Rexed, *The Gentlemen's Club: International Control of Drugs and Alcohol* (Chicago: Chicago University Press, 1975), which was an early attempt at rigorous analysis. Later work did not always keep up with these high standards. The gap has now been filled by McAllister, *Drug Diplomacy,* passim, which also has an extensive bibliography, in which work done in the last three decades can be followed.

21. See *Report of the International Narcotics Control Board, 1999* (New York: United Nations, 2000), chapter 1.

22. Ibid., 5–6, and note 38.

23. *Declaration on the Guiding Principles of Drug Demand Reduction,* adopted at the Special Session of the United Nations General Assembly Devoted to Countering the World Drug Problem Together, June 8–10, 1998 (Resolution S-20/3).

24. *The Single Convention on Narcotic Drugs of 1961* as amended by the 1972 Protocol (Vienna: United Nations, Treaty Series, vol. 976, no. 14152).

25. *The United Nations Convention against Illicit Traffic in Narcotic Drugs and Psychotropic Substances of 1998,* in Official Records of the United Nations Conference for the Adaptation of a Convention against Illicit Traffic in Narcotic Drugs and Psychotropic Substances, Vienna, November 25–December 20, 1988, vol. 1 (United Nations publication, Sales no. E.94.XI.5). Emphasis added.

26. United Nations, *Declaration on the Guiding Principles of Drug Demand Reduction,* adopted at the Special Session of the General Assembly Devoted to Countering the World Drug Problem Together, June 8–10, 1998 (Resolution S-20/3).

27. Ibid. (Resolution S-20/2, para 18).

28. Ibid. (Resolution S-20/4 E).

29. Virginia Berridge, "European Drug Policy: The Need for Historical Perspectives," *European Addiction Research* 3, no. 2 (1996), 219–25.

30. Richard Hartnoll, "Research on Illicit Drugs in Western Europe: An Overview," *European Addiction Research* 2, no. 1 (1995), 3–11.

31. Marcel de Kort and Dirk Korf, "The Development of Drug Trade and Drug

Control in the Netherlands: A Historical Perspective," *Criminal Law and Social Change, vol. 17* (1992), pp.123–144; David Downes, Contrasts in Tolerance: Post War Penal Policy in the Netherlands and England and Wales (Oxford, 1988); both cited in Berridge, "European Drug Policy," 220.

32. Berridge, "European Drug Policy," 221–22 and references therein.

33. Ibid.

34. cf. Musto, *The American Disease,* chapters 11 and 12, and the summary in his later article, "Opium, Cocaine, and Marijuana," 45–47; Virginia Berridge, "War Conditions and Narcotics Control: The Passing of Defence of the Realm Act Regulation 40B," *Journal of Social Policy* 7 (1978), 285–304; and Kohn, *Dope Girls,* passim.

35. Cf. Virginia Berridge and Griffith Edward, *Opium and the People: Opiate Use in Nineteenth-Century England* (London: Free Association Books, 1981).

36. Some interesting work is available, but not yet enough to build a comprehensive picture; cf. Piero Camporesi, *Bread of Dreams: Food and Fantasy in Early Modern Europe* (London: Polity Press, 1994); Richard Rudgley, *The Alchemy of Culture: Intoxicants in Society* (London: Lycaeum, 1993); Wolfgang Schivelbusch, *Tastes of Paradise: A Social History of Spices, Stimulants, and Intoxicants* (New York: Vintage Books, 1993); Jordan Goodman, Paul E. Lovejoy, and Andrew Sherratt, eds., *Consuming Habits: Drugs in History and Anthropology* (London: Routledge, 1995).

37. Berridge, "European Drug Policy," 223–24.

38. Karen Klaue, "Drugs, Addiction, Deviance, and Disease as Social Constructs," *Bulletin on Narcotics* 51, nos. 1 and 2 (1999), 45–55.

39. The views expressed in this chapter are those of the author and do not necessarily reflect those of the United Nations.

13

The European Union and Drug Control

Issues and Trends

Tim Boekhout van Solinge

National drug policies in the countries of the European Union have been changing considerably since the end of the twentieth century. In the 1980s, the member states began to develop harm reduction policies as a response to the problem of a growing number of intravenous drug users who had been infected by the HIV virus. Because of this public health threat, the traditionally repressive law enforcement approach toward illicit drugs was gradually abandoned and more pragmatic ways to deal with the drug question were defined. At the end of the decade it became clear that this pragmatic approach was being applied not only to the problematic intravenous drug users, but to the recreational users as well. Especially with regard to the most popular illicit drug, cannabis, decriminalization has become the general tendency in most European countries since the late 1990s. National drug policies in Europe—generally speaking—have undergone a shift from an emphasis on law enforcement toward a public health approach. This has included a policy of decriminalization for the possession of small quantities of cannabis and has involved an increasing pragmatism in dealing with the drug question.

This change of focus within the countries of the European Union can also be noted in the position taken by the European Union as an institution or European organization. In the three main EU institutions where drug policy is being debated, the Council, the Commission, and the European Parliament, one can observe a decreasing support for the traditional repressive approaches. This is most clearly reflected in the European Union's attitude toward the question of cocaine production and trafficking in Colombia, where the Union has distanced itself from the positions taken by Colombia and the United States.

The drug policy developments that have been taking place over the last few years in the countries of the European Union have made the outspoken, pragmatic, and nonpunitive Dutch approach toward illicit drugs no longer the exception it used to be. Looking back, the Netherlands should rather be considered a European forerunner, the first country that has developed a harm reduction strategy and a liberal policy toward cannabis use. We will look at the Dutch case in more detail and against the background of the more general changes in the European drug policy landscape later in this chapter.

European Drug Policy Developments

The shift in drug policy from a criminal orientation toward a public health orientation has meant a considerable paradigm change in the way of thinking about illicit drugs. Before, drugs were considered as something completely undesirable that should be banned from society. The present attitude of the European countries can best be summarized as "living with drugs at the least social and medical costs." Its implications are that the use of illicit drugs has been accepted more or less as a fact of life that should be dealt with practically and no longer fought against at any price.

Recreational drug use in the Western World increased in the 1990s. Not only the traditional and known substances were being used. "New" drugs such as Ecstasy (MDMA) and amphetamines have become increasingly popular. In response, the more pragmatic and less punitive approach with regard to hard or injectable drugs, developed in the 1980s and 1990s, was being extended to recreational drugs. Experimental drug use had increased in many countries in those decades, and it was clear that punitive measures had made no impact. For cannabis, the most widely used illicit substance, European authorities decided to recommend a less punitive, more lenient, and tolerant approach. The annual report of the European Union's European Monitoring Center for Drugs and Drugs Addiction (EMCDDA) in Lisbon has reported a clear shift toward decriminalization in most member states at the end of the 1990s. Some countries have developed a policy of harm reduction for the fashionable synthetic drugs such as Ecstasy and amphetamines. By informing people about the real risk of use, and by modifying the circumstances under which the substances are being used, the risk of fatalities can be reduced. In 1997, the European Union installed an early warning system that identified the risks of new drugs that appear on the market, followed by recommendations concerning the action to be taken.

The policies of individual European countries with regard to cannabis have been changing quite drastically over the last few years. Before the 1990s, the Netherlands and Denmark were the "European exceptions" in the sense that they were the only countries where cannabis was openly sold. Today, other countries are relaxing their practices and policies as well. In

1993, the German federal constitutional court decriminalized small-scale possession of cannabis. The quantity allowed differs per state and varies from 3 to 30 grams. In January 2001 the Belgian government decided to decriminalize the possession of small amounts of cannabis. In July 2001, Portugal decriminalized the use and possession of limited amounts of all illicit drugs for personal use, including cocaine, heroin, and amphetamines. Portugal used to have one of the most serious drug problems in Europe and decided to change its policy and focus on the social and health aspects of drug abuse.

The United Kingdom has the highest cannabis use rate in Europe. The debate about decriminalization or legalization has been going on for quite a number of years. Moreover, over the last few years, a growing number of politicians—Conservative as well as Labour—and senior policemen have called for cannabis decriminalization. A House of Commons committee concluded in May 2002 that "the time had come for international treaties to be reconsidered" and that a "discussion should be initiated on alternative ways, including the possibility of legislation and regulation to tackle the global drugs dilemma."[1] Recently, British Customs has been giving cannabis a lower priority, focusing on the seizure of hard drugs instead. People caught with marijuana are no longer arrested, but receive a warning. In 2002, cannabis selling points have sprung up in different parts of the United Kingdom. They have received the support of some politicians and enjoyed wide media attention. Here also, the focus of drug policy measures has been changing. Drugs are increasingly being considered a health issue instead of a criminal problem. Instead of punishing drug users, the aim of policy is now to help them and have them treated. A call by British chief constables in May 2002 to expand treatment to heroin and cocaine users instead of punishing them with a formal caution or a conviction was welcomed by Home Office ministers.[2]

Cannabis decriminalization in the countries of the European Union appears to be part of a larger international trend. Switzerland has decided to go beyond the EU countries in liberalizing its cannabis policy. In practice, the use and small trade from hemp stores had already been decriminalized. Now the Swiss government has proceeded to propose to Parliament the decriminalization of the use, cultivation, and possession of cannabis.

Similar changes in policy and practice can be noted outside Europe. In Canada, Australia, and New Zealand, the issue of cannabis decriminalization or legalization is hotly debated. In Jamaica, where the use of cannabis has been widespread for some 150 years, the Senate unanimously decided in the year 2000 to install a national commission to study the ganja (marijuana) question and to recommend possible policy changes. In August 2001 the National Ganja Commission recommended decriminalizing private use and possession.

The European Union's Position on Drugs

The European Union had been developing its own drugs policy when the Treaty of Maastricht took effect in 1993.[3] Since then, the drug issue has been on the agenda of numerous EU forums. The decision-making powers of these forums depend on the aspect of the drug problem that is being discussed. This has to do with the "three-pillar" structure—each pillar corresponding to the European Union's different policy areas—introduced by Maastricht. The first pillar consists of the "old" European Community (EC), the second deals with the Common Foreign and Security Policy, while the third deals with Justice and Home Affairs. Drug issues are being discussed in all three pillars. The first pillar operates according to the Community method; here the Commission plays an important role and possesses the right of initiative. The second and third pillars operate according to the intergovernmental method, which means that member states arrive at agreements through joint consultations, with the Commission having a far less prominent role. Despite the differences in the right of initiative, it is always the Council, in which the member states are represented, that takes the final decision. The powers of the European Parliament are relatively limited. It participates in decision making, but only in those policy areas that are subject to the codecision procedure, and in which the Council and Parliament have to reach agreement. As far as drugs are concerned, this applies only to certain health-related aspects.

In the first pillar, drug issues are discussed primarily within the framework of public health and development cooperation. In accordance with the European Union's principle of subsidiarity—basically meaning that Community action is taken only if it adds value to policymaking at the national level—public health has been largely a matter of domestic policy for the member states. Complementary measures by the Commission concern in practice mainly the realms of preventive action and the dissemination of information. In the first pillar, other aspects of the drug problem such as the precursor trade and money laundering are dealt with. In the second pillar (Common Foreign and Security Policy), drug issues are often discussed with third countries and international organizations. The third pillar (Justice and Home Affairs) deals extensively with drug issues, particularly in relation to the fight against organized crime and drug trafficking.

Drug issues are increasingly included in negotiations with countries outside the European Union and have become part of the activities in the field of development cooperation. The European Union maintains a policy requiring third countries to demonstrate adequate action in combating drugs as a condition for cooperation. This applies not only to potential member countries, but to all those countries that want to do business with the European Union.

It is in this area of external relations that the European Union has become particularly active in drug-related matters.[4] The very fact that most EU measures on drugs are defined by the second and the third pillar—and not by the first pillar, of which public health is a part—could suggest an emphasis on a punitive approach. However, this is not the case. The principle of subsidiarity dictates that public health matters will be left to the member countries themselves. Drug issues will be found in the second pillar of Common Foreign and Security Policy, and in particular in the third pillar of Justice and Home Affairs.

It is difficult to speak of a "European Union drugs policy." Some analysts maintain that such policy would be the sum of the measures taken by the Commission, the Council, and the Parliament. Others note that it is difficult to speak of a supranational "policy" in an area that still primarily belongs to the competence of the member states. Although the European Union has been taking complementary measures, these still do not add up to a coherent and comprehensive approach, and it has remained unclear which body would be responsible for developing one. However, the fact that the European Union presented its third Action Plan to Combat Drugs in 1999 suggests the presence of a coordinated and influential policy in the area of counter-narcotics action. This suggestion has been reinforced by the debate on the harmonization of anti-drugs legislation and its implementation, which has been widely commented upon in the media. Harmonization proved to be a politically sensitive issue, too difficult to achieve on the short term. Expanding practical cooperation in this area to the effect that member countries will join forces and elaborate common solutions when faced with common practical problems proved to be more realistic. This is the course set for the near future, although the issue of harmonization may return to the agenda later on.

The fight against drugs has the highest priority, at least in the rhetoric of the European Union. Yet, the budgetary allotments to counter-narcotics actions are relatively small: a mere 50 to 55 million U.S. dollars. The total external expenditure on anti-drug action in recent years has been about 20 million dollars annually.[5] Documents of the European Union proclaim support for a balanced approach to supply and demand reduction in all sectors. They increasingly stress the importance of reducing demand through preventive measures. However, concrete strategies leading to a decline in drug use have yet to be worked out. This is a difficult area to deal with given the social, cultural, and economic parameters of the issue. Recreational drug use among young people appears to be a part of an international youth culture, while problematic drug use is increasingly bound up with socioeconomic factors, such as social marginalization, and medical conditions, such as mental illness. Anti-drug measures are "contracted out" and imposed on other countries as a condition for cooperation. Despite the claims of having a balanced approach, the European Union's actual policies have remained heavily focused on supply reduction. Policy developments in this area continue to show strong inconsistencies. While there is a clear trend within the European Union toward decriminalization, the European Union's external policy insists that third countries should be taking more punitive measures.

Yet the way the European Union pressures source countries to take measures in order to limit the flow of drugs to the consumer countries has been substantially different from the position taken by the United States in this area. The drug control strategy of the European Union member states includes an emphasis on the health and social aspects, over repressive, let alone military, options. This position is reflected by the European Union's stand on cocaine production and trafficking in and from Colombia. Plan Colombia, designed by the Colombian and U.S. governments to curb the Colombian drug trade, has a strong military dimension. The European countries view Colombia as experiencing a humanitarian crisis solvable only through social development. They condemn the militarization of the anti-drug action and thus have been reluctant partners to the project. To distance itself from Plan Colombia and the war strategy chosen by Colombia and the United States, the European Union decided in October 2000 to channel its aid package of 250 million U.S. dollars to programs run by nonprofit groups working for human rights, judicial reform, and economic development instead of donating it directly to the Colombian government. The European Union's reticence with regard to the military approach was underlined by the European Parliament Resolution of February 1, 2001, that rejected Plan Colombia in clear statements with a vote of 474 in favor and only 1 against. The resolution denounced the chemical spraying of drug crops and underlined the incompatibility of the U.S. strategy with the European developmental approach. It explicitly warned that several dimensions of Plan Colombia contain aspects that run counter to the cooperation strategies and projects to which the European Union had already committed itself, jeopardizing its development cooperation programs.[6] It concluded that Plan Colombia had not been the product of a process of dialogue between the various partners in society and that "stepping up military involvement in the fight against drugs involves the risk of sparking off an escalation of the conflict in the region," considering that "military solutions cannot bring about lasting peace."[7] Decision-making procedures in the European Union are rather complex. The three-pillar structure, and the fact that the Commission, the Council, and the Parliament each are involved in policymaking does not make these procedures easy to comprehend. As far as the European Union's decision making on drugs is concerned, it is important to realize that at this moment, the fifteen member states are still making most of the decisions. These decisions are made in the

Council, where the member states meet and discuss all drug issues through the transpillar Horizontal Drug Group. The fact that each individual member state will remain responsible for most of the decisions to be taken on drug issues means that the major drug policy changes that have been occurring in the countries of the European Union will affect the general position of the European Union in these areas. The member states' shift toward decriminalization, harm reduction, and more health-oriented approaches has meant that the Netherlands is no longer the European Union's maverick. Sweden, persisting in the idea of a drug-free society and resisting any official reference to harm reduction in documents of the European Union, now has become the exception.

The general attitude toward drugs in most European countries has changed. The Netherlands has led the way. Many of its policy measures were first controversial, but now have become generally accepted. How have these policies come about? Why did this country decide to have a liberal drugs policy in the first place? What were the considerations?

The Dutch Drug Policy: Origins and Development

On a visit to the Netherlands one is likely to meet an illicit drug scene one way or an other. For most foreigners, a visit to the Netherlands will mean a visit to its capital, Amsterdam. The visitors will see many cannabis cafes, the so-called coffee shops where cannabis can be used and bought in small quantities. Users of heroin and crack-cocaine can also be seen in the busy inner city streets. A new phenomenon in the tourist areas of Amsterdam's historical inner city is the smart shop. These shops sell many different kinds of non-illegal mind-altering substances, varying from energy drinks to psychedelic (magic) mushrooms. The presence and visibility of drugs, combined with the legalized prostitution phenomenon concentrated in Amsterdam's red light district, may give people the impression that the Netherlands has become a Sodom and Gomorrah, a place where the authorities seem to have surrendered and are now allowing everything. However, this is not the case, but why would a country pursue such a lenient and liberal drug policy?

National drug policies in the Netherlands are closely related to other policy concerns and are also influenced by social and cultural traditions that have developed over time. One of these traditions concerns a critical attitude toward criminal law as an effective means to respond to undesirable social phenomena in society. Especially for the people of the United States, who share a different and more punitive tradition with extensive use of criminal law enforcement as a control mechanism, such an approach is sometimes hard to understand. From a Dutch perspective, there has never been a question of surrender by the authorities, which would have led them to pursue a tolerant and permissive policy toward illicit drugs. Present Dutch drug policy has been the result of well-considered political decisions, based on principles that are deeply rooted in Dutch society. The extent of drug use in Dutch society—not particularly high compared to other Western countries—has not played a role in the decision-making process. As in most Western societies, Dutch authorities were confronted in the late 1960s with a new phenomenon: the use of illicit psychoactive substances among young people, mostly cannabis (marijuana and hash), and to some extent LSD and heroin. In 1968 the Dutch authorities installed a government commission, the Baan Commission, with the purpose of studying the phenomenon and formulating policy recommendations. From the beginning, sociological views of this phenomenon have influenced the perspectives on drug use and have inspired the policy measures following from them. This influence is present in the work of the Baan Commission, and that of another commission preceding Baan, the Hulsman Commission.[8] Sociological labeling theory has been especially influential in their analyses. Following this theory, the Baan Commission stated that if society stigmatizes deviant behavior, such as drug use, the risk will arise that this behavior will intensify. This, again, will make the return to a socially accepted lifestyle more difficult. The Baan Commission explained drug use in a social context, pointing to special characteristics of the youth culture and other subcultures as important determinants of the functions of drug use.[9]

The Baan Commission's report devoted wide attention to cannabis, the illicit substance most used. It described cannabis as relatively benign with limited health risks, and not directly leading to the use of other, heavier substances. It presented a classification of different drugs on the basis of a risk scale based on medical, pharmacological, socio-scientific, and psychological data and recommended making a distinction between cannabis and those other illicit drugs that were considered an unacceptable health risk. It generated the distinction between so-called "soft drugs" (that is, cannabis), and "hard drugs" (amphetamines, heroin, cocaine, Ecstasy, LSD, and so on).

The Netherlands has not been the only country that installed a government commission to study the drug phenomenon. Other governments did the same thing: in the United Kingdom with the Advisory Committee on Drug Dependence (1969), in the United States with its National Commission on Marihuana and Drug Abuse (1972), and in Canada with the Government Commission of Inquiry into the Non-Medical Use of Drugs (1970).[10] The recommendations of the Dutch Baan commission did not differ substantially from those of the other national commissions. The Dutch case was not exceptional: a government commission was installed to study the phenomenon and like the others it recommended to decriminalize. The Dutch became a deviant case because the recommendations were readily followed by (long-term) policy measures accompanied by a formal change in strategy, while the others did not proceed in that direction. The big change in Dutch drug policy concerned the revision of the Dutch Opium Act in 1976. This revision produced a formal legal distinction between illicit drugs posing an unacceptable health risk (List I) and cannabis products (list II). Subsequently, the legal expediency principle opened up the way to decriminalize small-scale possession and sales from the coffee shops. The expediency principle does allow prosecutors in certain cases to refrain from prosecution of criminal offenses in the public interest. For cannabis it was decided by the College of Prosecutors-General that the expediency principle should be applied systematically if the quantity in possession did not exceed 30 grams, approximately 1 ounce. The reason behind it is that public health interests (the protection of the citizens) are considered more important than criminalizing citizens for the possession and/or consumption of small quantities of cannabis.[11]

At the time, the policymakers did not intend to create a system of outlets selling cannabis. However, the expediency principle offered a few youth centers the possibility to allow a "house dealer" on their premises. Such a dealer would make sure not to carry more than the "allowed" decriminalized quantity of 30 grams. This system of house dealers opened the way to a new type of selling outlets, the so-called coffee shops, which also started selling cannabis in small quantities, also from a stock not exceeding 30 grams.

Finally, two more factors should be mentioned as having influenced the direction of Dutch drug policy. One is the strong libertarian tradition in the Netherlands. In Dutch practice this has included a strong notion of individual freedom. The other is the critical attitude toward the use of penal law as a way to solve social problems. To arrest and punish people, and burden them with a criminal record, was considered more harmful than the illegal act of possessing drugs in small quantities. The same effort to decriminalize was applied to other illicit substances as well. The College of Prosecutors-General defined the subsequent decriminalized quantities: for heroin and cocaine this is half a gram, for LSD one trip, and for amphetamines and Ecstasy one tablet.

The need to separate the markets of cannabis on the one hand, and those of other, more dangerous drugs on the other, has been the main argument in defense of the small-scale sale of cannabis in coffee shops. Allowing people to buy and use cannabis in specific outlets where no other illicit drugs would be allowed would prevent consumers from easily entering into contact with these other drugs.

Since the early 1970s, Dutch drug policy has been defined as a health-oriented policy. The emphasis has been on the health aspects, not on law enforcement. Even though Dutch drug policy, like most national responses toward the drug problem, is a combination of health and law enforcement, in the Dutch case the health aspects are clearly emphasized. This also means that the Ministry of Health is the primary agency responsible for dealing with drug problems. Different ministries are responsible for aspects of drugs policy, but the Ministry of Health is responsible for their coordination.

The Dutch system has a strong public health approach with an important role of health care at the local level, a system that goes back to the early twentieth century. This system has been very effective in identifying certain health problems or threats related to drug use, and in defining workable solutions. When in the 1970s some heroin users started developing drug related problems, local health authorities took action. They introduced methadone programs and started a needle exchange to prevent the spread of AIDS, all under the banner of harm reduction.[12]

Dutch Drug Policy Debates

The use of hard drugs such as heroin and crack-cocaine and the accompanying marginalized lifestyles may be socially and medically damaging for the individuals concerned, but it has not become a public health problem. Heroin arrived on the Dutch market in the early 1970s. From the beginning until the mid 1990s, drug addiction concerned in almost all cases heroin, in some cases amphetamines or cocaine. The number of heroin addicts increased from ten thousand in 1977 to thirty thousand in 1983. Since then, their numbers have been stable, with probably some decrease in the last few years. The number of problematic users or drug addicts is currently estimated to be around twenty-five thousand. Through the years, their mean age has increased (thirty-nine years in 1997). The influx of young users is low. The general picture is one of a relatively stable, aging population of heroin addicts with a low incidence of new cases and a low mortality rate from infectious diseases, such as AIDS. In the Netherlands no proof can be found that would support the stepping stone hypothesis, according to which cannabis users would progress toward the use of hard drugs such as heroin or cocaine.

A new development since the mid-1990s concerns the increased use of crack-cocaine among hard-core drug addicts, most of them users of heroin. Before, cocaine was often used as a side substance accompanying the more dominant heroin. Now heroin has become the side substance to the more dominant cocaine. The increased use of crack-cocaine can also be noted in other European countries. In the United States, this development occurred a decade earlier. As in the United States, the crack phenomenon in the Netherlands is related to social marginalization.[13] Considering the U.S. experience with crack-cocaine, and the decrease in its popularity to the advantage of more "classic" heroin, the role of crack-cocaine in the Dutch hard-core drug scene may also be assumed to be a temporary phenomenon.

In 1995, the government presented a report that included an evaluation of twenty-five years of Dutch drug policy. The report led to some aspects—already existing in practice—becoming officially regulated, while other aspects of the drug policy became more repressive. The new policy toward the use of heroin reflects this combination of regulation and repression. Also in 1995, the government decided to start an experiment with the legal prescription of heroin to chronic long-term users who had tried kicking the habit several times in their long career of heroin use. It was first decided to start a pilot project in the cities of Amsterdam and Rotterdam in which fifty heroin users would participate. If the pilot were positively evaluated, the project would be extended to include some six hundred to seven hundred users. In the late 1990s, the pilot project was positively evaluated and it was gradually extended to other cities with more users participating.[14]

At the same time, the policy toward heroin users has become more repressive, with a shift of focus toward the reduction of nuisance. For those drug addicts committing many petty crimes, a new penal measure of compulsory treatment has been introduced. Hence, the new policy measures include on the one hand an extension of the treatment system of medically prescribed heroin, while on the other hand becoming less tolerant and more repressive toward those heroin users who are causing nuisance and committing petty crimes.

The most prominent issue in the Dutch drug policy debates over the last years has been the semilegal status of cannabis and coffee shops. Before the 1995 governmental debate it was thought by many that the government would proceed with the cannabis policy and put an end to the ambiguous situation concerning the coffee shops, which are allowed to sell to consumers, but where the trade to provision them remains formally illegal. The original intention of the government in 1995 was to investigate the possibility of resolving this ambiguity by allowing a legal supply of cannabis to coffee shops. This plan met with harsh criticism from other European Union member states, led by France. Eventually a compromise was reached through which the coffee shops would be subjected to a licensing system and would have a more formal and clear structure. Most of the hash and marijuana sold in coffee shops is imported: hash from Lebanon, Morocco, and India or Afghanistan, and marijuana from Jamaica, Colombia, and Thailand. Gradually, however, Dutch homegrown marijuana, usually grown by using hydroponic techniques, has managed to get a large slice of the market. Originally supply was organized by small-scale cultivation. However, larger criminal organizations have increasingly taken control in this area, presenting a new challenge to law enforcement.

Conclusion

The developments in European drug policy have been showing decreasing support for the traditional punitive way to deal with illicit drugs in favor of a more pragmatic and lenient approach. Traditionally, the drug problem has been viewed as a criminal problem. At present, however, the dominant view of the countries of the European Union is that drug use is primarily a health issue. Law enforcement practices have changed, even though most European Union member states have not modified their former drug legislation.

The question of whether a truly European drug policy will materialize in the future is hard to answer. For the time being, the member states have been pursuing policies of their own. In drugs, as well as in other policy areas, forging agreements and achieving harmonization have remained complicated procedures. Political debates often fail to address the issue of exactly what should be harmonized. After all, the drug policy has dimensions that need to be discussed in all three pillars. This makes it very difficult to achieve uniformity. Questions of principle add to the problem. Harmonization has proven to be a politically sensitive issue involving national cultures and traditions, including the role of health care, the role of the police, and the criminal law system, the acceptance of legal drugs and medicine in society, and the way in which a society responds to deviant behavior. A new wind is blowing in the countries of the European Union in the area of drug policy. Instead of insisting that drug use should be fought and drugs be banned from society, the increasingly popular harm reduction paradigm maintains that it is better to "live with" drugs at the least social and medical costs. The emergence of harm reduction as an acceptable European model has meant a considerable policy change from the past. The use of certain illicit drugs has now been accepted as a fact of life for policymakers. However, a general reconsideration of the illegal status of all drugs is not contemplated, although cannabis use is being decriminalized and the use and possession of small quantities of heroin and cocaine have met a more tolerant stance. The situation that has arisen is not always consistent. The European Union refers to the UN drug conventions as the common basis for EU drug policy. These conventions state that all cultivation, trade, and possession of illicit drugs for other than medical and scientific purposes are not allowed. In practice, however, and especially at the local level, the countries of the European Union have been increasingly distancing themselves from this UN policy line. At the international level, the European Union has also been distancing itself from the U.S. strategy with its emphasis on repression and the use of military means.[15]

Future developments in the European Union's drug policy will depend on policy developments at the local level in the member states. This is not to say that everyday practice will automatically be translated into policy in Brussels. In the long term, however, solutions adopted in the member states are bound to influence the general policy of the European Union. This is conditional, of course, on agreements between member states—especially in the third pillar—and the space left to countries to experiment and find out which approach works best.

Within the European context, the Netherlands presents an interesting case. It has experimented with a pragmatic and liberal drug policy since the 1970s. In hindsight, the country has been a trailblazer for the other countries in the European Union. In recent days, however, Dutch drug policy has become much less a European or international exception. Paradoxically, the changes in the European Union have been such that Sweden has become a deviant case, as the only European member state that persists in the goal of a drug-free society, resisting any formal harm reduction measures.

Notes

1. "Reform of United Nation Drug Conventions on the Agenda," Amsterdam, Transnational Institute press release, May 23, 2002.

2. "Change of Policy Asked For," *The Guardian,* May 3, 2002.

3. Cf. Tim Boekhout van Solinge, *Drugs and Decision-making in the European Union* (Amsterdam: CEDRO/Mets and Schilt, 2002), passim.

4. Ibid.

5. Ibid. These amounts do not represent the entire budget on counter-narcotics action, as other budget lines are operating in addition to those discussed here.

6. Martin Jelsma, *European Parliament Rejects Plan Colombia* (Amsterdam: Transnational Institute, 2001), passim.

7. *European Parliament Resolution,* no. B-5–0087/2001, February 1, 2001.

8. The Baan Commission's report was presented to the minister of health in February 1972. The work of the Baan Commission and the Hulsman Commission has been analyzed in Peter D. A. Cohen, "The Case of the Two Dutch Drug Policy Commissions: An Exercise in Harm Reduction, 1968–1976" (paper presented at the 5th International Conference on the Reduction of Drug-Related Harm, Toronto, March 1994). Also, Tim Boekhout van Solinge, "Dutch Drug Policy in a European Context," *Journal of Drug Issues* 29, no. 3 (1999), 511–28.

9. Baan Commission's report.

10. Advisory Committee on Drug Dependence, *Cannabis* (London: Her Majesty's Stationary Office, 1969); National Commission on Marihuana and Drug Abuse, *Marihuana: A Signal of Misunderstanding* (Washington, D.C.: U.S. Government Printing Office, 1972); Canadian Government Commission of Inquiry, *The Non-Medical Use of Drugs* (Ottawa: Information Canada, 1970); see also Lynn Zimmer and John P. Morgan, *Marihuana Myths, Marihuana Facts* (New York: The Lindesmith Center, 1997).

11. Wim van den Brink, Vincent M. Hendriks, and Jan van Ree, "Medical Co-prescription of Heroin to Chronic, Treatment-Resistant Methadone Patients in the Netherlands," *Journal of Drug Issues* 29, no. 3 (1999), 587–607.

12. Ibid.

13. Craig Reinarman and Harry G. Levine, eds., *Crack in America: Demon Drugs and Social Justice* (Berkeley: University of California Press, 1997), passim.

14. For details concerning these experiments, see Van den Brink et al., "Medical Co-prescription of Heroin," passim.

15. "Europe Moves Drug War from Prisons to Clinics," *Washington Post,* May 2, 2002.

V

Drugs, Transnational Crime, and International Security

14

Globalization and Transnational Organized Crime

The Russian Mafia in Latin America and the Caribbean

Bruce Michael Bagley

"Russian organized crime groups pose a unique law enforcement challenge, jeopardizing public safety throughout the world through their transnational criminal enterprises. Worldwide money-laundering activity from Cyprus to the Cayman Islands and from Vanuatu in the Pacific to Venezuela; the assassination of American businessman Paul Tatum in Moscow; financial scams in New York; car theft rings in Europe; narcotics trafficking and money-laundering alliances with Colombian and Nigerian drug lords and the Italian mafia represent but a few of the tentacles extended by Russian organized crime networks throughout the world. Currently 200 large Eurasian criminal organizations operate worldwide and have formed alliances with their criminal counterparts in 50 countries (including 26 United States cities)."[1]

In the post–Cold War period, Russian transnational organized crime has become a new phenomenon, rapidly expanding its activities throughout the global system. Latin America and the Caribbean have become one of its areas of operation. Although the evidence currently available in the public realm is primarily journalistic and often anecdotal, it is, despite these limitations, sufficient to support the conclusion that the linkages or "strategic alliances" between various Russian organized crime groups and major transnational criminal organizations in Latin America and the Caribbean in 2001 are already substantial and expanding rapidly. Moreover, it raises the specter that, at least in some key countries in the region (for example, Colombia, Mexico, and Brazil), the alliances between home-grown and Russian criminal organizations may provide domestic criminal and/or guerrilla groups with access to the illicit international markets, money-laundering facilities, and illegal arms sources that could convert them into major impediments to economic growth and serious threats to democratic consolidation and long-term stability at home.

Organized crime[2] flourishes best in the contexts provided by weak states.[3] In the wake of the complete collapse of the Soviet Empire in 1991, the new Russian state that assumed power in Moscow was from the outset a weak state and its institutional weakness led Russia, along with most of the other fourteen independent states that emerged out of the former Soviet Union (for example, the Ukraine, Belarus, Georgia, Estonia, Latvia, Lithuania, Armenia, Azerbaijan, Tajikistan and Kazakhstan), to become hotbeds of organized crime over the decade of the 1990s.[4]

Weak States and Organized Crime

The longstanding institutional weaknesses of most states in Latin America and the Caribbean, in combination with the existence of a highly lucrative underground drug trade in the Western hemisphere, made the countries in that corner of the world system especially attractive targets for Russian transnational criminal enterprises. The lack of transparency and effective state monitoring in the banking systems of many Latin American and Caribbean nations left them particularly vulnerable to penetration by Russian money launderers. Their corrupt and ineffective law enforcement institutions and judicial systems allowed Russian crime groups to operate outside of the law with virtual impunity. Indeed, the dubious practice of a number of the smaller states in the region (e.g., Dominica, Panama, Uruguay, and Paraguay) of "selling" citizenship literally provided an open invitation to Russian crime groups to establish themselves in the hemisphere. As Tom Farer notes, when states are weak, but act as if they were strong, "spewing out laws and regulations purporting to regulate, inhibit, and tax private activity" without the will or capacity to enforce the law, they inevitably create spaces or niches between reality and legality that can be and frequently are exploited by organized crime.[5]

The ongoing processes of globalization unquestionably facilitated the transnationalization of Russian mafia activities over the last decade. In broad strokes, globalization refers to the "shrinkage" of distance on a global scale through the emergence and thickening of "nets of connections"—economic, technological, social, political, and environmental.[6] Of course, as many skeptics have noted, the recent transformations in the world system are by no means completely new.[7] What is novel about them in the contemporary period are their extensity, intensity, velocity, and impact on states and societies around the globe.[8] Russian transnational criminal organizations (like other international criminal and terrorist networks) have been able to exploit the increased ease of international travel, the liberalization of emigration policies, the expansion of international trade, the spread of high technology communications systems, and the underregulation of international financial networks (via sophisticated money-laundering techniques) to extend their criminal enterprises well beyond the borders of their own country.[9]

For historically weak states such as those in Latin America and the Caribbean, their accelerating insertion into the global economy over the last several decades, with particular intensity in the post–Cold War era, has generally required painful fiscal austerity measures on the part of national governments and a severe "downsizing" of the state in general. Under the banners of the "Washington consensus" and neoliberal market reforms, state penetrative, extractive, and regulatory capacities throughout the region, which were never particularly strong, suffered dramatic erosion in the aftermath of the 1982 regional debt crisis. As a result, state authorities in the 1990s often found themselves bereft of the financial and institutional resources essential for combating the rise and expansion of transnational organized criminal activity within their national territories. Law enforcement agencies throughout Latin America and the Caribbean remain woefully inadequate, underfunded, and corrupt. Courts and prison systems are outdated and overwhelmed. And high-level political corruption has continued, or even worsened in many cases, despite the neoliberal belief that wholesale liberalization would—once the initial transition phase had been complete—"reduce the range of illicit and concealed profit opportunities available to the holders of political power."[10] Ill prepared as they were in the past to combat transnational organized crime, as a result of almost two decades of neoliberal reforms most states in the region are even less capable today.

The tendency of neoliberal reforms to exacerbate the gap between rich and poor in many Latin American and Caribbean countries and to heighten the poverty and misery of those subordinate classes not effectively linked to export sectors—the principal "losers" in the processes of globalization—quite predictably has generated rising resistance to globalization among the disadvantaged and intensified popular demands for policy reforms and fuller democratization across the region. Yet, in the context of globalization, the scope of autonomous state action in most developing countries is significantly constrained and ameliorative policies are often viewed as inefficient and unacceptable. Confronted with the overwhelming power of globalized production and international finance, including heavy international debt burdens, most Latin American and Caribbean political elites have been reduced to negotiating from positions of weakness the terms of their progressive national integration into the global capitalist system. Unable to oppose stronger transnational forces and unwilling to adopt more flexible systems of democratic political representation designed to modernize and legitimate the state, governmental and party elites have generally striven, instead, to preserve the fundamental structures of power and domination intact while resisting grass-roots pressures for greater socioeconomic equality and democracy via selective state cooptation (to restrict mounting dissent) and systematic state coercion (to repress outbreaks of protest and praetorianism).[11]

In most of Latin America and the Caribbean, the dynamics of globalization over the last two decades have resulted in almost ideal conditions for the rapid penetration and spread of transnational organized crime. On the one hand, the hundreds of millions of under- or unemployed poor provide a vast seething cauldron in which criminality of all sorts can and does incubate and multiply.[12] Indeed, engagement in criminal activities, including forms of organized crime, on the part of many of the disadvantaged in the region can be seen as a rational survival strategy in the face of otherwise severely limited life opportunities. On the other hand, the weak, often corrupt, and frequently illegitimate states typical throughout the hemisphere have routinely proven unable to address adequately the desperate needs of these "marginalized" segments of their populations or to prevent the spread of common criminality. They have been even less able to halt the rise or impede the spread of more sophisticated and technologically adept transnational organized crime.[13]

The Rise of Russian Organized Crime

While there were preliminary indications of the rise of organized crime in the former Soviet Union by the early 1970s (for example, the infamous Odessa gang and the burgeoning "shadow" economy), the organizations that today are generically known as the Russian *mafiya* (mafia) or Russian organized crime first began to appear in the mid-1980s in the context of the last Soviet president's—Mikhail Gorbachev's—famous program of economic opening known as *perestroika* (restructuring). *Perestroika* not only paved the way for the establishment of legal private enterprise in the Soviet Union, it also created new opportunities for criminal activity of all sorts as the Soviet grip on the economy weakened. Emergent Soviet criminal gangs gained added impetus during this initial period of restructuring from the parallel policy of *glasnost* (openness), which was first advanced by Gorbachev's chief political adviser, Alexander Yakolev, and which rapidly undercut Communist Party authority and centralized state control over the political process. Misguided economic polices calling for use of the "initiative and drive" of the black market or "shadow" economy put forward by key Gorbachev advisers such as Stanislav Shatalin and Abel AgAnbegyan further stimulated the growth of criminality during Gorbachev's final years in office.

The Soviet leadership failed to foresee clearly the consequences of these reforms and, thus, unintentionally created the "breeding grounds" for the rise of a new wave of organized crime in the former Soviet Union. The early beneficiaries of Gorbachev's reforms were generally small criminal gangs and petty smugglers who, within a few years, managed to develop vast, although generally informal, criminal networks. Among the most lucrative of the pioneering criminal ventures launched by the new Russian mafiosos were extortion schemes or "protection" rackets directed at the country's emergent capitalist class or "new rich" in which "taxes" were collected in exchange for protection from other criminal gangs, for help in getting rid of unwanted competitors, and for assistance in collecting on bad debts. The theft and clandestine sale of state property also quickly became a major Russian mafia enterprise.[14] By 1991, despite the frenetic efforts of Gorbachev and his fellow Communist Party reformers to regulate their country's economic and political opening through legislative reforms, the Soviet state effectively lost control of the process and ultimately disintegrated. Set against a backdrop of historically weak legal institutions and declining Soviet administrative authority, the opening of the Soviet economy proved to be an essentially chaotic process. What limited order was achieved during the period of transition came not from the state, but rather from a group of "coordinators" or "godfathers"—often known as the thieves-in-law—who ensured the stability of the emergent system of organized criminality and, to a degree, coordinated the diverse elements of it. Among the key services the thieves-in-law provided were protection of pseudo-businessmen from extortion by rival gangsters, division of spheres of influence among rapidly proliferating mafia organizations, assistance to criminals in the disposal of stolen state property and the laundering of the proceeds, and the facilitation of contacts between criminal bosses and corrupt officials in the "new" Russia. Ten years after the collapse of the Soviet Union, the thieves-in-law continue to operate in Russia and several other post-Soviet independent states in eastern Europe, making organized criminal activity in much of the region virtually untouchable by domestic or international law enforcement.[15]

Western donor nations generally and the United States specifically may have contributed indirectly to undermining or weakening the Russian state and others in eastern and central Europe in the 1990s through their misdirected aid policies. Fearing that Communist Party bureaucratic holdovers might seize control of, or improperly divert, Western assistance flows into Russia and other former Soviet bloc countries, whenever possible most international donors channeled their assistance through nongovernmental organizations (NGOs) rather than through existing state institutions. The intent was to help strengthen the region's embryonic civil societies in the post-Soviet period while undercutting entrenched and corrupt bureaucratic authorities. Good intentions notwithstanding, such policies, in practice, did not prevent Western aid resources from being siphoned off by the region's proliferating organized crime groups and may even have facilitated criminal enterprises of various sorts by circumventing state controls altogether. Simultaneously, such aid practices unquestionably further reduced the authority and impact of already debilitated state institutions while limiting international donors' leverage in support of effective institutional reforms.[16]

While recognizing the significance and impact of Russian organized crime both within contemporary Russia and abroad, analysts such as Rensselaer Lee caution observers not to "inflate" the extent of the Russian mafia's activities disproportionately: "If organized crime is as ubiquitous as these writers suggest, the concept loses much of its organizational shape. Instead of defining violent and lawless subgroups, it begins to encompass much of the Russian state and society. For example, the so-called shadow economy in Russia is indeed large, accounting for some twenty to forty percent of the country's gross domestic product, according to different estimates. Yet most of this share consists of legal production and commercial activity unregistered and hence untaxed rather than traditional mafiya pursuits (drugs, extortion, weapons trafficking, and the like)."[17]

Lee also points out that Russian organized crime is neither monolithic nor necessarily hierarchical, especially abroad. Indeed, "much of the heavy lifting in international illegal commerce, from heroin trafficking to the smuggling of radioactive material and counterfeit money, is done by ad hoc criminal coalitions with few apparent resources, little formal structure, and uncertain connections with the political or official upperworld. Such groups commonly coalesce for one or two deals, divide up the proceeds and then disband."[18] The United States Government Interagency Working Group on international crime observes that over the latter 1990s the traditional domination of the "thieves-in-law" or "godfathers" of Russian crime gradually began to yield to a new breed of more "flamboyant, aggressive and politically savvy . . . Russian criminals . . . well versed in modern technology and business practices that allow them to operate efficiently across international borders."[19] Perhaps the most powerful of this new breed of Russian crime syndicates in terms of wealth, influence, and financial control is the Solntsevo group known as Solntsevskaya. It dominates Moscow's criminal underworld—including the drug market—and is reputed to have extensive worldwide operations involving arms and narcotics trafficking and money-laundering operations.[20] These overseas contacts and alliances do not, however, signal the emergence of a vast, centrally directed Russian underworld empire. Rather most Russian international criminal networks appear to be made up of "alliances of convenience" that are temporary and impermanent, not long-term and strategic.[21]

With the transition from the presidency of Boris Yeltsin to that of Vladimir Putin in 1999–2000, the political pendulum in Russia may have begun to swing back toward the construction of a stronger Russian state, one perhaps more authoritarian than democratic.[22] Public opinion in Russia has exhibited overwhelming concern in recent years with the construction of a "strong state" capable of reining in rampant lawlessness and corruption. Putin himself has repeatedly referred to the need for imposing "the dictatorship of law." Skeptical observers, however, note that President Putin himself is the product of the very oligarchical system created under Yeltsin and that he has publicly rejected the popular idea of investigating the results of Russia's highly questionable privatizations of former state-owned enterprises during the 1990s for legal improprieties, cronyism, and corruption. If, as Margaret Beare emphasizes, "the meaning of the 'dictatorship of law' should turn out to be protection of the gains of the beneficiaries of the legal vacuum, then the main sources of Russian organized crime and corruption are likely to remain unaffected."[23]

As of the late 1990s, the Organized Crime Control Department of the Russian Federation Ministry of Interior (MVD) reported that more than 8,000 Russian/eastern European/Eurasian criminal groups and some 750–800 thieves-in-law made up the so-called "Russian *mafiya*." As of 2001, between 200 and 300 of these Russian mafia groups (varying in size from a few dozen to several hundred members) operated transnationally, many in the Western Hemisphere. In addition, at least 150 ethnic-oriented Russian criminal groups had also been identified, including Chechens, Georgians, Armenians, and Russian-Koreans, of which at least 25 were active in various parts of the United States, the Caribbean, and Latin America.[24]

From a geostrategic perspective, the international expansion of Russian organized crime during the 1990s essentially reflected a three-pronged pattern. The first prong focused on the newly independent states of the former Soviet Union, or what the Russians call their "near abroad." The remnants of Soviet infrastructure and networks provided an ideal "highway for crime" that allowed easy access to new markets outside of Russia proper via linkages with local former KGB operatives and other corrupt members of the former regime. Many previously honest Soviet-era officials also proved open to *mafiya* "bribe or barter" deals owing to their precipitous and painful loss of power, prestige, and income. Beyond establishing a foothold in these new markets, a second attraction of expansion into the near abroad was that it permitted easy access to western Europe and the European Union through eastern and central Europe. It also facilitated Russian mafia access to the conflict-ridden Balkans, south into the Caucasus and onto Iran, Turkey, and Iraq, and, perhaps most important of all, into central Asia with its linkages to sources of heroin in Afghanistan and Pakistan.[25]

Russian criminal penetration throughout the near abroad advanced rapidly over the decade, literally overwhelming these newly created states and their embryonic law enforcement institutions. As of the early 2000s, however, growing awareness of the severity of the threat that mafia corruption and criminality had come to pose to institutional viability and state security led governmental authorities across the region to embark on aggressive campaigns against organized crime and attendant bureaucratic and political corruption. How successful these efforts will ultimately prove to be remains very much an open question.[26]

A second, parallel prong or target of the Russian mafia's expansion abroad was Asia. In the early 1990s various Russian mafia groups sought to forge arrangements or alliances with Chinese "triads" both on the mainland (specifically Shanghai) and in Macao, Hong Kong, and even Malaysia.[27] Using the port of Vladivostock as their base of operations and exploiting contacts among corrupt Russian state officials *(apparatchiks)* and naval officers stationed there, these mafia groups strove to take advantage of the growing legal shipping trade between this key Russian port and the lucrative Chinese and Korean markets. Contrary to expectations, however, the Asian gambit did not prove as profitable as initially anticipated. This was due in part to failure of Sino-Russian and Russian-Korean trade to grow as rapidly as first hoped. The Russian mafias also found working with their Chinese criminal counterparts more difficult than they had initially assumed. The Chinese gangs were both wary of the Russians and skeptical of the potential benefits of working with them. In practice, the entrenched and powerful Chinese triads kept to themselves. Close ties with corrupt Chinese Communist Party officialdom and deep involvement with the operations of the Chinese military (the Peoples' Liberation Army, or PLA) and its vast network of enterprises effectively negated any real possibilities for close collaboration between the Russian and Chinese mafias, at least in the medium-term.[28]

The third prong of the Russian mafia's strategy of expansion abroad over the 1990s focused on penetration of the Western Hemisphere, initially the United States and Canada. By the mid-1990s, frustrated by the disappointing results of their Asian strategy, Russian organized crime groups became increasingly interested in and focused on new opportunities for criminal activity in Latin America and the Caribbean. Specifically, they realized that the region offered open markets for Russian and Soviet-bloc arms in exchange for drugs to be smuggled back to Europe and Russia and easy access to global financial networks for money-laundering purposes. Moreover, the region's relatively weak states and deeply imbedded "culture of corruption" provided a familiar environment reminiscent of the one in post-Soviet Russia in which Russian criminal organizations had originally arisen and flourished. In effect, the Russian mafia adapted the previous Soviet-era tactics of forging ties in the Americas via attractive offers of cheap weapons and "technical assistance." This time around, however, the technical assistance proffered was in the realm of money laundering rather than in the use of sophisticated Soviet weaponry.

Russian Mafia Activities in Latin America and the Caribbean

Given their common interests in illicit profits and avoidance of national and international law enforcement authorities, there is a "natural" tendency for Russian (or Italian, Asian, or North American) criminal organizations to forge alliances or partnerships with their South American and Caribbean counterparts when operating in the region. Such links allow the Russians, along with other transnational crime groups, to carry out criminal activities in the region with a relatively low profile, to avoid detection by authorities, and to reduce their risks of arrest, infiltration, and loss of profits.

According to Interpol, in Latin America and the Caribbean to date the Russian mafia has been primarily attracted to and involved in activities such as drug trafficking, money laundering, and arms trafficking.[29] Although Russia and eastern/central Europe only account for approximately 10 percent of world drug sales (approximately 15 billion U.S. dollars total), the market there is growing fast and the profits are already huge.[30] The drug market is even bigger in western Europe (perhaps 50–60 billion U.S. dollars), where the Russians are also deeply engaged. Closely linked to their drug smuggling activities is their growing involvement in arms trafficking into Latin America, often in arms-for-drugs deals with drug-trafficking rings (or cartels) and guerrilla organizations. Finally, in light of weak state enforcement and regulatory capabilities throughout the former Soviet Union and the incipient institutionalization of the financial and banking systems in Russia and most of eastern Europe, Russian criminal organizations, working under the sponsorship and protection of thieves-in-law, have been able to offer relatively low-risk money-laundering services to a variety of South American drug traffickers, sometimes charging as much as 30 percent of the proceeds.[31]

Alongside these three core criminal activities, there is also some (admittedly spotty) evidence of expanding Russian involvement with other Latin American criminal enterprises such as prostitution, international traffic in women, child pornography, usury, extortion, kidnapping, credit card fraud, computer fraud, counterfeiting, and auto theft, to mention only the most prominent. The actual extent of Russian *mafiya* involvement in such criminal activities in Latin America is, of course, difficult to specify with precision and undoubtedly varies from country to country. The sections that follow provide summary descriptions of the principal features of Russian criminal activity in the major countries and subregions of Latin America and the Caribbean.

Mexico

Interpol reports indicate that a variety of Russian criminal organizations, operating through literally "hundreds" of small cells, are engaged in a wide range of illegal activities in Mexico. Russian mafia groups such as the Poldolskaya, Mazukinskaya, Tambovskaya, and Izamailovskaya, all linked to one of Russia's major transnational criminal organizations—Vory versus Zakone (or "Ladrones de la Ley" [Thieves of the Law])—are among the most active. The Moscow-based Solntsevskaya gang is also reported to be present in Mexico as are other mafia gangs from Chechnya, Georgia, Armenia, Lithuania, Poland, Croatia, Serbia, Hungary, Albania, and Rumania. Their major activities include drug and arms trafficking, money laundering, prostitution, traffic in women from eastern and central Europe and Russia, emigrant smuggling, kidnapping, and credit card fraud.[32]

Linkages with one or more of the seven principal Mexican criminal organizations or cartels operating in the country allow these Russian gangs to obtain drugs (especially cocaine, heroin, and methamphetamines) at low prices and under relatively secure circumstances (often in resorts, hotels, or houses protected and owned by their Mexican associates). Over the past five years, Pacific Ocean smuggling routes have increasingly supplanted the more closely monitored and congested Caribbean as the cocaine traffickers' most lucrative smuggling option. More than half of all the cocaine entering the United States is now believed to come up the Pacific side. Seizures of South American cocaine bound for Mexico and the United States more than doubled between 1999 and 2000 alone. This upsurge in confiscations was both a function of the overall increase in drug flows through the eastern Pacific, especially from Colombia, and a result of a major redeployment of the U.S. Coast Guard's Pacific Coast forces away from their traditional mission of fisheries enforcement to support for U.S. military counterdrug operations. It also reflects the greater cooperation and information sharing between U.S. law enforcement and the Mexican navy evident in the last two years.[33]

Nonetheless, drug traffickers' techniques in the Pacific are even more challenging to law enforcement authorities than those traditionally employed in the Caribbean. First, the Pacific is open ocean and, hence, comparatively much more difficult to patrol than the smaller and more confined Caribbean. Second, cocaine in the Caribbean is usually transported in open speedboats that are relatively easy to detect because of their oversized engines and extra fuel containers. In the Pacific, in contrast, cocaine is commonly hidden in the hulls of fishing boats or on board huge container ships that are inherently more difficult to identify and search.[34]

A May 3, 2001, U.S. Coast Guard seizure (off the Pacific coast 1,000 kilometers south of Acapulco and 1,500 miles south of San Diego) of a Russian/Ukranian-manned, 152-foot, Belize-flagged fishing trawler named the *Svesda Maru* loaded with 12 tons of Colombian cocaine provided dramatic new evidence of Russian mafia involvement in drug trafficking in Mexico.[35]

Suspecting that the boat may have been involved in drug smuggling, U.S. authorities boarded the vessel on April 28 and spent some five days looking for contraband. The 12 tons of cocaine were eventually found in the ship's fuel tanks after a U.S. Coast Guard structural engineer performed "soundings" of various cavities in the vessel. It proved to be the largest cocaine seizure in U.S. maritime history.[36] Authorities of the United maintain that the crew, comprised of eight Ukrainians and two Russians, must have had the permission of the Tijuana cartel (led by the infamous Arellano Felix clan) to ship so much cocaine to the West Coast of the United States.[37] According to San Diego-based DEA agent Errol Chavez, the nationalities of the *Svesda Maru* crew are an "indication that there is direct involvement or some kind of association between Russian organized crime and members of the Arellano Felix organization."[38] Previous revelations in November 2000 by the Mexican attorney general's office to the effect that Mexican authorities had uncovered proof that Tijuana's Arellano Felix gang had provided Russian military hardware and cash to Colombia's FARC guerrillas in exchange for large shipments of cocaine also pointed to a pattern of deepening Russian mafia involvement in the Colombian-Mexican drug connection.[39]

Officials in Southern California reportedly suspect the Russian and Ukrainian crew of the *Svesda Maru* of belonging to a Russian organized crime syndicate based in Los Angeles, where between six hundred and eight hundred known Russian crime figures live, mostly in the North and West Hollywood areas. A 1999 California Department of Justice report found that Russian crime groups based in Los Angeles had formed alliances with La Cosa Nostra in North America, Colombian cartels in South America, and the Sicilian mafia in Europe.[40] Prior to this May 2001 seizure, however, Mexican authorities claimed that Amado Carillo Fuentes (alias "El Senor de los Cielos" or "Lord of the Skies") of the Juarez cartel had forged the only known Mexican-Russian criminal alliance just prior to his death in 1997.[41]

The vast bulk of the South American cocaine that transits through Mexico is unquestionably destined for the U.S. market. Russian organized crime has not, however, been a major player in illicit cocaine trafficking into the United States, at least to date. Russian involvement in cocaine smuggling through Mexico appears to be destined principally toward western European, Russian, and eastern European markets. Multiple drug smuggling routes out of Mexico are available to Russian gangs. One well-known route takes drugs from Mexico in cargo ships across the Pacific to the port of Vladivostock in the Russian Far East and thence into the Russian interior. A second Pacific route ships drugs down the west coast of South America, around the Cape of Good Hope, and then across the south Atlantic to European or Russian ports (known by Russians as the western route). A third route carries Russian drug shipments in vessels embarking from Mexico's east coast out through the

Gulf of Mexico and the Caribbean Sea across the Atlantic to ports in Spain, Portugal, Sicily, and the Baltic Sea (the Baltic route). There is little reason to believe that Russian criminal groups have sought to smuggle cocaine destined for European or Russian/east European markets through U.S. territory, basically because the costs of doing so are prohibitive and the risks of running afoul of U.S. law enforcement authorities quite high.

Central America

The seven relatively small transit countries of Central America (with the exception of Panama) until recently received far less attention from Russian mafia organizations than Mexico. Nonetheless, in 2001 the two large cocaine seizures on ships in the eastern Pacific off Central America manned by mixed crews of Russian, Ukrainians, Salvadorans, and Nicaraguans led authorities throughout the isthmus to sound the alert. Indeed, in March 2001 Interpol warned that a number of citizens of the former Soviet Union linked to organized crime had taken up residence in various countries in the subregion. As drug trafficking along the Pacific coast between Colombia and Mexico intensifies, many observers fear that Russian organized crime will become increasingly active throughout Central America as well.[42]

In the early 2000s, conditions in Central America were particularly conducive to the expansion of Russian and other types of international organized crime owing to the widespread poverty in the subregion (up to three-fourths of the roughly 30 million Central Americans live on less than two dollars per day) and the weakness and illegitimacy of political institutions throughout the isthmus. Drug trafficking is Central America's most profitable criminal enterprise. In 2000 the DEA reported that of the estimated 645 metric tons of cocaine smuggled into the United States some 425 metric tons passed through the Central America-Mexican corridor.[43] This huge volume of Colombian (and to a lesser extent Peruvian) cocaine shipped through the subregion has fueled an explosion of some 2,000 youth gangs and related gang violence in recent years, especially in Nicaragua, Honduras, El Salvador, and Guatemala.[44] The combined gang membership in these four counties is estimated at about 400,000 youths, composed primarily of males between twelve and twenty-four years old. Honduran police, for example, have confirmed the existence of 489 different youth gangs and Guatemalan officials have identified some 500 in their country with more than 100,000 active members in all. Many of these gangs, or *maras* as they are known in the subregion, are led by youths or adults who previously belonged to gangs in the United States but were convicted of felonies and deported back to Central America. A number of these gangs, such as El Salvador's ruthless and widely feared Mara Salvatrucha, also have branches in major American cities, engage in drug and arms trafficking, and carry out contract murders for Mexican and Colombian drug organizations.[45]

These linkages with Colombian and Mexican cartels have allowed the Central American gangs to upgrade their arsenals and build more sophisticated criminal organizations than ever before. Their ties to organized crime in U.S. cities, along with their links to Mexican and Colombian cartels, have facilitated their growing contacts with Russian organized crime in recent years, especially in the areas of arms and drug trafficking and money laundering. As a result, violent local Central American gangs with international connections, financed by drug money, and equipped with Russian AK-47 assault weapons and rocket-propelled grenades, are currently challenging—and sometimes overwhelming—civilian law enforcement agencies throughout the isthmus.[46]

The governments of the subregion have attempted to contain their spiraling crime waves, but they each face serious national budgetary constraints that have (and will for the foreseeable future) limit their capacity to respond effectively. The Salvadoran and Honduran governments opted in 2000–2001 to draw on their military forces to reinforce their inadequate civilian law enforcement institutions. After a bloody prison riot in June 2001, President Portillo of Guatemala declared that his government would seek augmented security assistance from the United States, the United Kingdom, and Israel, among others. Both the Nicaraguan and Costa Rican governments have also recently pledged to crack down on criminal activity in their countries as well. As a result, civilian law enforcement throughout Central America is likely to become progressively more militarized over the next few years. However, national economies across the subregion are so hard-pressed that increased budgetary outlays on security and law enforcement will inexorably reduce social spending. Such reductions, in turn, could prove socially explosive and politically destabilizing. Moreover, heightened military involvement in the fight against drug trafficking and organized crime in the subregion could lead to the contamination and corruption of their armed forces, as it has in Mexico, Peru, Bolivia, and elsewhere in Latin America during the last two decades.[47]

Colombia, the Caribbean, and the Andean Region

Russian mafia groups operating out of Los Angeles, New York, Miami, and Puerto Rico, among other U.S. cities, have formed a variety of alliances with Colombian trafficking organizations since at least 1992 to acquire cocaine for delivery to Europe and the territories of the former Soviet Union and to provide arms to Colombian narcotraficantes and guerrilla organizations.[48] Russian organized crime groups have also opened more than a dozen banks and front companies across the Caribbean to launder hundreds of millions of dollars from drug sales and other criminal activities.[49]

Indeed, U.S. undercover operations since the mid-1990s have detected various attempts by Russian crime groups to sell Colombian drug traffickers submarines, helicopters, and surface-to-air missiles.[50] At least two Russian combat helicopters, along with quantities of small arms, were sold to the Cali cartel in the mid-1990s. In the late 1990s Russian vessels docked repeatedly at the Caribbean port of Turbo in northern Colombia to offload shipments of Russian AK-47 assault rifles and rocket-propelled grenades for the FARC guerrillas and, possibly, for right-wing paramilitary bands, in exchange for cocaine. The discovery of a partially built submarine in a suburb just outside of Bogotá in late 2000, based on Russian plans and specifications, added to speculation about a growing Russian connection with the Colombian drug trade, even though no direct involvement of Russian criminal figures in this case was ever demonstrated.[51]

The microstates of the Caribbean have proven especially attractive to Russian criminal syndicates. Already entrenched in Europe, where there is a lucrative growing market for cocaine, and in Russia and other former Soviet bloc countries, Russian criminal organizations increasingly resorted to the use of various Caribbean nations as both transit points for drugs and arms-smuggling activities and as easy-access money-laundering sites for their expanding international operations from the mid-1990s on.[52] With strict bank secrecy laws and lax financial enforcement mechanisms, such Caribbean islands as Antigua and Aruba, where Russians opened several offshore banks in the mid-1990s, offered attractive havens for laundering large sums of money from Russian mafia operations. Panama, Costa Rica, and the Cayman Islands have also served as Russian money-laundering sanctuaries as well.[53] Intensified U.S. government and international pressures on these Caribbean and Central American havens over the late 1990s and early 2000s have made operations more difficult for Russian *blanqueadores* (launderers) in recent years but have by no means halted Russian (and other international organized crime) laundering activities in the subregion altogether.[54]

Russian mafia money-laundering schemes have certainly not been limited to the Caribbean and Central America. The weakly institutionalized and poorly regulated Russian financial system is itself widely recognized as a money-laundering paradise.[55] The 10 billion dollar Bank of New York Russian money-laundering scandal that rocked the United States in 1998–1999 clearly revealed that U.S. banking institutions were not immune from penetration and manipulation by Russian crime groups either.[56]

The August 2001 indictment in western Europe of a onetime business associate of incumbent Russian president Vladimir Putin on charges of money laundering and fraud raised serious questions about Putin's earlier role in an obscure Russo-German property development company. The firm, called the St. Petersburg Real Estate Holding Company (known by its German acronym, SPAG), has not yet been charged, but European and American intelligence sources suspect it is linked to the laundering operations of Russian mobsters and Colombian drug dealers. Until he was inaugurated as Russia's president, Putin was on SPAG's advisory board and, even after becoming president, he reportedly maintained close relations with the former head of SPAG's Russian operations, Vladimir Smirnov. To date, there is no public evidence that Putin ever received any money from SPAG. Officials of the United States believe, rather, that Putin helped SPAG in the expectation of future political support from some of the company's influential Russian backers. The Putin-SPAG connection may reflect the ongoing influence of Russia's infamous criminal godfathers or thieves-in-law.[57]

Indicating a major new phase of Russian mafia involvement in the Colombian cocaine trade, during 1999–2000 a new Russian smuggling ring (linking corrupt Russian military figures, organized crime bosses, and diplomats directly with Colombia's FARC guerrillas) moved regular shipments of up to 40,000 kilograms of cocaine to the former Soviet Union in return for large shipments of Russian and eastern European weaponry. According to U.S. intelligence officials, this major Russo-Colombian smuggling operation reportedly worked as follows:

1. Russian-built IL-76 cargo planes took off from various airstrips in Russia and the Ukraine laden with anti-aircraft missiles, small arms, and ammunition.
2. The planes, roughly the size of Boeing 707s, stopped in Amman, Jordan, to refuel. There, they bypassed normal Jordanian customs with the help of corrupt foreign diplomats and bribed local officials.
3. After crossing the Atlantic, the cargo jets used remote landing strips or parachute airdrops to deliver their cargo to FARC.
4. The planes returned loaded with up to 40,000 kilos of cocaine. Some was distributed as payment for the diplomatic middlemen in Amman and sold in the Persian Gulf. The rest was flown back to the former Soviet Union for sale there or in Europe.[58]

A senior U.S. intelligence source identified Luiz Fernando Da Costa (alias Fernandinho or Fernando Beira Mar), one of Brazil's biggest drug capos until his capture by Colombian military forces in early 2001, as a key player involved in the delivery of these Russian arms shipments to FARC. Within Colombia, Fernandinho apparently coordinated the arms deliveries to FARC through his base in the town of Barrancomina, Vichada, also the headquarters for FARC's Sixteenth Front led by Tomas Medina Caracas (alias el Negro Acasio) and a major FARC-run cocaine-processing center.[59]

Da Costa also ran arms into Brazil and Colombia out of the town of Pedro Juan Caballero in Paraguay where he worked with Fuad Jamil, a Lebanese businessman operating in the same Paraguayan town. Indeed, U.S. sources claim that Hezbollah, the Iranian-backed, Lebanon-based, militant Shiite organization best known for its guerrilla activities against Israeli troops in southern Lebanon, may also have been involved. Hezbollah has roots among the Arab immigrant communities of Paraguay, Ecuador, Venezuela, and Brazil and frequently uses legitimate business operations to cover illegal arms transfers.[60] In addition to the Brazilian connection in this Russian arms-for-cocaine smuggling operation into Colombia, there was also a Peruvian connection as well. As early as May 1996, U.S. police had seized 383 pounds of Peruvian cocaine—with a U.S. street value of roughly 17 million U.S. dollars—on a Peruvian air force DC-8 transport plane en route to Russia through Miami. Thirteen Peruvian air force personnel were arrested in that incident. In July 1996, 280 pounds were found on two Peruvian navy ships, one in Vancouver, Canada, and the other in the main Peruvian port of Callao. In fact, scores of Peruvian officers were investigated, and dozens arrested, on drug and arms trafficking charges throughout the decade.[61]

According to Vladimiro Montesinos, the former director of the Peruvian National Intelligence (Servicio de Inteligencia Nacional, or SIN), on at least four separate occasions in 1999 Russian black-market arms acquired in Amman, Jordan by two Peruvian brothers of Lebanese descent (Luis Frank Ayabar Cancho and Jose Luis Ayabar Cancho) were clandestinely transported by plane from Amman to Colombia. In all, Montesinos claimed, a total of ten thousand AKM Kalashnikov automatic rifles manufactured in East Germany were delivered to FARC through this Peruvian network. The planes made refueling stops in various countries in the Caribbean, including Trinidad and Tobago, then proceeded to drop their arms shipments by parachute into guerrilla-held territory in Colombia, and finally landed in the Peruvian city of Iquitos, which is located in the upper Amazon basin.[62]

In fact, Montesinos himself was behind this arms-smuggling ring. Information about his arms-smuggling deals ultimately leaked out in July 2000 after customs officials in Trinidad and Tobago detained one of the flights following a routine inspection that uncovered Russian missiles, rifles, and parachutes instead of the medical supplies listed on the cargo manifest.[63] When first confronted with this information, the Peruvian foreign minister initially denied that the plane belonged to the Peruvian government. Several hours later, Peruvian president Alberto Fujimori rectified the foreign minister's account and officially identified the plane as Peruvian property. The plane was then released and sent on its way. However, the international scandal that followed public revelation of Montesinos's personal involvement in this illicit operation eventually led to his downfall and, ultimately, to the collapse of the Fujimori government itself in August 2000.[64]

For their part, as a result of the FARC documents captured by the Colombian military in Barrancomina during Operation Gato Negro, the Ayabar brothers stand accused by Colombian and Peruvian authorities of exchanging Russian arms for Colombian cocaine from FARC. Following their arms deliveries, the brothers allegedly transported the cocaine by plane from Colombia to the Atlantic coast of Surinam, where it was then loaded on to cargo ships and camouflaged in shipments of honey for export. The cocaine was reportedly destined for sale in the drug markets of western Europe and Russia.[65]

The scale of these arms-for-cocaine smuggling operations underscores the enormous challenge law enforcement authorities face in Russia and throughout the independent states of the former Soviet Union, where in many cases Soviet-era intelligence operatives made virtually seamless transitions from Cold War espionage or military intelligence operations into organized crime.[66] According to U.S. intelligence officials: "The source of the weapons [smuggled into Colombia from Russia] is both organized crime and military. There is a tremendous gray area between the two in Russia and the Ukraine."[67]

Although the smuggling operations described above were broken up by national and international law enforcement authorities by mid-2000, the continuation of rampant lawlessness and organized crime activity in present-day Russia and other countries of the former Soviet bloc means that new arms-for-drugs schemes could emerge at any time, if they have not already done so. Indeed, the Russian government's current policy of aggressively promoting military weapons exports, especially to Latin America, to earn badly needed foreign exchange, while systematically ignoring or overlooking pervasive corruption within the Russian military itself, virtually guarantees that such deals will be repeated in the future.[68]

In August 2001 at El Dorado airport in Bogotá, Colombian authorities arrested three members of the Irish Republican Army (IRA) traveling under false passports on suspicion that they were in the country to train FARC guerrillas in the use of explosives and urban terrorism tactics. Niall Connolly—one of the men arrested—had been the official representative in Cuba of Sinn Fein, the political party associated with the IRA in Northern Ireland, since 1996. A second, James Monaghan, was formerly a member of Sinn Fein's executive committee and, until his arrest, the IRA's "director of education," who was responsible for developing new weapons and training IRA members in their use. The third, Martin McCauley, who along with Monaghan had served time in British prisons for terrorist acts in Great Britain, had reportedly been sighted previously in Colombia with FARC guerrillas as early as 1998. While the scope of the IRA's linkages to FARC still remains unclear, the capture of these three IRA militants in Colombian territory reveals unequivocally that FARC's international linkages extend beyond drug traffickers and transnational organized crime groups to international terrorist organizations as well. With the recent IRA decision (in the wake of the September 11, 2001,

278 / Bruce Michael Bagley

terrorist attacks on the United States and the subsequent pressure from Irish-Americans to accede to Sinn Fein's pleas) to initiate disarmament to save the Northern Ireland peace process from collapse, the possibility of recalcitrant, out-of-work IRA radicals signing on as "advisors" to FARC in the future cannot be discarded. Unfortunately, many IRA factions in Northern Ireland appear less interested in consummating the peace agreement than in profiting from their evolving interests in international criminal activities.[69]

Throughout the 1990s and into the early 2000s a booming trade in the "designer" or "club" drug commonly known as Ecstasy (MDMA) burgeoned in the United States and in many cities in Latin America, providing additional profit-making opportunities for Russian criminal organizations operating in the Western Hemisphere.[70] Most of the world's supply of Ecstasy is manufactured in the Netherlands and Belgium, although there is mounting evidence that production has begun to spread to Russia and several eastern European states. For the last decade, Israeli and Russian MDMA trafficking organizations have dominated the MDMA market in the United States. But the high profitability of the trade has begun to attract other drug-trafficking organizations based especially in Colombia, the Dominican Republic, Mexico, and Asia. Such groups, possibly through temporary alliances or via Ecstasy-for-cocaine deals, are likely to make inroads into Israeli and Russian control of the MDMA trafficking networks during the next few years. Even as such inroads are made, however, most observers believe that Europe, because of its technological prowess in Ecstasy production, is likely to remain the primary source region for Ecstasy, at least in the near and medium term.[71]

Dominican drug-trafficking organizations in alliance with Colombian cartels have been deeply involved in the cocaine trade along the U.S. east coast for more than a decade. In the mid-1990s, the Dominicans became the first Latin American smugglers to assume a major role in MDMA distribution. Some Colombian and Mexican crime groups have also become involved in recent years. The MDMA traffickers targeting U.S. or Latin American markets commonly employ couriers or "mules" traveling by plane from Europe to cities such as Miami, Santo Domingo, Bogotá, or Mexico City, but larger quantities shipped by sea on cargo vessels have been confiscated as well. The couriers either ingest (swallow) MDMA pills wrapped in plastic balloons or condoms or strap them to their persons or luggage. The DEA believes that Dominican and Colombian crime groups may have begun cocaine-for-MDMA deals with European, Israeli, and Russian traffickers and that such exchanges are likely to increase the availability of MDMA in the United States and elsewhere in the hemisphere substantially in coming years.[72]

Cuba

In contrast to the weak, democratic, and capitalist states of the insular Caribbean that proved uniformly easy prey for Russian transnational organized crime during the 1990s, the highly centralized and authoritarian Communist state of Fidel Castro's Cuba remained essentially immune from Russian criminal penetration over the decade. In the late 1980s, the Cuban government had been linked with Colombian drug traffickers when General Ochoa, a prominent and popular Cuban military commander in Angola, and other Cuban officers under his command reportedly engaged in drug-smuggling activities to underwrite their poorly funded troops in Angola and, allegedly, to enrich themselves personally. Prior to Ochoa's high-profile trial in Havana on drug-trafficking charges and his subsequent conviction and execution, Fidel and his brother Raul, head of the Cuban armed forces, were widely rumored to have at least condoned Ochoa's drug-smuggling activities as a way of circumventing the U.S. embargo against Cuba and obtaining badly needed hard currency to support the Cuban military presence in Africa. Whether such accusations against the Castro brothers were true or not remains unresolved. Whatever the truth of the matter, however, Ochoa's considerable following among Cuban troops in Angola and among veterans at home, the increased autonomy from the Castros and the Cuban high command that drug money conferred upon him, and the intense international opprobrium that accompanied international revelation of high-ranking Cuban military officers' roles in illicit drug-trafficking operations apparently led the Castro regime to put an end to Cuba's involvement in the trade by the early 1990s.

Despite some thirty years of close Cuban-Soviet relations during the Cold War following the Cuban revolution in 1959, the 1991 collapse of the Soviet Union, the concomitant end of Communist Party rule in Russia, and the progressive termination of former Soviet subsidies to Cuba under Russia's first president, Boris Yeltsin, severely strained Cuban-Russian relations throughout the 1990s. Ironically, latent Cuban antipathy toward Russians, unmistakably present among Cubans even at the high point of Cuban-Soviet cooperation in the 1970s and 1980s, grew more palpable over the 1990s, effectively making Cuba an inhospitable prospective host country for Russian criminal organizations seeking to establish themselves in the Caribbean.[73] The wariness and vigilance of the Cuban state in the wake of the Ochoa affair regarding any involvement of Cuba in international drug trafficking also militated against the establishment of Russian mafia operations in Cuba. Finally, the U.S. embargo against Cuba and the country's limited participation in the global capitalist economy meant that Cuba held little attraction for Russian mafiosos intent upon establishing bases for their transnational criminal activities in the region.

Without massive Soviet subsidies to keep the Cuban economy afloat (estimated as high as 10 billion U.S. dollars annually at the outset of the 1980s), Castro and the Cuban Communist leadership were forced during the 1990s to seek foreign investment from Europe (especially Spain) in the state-owned tourist industry to help diversify the failing national economy. One consequence of the growth of foreign tourism in Cuba over the decade was the emergence of an illegal drug market (along with prostitution) to service the burgeoning tourist trade. Small Cuban criminal gangs working with traffickers from Colombia, neighboring Caribbean countries such as Haiti, the Dominican Republic, and Jamaica, and even Mexico smuggle drugs into Cuba for distribution and sale within the country or for transit to Europe. Cuba's repressive state security apparatus has, however, been quite successful both in preventing the rise of powerful domestic organized crime groups and in disrupting efforts by Russian or other transnational criminal organizations to use Cuban territory as a transit point for large-scale drug trafficking into Europe.

Nonetheless, given the Cuban economy's severe economic problems over the decade, including the scarcity of expensive imported petroleum, the Cuban navy and coast guard have been unable to afford the equipment or fuel needed to patrol Cuban waters out to the twelve mile territorial limit effectively. The resulting gaps in Cuban coastal patrols have allowed Colombian traffickers to use Cuban waters as a handy drop-off point for drug shipments (drugs are either tossed over the sides of ships or parachuted from low flying airplanes into the sea) destined for the U.S. market. After a prearranged drop, traffickers based in the United States operate "fast boats" to pick up the drugs and transport them into South Florida, avoiding detection by U.S. authorities under the cover of darkness or in the confusion of weekend and holiday pleasure boat traffic. Although the Cubans repeatedly approached Washington with proposals for closer U.S.-Cuban cooperation and information sharing in the area of drug trafficking during the 1990s, their offers were regularly rebuffed by hardliners in the U.S. Congress who reject any form of collaboration with the Castro regime out of hand, including cooperation in the area of drug control.

Brazil and the Southern Cone

Since the mid-1990s there have been a variety of press reports hinting at growing Russian organized crime involvement in drugs and arms trafficking and money laundering in Brazil and the four Southern Cone countries. The half dozen or so highly publicized arrests of Russian and other former Soviet bloc crime figures that have taken place in recent years in the nations of the subregion have lent some credence to these journalistic alarms.[74] Nonetheless, a mid-2000 report on the Russian mafia prepared by Argentine national security officials found that there was no credible evidence indicating that Argentina had yet been seriously affected by Russian criminal organizations. According to one highly placed source at the Argentine Interior Ministry, "If you ask me officially, I would have to say that there is no record of the presence of the Russian mafia in Argentina. The truth is that no one investigates mafias in Argentina, but that does not mean that they are not here."[75] Russian mafia presence in Argentina (specifically Chechen gangs) has been linked primarily to the use of Argentina as a transit country for Andean cocaine shipments to Europe (in fishing trawlers and cargo ships), arms trafficking to Brazil and Colombia, and money laundering. In the so-called "tri-border" area where Argentina, Brazil, and Paraguay meet, Argentine intelligence sources have detected contacts between Chechen separatist groups and "Islamic terrorists" and suspect Chechen use of these networks for arms-smuggling purposes.[76] The Argentine border with Paraguay is notorious for contraband of all types and provides virtually ideal conditions for Russian mafia operations.[77]

In June 2000 the Brazilian daily newspaper O Globo reported growing participation of Russian mafia groups in the recruitment of Brazilian women for prostitution in Europe, especially Spain, and Israel. Russian criminal networks were also reported to be responsible for the smuggling of Russian AK-47s and Soviet rocket launchers into the *favelas* of Rio and São Paulo in exchange for Colombian cocaine. General Rosso Jose Serrano, former head of the Colombian national police, claimed that Russian criminal networks were also smuggling arms through Brazil to Colombia using the same contraband routes that had been developed for smuggling cocaine out of Colombia to Brazil and on to Europe.[78]

Brazil's continuing role as a major cocaine transit point has resulted in cheap cocaine flooding the country. Along Brazil's long, unprotected borders with Bolivia, Peru, and Colombia, refined cocaine costs just 2,000 U.S. dollars per kilo or less. In Brazil's major urban areas, such as Rio de Janeiro or São Paulo, a kilo goes for as little as 4,000 U.S. dollars, or 80 percent less than the street price in New York or Chicago.[79] As a result of surging drug trafficking, violent crime rates have soared in Brazil's major urban centers and many of the country's sprawling urban slums have become armed camps run by "drug commands" or gangs that often act as alternative governments in their neighborhoods.

Drug-related corruption has also permeated the Brazilian national economy and political system. In 2001, a Brazilian congressional investigation into corruption linked 827 prominent Brazilians to drug trafficking and money laundering, including 2 national congressmen, 15 state legislators, 4 mayors, 6 bank directors, and scores of police officers and judges.[80] This environment of pervasive official corruption has proven highly propitious for the rapid expansion of Russian organized crime groups alongside Brazil's own homegrown criminal organizations.

Uruguay reportedly became the preferred site for Russian money-laundering activities in the Southern Cone during the 1990s because of the country's comparatively weak banking regulations. Lax Uruguayan law enforcement has allowed Russian mobsters to take control of a number of Uruguayan banks and to obtain Uruguayan visas and passports with relative ease. The Russian mafia also reportedly uses the Bolivian banking system for laundering purposes for the same reasons.[81]

On January 17, 2000, at the Chilean port of Africa on the Pacific coast, Chilean customs personnel seized 9 tons of Colombian cocaine on the Panamanian-flag merchant ship *Nativa*. Captained by a Colombian, the ship's crew was made up of Ukrainians. This seizure was fifteen times larger than any previous cocaine confiscation carried out by Chilean authorities and five times larger than any ever made by Argentina. In both countries it was viewed as an ominous indicator of rising joint Colombian and Russian drug trafficker use of Pacific coast and Southern Cone routes for drug smuggling to Europe and former Soviet bloc countries.[82]

Conclusions: The Impact of Russian Organized Crime in Latin America and the Caribbean

The Russian mafia's rise to prominence at home over the past decade and a half is directly attributable to the collapse of the former Soviet Union and the extreme weakness of the contemporary Russian state and its key economic and law enforcement institutions. The intensity and velocity of globalization in the post–Cold War era facilitated the rapid expansion of Russian organized crime abroad. The limitations and deficiencies of international law enforcement agencies and arrangements (global governance) permitted Russian crime groups to operate almost unfettered in the global system. Geography, drugs, weak state institutions, and widespread corruption, poverty, and violence made many Latin American and Caribbean nations especially vulnerable and attractive targets for Russian crime groups. In 2001, the specter of deepening penetration by Russian transnational criminal organizations into most, if not all, of Latin America and the Caribbean loomed ominously.

What are the consequences of this deepening penetration likely to be? To answer this question, it is first useful to clarify that Russian criminal organizations are, by and large, comprised of neither terrorists nor revolutionaries. They seek illegal profits from illicit criminal activities within the global capitalist system and protection from legal prosecution, not the overthrow of existing states. Their criminal enterprises tend to be decentralized and loosely structured rather than hierarchical and tightly disciplined. Their preferred criminal strategies involve the formation of opportunistic and temporary, rather than strategic and permanent, alliances with domestic criminal groups and political authorities that allow them to operate without running afoul of local or international law enforcement. Their preferred tactics run to bribery, extortion, and intimidation rather than to indiscriminate violence and murder, although when pressed they certainly have proven to be ruthless. They do not, therefore, as a rule constitute direct threats to the stability and security of the Latin American and Caribbean states within whose territory they operate.

The dangers and risks to Latin American governments and societies that emanate from expanding Russian *mafiya* activities within and outside their national borders are usually more indirect than direct, although nonetheless real because of their obliqueness. In Colombia, for example, Russian mafia arms-for-cocaine smuggling operations have unquestionably upgraded the FARC guerrillas' arsenal and enhanced their firepower vis-à-vis the Colombian police and armed forces, thereby contributing to the intensification of the country's internal conflicts. The fact that the Russian mafia appears equally willing to sell arms to Colombia's right-wing paramilitaries may underscore their lack of ideological involvement in Colombia's decades-old civil strife, but it in no way mitigates the profoundly negative consequences that their illicit activities hold for Colombian political stability and state security. The Russians' international money-laundering services are provided in a similarly nonpartisan fashion—for a price, they will launder drug trafficker, guerrilla, or paramilitary money on an equal opportunity basis. In doing so, of course, they facilitate the clandestine movement of the narco-dollars that help underwrite the on-going violence in Colombia.[83]

Even for those Latin American countries not engulfed in civil wars such as the one raging in Colombia, Russian illegal arms trafficking and arms-for-drugs deals in alliance with local criminal gangs significantly increase the firepower available to violent elements of society and make them more difficult and dangerous for law enforcement to control. Brazil's *favelas,* for instance, have become virtual war zones, at least in part as a result of Russian drug and arms-trafficking links with local criminal organizations in that country. Likewise, the Central American *maras* have become progressively better armed and threatening to social stability and state security throughout the isthmus as a result of their linkages with Russian (along with Mexican, Colombian, and North American) transnational organized crime groups.

The Russian mafia is not, by any means, the only source of weapons in the region. The United States itself is a major purveyor of small arms throughout Latin America and the Caribbean and elsewhere in the world.[84] But given the political chaos and relative availability of black-market arms in Russia and most other former Soviet bloc countries, Russian crime groups enjoy significant comparative advantages in this clandestine market and, thus, have emerged as major players in the international illicit arms trade.[85] The consequences for Latin America and the Caribbean are visible on a daily basis in the surging rates of gang warfare and violent crime registered in every major urban area in the region.

Independent of the arms black market, the Russian mafia's criminal strategies and tactics for penetration into the region are inherently, even if indirectly, threatening to institutional stability and state security. Russian crime groups do not normally seek to displace the local criminal organizations in each Latin American or Caribbean country, but rather try to cooperate with them in order to facilitate their own illegal operations and to elude detection and arrest. In doing so, they clearly strengthen the local crime groups with which they affiliate by providing them with expanded markets in Europe and Russia for contraband such as cocaine, heroin, and methamphetamines, by sharing new smuggling routes into (and networks of protection and distribution in) these lucrative markets, and by helping to launder the profits derived from their illicit enterprises through Russian channels at home and abroad. The Russian mafia's "marriage of convenience" with the Arrellano Felix cartel based in Tijuana, Mexico illustrates the dangerous potential of such alliances. The May 3, 2001, 12-ton cocaine seizure on the Russian- and Ukrainian-crewed *Svesda Maru* constituted the largest cocaine bust in U.S. maritime history. The money and arms obtained by the Arrellano Felix mob through its linkages with Russian crime groups unquestionably make the Tijuana cartel wealthier, more able to purchase Mexican police and political "protection" through bribery, and better armed and equipped to ward off rival gangs or to resist Mexican and U.S. law enforcement efforts mounted against them.

The Russian's preferred tactics of bribery, blackmail, and intimidation tend to exercise corrosive pressures on key private and public sector institutions, thereby undermining individual states' abilities to preserve a stable economic and social environment, effective law enforcement capacity, and "level playing field" required to promote legal business activity and attract the foreign investment that is essential to long-term economic growth. Traditional and long-standing patterns of patrimonial rule, personalism, clientelism, and bureaucratic corruption throughout Latin America have encouraged and facilitated Russian crime groups' use of these favored tactics (as they have for domestic criminal organizations as well). Time and again, many (although certainly not all) police and customs officials, military officers, judges, politicians, and businessmen have proven susceptible to such tactics in large and small countries alike throughout the region.[86]

The Russian mafia's expanding presence in Latin America and the Caribbean does not currently constitute a direct security threat either to the individual states of the region or to the United States. It does, however, contribute indirectly to the entire region's growing economic, social, and political turmoil and insecurity and thus poses a major challenge to economic growth, effective democratic governance, and long-term regime stability throughout the hemisphere.

In the future, however, Russian and other transnational crime networks in Latin America and the Caribbean could become more directly threatening to state security throughout the region and in the United States itself. Networks initially created to move drugs and light arms might conceivably be reconfigured to move heavy weapons such as fighter aircraft or submarines, to disseminate nuclear, chemical, or biological weapons of mass destruction, or to smuggle contract assassins and/or members of the Al Qaeda terrorist network if there were enough profit to be made in doing so.[87] In late October 2001, for example, rumors surfaced in both the Colombian and U.S. press that some Colombian drug traffickers had been approached by representatives of "Arab groups" with a proposal to pay the traffickers to mix cocaine with anthrax before smuggling it into the United States. Authorities in the United States immediately dismissed such reports as lacking in credibility. While such reconfigurations are conceivable, the logic of the underground market place—high profits and limited risks—militates against transnational organized crime groups participating in such terrorist schemes, unless the profits involved promised to be so huge as to make them irresistible. Drug traffickers are not, as a rule, interested in destroying their own markets or exposing themselves to intense international persecution. To date, there is no credible evidence that such reconfigurations have yet occurred anywhere in Latin America or the Caribbean.[88]

The trend toward blurring the distinction between organized crime and terrorist groups is most pronounced in the states of the former Soviet Union. In the case of the Chechen "terrorists," for example, it is not entirely clear whether they are more interested in creating an independent nation-state or in perpetuating regional instability so that they might continue to profit from the drug trade and other criminal enterprises. Similarly, while some members of the Islamic Movement of Uzbekistan are devoted to promotion of a militant and extremist brand of Islam, most appear primarily focused on profiting from the central Asian and Afghan drug trade. For the right price, however, either group could probably be convinced to work for Osama bin Laden and the Al Qaeda terrorist network, if they are not part of it already.

As with other forms of transnational organized crime around the globe, to meet the growing Russian mafia challenge successfully will require major institutional reforms in areas such as law enforcement, money laundering, border control, and anti-corruption measures at the individual country level, and sustained multilateral cooperation and intelligence sharing among state law enforcement agencies at the subregional, regional, and international levels.[89] It will also require a much clearer understanding on the part of political elites and law enforcement officials in every Latin American and Caribbean

286 / Bruce Michael Bagley

country of the transnational nature of the threats they face in their own nations and the consequent need to revise traditional and antiquated notions of national sovereignty and deeply ingrained but increasingly dysfunctional pseudo-nationalist rejection of international cooperation. To date, neither the requisite country reforms nor adequate multilateral-level coordination, much less the needed changes in mind-set, have been forthcoming.[90] As a result, Russian criminal organizations have been able to spread across the entire region virtually unfettered for more than a decade.

Initial developments in the international arena in response to the devastating September 11, 2001, terrorist attacks on the United States suggest that a new momentum behind greater multilateral cooperation might materialize in coming months and years. Specifically, the additional impetus given by the United States to the multilateral aspects of law enforcement in its prosecution of the "war" on global terrorism could ultimately usher in a new era of international coordination against terrorism and organized crime. To combat this new stage of global terrorism effectively will unquestionably require the construction of new multilateral mechanisms for the international monitoring and policing of terrorist movements, illegal weapons sales, illicit capital flows, and money laundering.

The two common elements shared by global terrorism and transnational organized crime—money laundering and proliferation—may finally catalyze serious and sustained multilateral coordination in international law enforcement. The current enthusiasm for multilateral efforts could, however, quickly evaporate. The real key to success in both the "war" on terrorism and the fight against transnational organized crime will be whether or not the international community has the will and capacity required to design and institutionalize effective systems of multilateral coordination and cooperation over the long haul. The states of Latin America and the Caribbean will be called upon to play major roles in this process. Failure to act promptly and effectively is likely to carry a high price tag in terms of the erosion of domestic prosperity and stability within individual nation-states and the imposition of major costs on recalcitrant states via international pressures and sanctions applied either unilaterally by the United States or multilaterally by the international community.

Notes

1. Center for Strategic and International Studies (CSIS), *Russian Organized Crime* (Washington, D.C.: CSIS, 1997), passim.

2. The Federal Bureau of Investigation (FBI) defines organized crime as "a self perpetuating, structured and disciplined association of individuals or groups, combined together for the purpose of obtaining monetary or commercial gains or profits, wholly or in part by illegal means, while protecting their activities through a

pattern of graft and corruption." CSIS, *Russian Organized Crime*, 23–24. Transnational crime is defined as crimes or offenses whose inception, prevention, and/or direct or indirect effects involve more than one country. Gerhard O. W. Mueller, "Transnational Crime: Definitions and Concepts," *Transnational Organized Crime* 4, nos. 3 and 4 (1998), 14.

3. The term "weak" state as used here refers not to the type of regime (for example, authoritarian or democratic), or to the form of government (for example, unitary or federalist), or to institutional arrangements (for example, presidential or parliamentary political systems). Rather, it refers to the institutional capacity of the state, whatever its form, to penetrate society, extract resources from it, and regulate conflicts within it. Specifically, the term refers to the ability of state authorities to govern legitimately, to enforce the law systematically, and to administer justice effectively throughout the national territory. Understood in this fashion, Latin America has produced no strong states. Not even the Mexican state during the seventy-one years of single-party domination and inclusionary authoritarianism under PRI rule or the Brazilian state during the decade plus of military rule and bureaucratic authoritarianism can be accurately classified as strong states according to this definition. Of course, the weak/strong dichotomy encompasses an underlying continuum or range of possibilities. Some Latin American and Caribbean states are clearly weaker than others. Thus, it is valid to argue that both the Mexican and Brazilian states are "stronger" than, say, the Haitian or Paraguayan states.

4. CSIS, *Russian Organized Crime*, 23–49; Michele Aglietta and Philippe Moutot, "Redeployer les Reformes: Comment Adapter la Strategie de Transition," *Economie Internationale: La Revue du Cepii*, no. 54 (1993), 67–104.

5. Tom Farer, "Conclusion: Fighting Transnational Organized Crime: Measures Short of War," in Tom Farer, ed., *Transnational Crime in the Americas* (New York: Routledge, 1999), 251.

6. Robert O. Keohane, "Governance in a Partially Globalized World," *The American Political Science Review* 95, no. 1 (2001), 35–60.

7. Giovanni Arrighi, *Globalization, State Sovereignty, and the "Endless" Accumulation of Capital* (Binghamton, N.Y.: Fernand Braudel Center, 1997).

8. David Held, et al., *Global Transformations: Politics* (Stanford, Calif.: Stanford University Press, 1999), 1–31.

9. For analyses of the impact of globalization on transnational organized crime, see Nikos Passes, "Globalization and Transnational Crime: Effects of Criminogenic Asymmetries," *Transnational Organized Crime* 4, nos. 3 and 4 (1998), 22–56; Phil Williams, "Organizing Transnational Crime: Networks, Markets, and Hierarchies," Ibid., 57–86. Russian money laundering amply demonstrated the financial sophistication of the Russian mafia by successfully obscuring its illicit transactions within the larger movement of capital into and out of emerging markets by timing them to the speculative capital shifts that occurred during the Mexican peso crisis (1995), the Thai bhat crisis (1997), and the Turkish lira crisis (2001), among other recent currency crises.

10. Laurence Whitehead, "High-level Political Corruption in Latin America: A 'Transitional' Phenomenon?," in Joseph S. Tulchin and Ralph H. Espach, eds., *Combating Corruption in Latin America* (Washington, D.C.: The Woodrow Wilson Cen-

ter Press, 2000), 108; see also Luigi Manzetti, "Market Reforms Without Transparency," in Ibid., 130–72; Edmundo Jarquin and Fernando Carillo Flores, "The Complexity of Anti-Corruption Policies in Latin America," in Ibid., 193–204.

11. James H. Mittleman, "The Dynamics of Globalization," in James H. Mittleman, ed., *Globalization: Critical Reflections* (Boulder, Colo.: Lynne Rienner Publishers, 1997), 6–10; Robert Cox, *Production, Power, and World Order: Social Forces in the Making of History* (New York: Columbia University Press, 1987), 20–42.

12. Of the 500 million people who reside in Latin America, 89 million live in extreme poverty, and almost one-half are considered poor. According to the United States Economic Commission for Latin America and the Caribbean, the proportion of people living in poverty decreased modestly in Latin America in the 1990s after the disastrous "lost decade" of the 1980s, but the number is likely to grow again as the United States, Latin America, and most of the world economy fall into recession in 2001–2002. Clifford Krauss, "Economic Pain Spreads from United States Across Latin America," *New York Times,* October 14, 2001.

13. Of course, only a small proportion of the poor in Latin America (as elsewhere around the globe) resort to criminality of any sort and even smaller numbers actually become involved in organized crime. In fact, the poorest of the poor are generally ill-equipped to engage in organized criminal enterprises because such activities require relatively higher levels of education, technical know-how, access to financial resources, and familiarity with bureaucratic-administrative procedures and police and political contact than the abjectly poor have at their disposal. For a discussion of the characteristics of modern large-scale criminal organizations see Letizia Paoli, "Criminal Fraternities or Criminal Enterprises," *Transnational Organized Crime* 4, nos. 3 and 4 (1998), 88–108.

14. Margaret E. Beare, "Russian (East European) Organized Crime around the Globe" (paper presented at the Transnational Crime Conference, Canberra, Australia, March 9–10, 2000), 1–2.

15. Ibid., 2–4. Some estimates suggest that as much as 40 percent of Russian GDP is presently controlled by organized crime and as many as 90 percent of all Russian business enterprises are obliged to make protection payments to one or another group of Russian mobsters.

16. See, for example, Janine R. Wedel, "United States Assistance for Market Reforms: Foreign Aid Failures in Russia and the Former Soviet Bloc," *The Independent Review: A Journal of Political Economy* 4, no. 3 (2000), 393–417; Janine R. Wedel and Gerald Creed, "Second Thoughts from the Second World: Interpreting Aid in Post-Communist Eastern Europe," *Human Organization* 56, no. 3 (1997), 253–64.

17. Rensselaer W. Lee III, "Transnational Organized Crime: An Overview," in Farer, ed., *Transnational Crime in the Americas,* 4. As Richard Giragosian noted in comments on an early draft of this paper, it is important to realize that this type of corruption undermines the ability of the Russian state to collect taxes, to ensure fiscal and economic stability, to pursue effective market reforms, and to consolidate governmental authority.

18. Ibid., 2; also Williams, "Organizing Transnational Crime," 72–78.

19. United States Government Interagency Working Group, *International Crime Threat Assessment* (Washington, D.C.: U.S. Government Printing Office, 2000), 74.

20. Ibid., 74–75. The second major Russian gang is the Dolgopruadnanskaya. In Moscow the Ostankino and Lubertsy clans are also significant players. Chechens and Georgians have a disproportionately large role in the Russian underworld. The largest Chechen mafia is known as the Obshina. "So Who Are the Russian Mafia?" *BBC Online Network,* April 1, 1998.

21. Gregory F. Treverton, "International Organized Crime, National Security and the "Market State," in Farer, *Transnational Crime in the Americas,* 52.

22. For discussion of the nature of the Russian political regime ten years after the breakup of the Soviet Union see Lilia Shevtsova, "Russia's Hybrid Regime," *Journal of Democracy* 12, no. 4 (2001), 65–70; Archie Brown, "From Democratization to 'Guided Democracy,'" *Journal of Democracy* 12, no. 4 (2001), 35–41.

23. Beare, "Russian (East European) Organized Crime," 5; Stephen Hanson, "Putin and the Dilemmas of Russia's Anti-Revolutionary Revolution," in Dick Clark, director and moderator, *Russia under Putin and United States-Russian Relations,* Twenty-Sixth Conference, August 19–26 (Washington D.C.: Aspen Institute, 2001), 21–28.

24. Louis J. Freeh, "Statement for the Record," by Louis J. Freeh, Director Federal Bureau of Investigation, on international crime before the United States Senate, Committee on Appropriations, Subcommittee on Foreign Operations, Washington, D.C., April 21, 1998.

25. Camille Verleuw, *Trafics et Crimes en Asie centrale et au Caucase* (Paris: Presses Universitaires de France, 1999), 1–60. Afghanistan is a major source country for the cultivation, processing, and trafficking of opiate and cannabis products. In 2000, it produced more than 70 percent of the world's supply of illicit opium. In 2001, it produced only 74 metric tons of opium versus 3,656 tons in 2000. Nonetheless, the United Nations estimates that up to 60 percent of Afghan opium has been stored for future sales. In late 2001 reports of heroin shipments north from Afghanistan through the central Asian states to Russia increased dramatically. Tajikistan is a frequent transit point or storage area for Afghan opium and heroin. While some Afghan heroin is used in Russia, most transits Russia and is ultimately smuggled to the major consumer markets in the West. Asa Hutchinson, *Remarks by Asa Hutchinson, Administrator, Drug Enforcement Administration, before the House Committee on Government Reform, Subcommittee on Criminal Justice, Drug Policy, and Human Resource, Regarding "Drug Trade and Terror Networks"* (Washington, D.C.: U.S. Government Printing Office, 2001).

26. Susan Eisenhower, "Putin's Policies toward the 'Near Abroad,'" in Clark, *Russia Under Putin,* 29–34.

27. For a history of opium trafficking and the roots of organized crime in Asia during the first half of the twentieth century, see William O. Walker III, *Opium and Foreign Policy: The Anglo-American Search for Order in Asia, 1912–1954* (Chapel Hill: University of North Carolina Press, 1991), 222.

28. Ko-Lin Chin, Sheldon Zhang, and Robert J. Kelly, "Transnational Chinese Organized Crime Activities: Patterns and Emerging Trends," *Transnational Organized Crime* 4, nos. 3 and 4 (1998), 127–54.

29. Doris Gomorra/Grupo Reforma, "Redes de la Mafia Globalizada en Mexico," *Reforma,* May 16, 2001.

30. "A Survey of Illegal Drugs: Stumbling in the Dark," *The Economist,* July 28, 2001, 3. Speaking to a special meeting of the Russian Security Council on September 28, 2001, President Putin stated that the drug problem in Russia has become so serious that it "threatens the country's national security both directly and by providing funds to terrorists." Russia registered 243,000 drug-related crimes in 2000, 12,000 of which were committed by organized gangs. Victor Yasmann, "Putin Says Drug Problem Threatens Russian National Security," RFE/RL *Security Watch* 2, no. 39 (October 10, 2001), 8.

31. "Q&A: Who's Behind Russia's Money-laundering," BBC *Online Network,* October 19, 1999.

32. Gomorra/Grupo, "Redes de la Mafia," passim.

33. Molly Moore, "Cocaine Seizures by United States Double in Pacific Ocean: South American Cartels Abandon Caribbean for More Lucrative Route," *Washington Post,* September 3, 2000, A24.

34. Ibid., A24. Officials with the DEA estimate that 65 percent of the cocaine produced in South America reaches U.S. cities via the United States-Mexico border and is smuggled across by Mexican cartels (based principally in Tijuana, Juarez, Sinaloa, Matamoros, and Guadalajara) acting in alliance with Colombian suppliers. Jerry Seper, "Mexicans, Russian Mob New Partners in Crime," *Washington Times,* August 13, 2001, 6; Alfredo Joyner, "Tambien en Estados Unidos Hay Cartels de la Droga," *Milenio Diario de Mexico,* September 18, 2001, 1.

35. A previous bust of a ship called *Forever My Friends* made by the U.S. Coast Guard in the eastern Pacific on March 6, 2001 involved ten Russian crew members smuggling 8 tons of cocaine to Mexico. "Ship and Suspects in Major Cocaine Bust Arrive at San Diego," CNN.Com., May 14, 2001.

36. "Record Cocaine Haul," BBC *News,* May 14, 2001.

37. Rene Gardner y Victor Fuentes/Grupo Reforma, "Operand los Arellano con Mafia Rusa-DEA," *Reforma,* May 14, 2001, 3; "Accord with United States Won't Stop Mexico's Drug Cartels," Stratfor.com, July 31, 2001.

38. Gretchen Peters, "Mexico: Drug Trafficking in the Pacific Has a Distinct Russian Flavor," *San Francisco Chronicle,* May 30, 2001, 4.

39. Ibid.

40. "Accord with United States," Stratfor.com.

41. Abel Barajas/Grupo Reforma, "Desconocen Vinculos Arellano-Rusos," *Reforma,* May 18, 2001, 3.

42. "Investigan Mafia Rusa en Centro America," *La Prensa Gráfica,* March 9, 2001, 1.

43. "Special Report: Central America's Crime Wave," Stratfor.com, August 29, 2001, 2–3.

44. Much of the total wave of violent crime engulfing Central America's fragile democracies, discouraging foreign investment, and slowing economic growth is directly related to youth gang activity. In El Salvador, for example, national police authorities reported 735 homicides between January and April 2001, of which 599 were related to gang violence and drugs. The Salvadorian government estimates that crime costs the country the equivalent of 13 percent of GDP annually. Ibid., 2.

45. Ibid., 2.

46. Ibid., 2–3.

47. Ibid., 3; Bruce Bagley, *Myths of Militarization: The Role of the Military in the War on Drugs in the Americas* (Coral Gables: University of Miami, North-South Center, 1991), 16–23.

48. The first "summit" meeting between the Cali cartel and Russian mafia capos reportedly took place in Moscow in late 1992, although there is evidence that Colombian cocaine was being shipped by the Cali cartel to Russia and other East bloc countries as early as 1991. Patrick L. Clawson and Rensselaer W. Lee III, *The Andean Cocaine Industry* (New York: St. Martin's Press, 1998), 87. Prior to the forging of this Russian connection, in the late 1980s and early 1990s the Cali cartel had first established "a very effective alliance with Sicilian criminal organizations that was instrumental in opening up the European market for Colombian cocaine. It allowed the use of existing drug distribution routes in Europe, and was effectively a strategic alliance that allowed Colombian organizations to diversify into a new market at a time when the U.S. cocaine market had become saturated." Williams, *Organizing Transnational Crime,* 64. For a detailed discussion of the nature of the alliance between the Colombian cartels and Italian groups, see Clawson and Lee, *The Andean Cocaine Industry,* 62–89.

49. Douglas Farah, "Russian Mob, Drug Cartels Joining Forces: Money-laundering, Arms Sales Spread Across Caribbean," *Washington Post,* September 29, 1997, A1, A16; Juanita Darling, "Colombian Cartels Find New Drug Paths to United States," *Los Angeles Times,* November 17, 1997, A1.

50. In a February 1997 meeting between a Russian mobster (Ludwig Fainberg, also known as Tarzan) and representatives of the Cali cartel that took place at a Russian mob-owned strip club called Porky's located in Miami, Florida, Tarzan offered to provide a Soviet Tango-class diesel submarine, along with a full crew, to the Cali cartel for 5.5 million U.S. dollars for use in transporting cocaine from the Pacific coast of Colombia to Mexico or California. Fainberg was, however, subsequently arrested and the deal was never consummated. "La Cocavodka," *Revista Semana,* no. 805, October 5–12, 1997; Mireya Navarro, "Russian Submarine Drifts into Center of Brazen Drug Pilot," *New York Times,* March 7, 1997, A22; Tammerlin Drummond, "Enter the Redfellas: Are Russian Mobsters Dallying with Drug Lords?," *Time,* July 14, 1997, 48.

51. Sue Lackey with Michael Moran, "Russian Mob Trading Arms for Cocaine with Colombian Rebels," MSNBC.com., April 9, 2000; Kirk Semple, "The Submarine Next Door," *New York Times Magazine,* December 3, 2000, 18; "Investigación: Yellow Submarine," *Revista Semana,* 3–5. In April 2001, Colombian police reportedly seized 1.5 pounds of enriched uranium of a type used in Soviet submarines that may have been obtained from elements of the Russian mafia. Matthew Campbell, "Bogota Police Foil 'Atom Bomb' Sale," *New York Times,* April 29, 2001, 22.

52. Around 200 metric tons of cocaine are smuggled into Europe annually, despite seizures of dozens of tons en route. Agence France Presse, "European Trade in Cocaine on the Increase," *Yahoo! News,* August 8, 2001.

53. Farah, "Russian Mob," A16; Susan Roberts, "Small Places, Big Money: The

Cayman Islands and the International Financial System," *Economic Geography* 1, no. 3 (July 1995), 58–72; Anthony P. Maingot, "The Decentralization Imperative and Caribbean Criminal Enterprises," in Farer, ed., *Transnational Crime in the Americas,* 143–70.

54. See, for example, R. T. Naylor, *Hot Money and the Politics of Debt* (Montreal: Black Rose Books, 1994); Robert E. Grosse, *Drugs and Money: Laundering Latin America's Cocaine Dollars* (Westport, Conn.: Praeger, 2001); and Jack Blum, "Offshore Money," in Farer, ed., *Transnational Crime in the Americas,* 57–84. Blum is particularly critical of Panama: "Free-trade zones such as the Colon free-trade zone in Panama have become centers for illegal commercial and financial activity. One of the most important branches of the BCCI was in the Colon free-trade zone, which was then and continues to be a center for the smuggling of goods and weapons all over the hemisphere" (p. 83).

55. CSIS, *Russian Organized Crime,* 36–40; Ilene R. Pursher, "Worldwide Webs: Mafia's Reach Grows," *Christian Science Monitor,* October 8, 1997, 12; Stephen Handelman, *Comrade Criminal: Russia's New Mafia* (New Haven: Yale University Press, 1995).

56. GAO, *Suspicious Banking Activities: Possible Money-laundering by United States Corporations Formed for Russian Entities* (Washington, D.C.: United States General Accounting Office, GAO-0 1-120, October 2000), 12.

57. Mark Hosenball and Christina Caryl, "A Stain on Mr. Clean," *Newsweek,* September 3, 2001, 48. German reunification in the early 1990s provided Russian organized crime groups with golden opportunities, often in collusion with former East German Communists, to establish legitimate fronts for mafia activities such as prostitution, drug smuggling, and money laundering in Germany. Personal interviews with convicted Colombian drug traffickers conducted during August and September 2001 in Miami, Florida revealed that Germany was still a preferred site for laundering and investing their drug profits.

58. Lackey, "Russian Mob Trading Arms for Cocaine," 2. Hundreds of thousands of kilos of Colombian cocaine at 50,000 U.S. dollars per kilo in Europe were reportedly smuggled via this route in 1999–2000.

59. Ibid., 3; "Narcotráfico: La Prueba Reina," *Revista Semana,* April 2, 2001, 26–29.

60. Lackey, "Russian Mob Trading Arms for Cocaine," 3–4; "Frontera Investigada," *Revista Semana,* October 22, 2001.

61. Anthony Faiola, "United States Allies in Drug War in Disgrace: Arrests of Peruvian Officials Expose Corruption, Deceit," *Washington Post,* May 9, 2001, A01.

62. "Montesinos Vendia Armas a Guerrilla y Paramilitares," *Revista Cambio,* September 4, 2001, 3–5.

63. Although Montesinos identified only four contraband flights, Luis Frank Ayabar claimed that up to twenty flights actually took place between 1999 and 2000 and as many as forty thousand rifles may have been delivered to FARC. Subsequent revelations indicated that Montesinos might also have been responsible for selling at least four Soviet-made Sam-16 surface-to-air missiles to FARC. "El Arsenal Oculto," *Revista Cambio,* October 22, 2001, 3.

64. In the first six months following Fujimori's fall, eighteen generals and more than seventy of his government's high-ranking military and intelligence officials were arrested and jailed for corruption, drug smuggling, and arms trafficking.

65. "Montesinos," *Revista Cambio,* passim.

66. J. Michael Waller, "The KGB and Its 'Successors,'" *Perspective* 4, no. 4 (1994), 17–18; Richard F. Staar, "Russia's Military: Corruption in the Higher Ranks," *Perspective* 9, no. 2 (1998), 4.

67. Laskey, "Russian Mob Trading Arms for Cocaine," 6.

68. CSIS, *Russian Organized Crime,* 32–33. In the wake of the September 11, 2001 terrorist attacks on the United States, for example, insistent but unconfirmed press and radio reports alleging Russian mafia sales of Soviet era weapons of mass destruction to Osama bin Laden and his Al Qaeda terrorist network and nuclear materials to the Taliban in Afghanistan surfaced repeatedly in the United States and several western European countries. See "Moscow Angered by United States Paper's Linking Russian Mafia to Bin Laden," RFE/RL *Security Watch* 2, no. 39 (October 10, 2001). While the possibility of terrorist groups such as Al Qaeda going fully nuclear appears small, combining conventional explosives with radioactive materials such as cesium-137 or cobalt-90 to contaminate key urban centers in the United States or Europe, perhaps for decades, is already within their capabilities.

69. "Colombia 'IRA' Witness Disappears," BBC *News,* October 23, 2001; Warren Hoge with Mirta Ojito, "Sinn Fein, for First Time, Asks IRA to Begin Disarming," *New York Times,* October 22, 2001, 3; Warren Hoge, "IRA Relents on Arms, Saves Peace Accord," *New York Times,* October 24, 2001, 3; Tamara Makarenko, "Transnational Crime and Its Evolving Links to Terrorism and Instability," *Jane's Intelligence Review,* November 1, 2001, 5–6.

70. The drug MDMA has been around since 1914. But it was not actually used until the 1970s, when a small group of psychiatrists discovered the drug's capacity to dissolve patients' fear and defenses. By the early 1980s, entrepreneurs coined the name "Ecstasy." In 1985, growing recreational use of the drug in the United States, combined with preliminary research findings of potential brain damage and other attendant dangers, prompted the U.S. government to ban MDMA for both medical and recreational use. Marsha Rosenbaum and Steve Hellig, "Examining the Use and Abuse of Ecstasy," *San Francisco Chronicle,* February 2, 2001, 12.

71. Joseph D. Keefe, "Statement before the Senate Governmental Affairs Committee" (Washington, D.C.: United States Department of Justice, Drug Enforcement Administration, 2001), 4.

72. Ibid., 5.

73. The rancor between Castro's Cuba and Putin's Russia boiled into public on October 17, 2001, when President Putin, without consulting Havana, suddenly announced that Russia would close its large eavesdropping center in Cuba. The Lourdes base, one of the last relics of the Cold War still operating in Cuba, was built by the Soviet Union in 1964 and housed an estimated fifteen hundred Russian and Cuban military personnel. Putin's decision to close the Cuban facility, along with a similar Pacific electronic reconnaissance post at Cam Ranh Bay in Vietnam, left Cuba no room for negotiations. Putin unilaterally declared that the posts were to be closed for

budgetary reasons, because of their declining significance for Russia in the post–Cold War era, and to shift Russian military assets to the fight against international terrorism. Cuba's anger reflected its frustration at yet another economic blow from Russia, which had paid 200 million U.S. dollars annually in rent for use of the Lourdes facility. Susan B. Glaser, "Russia to Dismantle Spy Facility in Cuba," *Washington Post,* October 18, 2001, A34; Kevin Sullivan, "Cuba Upset by Closure of Russian Spy Base," *Washington Post,* October 19, 2001, A26.

74. "Paraguay's Drug Trade Perilous Target for United States," Stratfor.com; Santiago O'Donnell, "La Argentina en la Mira de la Mafia Rusa," *La Nación,* September 24, 2000, l.

75. Ibid., p. 2.

76. The Paraguayan city of Ciudad del Este, located in the tri-border area some 350 kilometers from Asuncion, is often labeled the contraband capital of South America. It has a population of approximately five hundred thousand, of whom perhaps thirty thousand are Muslims, mostly of Arab descent. There is a drug trafficking-Islamic fundamentalism connection not only in the case of the Taliban, but also in the case of the Chechen separatists fighting for independence from Russia. General Shamil Basayev, the Jordanian-born fundamentalist leader of the Chechens, was trained in Afghanistan and had direct connections to Osama bin Laden in the 1980s. To finance their separatist movement, Basayev and his Chechen followers transported Afghan heroin through Abkhazia (a renegade province of Georgia that broke away with Russian military help in 1993) to the Black Sea or through Turkey to Cyprus and then on to Europe. In light of their goal of political independence, the Chechens can be differentiated from most other Russian organized crime groups. Guido Nejamkis/Reuters, "Preocupa Presencia Arabe en Paraguay," *El Nuevo Herald,* September 25, 2001, 4; Sharon LaFraniere, "Georgia Dispatches Troops Toward Separatist Region: Russia Bolsters Border with Abkhazia After Violence," *Washington Post,* October 12, 2001, A29.

77. The Paraguayan consul in Miami from June 1999 to May 2001, Carlos Weiss, is currently under arrest, accused of having sold more than three hundred passports, visas, and cargo shipment authorizations at up to 8,000 U.S. dollars a piece before he was fired in May. Some who received these documents are suspected of possible involvement in the terrorist attacks on the World Trade Center and on the Pentagon on September 11, 2001. According to a report by the Justice Department's inspector general released in February 2000, the Border Patrol "cannot accurately quantify how many illegal aliens and drug smugglers it fails to apprehend." James V. Grimaldi, Steve Fainam, and Gilbert M. Gaul, "Losing Track of Illegal Immigrants," *Washington Post,* October 7, 2001, A01; Gerardo Reyes, "Atentados en EU Reviven un Escandalo en Paraguay," *El Nuevo Herald,* September 20, 2001, 4; Larry Rohter, "Terrorists Are Sought in Latin Smugglers' Haven," *New York Times,* September 27, 2001, 6.

78. O'Donnell, "La Argentina en la Mira de la Mafia Rusa," 2.

79. A recent UN report estimated that about 900,000 out of Brazil's population of 170 million regularly use cocaine (0.7 percent). Although this percentage falls short of the U.S. consumption rate of around 3 percent (5.3 million), it exceeds consumption

rates in European nations such as France or Germany and makes Brazil the second largest cocaine-consuming nation in the world. Anthony Faiola, "Cocaine a Consuming Problem in Brazil: Drug-Fueled Violence Turns Slums into Urban Battle Fields," *Washington Post,* July 8, 2001, A01.

80. Ibid., A01.

81. O'Donnell, "La Argentina en la Mira de la Mafia Rusa," 3. For an analysis of the evolution of drug trafficking and international criminal activity in Bolivia from the 1950s through the 1990s, see Eduardo A. Gamarra, "Transnational Criminal Organizations in Bolivia," in Farer, ed., *Transnational Crime in the Americas,* 171–92. Personal interviews conducted by the author with high-ranking officials in Bolivia during July 2001 revealed that, despite the recent dramatic declines in Bolivian coca production under the former president, Hugo Banzer (who resigned from office on September 6, 2001, owing to severe illness from cancer), Russian and Italian mafia gangs—in conjunction with Peruvian and Bolivian traffickers—continue to use contraband routes across northern Bolivia to smuggle Peruvian and Bolivian cocaine into Brazil and, thence, onto cargo ships bound for Europe, especially Spain and Portugal, and Russia.

82. O'Donnell, "La Argentina en la Mira de la Mafia Rusa," 3.

83. For a discussion of the role of drug money in fueling Colombia's current conflicts see Bruce Bagley, "Narcotráfico, Violencia Política Exterior de Estados Unidos Hacia Columbia en los Noventa," *Colombia International,* no. 49–50 (2001), 5–38.

84. According to the Small Arms Survey, a Geneva-based organization, the United States is the leading exporter of small and light arms in the world, selling about 1.2 billion U.S. dollars of the 1998 worldwide total of 4 to 6 billion U.S. dollars. Colum Lynch, "United States Fight United Nations Accord to Control Small Arms: Stance on Draft Pact Not Shared by Allies," *Washington Post,* July 10, 2001, pA01; Tim Weiner and Ginger Thompson, "United States Smuggled into Mexico Aid for Drug War," *New York Times,* May 19, 2001, 6.

85. See R. T. Naylor, "The Rise of the Modern Arms Black Market and the Fall of Supply Side Control," *Transnational Organized Crime* 4, nos. 3 and 4 (1998), 220–22.

86. For an analysis of the relation between political corruption and governability with specific reference to the Colombian case, see Fernando Cepeda Ulloa, *Corrupción y Gobernabilidad* (Bogotá: 3R Editores, 2000). For analysis of the impact of organized crime on democratic governance in Mexico, see the essays in John Bailey and Roy Godson, eds., *Crimen Organizado y Gobernabilidad Democratica: Mexico y la Franja Fronteriza* (Mexico D.F.: Grijalbo, 2000).

87. James H. Anderson, *International Terrorism and Crime: Trends and Linkages* (Harrisonburg, Va.: William R. Nelson Institute for Public Affairs, James Madison University, 2000).

88. Gerardo Reyes, "Denuncian Mezcla con Cocaina en Colombia," *El Nuevo Herald,* October 24, 2001.

89. For detailed discussions of how to respond more effectively to the challenges of transnational organized crime at the international level, see Giuseppe de Gennaro, "Strengthening the International Legal System in Order to Combat Transnational

Crime," *Transnational Organized Crime* 4, nos. 3 and 4 (1998), 259–68; Roy Godson and Phil Williams, "Strengthening Cooperation against Transnational Crime: A New Security Perspective," Ibid., 321–55.

90. For examples of the difficulties that continue to plague effective international law enforcement efforts on different fronts, see William F. Wechsler, "Follow the Money," *Foreign Affairs* 80, no. 4 (July/August 2001), 40–57; Lester M. Joseph, "Money-laundering Enforcement: Following the Money," *Economic Perspectives: An Electronic Journal of the United States Department of State* 6, no. 2 (May 2001), 11–14; Phil Williams, "Organized Crime and Cybercrime: Synergies, Trends, and Responses," Ibid., 22–26.

15

The War against Drugs and the Interests of Governments

Alain Labrousse

The *World Drug Report 2000* published by the Office for Drug Control and Crime Prevention (ODCCP) has presented facts and figures supporting the idea that substantial progress has been made in the fight against drug production and trafficking.[1] The report notes: "The end of the Cold War and the emergence of real processes for peace in a number of hitherto insoluble conflicts have softened the tensions within the international system, making cooperation [in the area of drug control] a more practical enterprise."[2] This position is a rather optimistic one. The end of the Cold War, in fact, fostered the appearance of pseudo-states within which political corruption became institutionalized, which triggered new regional conflicts. The fight against drug production and trafficking has become even more complex because of the economic and geopolitical interests of governments. The western-industrial countries in particular, leaders in the war against drugs, have been most inconsistent in their drug policies toward their allies or clients when their own interests are at stake.

The claim that illicit drug production has been declining significantly is based on a selective use of data. When the ODCCP reported that coca cultivation had declined in Bolivia and Peru between 1995 and 2000 (from approximately 150,000 hectares to 50,000 hectares), it failed to mention that this reduction had been offset by an increase in areas under cultivation in Colombia (from 40,000 to 160,000 hectares). World production of opiates has increased (from 4,000 to 5,000 tons between 1998 and 2000) to levels where the drug traffickers themselves pushed for a production freeze in Afghanistan in order to maintain price levels. In July 2000, Mulla Omar, leader of the Taliban, ordered the complete eradication of poppy crops in a country that until then had been the world's number one opium producer. At the time when poppy seeds are planted, technicians from European NGOs observed emissaries of the emir[3] touring the villages and spreading the message that the terrible drought that had struck the country was a punishment from heaven to those cultivating that impious plant. Uncooperative peasants were imprisoned in Djelalabad, capital of the province of Nangahar. A field survey among Pakistani and Afghan opium traders revealed that the central Asian mafia paid the Taliban for its assistance in controlling supply, preventing the market from being flooded with opium and heroin after the record harvests of 1999 and 2000.[4] Financial compensation was offered for organizing the production freeze for at least one year.

The production of cannabis derivates has been growing constantly in response to increasing demand in western markets where their consumption has become commonplace. In 1999, Spain alone seized more than 400 tons of hashish from Morocco, where crops are estimated to cover 120,000 hectares in the Rif mountains and beyond. In other western European countries, authorities continue to seize large quantities of hashish produced in Pakistan, Afghanistan, and Nepal. Mexico, Colombia, Jamaica, Trinidad and Tobago, Cambodia, and the countries of sub-Saharan Africa have become major exporters of marijuana.

Although the replacement of natural drugs with synthetic substitutes is not yet on the agenda, the production of and trafficking in synthetics are growing exponentially. In Europe, the number of seizures by law enforcement authorities increased by 38 percent between 1997 and 1998. In the United Kingdom, an annual average of nearly 3 tons of pills was captured. In the Netherlands, an average of 1.5 tons was seized. France has become the hub for trafficking in amphetamines and Ecstasy toward the United States, a trade controlled by Israeli rings. In the United States annual seizures amounted to 1.7 tons in the same period. Several eastern European countries, in particular Poland and the Ukraine, also have become important producers and traffickers.

Mafia Activities and Political Corruption

The profitability of drug trafficking has increased the ability of criminal organizations to penetrate the economic and political fabric of the states where they carry on their activities. They have followed the trend toward globalization from an early stage onward. Faced with an offensive by various states, the major organizations (the so-called "Colombian cartels," the Italian and Chinese "mafia," the Pakistani and Turkish "godfathers") decentralized and internationalized their structures in the mid-1990s to protect their operations from action by law enforcement authorities. The three or four major cartels in Colombia made way for at least forty medium-sized organizations. The dozen groups of the Camorra in Naples, counted in the 1980s, increased to approximately one hundred, with six thousand affiliates. These organizations simultaneously diversified their activities (trafficking in weaponry and the smuggling of human beings, diamonds, protected animal species, and so on) while delocalizing and strengthening their business ties with counterparts in other countries and on other continents. When the Turkish government cracked down on the casinos in the country, the *babas* (godfathers) transferred them to the Caribbean (Saint Martin in particular) and to Africa (Tanzania, among others). The Sicilian Cosa Nostra, which has been hit hard by law enforcement in the past decade, has stepped up its international presence, in particular in Brazil, Canada, eastern Europe, and South Africa. The Sicilian mafia has established solidly in Cape Town and Johannesburg, according to South African anti-mafia police forces. Its operations range from money laundering through dummy corporations and real estate deals to cocaine trafficking. They cooperate with Colombian traffickers and employ escaped Italian mafiosi.[5] The Russian mafia has stepped up its activities in recent years; several Latin American countries have to deal with an increasing presence of Russian mafia in their countries.

All of the activities mentioned above are fostered by the relationships that criminal organizations maintain with local political powers. This does not only apply to "banana republic dictatorships" such as Myanmar and Equatorial Guinea and non-states such as Afghanistan, Paraguay, and Liberia, but also to countries that play key geopolitical roles in their regions, such as, for example, Turkey in Europe and Mexico and Brazil in Latin America.

Drugs in a Local Conflict

The increasing incidence of regional conflicts—a by-product of the end of the Cold War and the turbulence caused by the collapse of the Soviet Union—has considerable consequences for drug trafficking and large-scale crime.[6] During the Cold War, the major powers, prevented from diverting confrontation by deterrence, did so through their Third World allies. Drug money enabled certain countries to finance armed conflict instead of having to draw on secret funds. The end of the Cold War revealed that in most cases these conflicts lacked an ideological basis, and had produced ethnic, racial, and religious enmities. When the financial support by their powerful protectors came to an end, the warring parties went to look for alternative sources of finance and encountered them in various forms of trafficking, including drug trafficking.[7] In some thirty regional conflicts that occurred in the second half of the 1990s, the drug industry had a presence in different forms and on various levels.[8] Half of these conflicts have been taking place in Africa.

Conflicts like those in Colombia, Afghanistan, and Angola predate the Cold War and, with the withdrawal of sister parties and powerful protectors, they changed character, gradually sliding into predatory activities. The downfall of Communist regimes played an important role in causing the conflicts in Yugoslavia, Chechnya, Azerbaijan-Armenia, and Georgia.[9] In all these conflicts the combatants will search for funding in many different areas. They will traffic in oil, in drugs, in strategic metals, and virtually in anything that will give them a quick profit. Wide profit margins make drugs a particularly promising source of financing.[10] The taxes on drugs that were collected by the Taliban have been estimated at 100 million U.S. dollars per year.[11] This figure can be multiplied by three or four in the case of the FARC in Colombia. In a local conflict such as that of Casamance, in Senegal, the cannabis taxes levied in 1995 by the Mouvement des Forces Démocratiques de Casamance (MDFC) amounted to several millions of dollars.[12] It explains why in that case, several hundred barefoot combatants have acquired increasingly sophisticated weaponry over the years, and why, despite the peace accord signed with the government, they continue to confront the army, particularly in the cannabis—harvesting season. Kosovo presents one of the most significant examples of the role of drug trafficking in triggering conflict, as well as in creating the obstacles for its resolution. The connections between the UCK and drug traffickers are regularly confirmed by Italian law enforcement authorities.

Europe, Plan Colombia, and the United States

In the context of present regional conflicts with a drug-trafficking component, Plan Colombia should be carefully analyzed because it marks a significant difference in approach to the drug problem between Europe and the United States. All the elements of a lasting crisis are found in Colombia: internal conflict between Marxist guerillas and extreme right-wing militia members, with control over drug production and trafficking as one of the main issues at stake; a state attempting to restore civilian peace and take control of its territory; a foreign power—the United States—determined to intervene to put an end to drug trafficking at the risk of jeopardizing the peace negotiations.

The official objective of Plan Colombia is to combat drug trafficking, to support the peace process through negotiations with the main guerilla movement, the Revolutionary Armed Forces of Colombia (FARC),[13] and with the National Liberation Army (ELN),[14] and to promote the country's economic development, in particular through programs directed at the poor segments of the population. The overall cost of the plan was set at 7.5 billion U.S. dollars. The Colombian government has promised to contribute 4 billion dollars. The United States has decided to contribute 1.3 billion dollars. The remaining amount is to be contributed through bilateral channels (Spain,

Japan), multilateral financial organizations (World Bank, Inter-American Development Bank, Andean Financial Community, BIRR, and so on), and the European Union.

In Colombia, the plan has come under harsh criticism, not only by the guerilla movement, but also by development NGOs and human rights defense organizations. One object of criticism is the fact that approximately 70 percent of U.S. financing (1 billion U.S. dollars) will be used to reinforce the military potential of law enforcement. As part of the deal, sixty helicopters, including eighteen Blackhawk attack aircraft, were purchased from the United States. This action convinced FARC and ELN that, while pretending to fight drug traffickers, the U.S. government aims to sabotage the peace process and is preparing to wage war on them. Colombia and international NGOs (Amnesty International, America's Watch, WOLA, and others) have denounced what they consider "the logic of war," which is part of the plan and which will bring great suffering to the population in the affected areas. The plan has disturbed and divided the governments of neighboring countries, which fear the U.S. pressures toward the creation of a multilateral Latin American army force that once created would be asked to intervene in Colombia under the justification that guerillas and drug traffickers are undermining regional security. Such a plan had already been approved by Alberto Fujimori, the former president of Peru. It has met with strong opposition from Venezuela, whose nationalist president Hugo Chávez does not conceal his sympathies for FARC, Panama, and Brazil, which takes a dim view of any initiative that might compete with its role as a regional power.

The countries bordering on Colombia fear that a violent offensive against drug production in that country will scatter the local population, as well as guerillas and drug traffickers, across the Amazon region along the borders they share with Colombia. At a meeting in Bogotá in October 2000, the European Union clearly distanced itself from Plan Colombia, emphasizing that its contribution of 871 million U.S. dollars would be allocated to "institutional reinforcement" and "social development" programs outside the framework of Plan Colombia. The European Union—as explained in Martin Jelsma's chapter in this book—noted the differences between European aid and Plan Colombia, rejecting the inclusion of a military component and emphasizing the overall importance of support for the peace process and the preservation of human rights.

In March 2001, a meeting was held between representatives of twenty-six countries and FARC in the demilitarized zone that at the time still had been conceded to the guerillas. The United States did not attend,[15] but most countries of the European Union did, in the company of the Vatican, Switzerland, Canada, Japan, Mexico, Brazil, Venezuela, and others. Following the meeting, all participating countries reiterated their support for the peace process.

The European Union's increasing opposition to Plan Colombia has supported the elements in FARC's strategy tending toward mediation, reduced FARC's opposition to the presence of any international commission in the demilitarized zone, and put the seriously compromised negotiations back on track.

The Fight against Drugs: An Economic and Political Weapon

The compromises the rich countries make with drug-trafficking states are manifold. They are economically as well as politically inspired. Examples abound, above all those involving economic interests. During the 1990s, China and Poland readily agreed to be paid with heroin money for the weapons they sold to Myanmar. That country spent nearly 1 billion U.S. dollars to purchase combat aircraft from China at a time when its currency reserves did not exceed 300 million dollars.[16] There are strong suspicious that weapons sales by France to Pakistan in that same period were paid for by drug money.

The World Bank and the International Monetary Fund ask no questions about the origin of the funds that enable certain countries—in particular, Colombia during the 1980s—to pay their foreign debt. Certain European states and the European Union have turned a blind eye to the official protection of cannabis cultivation in Morocco because it has been contributing heavily to that country's economic equilibrium and would be extremely difficult to replace with an alternative source of income.[17]

The accusation of drug trafficking has also been used as a political weapon to destabilize or discredit a political opponent. The U.S. drug policy toward Iran exemplifies such a course of action. Iran's efforts to block the transiting of Afghan heroin (Iran lost nearly three thousand men in these fights over twenty years), did not prevent it from being "decertified" by Washington. The real motive had to do with its place on the American list of so-called "rogue states." In December 1998, Iran was removed from the list of "decertified" countries. The reason given was that "Iran is no longer a significant opium and heroin producer and has stopped being a transit country for drugs destined for the United States."[18] The action was generally interpreted as a goodwill gesture in response to the policy of openness displayed by President Mohamed Khatami since 1997.

The U.S. use of drugs as a political weapon has its imitators. Many Third World countries now use the drug issue in their fight with political opponents or with ethnic and religious minorities living within their borders. In Indonesia in the early 1990s, the province of Aceh, in northern Sumatra, saw its movement for independence fiercely repressed by the Indonesian central government armed forces, with a cannabis eradication campaign as an excuse. In Sudan, the fight against cannabis production, with support by the UNDCP, has enabled the Islamic government at Khartoum to intervene in recent years against the animist Beja tribe.[19] Charges concerning a state's involvement in drug trafficking are often used as blackmail to force compliance with certain policies desired by the other states.[20] In Syria, whose troops were deeply involved in hashish and heroin trafficking in Lebanon, the United States forced eradication campaigns on illicit drug crops in the Bekaa Valley in addition to exerting pressure on Syrian participation in the Middle East peace negotiations. A similar strategy has been used in Bolivia, where Washington forced President Hugo Banzer, who was responsible for serious human rights violations and the assassination of opponents in foreign countries as part of the "Condor Plan" during his 1971–1978 military government,[21] to support a complete eradication of illicit coca crops in exchange for silence on this past record.

Conclusion

The United States lost its seat on the board of the International Narcotics Control Board (INCB) in 2001. This action is probably the result of a combination of various interests. The negative vote of Latin American countries may have been motivated by their opposition to Plan Colombia and to the "certification" process. In addition, more structural changes, such as the development of synthetic drug production in the developed countries, are undermining some of the U.S. arguments in its crusade against source countries. With regard to substance abuse, the advance of "harm reduction" policies, contrary to those favoring the U.S. policy of a "drug-free world," is another sign of change.[22] However, the United States retains as allies two major specialized UN organizations in the fight against drugs—ODCCP and INCB—both of which have developed under its influence.

The U.S. position with regard to national policies on substance abuse and the international campaign against drugs has led to extreme positions among developing countries in Africa and Asia. An obvious reason has to do with the fact that they are nondemocratic societies—China, Malaysia, Saudi Arabia, and Iran are clear examples—that punish all visible deviance very harshly. However, there are also other motives. The fascination politicians have with the "American model" may count, in addition to an opportunism that pushes them to join in with what is perceived as the dominant position of the richest countries. We also see that sternly repressive policies may serve as a smokescreen for trafficking activities engaged in by the country's leaders. These countries will be prepared to support all anti-drug crusades, as long as their states will not be targeted. Against the background of these activities, the decision of the European Union not to support Plan Colombia has been a positive development, although the attitude of the individual European countries has not always been clear. Policies like those allowing money laundering in off-shore places such as Jersey for the United Kingdom and Saint Martin/Sint Maarten for France and the Netherlands create ambiguities and contradictions that create barriers in the fight against really serious drug crimes. This weakens the European effort to define a workable alternative to the War on Drugs.

Notes

1. The ODCCP absorbed the United Nations International Drug Control Programme (UNDCP).

2. ODCCP, *World Drug Report 2000* (Oxford: Oxford University Press, 2001), 4.

3. This is the title adopted by Mulla Omar.

4. Forty-five hundred tons in 1999 and thirty-two hundred tons in 2000; my field contacts confine that the Shinwari tribe, which resisted the Taliban decree, received money from them in order not to cultivate.

5. The most prominent godfather in the Cape Town region is Vito Palazzolo, a former banker for the Pizza Connection. After escaping from Switzerland, he sought refuge in South Africa, where he first worked for the apartheid regime and later rendered services to the Mandela government. He is one of the Cosa Nostra's most prominent leaders and has become an important South African business man. See "La Maffia Diversifie Ses Activités," in *La Lettre Internationale des Drogues,* no. 4, (2001), 4–6, published by the Association de Géopolitiques des Drogues (aegd).

6. Alain Labrousse and Michel Koutouzis, *Géopolitique et Géostratégies des Drogues* (Paris: Economica, 1996), 23–32.

7. Jean Christophe Ruffin, ed., *Économie des Guerres Civiles* (Paris: Hachette, 1996), passim.

8. See Observatoire Géopolitique des Drogues (OGD), "Conflicts, Drugs, and Mafia Activities" (communication to The Hague Press Conference, May 11–15, 1999). On most of the countries cited, the last three annual reports of the OGD may also be consulted (www.ogd.org).

9. Michel Koutouzis, "Drogues a l'Est: Logique de Guerres et de Marché," *ifri Politique Étrangère 195* (1998), 233–44.

10. From producer to consumer, prices are multiplied one thousand to twenty-five hundred times. See Alain Labrousse, *Drogues: Un Marché de Dupes* (Paris: Editions Alternatives), 78.

11. OGD, "Afghanistan," in *World Geopolitics of Drugs 1998–1999* (OGD: Paris, 2000), 35–37.

12. OGD, "Senegal," in *World Geopolitics of Drugs 1995–1996* and *World Geopolitics of Drugs 1997–1998* (OGD: Paris, 1998), 62.

13. The FARC has approximately fifteen thousand men. No cease fire was reached with this organization and military operations thus continue during the negotiations.

14. The ELN has fifteen hundred to two thousand combatants.

15. The reason mentioned was that FARC did not hand over for trial to U.S. au-

thorities the guerillas who had murdered three American development workers in February 1999.

16. This affair in particular was covered by Bertil Lintner, a journalist with the *Far Eastern Economic Review,* whose articles were reprinted in *Burma in Revolt: Opium and Insurgency since 1948* (Boulder, Colo,: Westview Press, 1999).

17. Eradication without any development alternative would result in an increased flow of migrants in Europe.

18. "Iran and Drugtrafficking," BBC News, December 17, 1998.

19. See on this subject OGD, "Sudan," in *World Geopolitics of Drugs 1997–1998,* 54–75.

20. The Israeli secret service also had files on Syrian military involvement in hashish and heroin trafficking.

21. Alain Labrousse, *La drogue, L'argent, et Les Armes* (Paris: A. Fayard, 1977), 366–70.

22. Sweden remains one of the last European supporters of this drug-free position.

16

Drugs and Transnational Organized Crime

Conceptualization and Solutions

Ybo Buruma

The problem of transnational organized drugs crime has been conceptualized in different ways, depending on the disciplinary focus of the researcher. Also, different intellectual communities have been proposing different solutions. Anthropologists, economists, and public analysts (to mention but a few) are inclined to pose different questions, to provide for different explanations, and to suggest different solutions, even though they have to deal with the same social phenomenon, and notwithstanding their interest in each others' findings. From the standpoint of criminal law, I am above all interested in the solutions proposed, which allows me to ignore the many differences represented within each of the aforementioned intellectual communities. That is the main reason why I will be discussing three "paradigms" involved in the study of transnational organized crime.

The concept "paradigm" is somewhat overused and ambiguous. Nevertheless, I have preferred it to the concept "model." This is because a model can be tested by empirical evidence, whereas a paradigm as a way of thinking in a certain intellectual community can merely be fruitful and plausible or not. A paradigm can generate scientific models, but I will not engage myself in a debate on the strength of different criminological models. A paradigm may also generate solutions to certain problems, in this case to the problem of transnational organized drugs crime. These solutions will be discussed by showing some of the strengths and weaknesses of the paradigms. I will describe the differences between the paradigms as precisely as possible, but I readily concede that many scholars will rightfully emphasize interdependency of the three paradigms among which I shall differentiate.

First, the "ethnic paradigm" will be discussed, which is the follow-up of criminological theories on alien conspiracies and still has its strength in a world defined by freedom of movement. Next, the "economical paradigm" will be dealt with, which defines crime in terms of criminal entrepreneurship in a world defined by freedom of capital. Finally, I will discuss the "political paradigm," which perceives organized crime in terms of its relationship with sovereign states and (decent) civil societies.

By focusing on each of these paradigms separately, we may appreciate that they each have a plausible basis, but we will also see that they each imply different targets to aim at in the fight against organized crime. We may appreciate that the smuggling and trafficking of migrants might be considered especially relevant in the ethnic paradigm, while money laundering fits the economical paradigm and corruption the political paradigm. However, we should also be mindful of the fact that each paradigm might blind us by giving rise to oversimplified theories, which fail to do justice to the full complexity of the phenomenon of transnational organized crime, and weaken us by solutions that are one-dimensional. For instance, we might ignore differences between countries of supply and countries of demand.

Writing about transnational organized crime, I will not deal with the difficulties regarding organized crime within a single country. The emphasis will be on crime that manifests itself in trade between countries of supply and countries of demand, especially with respect to drugs, although presumably the paradigms might also influence the way we look at terrorism or the trafficking of women. The basic idea of making a difference between countries of supply and countries of demand is highly problematic. For instance, what precisely is meant by the phrase "countries of demand" in relation to drugs? One would be inclined to characterize Pakistan and Colombia as countries of supply and the Netherlands and the United States as countries of demand. However, according to the *World Drug Report 2000*, Pakistan has 1.5 million heroin addicts (compared to totals of 1.2 million in Europe and 1 million in the United States) and there is an intensification of cocaine abuse in Latin America (up to 3.1 million habitual users of cocaine) while there is a decline in the United States (down to 7 million). Also, the Netherlands is a major producing country of amphetamine-type stimulants (11 percent of the world total).[1] In view of these simple figures, the customary way of thinking about countries of demand and countries of supply seems to be too simple. Nevertheless, I will not challenge conventional wisdom, although ultimately the discussion between "the West and the rest" might be more to the point.

The Ethnic Paradigm

Before going into the proposed solutions arising from the ethnic paradigm, I will try to make this paradigm a plausible one. It is one of the oldest ways of looking at organized crime in North America. In the period from 1890–

1920, many immigrants arrived from the Old World. Often starting their lives in ethnically defined groups, the first generations might have stuck to old social conventions. Later generations adapted to the new society and especially during the Depression, some of them tried their luck in crime in order to improve their social positions. Against this background, crime might be regarded as the product of people who do not share the basic values of their new homeland, and who have lost the firm ties of their own societies.[2]

After World War II, the influx of migrants in the ghettos in the United States, the *banlieus* in France, and the shanty towns in Asia and South America continued. Such poverty-ridden areas do not only harbor people without education or other qualities that would give them access to upward mobility. Over the years we have also seen many migrants with high personal qualities, but few legitimate possibilities that fit their skills. These often rootless people are tempted to take their chances in crime. Some of them, maybe only a minority, give in to such temptations and become criminals themselves. For a majority, however, crime is part of their daily lives, as victims or as acquaintances and bystanders. It is a well-known empirical fact that immigrant societies often become targets for criminals from their own midst, not only in the form of racketeering and extortion, but also as customers for the drug dealers.

Especially when in the late 1970s drug trade became one of the major lines of criminal activity, the relationship between ethnic groups in the United States of America and western Europe and their relatives in their countries of origin became a valuable asset in transnational organized crime. It became much easier to travel and in some respects it became easier to migrate, thus facilitating trade by bringing personnel from the countries of supply to the countries of demand.

This perspective gives rise to the idea of "the world as a global village without a police department."[3] It is true that some nationalities seem to be specializing in certain types of crime: the Dutch seem to concentrate on transporting soft drugs (hashish), and the Yugoslavs on violence. But even more interesting are the examples of pax mafiosa in which different ethnic groups form transnational coalitions.[4] A famous example is the supply of a submarine with twenty personnel by the Russian *mafiya* to the Colombian Cali cartel in exchange for drugs and a license to supply a part of the European market. Another example of this "dark side of globalization" (among many others) is the case of Ciudad del Este in Paraguay, where South American drug traffickers, Chinese triads, Japanese yakuza, Russian mafiosi, Italians, Nigerians, and even fundamentalist terrorists are conducting business with one another.[5]

With this in mind, transnational organized crime may be plausibly thought of in terms of ethnicity. A specific focus of concern in this respect is formed by the dangers of organized crime to what I call social integrity in countries of demand as well as supply. In the West, kids take the local drug boss as their role model and quit school. In Colombia, organized crime and narco-philanthropics can appear to hold a promise of a wonderful life for the under-privileged, as Gabriel García Márquez has so aptly described.[6]

Solutions from an Ethnic Perspective

A logical way of countering organized crime from the ethnic perspective is to concentrate on migration, fighting human trafficking into the countries of demand, while helping the countries of supply in fighting the production in their jurisdictions. In public rhetoric, there is a tendency within the ethnic paradigm to seek solutions in terms of fighting the "alien conspiracy" or, to go a bit further: we are good and they are bad.

Thus, from the perspective of the countries of demand, Plan Colombia, with its combination of eradication of crops and increased funding for alter-native development in Colombia, would seem to be preferable to actions in countries of demand. Of course, this perspective suggests that countries of demand need to look for suspects in certain ethnic communities and to try to minimize the influx of aliens. It is easy to see dangers and difficulties associ-ated with this perspective. A focus on certain ethnic minorities can lead to discrimination and violation of human rights. In addition, the same ethnic perspective teaches us a difficulty regarding the seizure of drugs. If the police want to confiscate drugs, they must bear in mind the possible consequences for the family of the suspects or for the group of ethnic relatives, and the dangers of stigmatization.

Moreover, the ethnic paradigm may give rise to oversimplification. First, ethnic groups may undergo displacement or demonstrate geographic flexibil-ity. Even if one considers, for instance, Colombian groups to be the enemy, it is clear that their actions will be taken over by other groups (for instance Mexicans of the Tijuana cartel operating in close coordination with the Co-lombian FARC). Second, this paradigm seems to ignore that the metaphor of the alien conspiracy is highly problematic in view of certain empirical data in countries of demand. In his chapter, Damián Zaitch presents data from field research, which indicates that—at least in the Netherlands—Colombian dealers prefer working with locals, who are better connected with the buyers; they prefer them over working with Colombians living there. Another ques-tion mark with respect to "alien conspiracy" has been placed by official Dutch and Belgian reports that criminal groups are more often cosmopolitic than monoethnic. In these so-called fluid multicultural networks, criminals of Dutch, Turkish, Chinese, and French descent can be found in one and the same group. Moreover, this way of looking at organized crime makes it hard to understand why there are so many "pure-Dutch" organized groups.[7]

The Economic Paradigm

In the 1970s and 1980s, criminological research showed that for many criminal activities, earlier ascribed to organized crime, the role of individual "criminal entrepreneurs" was more important than had previously been recognized. This discovery has been one of the main triggers for looking at organized crime from an economic perspective. Before going into the proposed solutions arising from the economic paradigm, four phenomena will serve to make this perspective a plausible one once more.

First, it is known that in criminal organizations normally investors are to be found as well as directors, bookkeepers, purchasers, transporters, sellers, and collectors who are ensuring that sellers pay the revenues to directors. This phenomenon has probably brought some authors to focus on corporative dimensions of organized crime.

Second, it became clear in the 1980s that an economic model would be useful not only because of this structural outlook of criminal organizations but also because of the sheer amounts of money involved. Crime is a billion dollar business: according to a Dutch report in 1995, the Dutch inland consumption of soft drugs (weed, hash) amounted to 0.4 billion U.S. dollars; export amounted to 1 billion, transit to 2 billion, and the overall participation in international trade to 6 billion U.S. dollars. These figures suggest that transnational criminal organizations may be multinational criminal enterprises.[8]

Third, it is the global movement of goods and money that made these illegal forms of trade possible during the last twenty years. Trade in illegal arms, drugs, and women is almost by definition international, not to mention trade in nuclear material or human organs.

Fourth, strategic alliances as well as diversification and geographic changes of markets can be understood from this economical perspective. Nowadays, Dutch drug traders are using the same types of joint ventures as their ancestors did during Holland's golden age in the seventeenth century. At one moment A, B, and C work together; a couple of months later—when C is in jail or has ripped off his fellow entrepreneurs—A and B continue with D. Each partner invests a certain amount in order to spread the risk.

Phenomena such as these seem to make the economic paradigm plausible. Moreover, it solves one of the problems related to the ethnic model. Thus, it helps understand why certain organizations, selling in the Netherlands, use Dutch transporters at the same time as Turkish buyers (in the countries of supply) and former-Yugoslav collectors of revenues generated by addicted street sellers. It also explains how Latin American sellers were able to find Dutch locals for a joint venture on the European market. Economic motives can be stronger than ethnic affiliations. Moreover, phenomena that seemed to be explained by an ethnic perspective, such as the aforementioned pax mafiosa, can also be understood in economic terms. People from Sicily and Cali have tried to cooperate in order to prevent Turkish and Pakistani criminals from dominating the European criminal market. In the United States, the Cali group worked together with Nigerians to challenge the market positions of the Chinese.[9]

A specific focus associated with this perspective in countries of demand as well as countries of supply is the danger for the integrity of the economy. The drive of criminals to invest their illegal revenues in noncriminal enterprises endangers the economy. In some source countries, the supply of criminally generated capital may have an impact on the national macroeconomic process along the lines of the "Dutch disease." In the countries of demand, the investment of illegally generated capital in noncriminal enterprises may endanger the integrity of the economy and change the roles of competition in unfair ways. Payments of protection money may create upward pressures on price levels in certain sectors. In this way, the protection by Cosa Nostra to construction companies in New York led to an enormous increase in real estate values in the late 1970s. These type of activities have led to a hardening of ordinary mores. In Russia, for example, doing business without having to pay for protection from the worlds of politics and crime has become almost impossible *(krysja)*.

Solutions from an Economic Perspective

A logical way of countering organized crime from the economic perspective is by focusing on funds, and especially money laundering.[10] The prime goal would be to hit organized crime where it can be felt, that is in their money-belts. In this perspective the seizure and confiscation of illegal proceeds are even more important than the arrest of criminals. However, in some countries of supply the economic significance of criminally generated money may make it hard for local authorities to take action along these lines. In countries of demand, where normally more profit is made, seizure and confiscation are easier from a political perspective. In countries such as the Netherlands, specific obligations exist for banks to report unusual cash deposits. The integration of illegal assets into the official economy is a more recent focus of fighting organized crime, by demanding certain official audits for companies who want to obtain government contracts or certain specific permits.

This brings us to the weaknesses of this paradigm. A key problem is that this perspective ignores the fact that a criminal's life is not merely defined by money. Criminals do not always act according to the logic of economic rationality. Moreover, in those situations where they do, they will use methods uncommon to the legitimate world. We only have to remember the ruthlessness of the Russian *mafiya*. Criminal enterprises are basically working in a hostile environment and ruthlessness is a way to survive in such an environment. This hostile environment is one reason not to overestimate the possibilities of investing illegal profits in countries of demand: the criminal competition may start extorting the criminal semi-legitimate entrepreneur. But even before there will be any profit, a criminal entrepreneur has his problems. If he cannot solve his disagreement with a supplier, he cannot go to court. There is much mutual deceit in this criminal business world, and it is hard to solve difficulties without the use of force. Sometimes, criminals will be competing with one another to death. Moreover, actions by the authorities leading to arrests or seizures of drugs or arms will intensify mutual distrust among cooperating criminals. This implies that the enterprise has to use a kind of organization that is not optimal in terms of efficiency. Cell-structured organizations will complicate the communication between the bosses and the subordinate personnel. Often the leaders may not know exactly what is happening as a result of this type of organization; rumors have it that this has been a problem for the Ah-Kong triad.

The Political Paradigm

The political paradigm regarding transnational organized crime focuses on the role of official government and civil society. In the old days, there may have been reason to speak about secret societies, and even today the yakuza and some Chinese triads have all the characteristics of these. I will not go into this. Instead, I will focus on the difficulties differentiating an underworld from an "upper world." An important line of reasoning in criminological theory stresses that one should always look at the symbiotic relations between organized crime and society (regardless of whether one looks at the career of the individual criminal, or at crime as a social phenomenon).

When considering the phenomenon of transnational organized crime in this line of reasoning, one should concentrate on the ability and willingness of authorities to counter organized crime, and the relationship between organized crime and ordinary civil society. Examples abound. Countries such as Columbia and Myanmar lack sovereign power in some of their regions: guerrilla organizations and war lords are in control (of these regions) and deliver drugs for arms. This also applied to the border area between Afghanistan and Pakistan in the early 1990s, and regions with a high level of economic and politic instability such as Chechnya and Kosovo.

In other countries it is not simply a matter of inability but also a matter of unwillingness on the part of national authorities to act against organized crime. In Taliban-controlled Afghanistan, and earlier in Bolivia, the national economies were highly dependent on the drug economy, which made these governments vulnerable (and even Mexico is generating more money from the export of drugs than the export of oil to the United States). In some countries, such as the Surinam of Desi Bouterse, the Panama of Noriega, or a number of (federal) states in Mexico, the government and/or the army itself are in change of the drug trade. One could say in these cases that a shadow economy is helping the ruling classes, much like the assistance organized crime used to give to the economically powerful to break strikes in the West or to provide luxury to party bosses in the former Soviet Union. Such a shadow economy also exists in countries with systems of tax collecting/protection money or otherwise high levels of corruption, such as Nigeria.

A specific problem exists with permissive countries such as the United States (arms trade), Switzerland and Luxembourg (money laundering), and the Netherlands (soft drugs). To be sure, in these countries organized crime is being countered, but there are constitutional or ideological circumstances hampering effective repressive action.

Howard Abadinski has shown that the illegal action that is part of organized crime does exist thanks to the dynamics of legal society.[11] Organized crime finds its outlets in the upper world where decent men are visiting prostitutes, fine children are using drugs, and legitimate corporations are dumping their chemical waste illegally. The underworld has been using the legal world as its market and supplier of raw materials, transportation, banking, legal services, and so on. Illegally accumulated profits are being used for investment in the legal sectors of the economy. Often, the activities will entail a considerable amount of corruption. Thus it is necessary to view organized crime as being part of a (national) civil society.

Next to the other two paradigms, this third one is also sufficiently plausible. Moreover, this paradigm solves a problem that has been associated with the purely economic paradigm. Criminal organizations basically compete in a hostile environment, and that is exactly why they need political backup, or, for that matter, must avoid any political adversary, which is also why it is interesting to focus on their relationships with legitimate society.

This paradigm shows the dangers of organized crime in terms of official and political integrity. In general, corruption will make a country vulnerable because the importance of people will exceed the importance of institutions with the possible result that the administrative goals of these institutions will be betrayed. Predatory rule by corrupt officials will hinder local development in countries of supply by imposing nonaccountable taxes. Counterstrategies of organized criminals in countries of demand will include attempts to bribe police and other officials in order to be tipped off before big busts. This form of corruption has been frustrating international cooperation in policing, generating distrust among law enforcement in the countries involved.

Solutions from a Political Perspective

A logical way of countering organized crime in this line of thought is by focusing on corruption and stressing administrative obligations for legitimate civil society. This will include an obligation to report on deliveries of drug precursors and deposits of excessively large sums of money.

However, this strategy also has its weaknesses. At the moment, in most countries of demand (or perhaps we should say in the greater part of the Western world) the underworld has not succeeded in entangling itself with the official upper world, nor with the top levels of civil societies: corruption is mostly incidental and serves short-term objectives. Some might even be tempted to say that organized crime in the West has never been a serious threat to economic and political power structures, but has complemented those structures. Also, in countries of supply one should not overestimate the criminal influence on the actions of authorities.

Conclusion

Since the Cold War, terrorism and organized crime have been viewed by public opinion in the West as the major threats to security. Some exaggeration may be involved, although it cannot be denied that in the last twenty years the level of organized crime has increased in a spectacular fashion. Increasing globalization has enabled transnational criminal enterprises to grow, to diversify internationally, and to exploit geographic differences. And in a world where the bases for international cooperation in dealing with contemporary challenges (the Internet, aids, the environment, terrorism, and drugs) have became more regionalized than during the Cold War, some countries have become safe havens of internationally operating crime syndicates, which, in the presence of a weak state, may align themselves with guerrilla movements and war lords.

Each of the paradigms, the three perspectives regarding transnational organized crime, implies certain solutions, depending also whether the situation in countries of supply or countries of demand is being focused upon. In countries of supply, bombing crops, occupying fiscal paradises, abducting corrupt presidents, and invading the countries that harbor leaders of criminal or terrorist organizations are radical options, however, with doubtful international legitimacy, even when accompanied by extensive humanitarian aid. They are to be viewed as modern types of warfare, including high-intensity conflicts with nonstate actors.

In the Western industrialized countries, the effects of organized crime have to be put into perspective, despite the present problems surrounding the affiliation with terrorism. Of course it would not be wise to disregard the dangers. At the same time, it should be recognized that organized crime involves a tiny minority of people. A considerable part of the illegally accumulated profits do not find their way to the legal economy but are spent in the underworld or are stashed away in other countries. The level of corruption in the West is rather moderate, and most of it has less to do with organized crime than with the worlds of high-level politics and big business.

The problems arising from the activities of transnational organized crime are much more acute in source countries, where the social, economic, and political integrity of society is being challenged. Fighting this development may lead to new problems, as the present War on Drugs is showing. The balance is not always a positive one.

The considerable weight of the negative dimensions has motivated several Western countries to redefine transnational crime involving the drug trade. They have begun to define the abuse of dangerous (or "hard") drugs as a health problem, and the drug production in source countries as "a crime." The consequences of such a redefinition do not always produce fairness and even-handedness in policy. Fumigating crops in Colombia while turning a blind eye on Wall Street coke snuffers (who are not a problem) while arresting East Harlem crack users (who are) does not convey an image of consistency. An assessment of the different paradigms has made clear the highly political motives behind law enforcement. In the post–Cold War world order, the need to combat transnational organized crime has become a legitimation for intervention by Western nations in countries of supply, in addition to a closure of their borders in order to prevent nonpromising foreign immigrants from entering. In the end, the best solutions in the fight against transnational organized crime and its involvement in drug trafficking may be clouded by the power relations between the West and the rest.

Notes

1. *World Drug Report 2000* (Oxford: Oxford University Press, 2001). According to a fact sheet of the American Bureau for International Narcotics and Law Enforcement Affairs (State Department) about 80 percent of the confiscated Ecstasy in the United States came from or through the Netherlands: cited in *Samenspannen tegen xtc*, policy paper of the Dutch Department of Justice, May 2001.

2. Donald Cressey, *Criminal Organization* (New York: Heinemann, 1972).

3. The quote is from Frank Ciluffo (Center for Strategic and International Studies) in Mike Brunker, *A Global Pillage without Police*, www.msnbc.com (August 31, 1999).

4. Manuel Castells, *The End of the Millennium* (Basingstoke: Blackwell, 1998).

5. Jeffrey Robinson, *The Merger: The Conglomeration of International Organized Crime* (London: Overlook Press, 2000), passim.

6. Gabriel García Márquez, *News of a Kidnapping* (London: Jonathan Cape, 1997).

7. Erwin R. Kleemans, et al., *Georganiseerde Criminaliteit in Nederland*, wodc-*rapport*, 1998, passim; Parlementaire commissie van onderzoek naar de georganiseerde misdaad in België, Belgische Senaat (1998–1999), 1:326–29.

8. Chris J. C. F. Fijnaut, Frank Bovenkerk, Gerard J. N. Bruinsma, and Herman G. van de Bunt, *Final Report on Organized Crime in the Netherlands on Behalf of the Parliamentary Enquiry Committee*, Official Papers II, 1995–1996, dossier number 24072, p. 52.

9. Pino Arlacchi, *Mafia Business: The Mafia Ethic and the Spirit of Capitalism* (Oxford: Oxford University Press, 1988).

10. Phil Williams, "Transnational Criminal Organizations: Strategic Alliances," *Washington Quarterly* (winter 1995), 58–74.

11. Howard Abadinski, *Organized Crime* (New York: Nelson-Hall, 1994).

VI

Conclusion

The Drug Industry, Its Economic, Social, and Political Effects, and the Options of Intervention and Control

Menno Vellinga

In just a few decades, drug production and trade have become big business in Latin America. One country after another has become involved in the production and trafficking of cocaine (Peru, Bolivia, Colombia), marijuana (Mexico, Jamaica, Colombia), opium (Mexico, Guatemala, Colombia), and other natural or synthetic drugs. Other countries have become participants in the drug trade (Haiti, Dominican Republic, Bahamas, Surinam, Ecuador, and Argentina), developed into banking centers where proceeds from the drug trade are being laundered (Panama, Bahamas, Uruguay), or served as exporters of precursor chemicals (Brazil).

Estimating the volume of all these activities and assessing their impact on the economy and society of the countries involved are not easy. Precise information on the size and structure of the industry has been hard to obtain. Data are manipulated for political reasons. They are either inflated or deflated—depending on the objectives to be pursued—in a way often bordering on statistical sensationalism. In addition, production and trade show considerable fluctuations as traffickers respond to repressive operations and changes in anti-drug policies. Finally, there are considerable differences in impact among individual drug-producing countries. The total amount earned by the Andean countries in cocaine production and trade at the height of the industry's development in the mid-1990s has been estimated at between 8 and 12 billion U.S. dollars. The corresponding street value in the United States and western Europe amounted at that time to a sum between 46 and 74 billion U.S. dollars. It is estimated that about 50 percent of the export income did find its way back to the source countries.[1] Since then, the price of cocaine has dropped substantially, while the growing participation of Mexican traffickers will reduce the share of the exporters from the Andean countries. Still, income through the drug industry for Colombia alone has been estimated at an average of 2.5 billion U.S. dollars per year in the 1990s.

The general economic effects of the drug industry's operations in the Andean countries can be divided into a spending effect and a structural effect. Both are closely interrelated and the overall impact will determine the balance between them. The drug industry has undoubtedly rendered a contribution to economic development in source countries but its macro-economic role has also been a source of headaches for policymakers. The inflow of narco-dollars has boosted hard currency reserves, facilitated the servicing of the foreign debt, and provided funds for infrastructural development. To launder the revenues derived from the drug trade, traffickers have invested in certain sectors of the economy, especially in construction, public utilities, and banking. In Colombia, they have also invested in industrial and service-oriented sectors of a more productive nature. In addition, the drug sector has created employment, which in the Andean region runs into the hundred thousands.

Analysts of the economic impact of the drug trade on source countries have alerted the leadership of those countries to the grave negative effects, including manifestations of "the Dutch disease."[2] Traditional export sectors suffer, as do in fact all other areas of the economy that are not directly connected to the production and trafficking of cocaine, resulting in a loss of output and employment and in a deteriorating trade balance. The continual influx of narco-dollars poses a danger of inflation, overvalued exchange rates for the national currency, a worsening of export positions, and reductions in economic growth. It also favors spending on imports rather than domestic goods.

In recent years, the general impact of the drug industry within the national economy of Peru and Bolivia has been declining. Together they still accounted for an estimated 25 percent of cocaine production in the year 2000, but the disruptive macroeconomic effects are lessening. The cocaine portion of the economy of Colombia, however, has remained considerable, and the sector continues to threaten the stability and integrity of the socio-political system. Colombia's economy is very different from other Latin American economies, and it is very probable that it would have been doing very well without the impact of the drug industry complex. In Peru and Bolivia the cocaine industry is no longer a threat to the state. The steady growth of the legal economy in the 1990s has opened opportunities outside the drug industry and also created the conditions for a repatriation of drug capital. The feverous activity in building construction in the big cities is undoubtedly linked to this phenomenon.

Strategies of Supply-Side Control

What can be done in the area of supply-side control given the interests involved? The most favored strategy today of controlling the supply side of the drug industry in source countries is alternative development. It has become the official development-oriented dimension of the supply-side strategy, next to precursor chemicals control, destruction of cocaine production facilities, intervention of shipments, and control of money laundering. It has been actively promoted by multilateral organizations, by the governments of source countries, and by those countries that have become a preferred destination of the cocaine traffic. The objective of alternative development is to create the economic and social conditions that will enable peasant households to realize sustainable levels of living that will eliminate the need for drug cultivation. The methodology is based on the integration of crop substitution, rural development, and law enforcement initiatives. The emphasis on each of these components has varied between regions and also between donors in the field of development cooperation: the United States has been leaning toward eradication by force, while the European countries have preferred an emphasis on integrated rural development. The strategy as such was defined at the end of the 1980s in response to the failure to control coca supply through both the narrowly defined crop substitution projects and the more broadly defined integrated rural development programs.

However, alternative development has not been very successful. General economic and sociopolitical dynamics in source countries, international pressures to produce quick results in coca crop reduction, and the economics of coca production itself undoubtedly have contributed to a negative development. Research on the microlevel has also shown that the results of alternative development programs are strongly affected by peasant household strategies and by the ability of program officers to take these strategies into account, to recognize the specific regional socioeconomic, cultural, and environmental circumstances that influence household drug crop cultivation, and to incorporate these insights into their programs.[3] Furthermore, despite considerable efforts to the contrary, coca cultivation has spread from the traditional areas to the colonization frontiers in Bolivia, Peru, and Colombia.

Alternative development was expected to be more effective than the other approaches by combining a broad strategy of regional development with a policy of law enforcement that was to go beyond simple repressive action. At the core of this strategy was the recognition that the supply side in coca-producing countries has complex economic, social, political, and cultural dimensions in addition to the agronomy and microeconomics of the industry. Thus, in the 1990s, the strategy of alternative development was widened to include the development process in those regions that feed the migration to coca-producing areas. At the same time, the growth of the legitimate sectors of the economy was supported through debt relief, balance of payments support, and preferential trade schemes. The idea behind these actions was that coca production feeds on marginal socioeconomic and ecological conditions in areas weakly integrated into the nation-state. A steadily growing legitimate economy in combination with a state apparatus responsible for providing basic needs would eliminate the necessity for drug crop cultivation. The international aid community wholeheartedly embraced alternative development as the strategy to control coca supply, and started financing programs in this area.[4]

The problems that presented themselves to the programs that actually were being executed are typical for coca-growing regions in Latin America. A transition to alternative crops is hampered by the inaccessibility of the regions, their distance from the markets, the lack of physical infrastructure (roads, water, electricity), the lack of technical assistance, and the lack of access to inputs (seedlings, fertilizer, pesticides, and so on). In short, the entire contextual support system for such a transition is often lacking, and even in the most favorable situations the competition with coca is not easy. For example, those in the Bolivian coca-producing region, the Chapare, who planted banana under optimal conditions (best soils, improved varieties, and high input of fertilizers, pesticides, and the like) have needed 2 hectares of bananas to match the gross income from 1 hectare of coca. Furthermore, the initial investment for bananas was 3 times as high as for coca and the use of labor was 1.7 times as high. Pineapple, presented as a crop with the potential to secure a competitive household income, has proved to be a similar case. The other alternative crops that were recommended by the programs have required extensive care and inputs in fertilizers and disease-controlling chemicals in addition to technical financial support and the organization of market outlets.[5]

Research concluded that the more successful alternative crops cultivated on the more fertile soils can produce comparable gross incomes, but would need a considerably higher investment in man-hours, next to costly inputs such as fertilizers and pesticides. In a situation of almost unlimited access to new land and wide possibilities for settlement, the amount of work expended to achieve a certain level of income is more important than the production per hectare. Agricultural labor contracted outside the household will be relatively expensive. Moreover, alternative crops suffer from the hot and humid conditions and require fungicides, pesticides, and herbicides. The gross annual income per hectare of coca will permit the household members to cultivate some subsistence crops and experiment with some alternative crops. It pays for the children's schooling and buys other staples and seeds, fertilizer, tools, and animals that cannot be self-produced. However, it is not enough to enable the household to advance up the social ladder and leave peasant life behind.

Crop substitution programs often operate with the objective of generating an annual gross household income that is not realistic and is outside the reach of most individual households. Profitability will remain at low levels due to low quality soils, lack of inputs, the problematic nature of some of the alternative crops, and the lack of technical assistance and other kinds of support, in particular the absence of banks and credit institutions. The small volumes of alternative crops that are being produced have difficulty finding a suitable market. Generally, the programs are introduced without extensive technical and economic feasibility studies, which includes assessing the marketability—either domestic or external—of the various crops that should replace coca. The ecological sustainability of the activities that were undertaken, including the management of forest resources, has never been a priority.[6]

These programs have failed to create an alternative for coca cultivation and those peasants who have participated should feel defrauded. The experience in each of the Andean countries has been very similar. It is clear that the consolidation of systems of production replacing coca cultivation involves a long-term process during which the cultivation of subsistence crops has to be guaranteed and support services have to be organized. Both are at the moment almost totally lacking.

Alternative Development: A Failed Strategy?

It is tempting to attribute the failure of alternative development to a deficient planning system operating with overly ambitious goals to be accomplished in an unrealistically short time span without adequate institutional support for the organization and development of those activities that could be alternatives to coca growing. And indeed, against the background of the accumulated international experience in rural development, it is hard to imagine a change of the agrarian structure and practices of an entire region in a few years without an adequate study of the viability of this strategy in terms of environmental factors, specific characteristics of the promoted crops, their economic productivity, markets to be developed, and institutional support.

However, this is too easy a conclusion. The program of alternative development within the present national and international political and economic conjuncture has many characteristics of a mission impossible. Despite all the rhetoric, financial aid for crop substitution as part of long-term development assistance has received less attention and a much smaller percentage of the program's total budget than law enforcement, military counter-narcotics support, and forced eradication. It is clear that a strategy that does not give proper attention to development issues will be dominated by the laws of economics. Where coca growing is suppressed, it will undoubtedly reappear in another neighboring area. The flexibility of drug traffickers will continue to contribute to a situation where coca growing moves from place to place.

Heavy international pressure to show results in terms of hectares of eradicated coca has worked against a development-oriented strategy based on detailed studies at the microlevel. These studies would have to analyze the motivations and circumstances determining household coca cultivation, the influence of development efforts and law enforcement interventions, and the priorities individual households take into account when considering the alternatives to the cultivation of coca.

Instead, coca growers have been approached as a homogeneous group; the diversity among them and the multifunctional role coca cultivation has had for the individual household have been ignored.[7] The socioeconomic differences among the peasant population, the differences in migration background, and the degree of permanence in settlement, all factors affecting crop decisions, are being ignored. Rather, alternative development programs have adopted a uniform approach, emphasizing a high economic return per hectare as the one and only motivating force in crop decisions. However, the motivations of individual households are varied and often will go beyond simple economic rationality.[8] This also helps to explain the variations in coca cultivation at the level of the household, as well as at the regional and subregional levels. In practice, compensation and crop substitution may primarily favor those households that are already better off and produce coca solely as a source of extra income. In those cases, social and legal pressures may work better. In the case of those totally dependent on their income from coca for survival, more attention should be given to the cultivation of food crops and off-farm employment.

Finally, to wipe out coca cultivation, to destroy the jungle labs, to track down the traffickers—and possibly to extradite them to the United States— is no simple affair in the political conjuncture of the Andean countries. Relationships between traffickers and politicians make control even more difficult. Under the present policies, the coca-cultivating peasant population has borne the brunt of the War on Drugs. The results in terms of a net reduction in hectares planted with coca have been questionable. The reduction in one place has led to the expansion in another area. The absence of substantial results from the supply-control strategies—contrary to what one would expect—does not seem to be a subject of major concern among the agencies involved. The policies that are being pursued continue to be internationally sanctioned despite widespread doubts concerning their effectiveness by multilateral organizations, the U.S. government, and the governments of source countries. For source countries these policies have created access to international development cooperation. Certainly in the case of Bolivia and Peru, this sector has become an important source out of which development projects in the coca regions can be financed. Paradoxically, one would need a constant and important presence of illegal cultivation of coca to guarantee continued access to these international sources of finding.

There is, however, an additional reason for continuing these policies. As we noted before, the concept of alternative development, as such, has a certain logic to it. Other policies that will deal effectively with supply-side control at the source are not easy to define and execute. Supply-side control finds itself trapped in a "Catch 22" situation in which most actions defined to combat coca production are producing the opposite results. The drug industry is a fiercely dynamic one run by entrepreneurs who are daring risk-takers. Their flexibility in adapting to changes in the conditions under which the industry operates has been formidable. Paradoxically again, the spectacularly increasing added value at the various stages of the commodity chain caused by interdiction programs in source countries may have increased the attractiveness of the industry for newcomers. Thus, interdiction may in practice turn into a coca price support program. Under these circumstances, coca-leaf-producing peasants are encouraged to increase yields on existing plots or move their coca to more inaccessible areas. Forcible eradication meets with strong resistance by the coca-growing peasants, their unions (Bolivia), or the guerilla movements that have offered them protection (Peru, Colombia). Finally, voluntary eradication and concomitant compensatory programs of alternative development provide the physical infrastructure (roads, water, electricity) that also serves the coca sector.

The Andean governments are crucial and essential actors in the implementation of programs of supply-side control. Although convinced of the necessity to respond to international pressures and to contribute to the drug control effort, their weakness has often made it difficult for them to comply. Each policy action affecting supply-side control has the tendency to generate a constituency that benefits from it and has an interest in having the policy sustained. These constituencies become entrenched and resist change. The state then avoids confrontation and turns to other urgent priorities in less controversial areas that have more public support.

What Can Be Done?

The lack of adequate information on the economic structure and functioning of the drug industry, its interaction with the formal economy, and its macroeconomic impact has hampered the definition of adequate policies. In the absence of such information, governments—and in particular the U.S. government—have opted for the "quick fix." To many policymakers, the relatively uncomplicated process of the cultivation of coca and its transformation into cocaine apparently requires an equally simple and straightforward response: Get the peasants to shift to other crops, rewarding them if they do and punishing them if they do not. Then, eliminate the producers and traffickers of cocaine by force and through military might.

The experience in supply-side control in the drug industry that has been accumulated over the years has taught us that the reality is much more complex than this diagnosis—on which the strategy of the War on Drugs has been built—suggests. Supply-side control in the coca-producing countries is confronted with the thousand-and-one correlates of underdevelopment. Coca cultivation and cocaine production feed on the poverty and lack of economic, social, and political stability in source countries. These are conditions that will never be remedied through a massive use of force, while using a limited number of isolated alternative development projects spread over an immense territory as a palliative. Moreover, the project approach, as such, given its limited scope and territorial definition, is totally inadequate as a means for addressing a problem that primarily concerns the functioning of the agro-sector as a whole, next to the state of affairs in the wider economy and the nature of state-society relationships. Drug control programs have been forced onto the respective governments, which—in turn—have forced them onto the drug-producing peasantry. International pressures dictated unrealistically short time spans for these programs and failed to organize adequate contextual support. Most organizations involved were hard-pressed for results. The War on Drugs has to be won and positive news of the front has to be communicated back to the base. Failure has been responded to by repression toward the coca growers. Through the years, they have been bearing the brunt of this "war" effort. The means of repression are often indiscriminate in their effects, affecting illicit as well as licit crops, as with the fumigation policy in Colombia.

These programs need to be phased out. This is not going to be an easy task because they include support for a wide range of institutions, such as police agencies, security forces, judiciaries, academia, the media, NGOs, and consultancy agencies, all of whom are committed to the continuation of the failed policies of the past. They should realize that supply suppression will not solve the problems with demand. It has accomplished nothing in the consumer countries and has caused great problems in the source countries.

Decriminalization or legalization would undo the drug mafia, but it would also hurt the hundreds of thousands of coca growers. Both stand to gain from a continuation of the current prohibition regimes. However, such radical actions on the demand side are not conceivable in the present international political conjuncture.

In fact, the short-term policy choices of the Andean governments are very limited. The Colombian government, especially, has lost the capacity to act decisively in this area. Its institutional weakness coupled to the lack of social cohesion and social control in civil society has made it unable to cope by itself with the problems that have arisen from a drug industry growing in response to an expanding demand in the United States and Europe. The more militarized approach in counter-narcotics action, supported by the United States and strongly opposed by the European Union, as included in Plan Colombia runs the danger of worsening this situation, generating adverse effects that threaten to plunge the country into civil war and expanding the conflict to the other Andean countries. For Colombia, the basic imperative remains the long-term process of strengthening the legitimate institutions of government, society, and the economy.

Short-term possibilities for "successful" counter-narcotics action lie in efforts to break up trafficking organizations, combat high-level corruption, and—above all—encourage the development of the legal economy in the drug-producing countries. "Success," however, may also have unintended affects. Breaking up the greater organizations has created the "advantage" of having to deal with hundreds of smaller refining and trafficking operations instead of the small number of large drug businesses whose economic power gave them access to the highest levels of government and whose capacity to use violence was on such a massive scale that the state would be undermined. However, the great number of smaller organizations has proven more difficult to trace and to control. Their greater flexibility in operations has posed significant problems to law enforcement.

Supporting the legal economy in source countries is probably the best manner, in the short-term, to reduce the relative importance of the narco-economy and, subsequently, its political weight. Such policy would require international aid, credit, and foreign investment, but—above all—major changes in trade regimes that will allow access to overseas markets. The European Union is already managing a system of generalized preferences that gives preferential access to the European market by the source countries involved in the War on Drugs. The system can be improved and its effectiveness increased. In spite of its flaws, it represents a promising way to go that also should be pursued forcefully by the United States, expanding the trade relations that form part of the Andean Trade Preferences initiative.[9] For the immediate future there are few other options open.

In the long-term radical solutions are necessary. These should be directed toward demand reduction and, on the supply side in source countries, toward massive long-term regional development efforts, operating on the basis of an intense participation by the communities and the households involved. The latter is in fact the only strategy that has never been tried, and one may assume that the international donor community will not be ready to finance it. Yet, it seems the logical way to go, given the fact that rural underdevelopment is at the heart of the problem and also because all other options have been exhausted. However, this approach would take more patience and good thinking than presently, realistically can be expected from the governments and international organizations participating in drug control activities. In the meantime, the War on Drugs has rapidly become the dirty business that one may expect from a real war. The violence, corruption, deceit, and damage to civil liberties in the effort to stamp out narcotics have been undermining the credibility of the claim to moral superiority made by the proponents of the War on Drugs. Moreover, foreign policy issues and other political interests, financial gain, and the creation of a mythology around the drug's medical and social effects have been involved from the start.[10]

The Search for Alternatives

Supply-side control in source countries cannot solve the problems with demand. Ending the War on Drugs will require decisive action on the demand side, but—also in this case—it is hard to be certain what kind of action that should be. The United States has been spending a total of 30 billion dollars in federal, state, and local money on drug control annually. Two-thirds of this amount has been dedicated to law enforcement activities, one-third to drug education or drug treatment. Domestic spending on illegal drugs has been estimated at 60 billion dollars a year. The total number of Americans behind bars for drug-related offenses is 400,000. At least 13 million Americans are estimated to be regular users, and there are no indications that this population is decreasing.[11]

In the various European countries, alternative drug policies—including some forms of decriminalization—are experimented with on a relatively large scale. The results are promising. All EU member states give action against drug traffickers the highest priority and, as far as their formal legal framework is concerned, not much difference can be noted among them. However, within the context of these laws, most member states have opted for pragmatic and flexible policies directed toward harm reduction. This has become a key concept, implying the reduction of harm to the user, his or her community, and the society at large.[12] While fighting the traffickers and the transnationally operating crime syndicates they are cooperating with, the strategies to reduce demand have shifted from repression toward prevention and care. Drug control policy has moved from the Ministries of the Interior to the Ministries of Health and/or Social Affairs. The EU member states are not fighting a war to achieve a drug-free society. Actually, unlike the U.S. strategy, documents of the European Union, while describing counter-narcotics action, are avoiding the concept of war with all its connotations.

The terrorist attacks of September 11, 2001 have drawn new attention to the drug money-laundering issue and the link between drug trafficking and terrorist organizations. "Follow the money" has become a new and promising strategy to trace the proceeds of the drug trade that are laundered through the off-shore banking sector and seek protection through bank secrecy. In the last few years, initiatives in this area have been taken already by the OECD, the IMF, and UNODCCP; the happenings of September 11th have given these actors a forceful impulse to continue.[13]

It is obvious that the sledgehammer approach to drug control as proposed by the War on Drugs is not working, and that core drug use may not be possible to eradicate at any price. Continuation of this strategy, however—as we noted earlier—serves a wide range of clientele, including anti-drug warriors, alternative development people, and the drug producers and traffickers who profit from inflated prices under prohibition. Changing the strategy toward a regime of "controlled liberalization" of drug use to be accompanied by a massive diversion of funds from the war effort toward anti-drug education, treatment, and research—which would be one solution—would meet with great problems internationally. Decriminalization would require the United States to abrogate a number of treaties prohibiting trade in narcotics and to redefine the bilateral agreements on the suppression of drug production signed with source countries.[14] After decades of having pursued policies of coercion, deceit, and encroachment on the sovereignty of these countries, this will not look like a very appetizing course for most politicians to pursue. The War on Drugs has maneuvered itself into a corner from which there will be no easy escape. It has become a prisoner of its own foibled policies. Yet the moment has arrived for international treaties to be reconsidered in addition to a radical turnaround in counter-narcotics strategy on the national level. There is no time to lose.

Notes

1. Patrick L. Clawson and Rensselaer Lee III, *The Andean Cocaine Industry* (New York: St. Martin's Press, 1996), 4–23; see also LaMond Tullis, *Unintended Consequences: Illegal Drugs and Drug Policies in Nine Countries* (Boulder, Colo.: Lynne Rienner, 1995), 2.

2. An interesting analysis of these macroeconomic effects is presented in *A Case Study of the Effects of Drug Production on LCDs: Bolivia, Coca, and the Dutch Disease?* (London: Economic Advisers Foreign and Commonwealth Office United Kingdom, 1990); also David Mansfield, *The Economic Impact of the Drug Trade* (London: Overseas Development Administration, 1996); Jurgen Schuldt, *La Enfermedad*

Holandesa y Otros Virus de la Economía Peruana (Lima: Universidad del Pacífico, 1994).

3. See David Mansfield, *Alternative Development: The Modern Thrust of Supply Side Policy* (London: Overseas Development Administration, 1996).

4. Clawson and Lee, *The Andean Cocaine Industry,* 148.

5. Data source, *Plan del Tropico, Cochabamba;* field interviews April/May 1996; also Menno Vellinga, "Alternative Development and Supply Side Control in the Drug Industry: The Bolivian Experience," *European Review of Latin American and Caribbean Studies,* no. 64 (1998), 7–26.

6. Cf. Alain Bojanic, "Balance Is Beautiful: Assessing Sustainable Development in the Rain Forest of the Bolivian Amazon" (Ph.D. diss., Utrecht University, 2001), passim.

7. Cf. Mansfield, *Alternative Development,* 14.

8. Cf. James C. Jones, *Farmers' Perspectives on the Economics and Sociology of Coca Production in the Chapare* (Binghamton, N.Y.: Institute for Development Anthropology, 1992), Working Paper, no. 77.

9. The system of trade preferences for Andean countries (ATPA), enacted in 1991, should be amplified; see "Programas de Fomento del Comercio Exterior: Estrategia Vital Contra el Terrorismo y el Narcotráfico," *Gestión* (Lima), October 13, 2001.

10. See "Ending the War on Drugs," *The Economist,* January 2, 1999, 25.

11. Ibid.

12. Gert Bogers, "The European Union and Policies of Drug Control" (paper presented at the Political Economy of the Drug Industry conference, Utrecht University, June 2001), passim.

13. Cf. "La Campaña de la UE y Otros Paises Contra el Lavado de Dinero," *La Jornada* (Mexico), September 20, 2001.

14. "Ending the War in Drugs," *The Economist,* January 2, 1999. According to a Rand Corporation Study cited in this article, when attempting to reduce domestic cocaine consumption, one should bear in mind that every dollar spent on treatment is seven times more effective than law enforcement and twenty-three times more effective than the dollar spent on blasting drug production in source countries. One could question the exactness of such calculations, but the message remains clear: Ending the War on Drugs will not only need a complete redefinition of strategies abroad, but it will even more so require a total shift in policies affecting demand in the user countries. See also Menno Vellinga, "The War on Drugs and Why It Cannot Be Won," *Journal of Third World Studies* 17, no. 2 (2001), 113–28.

Contributors

Luis Astorga is research associate in sociology at the Instituto de Investigaciones Sociales of the Universidad Nacional Autónoma de México (UNAM) in Mexico City. He has been a consultant on drug issues to international agencies and has published extensively on drug trafficking in Mexico, including *El Siglo de las Drogas* (1996).

Bruce Michael Bagley is professor of political science at the School of International Studies, University of Miami. He has written extensively on United States-Latin American relations, with an emphasis on drug trafficking and security issues. Publications include *Drug Trafficking Research in the Americas* (1997) and *Drug Trafficking in the Americas* (1995).

Tim Boekhout van Solinge is research associate in criminology on the Faculty of Law, Utrecht University. He has been involved in extensive research on alternative approaches to the drug problem and has authored many books and articles on these issues, including *Drugs and Decisionmaking in the European Union* (2002).

Ybo Buruma is professor of criminology on the Faculty of Law, University of Nijmegen. He has published many articles and research reports on fraud, corruption, and police practices in relation to investigations on the possibilities of cooperation between the army, police, and intelligence services of the member states of the European Union while combating transnational crime.

Hugo Cabieses is an economist at the Centro de Estudios Politicos y Sociales (CEPES) in Lima, Peru. He has been a consultant on drug issues to international agencies and, presently, to the national counter-narcotics agency.

Sandeep Chawla is presently head of research at the United Nations International Drug Control Programme (UNDCP) in Vienna. He has been development policy advisor to the United Nations for many years and has published widely in the area of social development. He holds a visiting teaching position at the University of Vienna.

Eduardo A. Gamarra is professor of political science and director of the Latin American and Caribbean Center at Florida International University. He has published numerous books and articles addressing drug issues, including *Entre la Droga y la Democracia* (1994), *Latin America Political Economy in the Age of Neoliberal Reform* (1994), and *Democracy, Markets, and Structural Reform in Latin America* (1995).

Ivelaw L. Griffith is professor of political science at Florida International University. He is a specialist on Caribbean and inter-American narcotics and security issues. He has authored numerous articles and several books on these issues, including *Drugs and Security in the Caribbean: Sovereignty under Siege* (1997) and *The Political Economy of Drugs in the Caribbean* (2000).

Martin Jelsma is research associate in political science at the Transnational Institute in Amsterdam. His many publications in the area of counter-narcotics policy include *Drogas, Poder, y Derechos Humanos en América Latina* (1998) and *Europe and the Plan Colombia* (2001).

Alain Labrousse is a sociologist and advisor to the Observatoire Francais des Drogues et des Toxicomanie (OFDT) in Paris. His publications include *La Drogue, l'Argent, et les Armes* (1991) and *Drogues: Un Marché de Dupes* (2000).

Rensselaer Lee is president of Global Advisory Services and a member of the Foreign Policy Research Institute in Philadelphia. He has published extensively on issues of narcotics trafficking and the criminal-political nexus, including *The White Labyrinth: Cocaine and Political Power* (1989), *The Andean Cocaine Industry* (1998, with Patrick Clawson) and *Smuggling Armageddon: The Nuclear Black Market in the Former Soviet Union and Europe* (1998).

Peter Reuter is professor in the School of Public Affairs and the Department of Criminology at the University of Maryland. Most of his research has dealt with alternative approaches to controlling drug problems, both in the United States and western Europe. He has been a consultant to numerous government agencies and foreign organizations in the field of drug control. His numerous publications include *Disorganized Crime: The Economics of the Visible Hand* (1983) and *Drugs: Learning from other Places, Times, and Vices* (2000, with Robert MacCoun).

Ernesto Savona is professor of criminology and director of the Research Center on Transnational Crime at the University of Trento, Italy. He is the author and editor of many books and articles on issues related to organized crime and international money laundering, including *Responding to Money Laundering: An International Perspective* (1997), *Organized Crime around the World* (1998), and *European Money Trails* (1998).

Francisco E. Thoumi is visiting professor at the Latin American and Caribbean Center at Florida International University. He has authored numerous books and articles on the drug trade and its effects on economy and society in Colombia. He is the author of *Political Economy and Illegal Drugs in Colombia* (1995).

Mariano Valderrama, a sociologist, is director of the Centro de Estudios Politicos y Sociales (CEPES) in Lima, Peru. He has published extensively on issues of international cooperation in Latin America, including *International Cooperation, Poverty, and Democracy* (2000) and *The Tower of Babel: NGOs, Foreign Aid, and Development* (2001).

Menno Vellinga is professor of development studies, director of the Institute of Development Studies (IDSUU) at Utrecht University, and visiting professor at the University of Florida. He is the author and editor of many books and articles on socioeconomic and sociopolitical aspects of development—including the drug problem—in Latin America. Recent publications include *Social Democracy in Latin America* (1994), *The Changing Role of the State in Latin America* (1998), and *The Dialectics of Globalization: Regional Responses to World Economic Processes* (2000).

Damián Zaitch is assistant professor of criminology on the Faculty of Law, Erasmus University, Rotterdam. He is involved in research on social control and terrorism, police-cooperation in Europe, and more recently on organized crime and drug policies in Europe and Latin America, resulting in *Traquetos: Colombians Involved in the Cocaine Business in the Netherlands* (2001).

Index